AF574236

ITALIAN COUNTRYSIDE

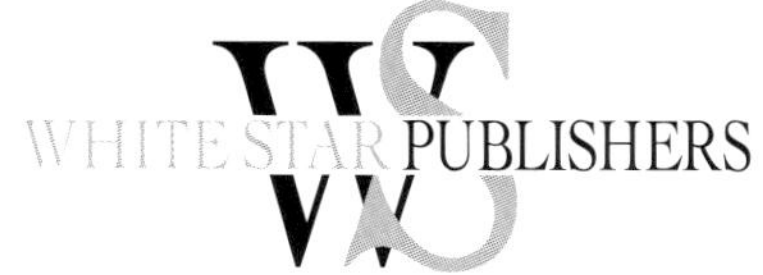

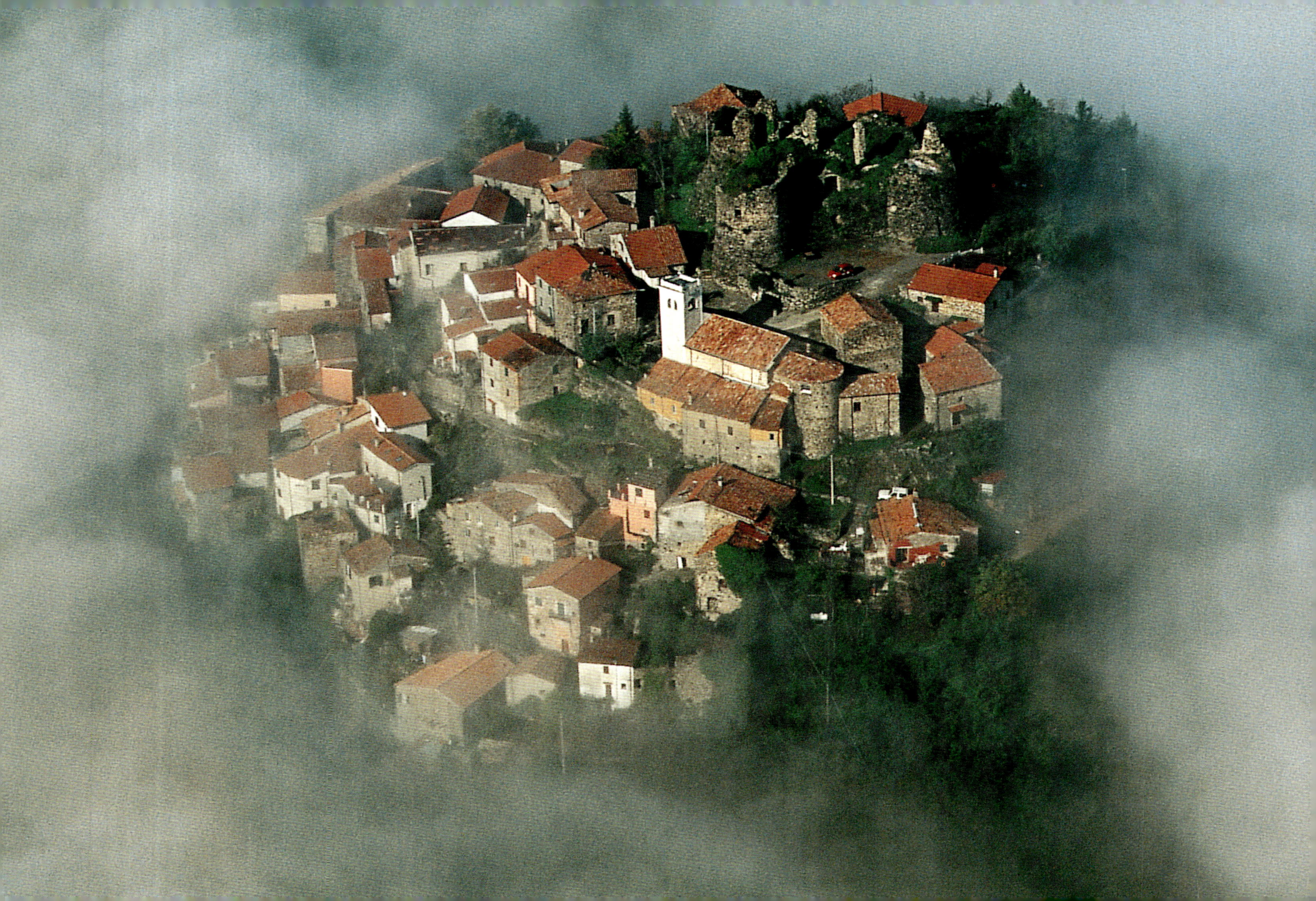

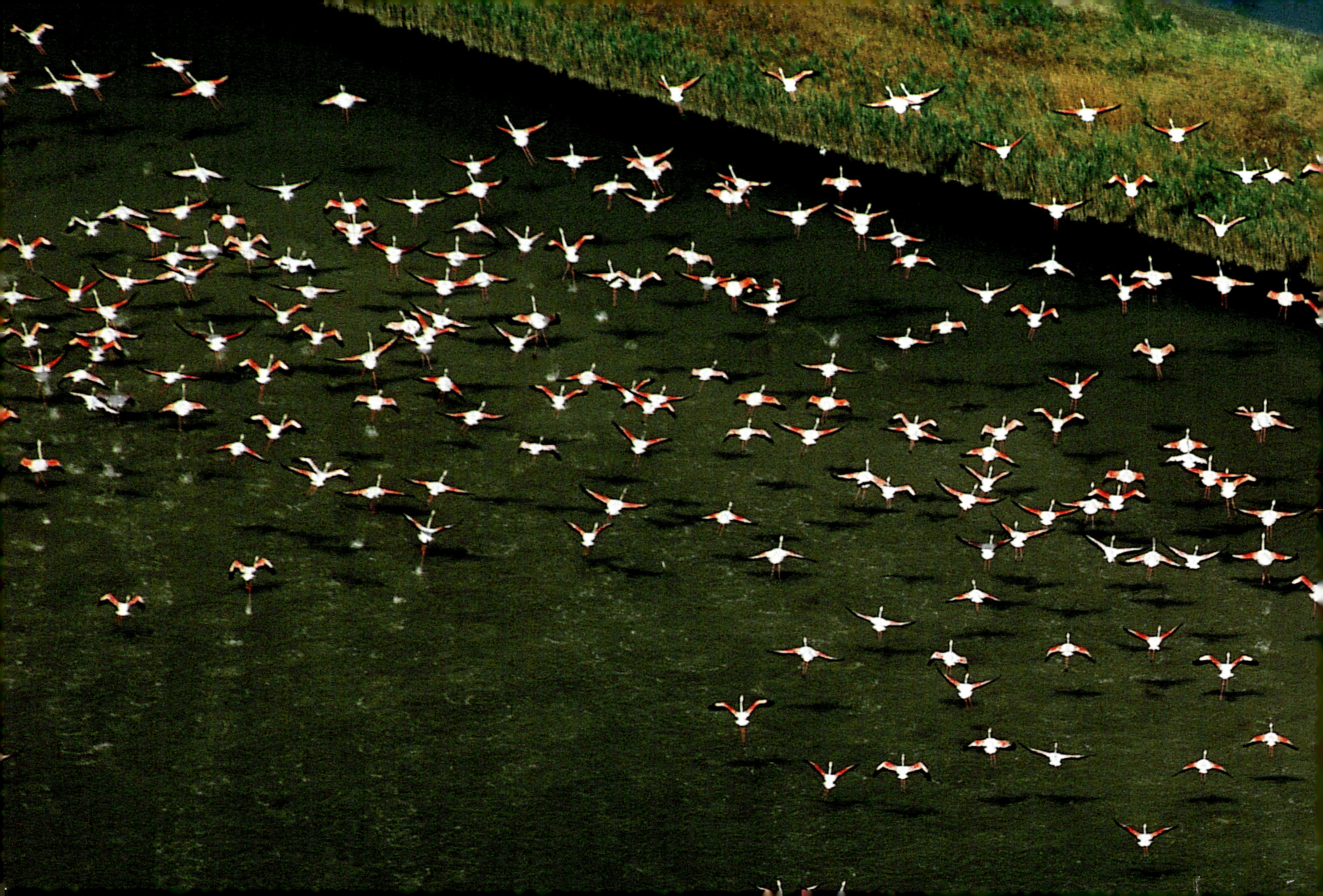

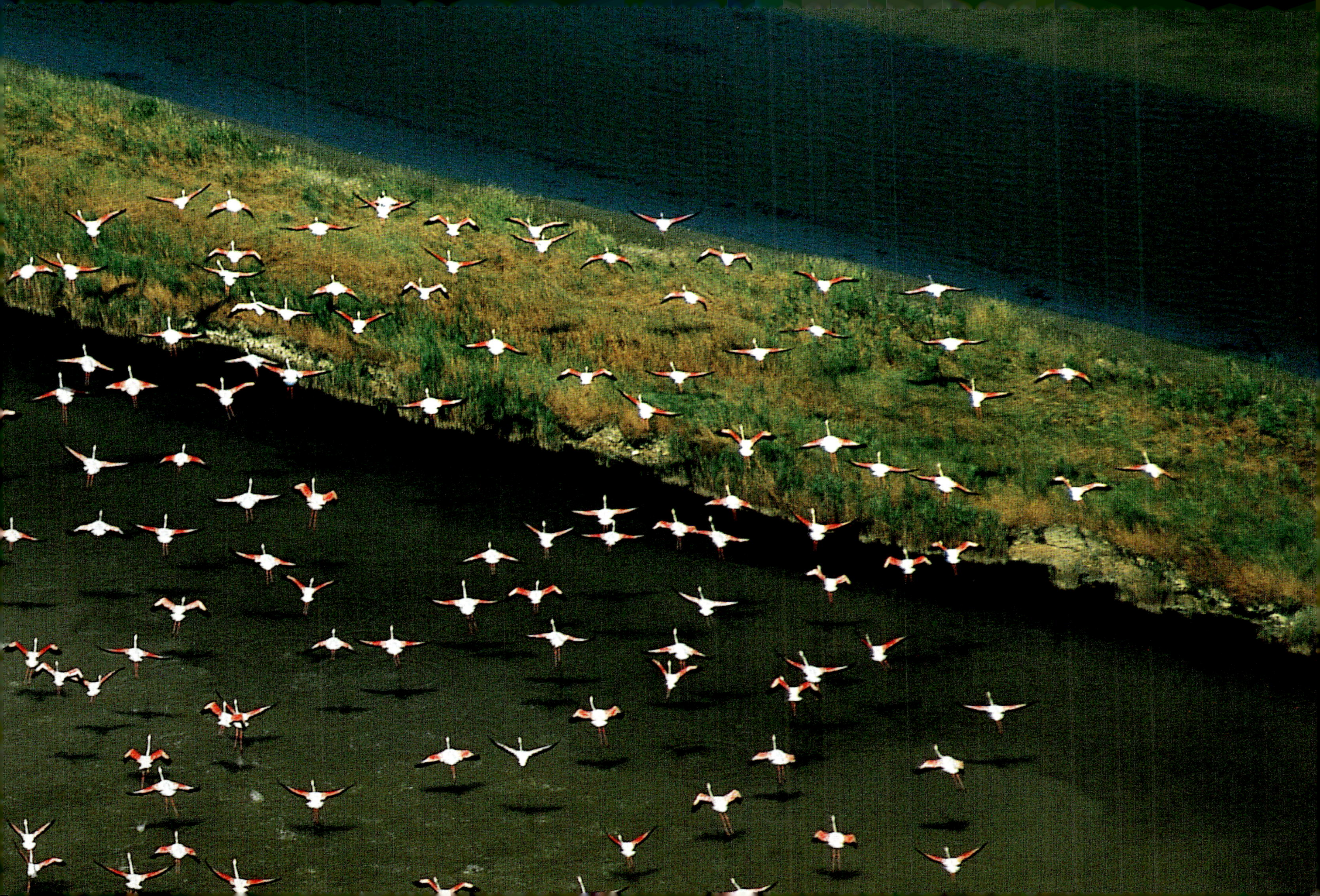

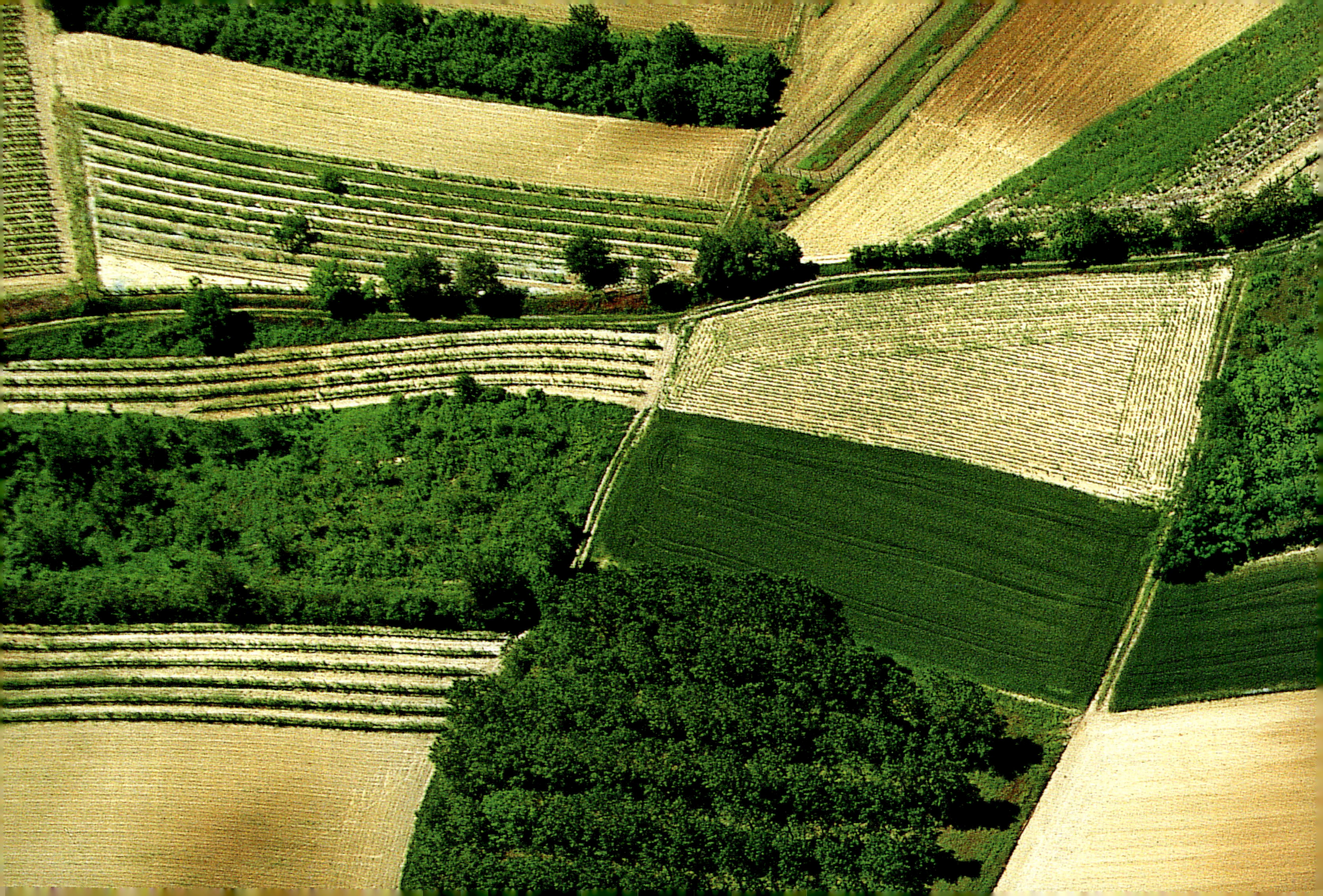

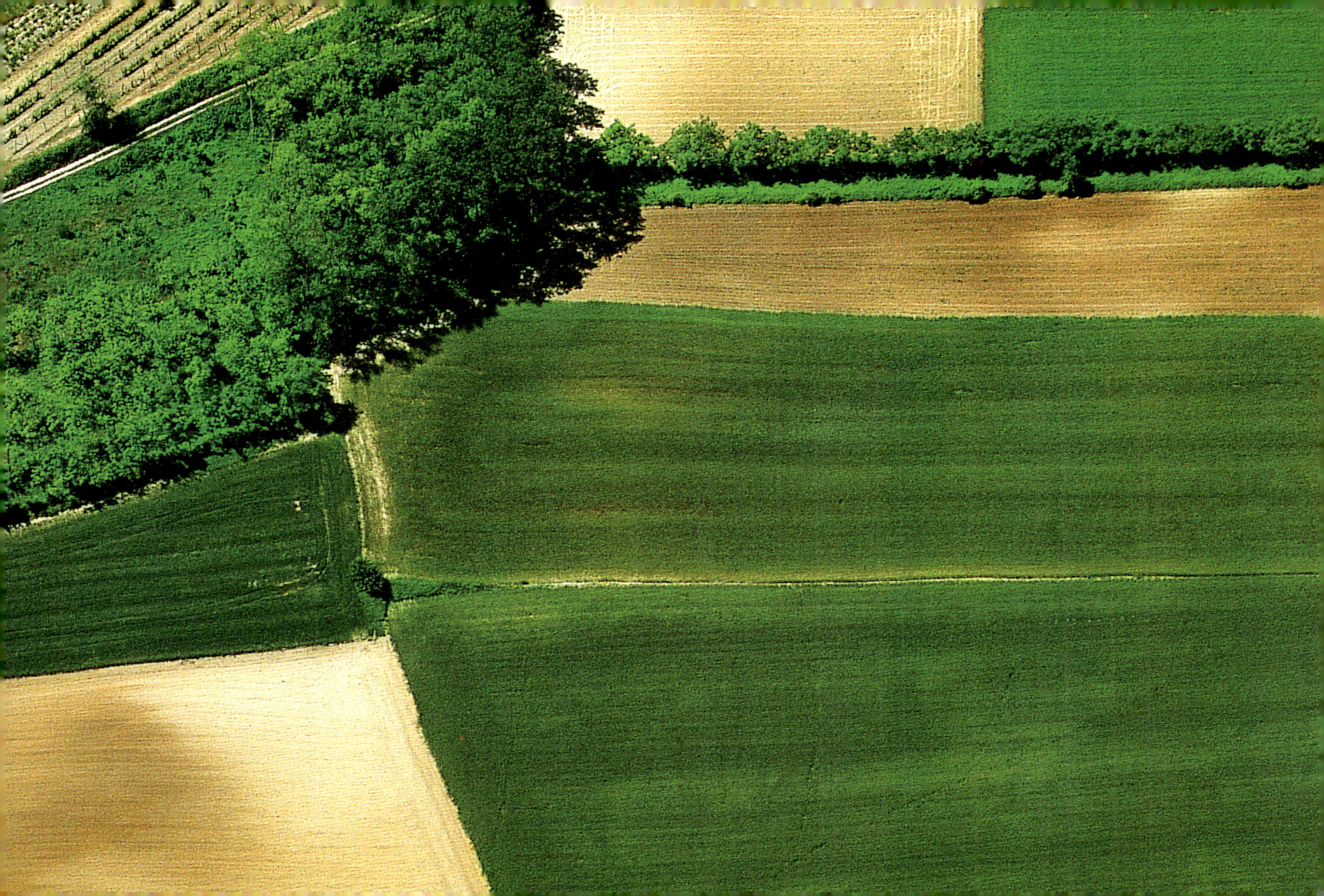

ITALIAN COUNTRYSIDE

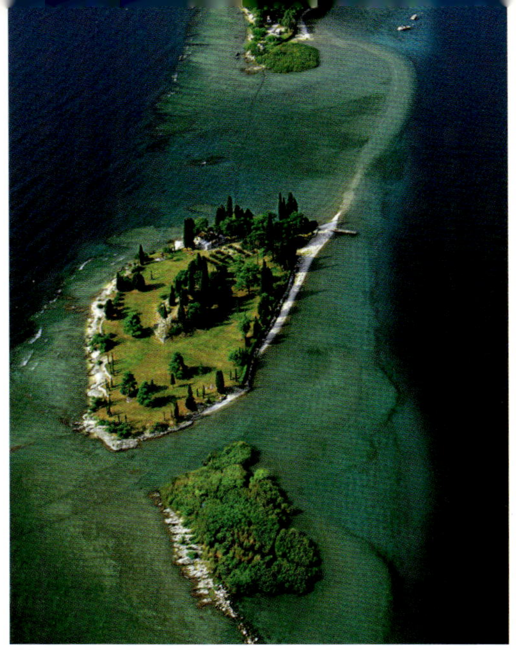

PHOTOGRAPHS
Antonio Attini

TEXT
Francesco Petretti

Contents

2-3 On the Via Francigena, the road that brought English pilgrims from Canterbury to Rome, stands Bibola (Massa Carrara province), an ancient village, its castle now in ruins.

4-5 Alongside the Valli di Comacchio, the now abandoned salt flats are the stopover point for thousands of pink flamingoes.

6-7 The hillsides of the Montferrat area (Alessandria) have traditionally been given over to the vine. This centuries-old practice has led to the creation of wines famous throughout the world.

8 Facing the Rocca di Manerba (Brescia) on Lake Garda is the Isola San Biagio, also known as "Rabbit Island."

9 On 2 July 2004, UNESCO added the Val d'Orcia (Siena) to its list of World Heritage Sites.

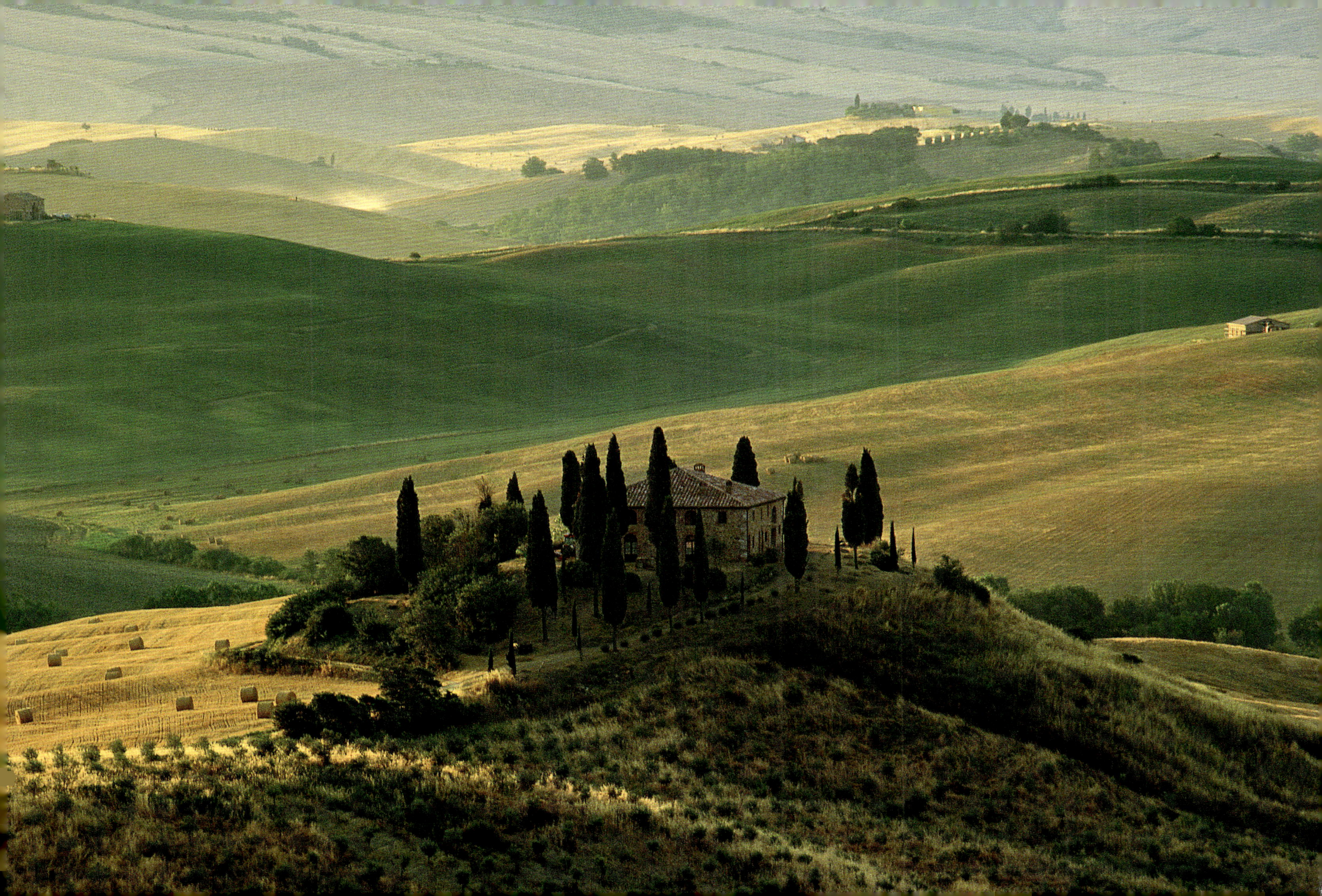

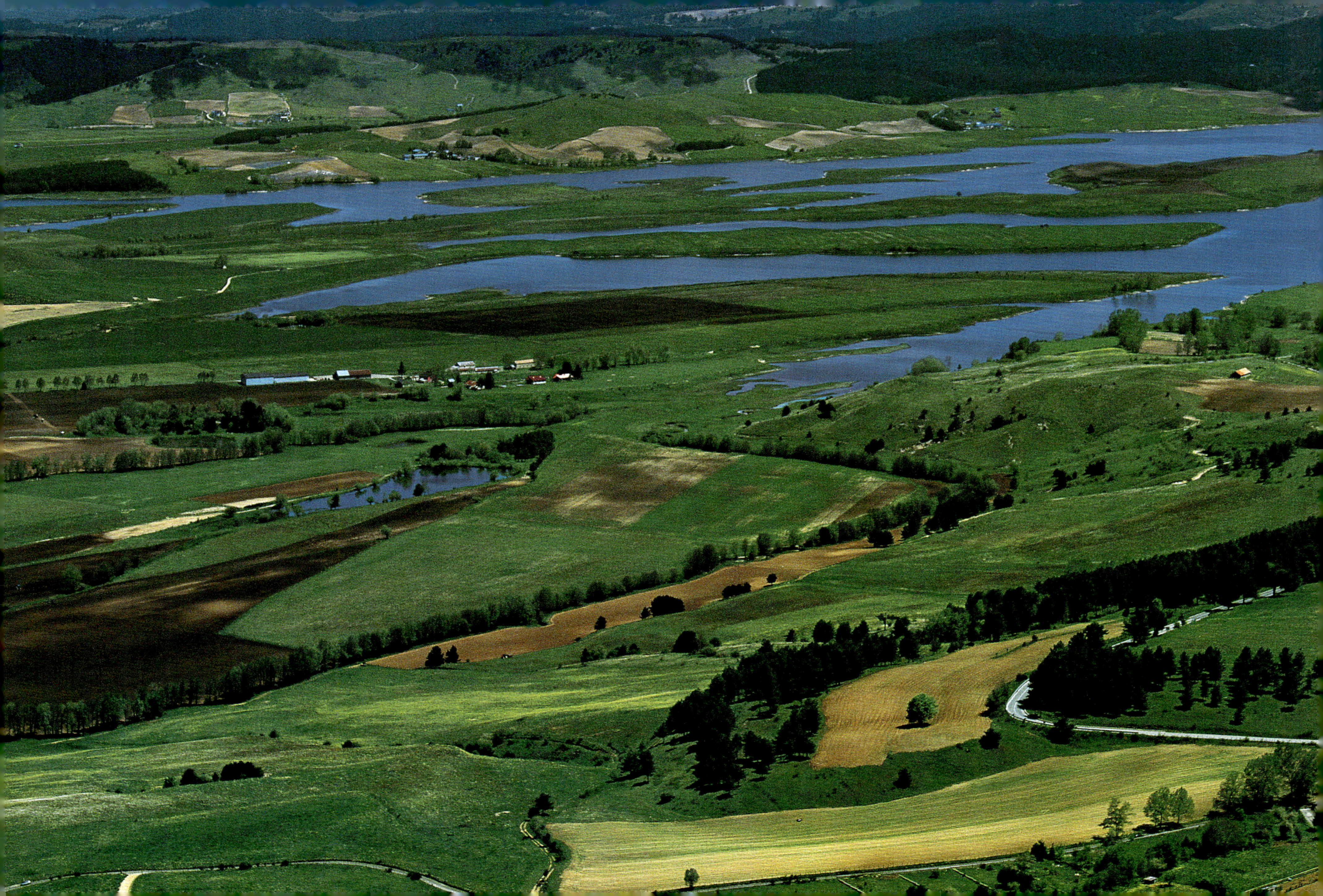

The Italian landscape is one of the most varied in Europe, thanks to its irregular, mountainous morphology, the extensive developments from north to south, its position at the center of the Mediterranean Sea, and the centuries-old efforts that humankind has made in changing it. In an area barely occupying 115,000 sq. miles (300,000 sq. km) – equivalent to little more than half of France – it ranges from the tundra of the high mountains, which possess the same look, the same wildlife and the same vegetation as the Lapland areas of the Scandinavian countries, down to the subtropical environment of the south of Italy, known as the Mezzogiorno, with has all the biological organisms typical of the North African Maghreb, and passing through all imaginable variations, from forests, to aquatic, to underground settings that are so characteristic of Europe. One passes from the highest of mountain peaks furrowed by glaciers to an immense chain of still active volcanoes, from fossil-rich downs abandoned by the seas millions of years ago to alluvial plains along the coast and to mountains built up from the skeletons of marine organisms over the millennia. In these areas the water-driven erosion of the rocks has produced the most impressive and imposing karstic effects, including deep and beautiful caverns looking like scenes from a fable, while the glaciers have molded the countryside into a series of shapes. Wherever one goes, the Italian countryside never ceases to amaze for the variety of its faces. With almost 58,000 species of animal and over 6000 forms of higher plant life, Italy, of all the nations in Europe, has the greatest biodiversity, many features of which have benefited from the labors of humankind over thousands of years to bring improvements to mountains, hills, plains, coasts, rivers and lakes, all of which have been subjected to colonization by peoples who have drawn upon the resources the peninsula has offered, often in the face of very great difficulties. For the most part mountainous, and with many extremely arid areas, the land has not always lent itself to agricultural exploitation and cultivators have often occupied themselves in a multitude of ways in order to snatch a crop from the stony reefs in Liguria, or the valleys of the Alps, or the torrid steppes of Puglia, and in so doing bringing life to those praiseworthy combinations of natural resources and human inventiveness. This is the dominating element so characteristic of the Italian countryside; it is the only ambience where a flock of sheep can graze under the arches of a Roman aqueduct or where a field of beetroot can grow amid the earthenware products of an ancient Etruscan settlement. Men have been living here for a very long time and it can be argued that Italy is one of the Mediterranean zones with the oldest civilization, where the Paleolithic and Neolithic peoples, together with the civilizations of the Etruscans and of Rome, along with those living in medieval as well as our own times, have transformed the woodlands into fields, drained the marshlands, created new lakes, built aqueducts and monumental buildings, excavated necropolises in the rock, defeated even

10 Lake Cecita, in the Sila area of Cosenza province, is not navigable; it was created for the irrigation of the surrounding cultivated fields (especially potato fields) and the generation of electrical energy.

the most inaccessible of mountain peaks with the new roads and buildings of holiday resorts, but above all else have managed to create a countryside in which the human and the natural elements have been flourishing in an impressive harmony. Even from a rural point of view, Italy can be proud of its extraordinary range of circumstances, which are a reflection of the variety of morphologies to be found in the land; from the sheer range of climatic conditions, from the highly complex histories of the civilizations which have succeeded each other in the various territories and which have led man to compete for the land with wildlife from the plains to the mountain tops, from the Alps to the Sicilian islands. It could be said that there is not a corner of the land that has not been the object, to some extent, of an agricultural or animal breeding initiative devised by humankind; the alpine meadows have been grazed right up to the perennial snowline, the same happens in the fields leading up to the Apennines, while the stone-built terracing climbs right up to the very edge of the craters of the volcanoes, as it does on the rockiest islands in the Tyrrhenian Sea. At a short distance from each other, an industrialized agriculture lives right alongside traditional agriculture. In these last years, Italian agriculture has been enduring a period of profound crisis. It is typified by the turbulent explosion of the industrial and service sectors, by the progressive urban migration of the rural population, by the depopulation of those areas already considered marginal in terms of the productivity (the mountains and hills) and by the pervasive changes in the markets

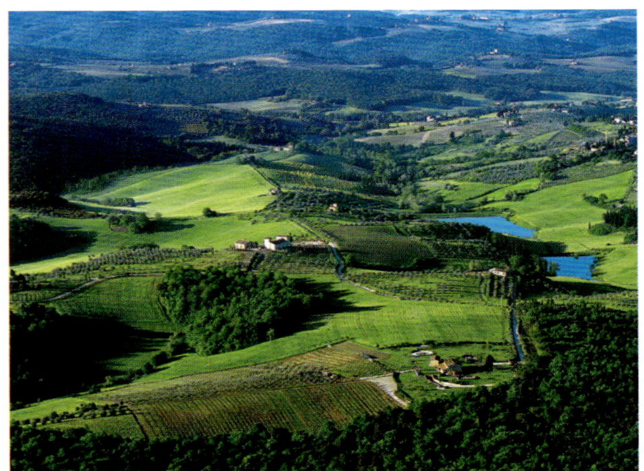

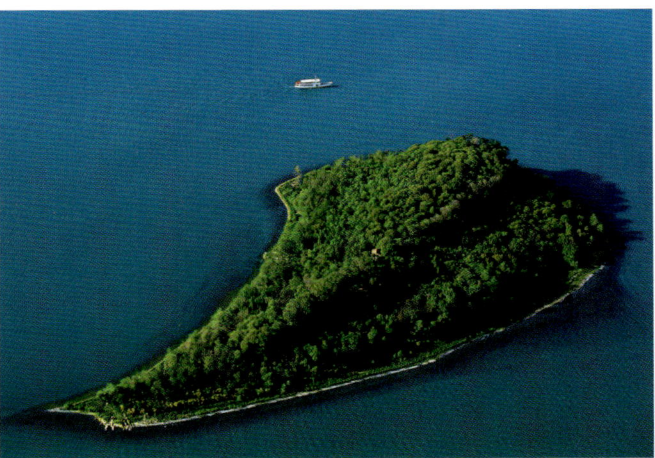

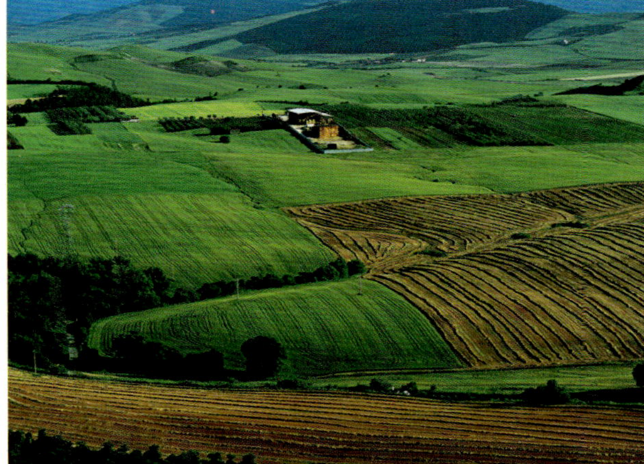

12 left From Tavarnelle Val di Pesa, the panorama is a gentle succession of green hills dotted with farmhouses and hotel buildings, some of which offer artificial lakes for fishing enthusiasts.

for agricultural products. This crisis is reflected in the decline in the agricultural population, in the disappearance of the small-scale cultivator, in the transformation of the agrarian countryside by the intensive adoption of yield-increasing methods in many areas, and the marginalization or even abandonment of other zones previously cultivated. Given the very considerable extent of these agricultural lands, these changes cannot fail to have a profound effect on the environment in its widest sense and on its flora and fauna in particular, tied as they are to the agricultural surroundings by thousands of years of adaptation. Some 50 percent of the animal and vegetable biodiversity of Italy is contained within, or depends to some degree on, the extensive agricultural zones which are still an important element of the Italian countryside, occupying approximately one half of the total cultivable areas, but this biodiversity is mostly concentrated in the hilly or mountainous zones. In Italy, just as in the rest of Europe, the conservation of the traditional agrarian countryside has now become one of the central themes of the new politics of the European environment, developed specifically by non-governmental associations and organizations of the European Union; these bodies have drafted a series of important provisions aimed also at arresting the decline in the varieties of cultivated crops and domesticated animals. Before the Second World War, over 400 varieties of grain were cultivated In Italy, but only 205 survive today. Of 40 types of crucifers, only 5 are still cultivated, while 80 percent of all the apples now grown are of only 3 varieties. The following pages present the Italian countryside from a somewhat privileged point of view, dividing it according to a number of important themes chosen in order to give a sense of order to the multiplicity and abundance existing in these settings and also to suggest a geographical itinerary similar to that followed by our photographers. We begin with the Po Valley which, with its 15,000 sq. miles (38,000 sq. km), is the largest of the Italian plains and indeed one of the most extensive in Europe. It takes in a range of natural habitats, as well as a number of environments heavily shaped by humankind, that are both unique and constantly changing. The second chapter is dedicated to the rivers, which are a characteristic feature of a large part of the Italian territory but which are among the natural environments most compromised by the intervention of humankind; their courses, often stripped of their arboreous and palustrine vegetation and frequently marked out by geometrically straight dykes or man-made structures composed of concreted heaps of stones and cement jetties, carry currents that are slack when the water is low but are given to unexpected surges when the level rises with the autumn and winter rains, and transform a river into a mere water conduit open to the skies, totally devoid of any fascination or any of its once rich variety, except, that is, for those stretch-

12 center L'Isola Minore on Lake Trasimeno (Perugia) is the smallest of the lake's islands and is totally deserted. It had been densely populated until the 1400s.

12 right In summer the countryside around Melfi (Potenza) becomes an incredible expanse of golden wheat, striking enough to be chosen as a set for the movie *I Am Not Scared* (2003).

es where humankind continues to live in harmony with the blue arteries of the Earth – areas that we have photographed and offer as illustrations. The third chapter is dedicated to the countryside of central and northern Italy and to all the multiple aspects which give it its character, in particular to those areas of hilly ground and where the alpine lakes of volcanic formation are to be found. The fourth and final chapter allows one to relive the journey that our photographers have made in the south of Italy – the so-called "Lands of the Sun" – with its mantle of vegetation typical of the Mediterranean scrub and of the garrigue where, as a response to the imperatives imposed by the climate, the countryside enjoys two seasons of fully blooming plant-life: in the autumn, and again in the early spring, when the rains are more plentiful. At such moments the countryside of the South becomes a riot of color: many species of orchid burst into flower producing specimens of extraordinary architectural complexity, including mirror bee orchids with their Prussian blue labellum, the humble but elegant yellow orchids and other orchids with violet spurs. Along with the orchids one can admire other flowers, such as the yellow and violet iris and the asphodel. The South possesses a fascination whose roots are buried in antiquity. These are lands which have been inhabited since time immemorial, leaving vestiges of civilizations that have used the reworking of stone as their major strength; stone has been used for the remarkable rural constructions in Apulia, for the *nuraghe* in Sardinia, the water tanks of Sicily and for the animal pens and dry walls of the Maremma. In these Lands of the Sun, there still exists today a countryside made up of a harmonious mix of unspoiled open space, cultivated areas and rural buildings as well as examples of perhaps a more subdued architecture but not for this less important and striking than the more magnificent buildings erected by mankind in this part of our peninsular. It is precisely the South of Italy, where the rural landscapes are seemingly more numerous than in the North and where the identity that has existed for centuries has been more faithfully preserved away from the major centers, that demonstrates how our journey in search of the beauties of the landscape is also an itinerary that takes us back into history; in fact it is quite possible to appreciate the profound changes that the handiwork of man has brought throughout the territory and recognize the thousands of years of exhausting, toil, which has been undertaken by generations of farmers and laborers in order to bring nature under control and so offer to us observers the magnificent spectacles that we have set out to find.

15 The countryside around Venosa (Potenza) offers a many-colored palette. This is the country of the Aglianico del Vulture DOC, the wine that in recent years has come to be known as "the Barolo of the South."

18-19 The hinterland of the Murgia (Basilicata) is an area of exceptional geological interest; it is composed of white limestone rich in traces of karst.

20-21 In 1999 UNESCO added the Po Delta Park to its list of World Heritage Sites.

22-23 A cottage in ruins in the countryside near Cagliari is evidence of the progressive abandonment of certain areas of the island.

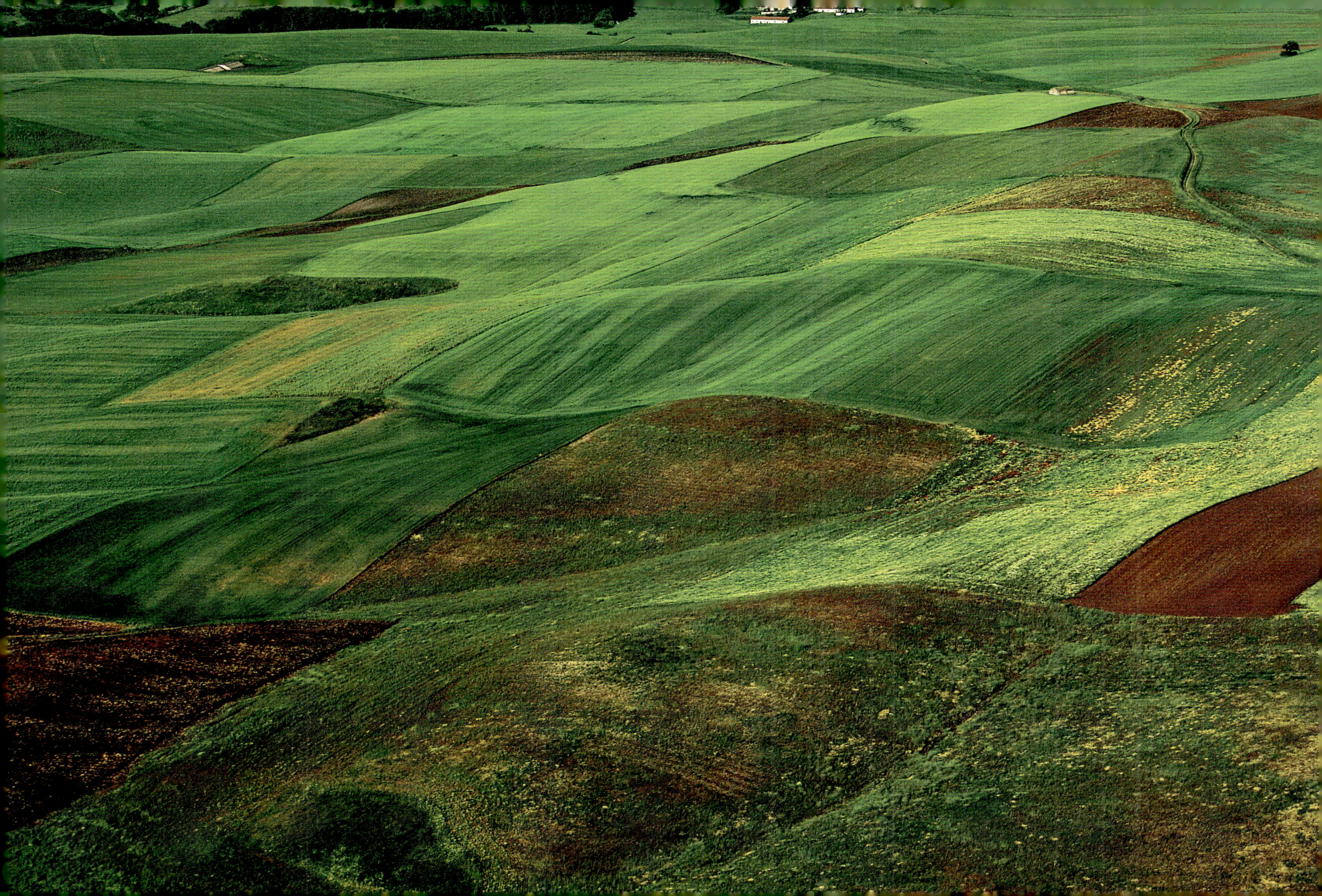

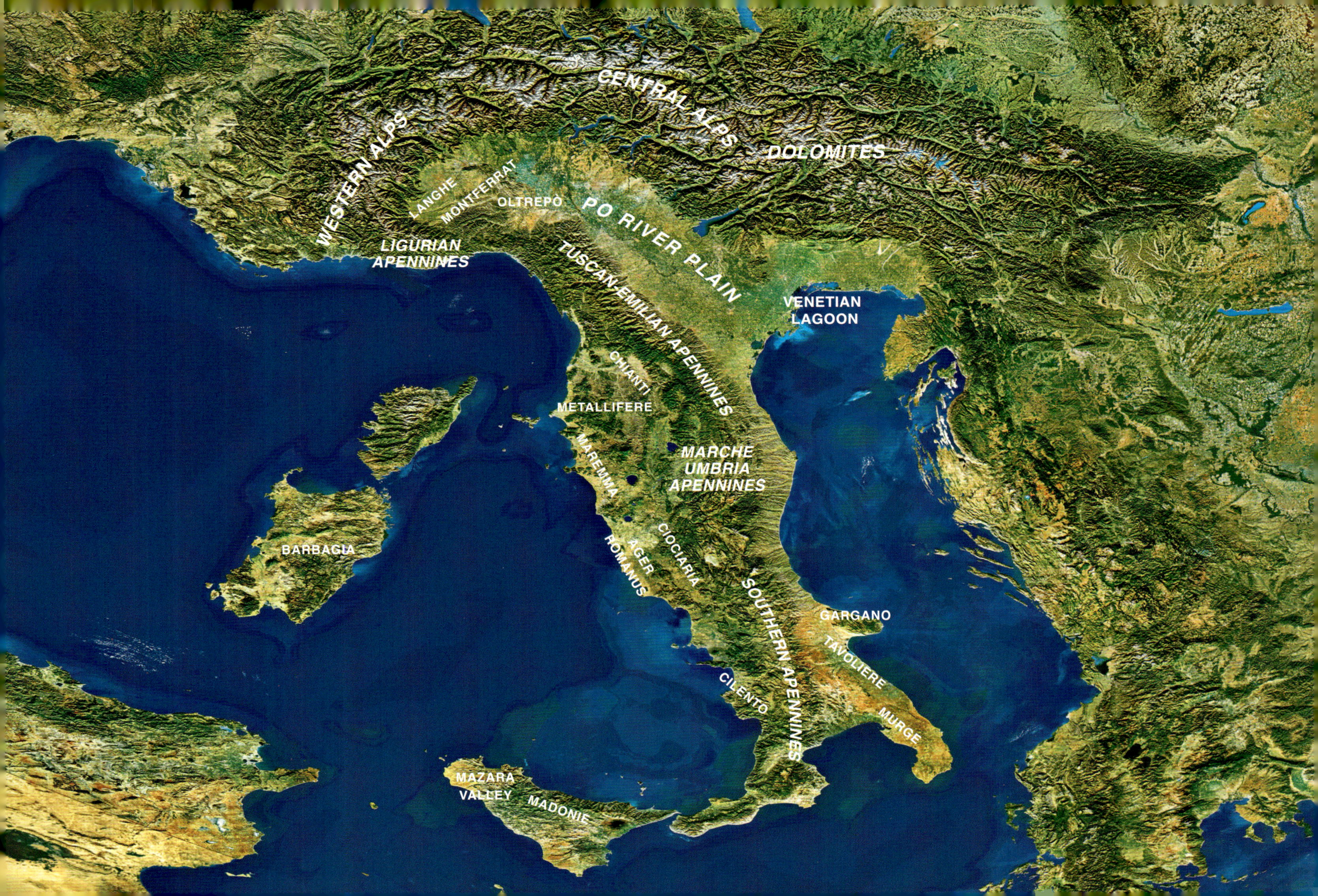
CENTRAL ALPS
DOLOMITES
WESTERN ALPS
LANGHE
MONTFERRAT
OLTREPÒ
PO RIVER PLAIN
LIGURIAN APENNINES
TUSCAN-EMILIAN APENNINES
VENETIAN LAGOON
CHIANTI
METALLIFERE
MAREMMA
MARCHE UMBRIA APENNINES
BARBAGIA
AGER ROMANUS
CIOCIARIA
SOUTHERN APENNINES
GARGANO
TAVOLIERE
CILENTO
MURGE
MAZARA VALLEY
MADONIE

Italian countryside key data

- Total Area: 116,346,5 sq. miles (301,338 sq. km).
- Population: 57,321,070 (most recent census).
- Density: 493/sq. mile (190/sq. km).
- Terrain: 43.3 % mountainous, 30.3 % hilly, 26.4 % flat.
- Principal Rivers: Po 405 miles (652 km), Adige 255 miles (410 km), Tiber 252 miles (405 km), Adda 195 miles (313 km), Oglio 174 miles (280 km), Tanaro 171 miles (276 km), Ticino 154 miles (248 km), Arno 150 miles (241 km), Piave 137 miles (220 km), Reno 131 miles (211 km), Sarca-Mincio 120 miles (194 km), Volturno 109 miles (175 km), Brenta 108 miles (174 km), Secchia 107 miles (172 km), Tagliamento 106 miles (170 km), Ofanto 106 miles (170 km), Ombrone 100 miles (161 km), Chiese 99 miles (160 km), Dora Baltea 99 miles (160 km), Liri-Garigliano 98 miles (158 km), Bormida 96 miles (154 km).
- Lakes and Lagoons: Lake Orta, Lake Maggiore, Lake Como, Lake Iseo, Lake Idro, Lake Garda, Lake Trasimeno, Lake Bolsena, Lake Vico, Lake Bracciano, Lake Albano, Lake Nemi, Lake Martignano, Lake Ampollino, Grado Lagoon, Marano Lagoon, Venetian Lagoon, Valli di Comacchio, Lake Lesina, Lake Varano, Alimini Lakes, Mar Piccolo of Taranto (Little Sea), Mar Grande of Taranto (Big Sea), Lake of Fondi, Sabaudia Lagoon, Burano Lake, Orbetello Lagoon, Lake Massaciuccoli, ponds of Cagliari, pond of Santa Giusta, Cabras Pond, Palude del Capitano.
- Principal Plains: Padana Plain (or Po Valley), Veneto-Friuli Plain, Valdarno, Lucca Plain, Maremma, Ager Romanus, Pontine Marshes, Volturno Plain, Sele Plain, Apulian Table, Salentino Plain, Sibari Plain, Plain of Gioia Tauro, Catania Plain, Campidano, Metapontina Plain, Nurra.
- Agricultural Activity: the most recent census (2000) registered nearly 2.5 million working farms, with a drop of approximately 14% when compared to 1990. 49% of workers employed in agricultural labor are located in the South, while the remaining 51% are distributed between the North (38%) and the Center (13%).

This satellite photograph, as reworked by computer, shows a view of the Italian peninsula and of the principal rural areas that give it its character. The image is distorted by the perspective and by the curvature of the earth's surface, resulting from the relatively low position of the satellite.

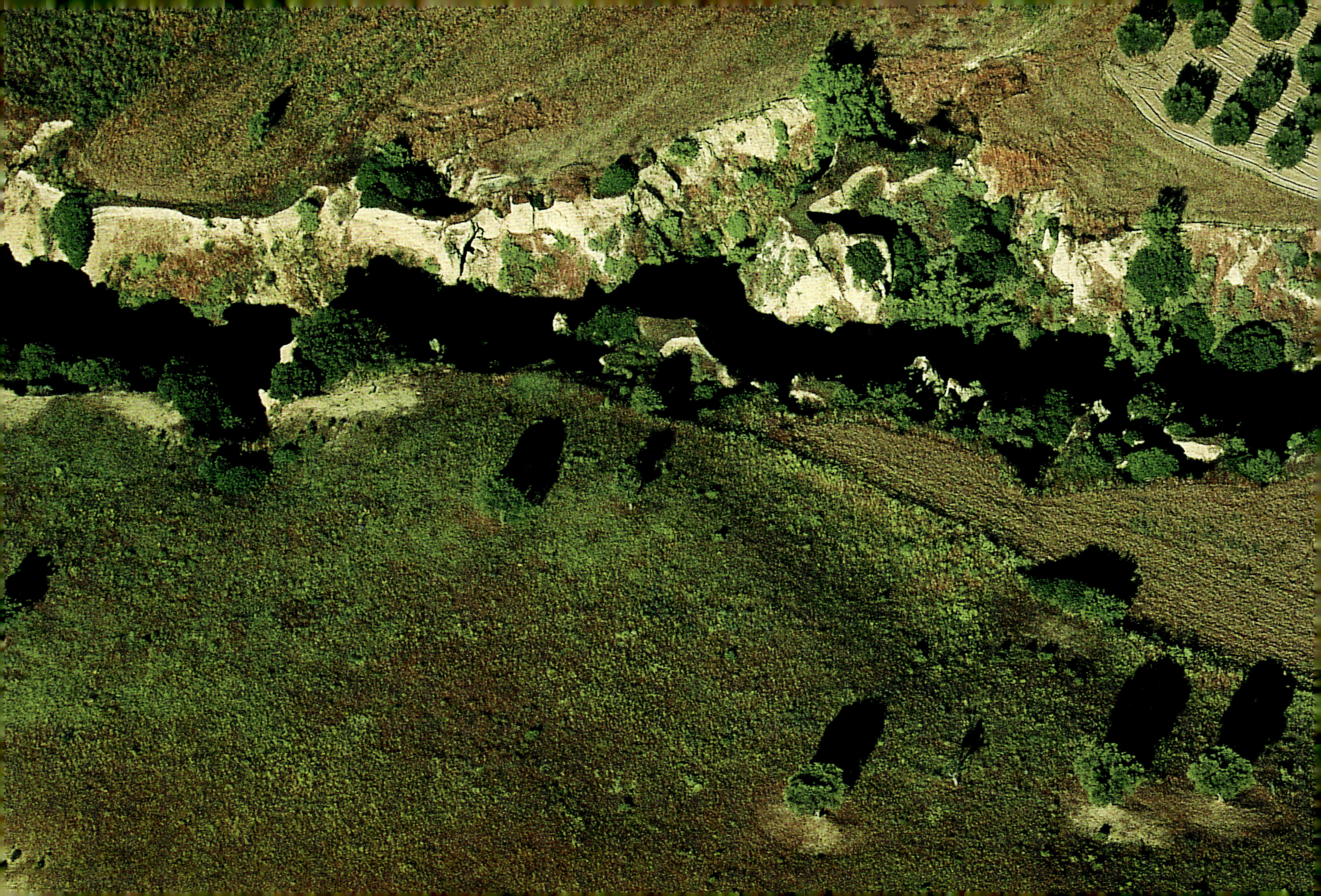

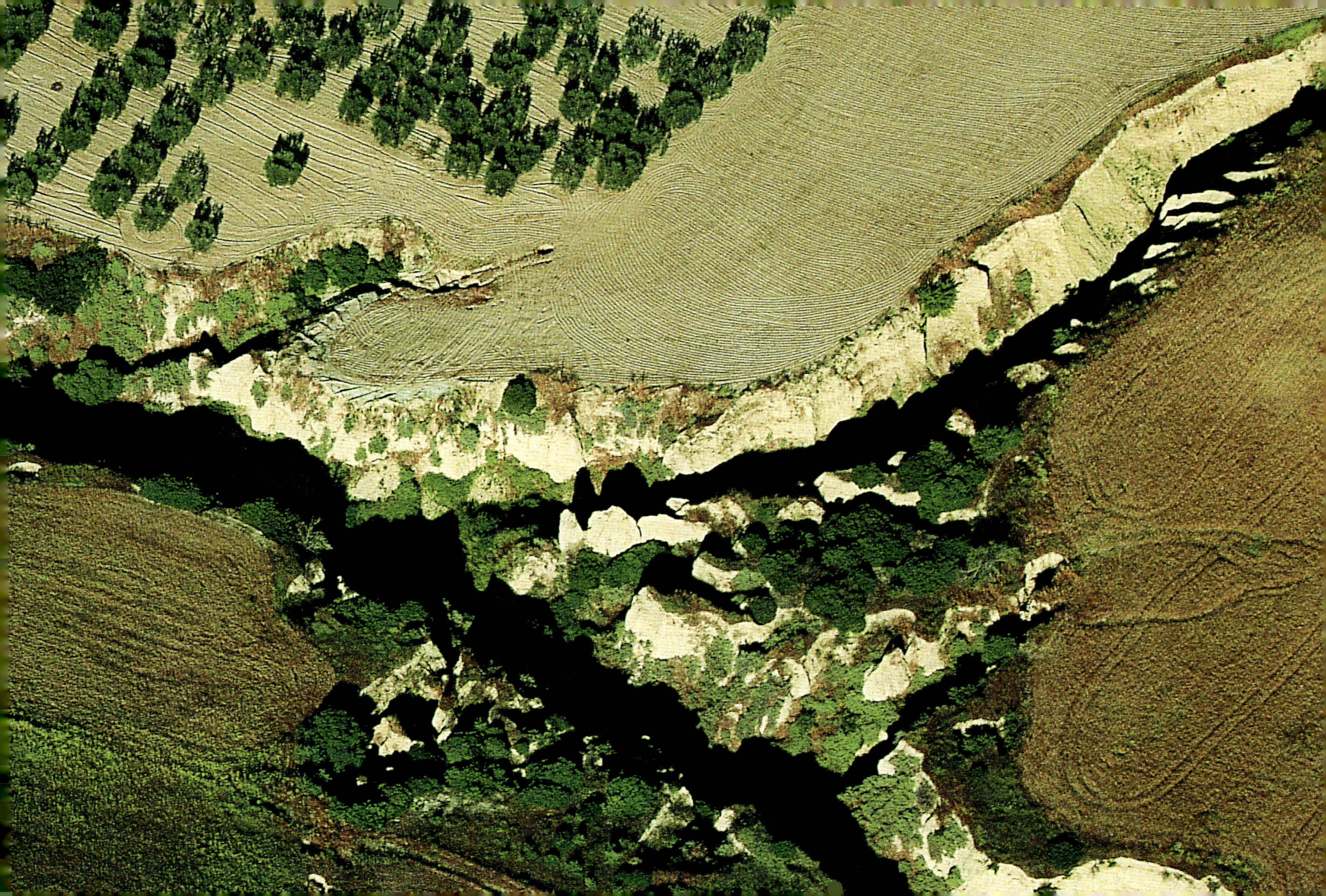

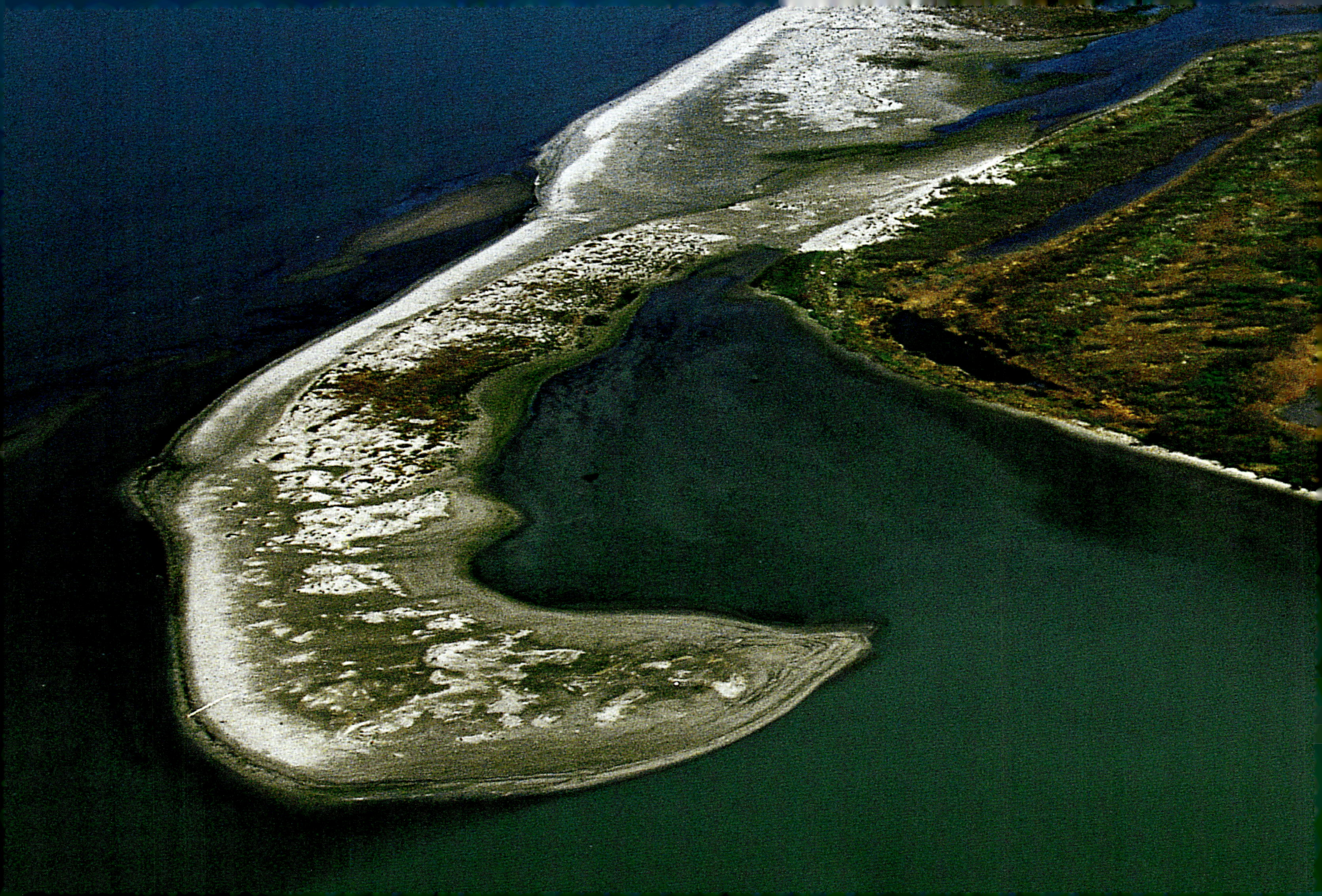

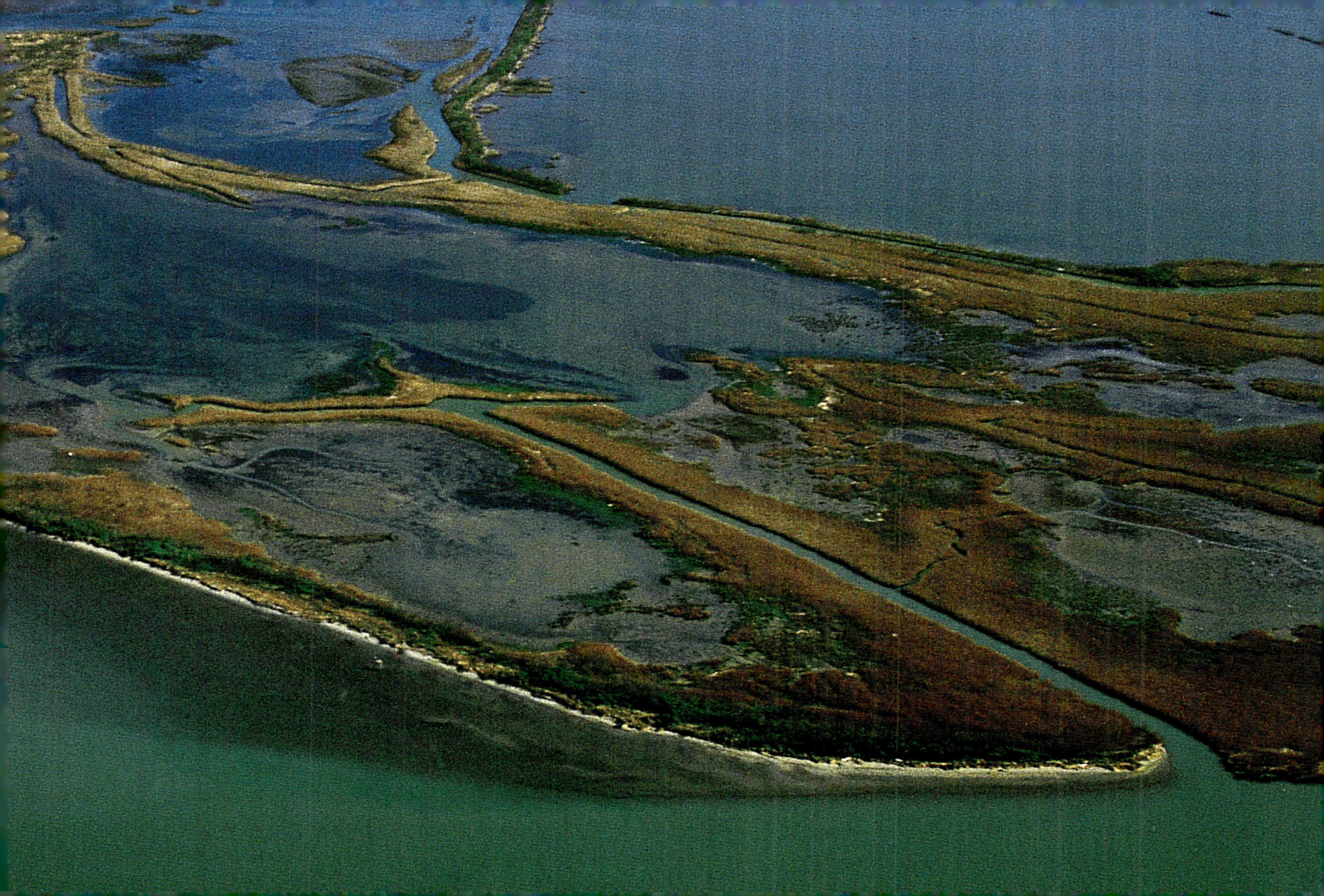

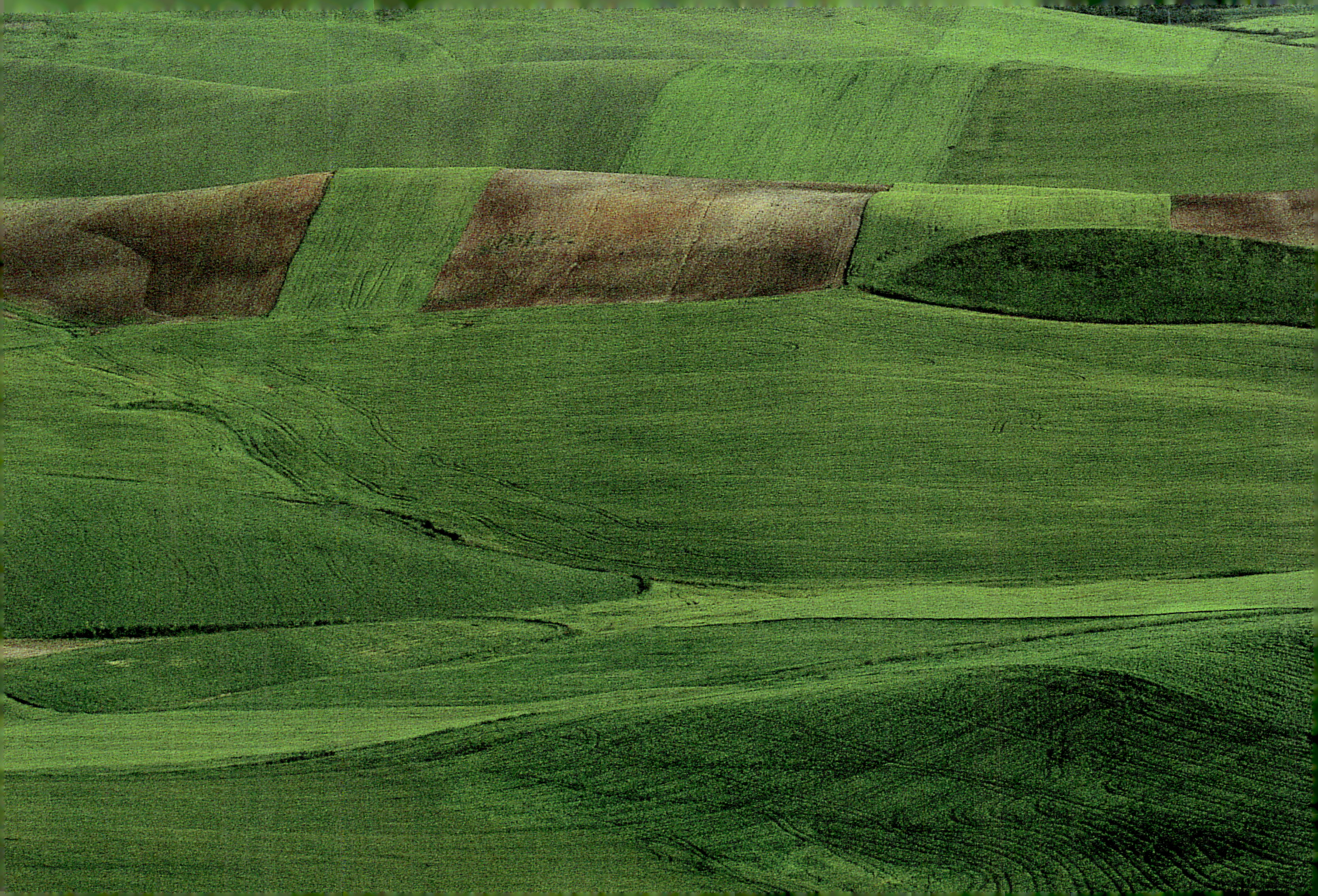

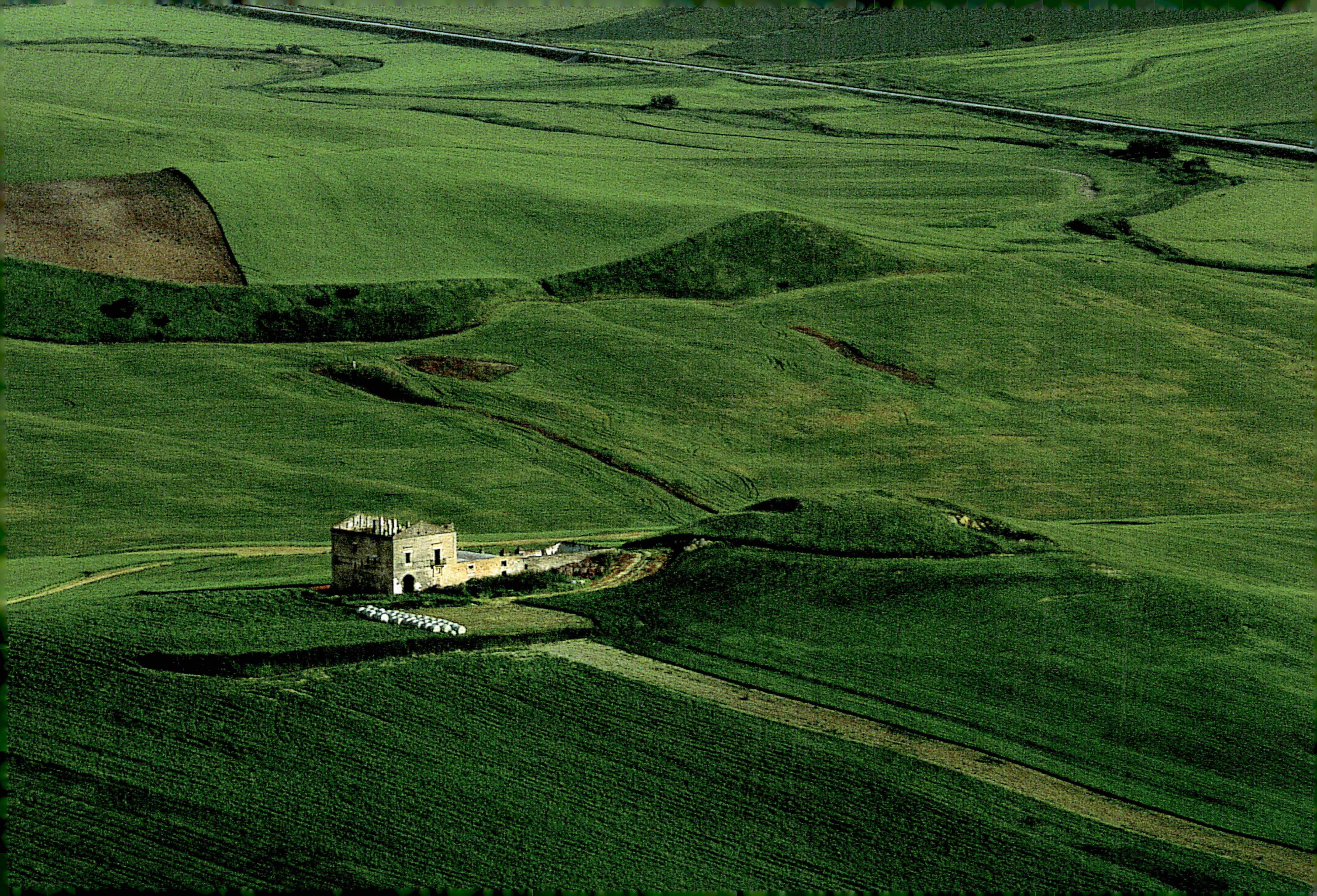

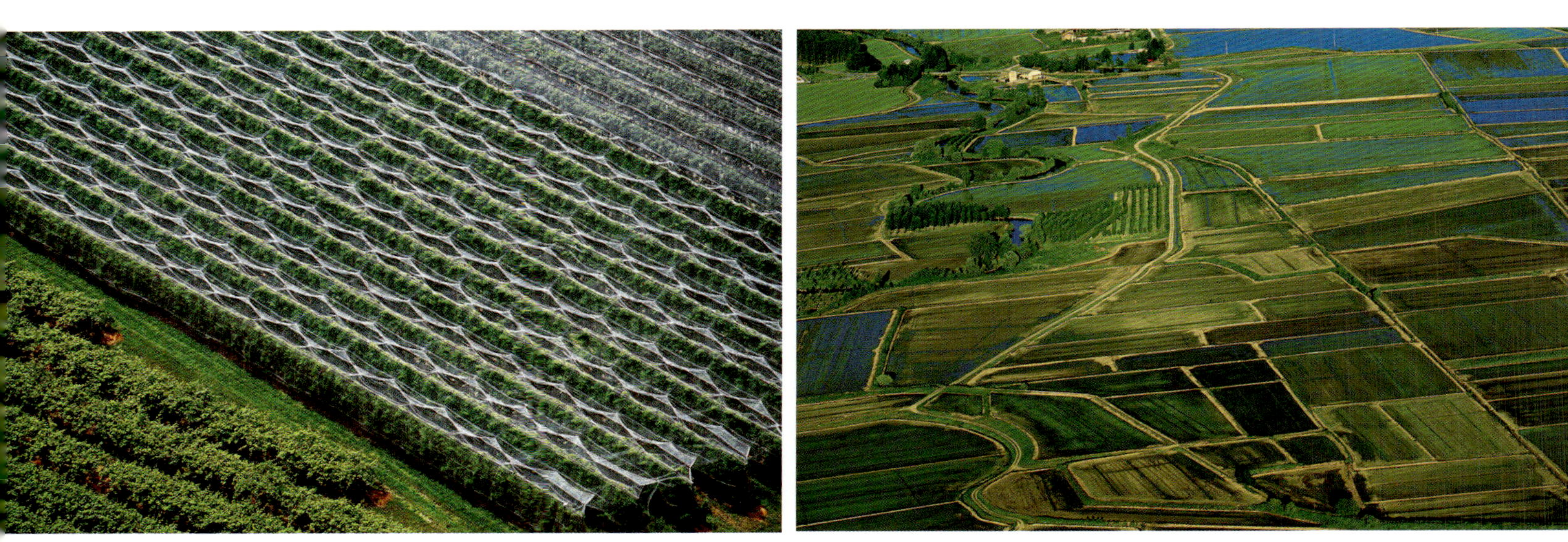

THE PO VALLEY

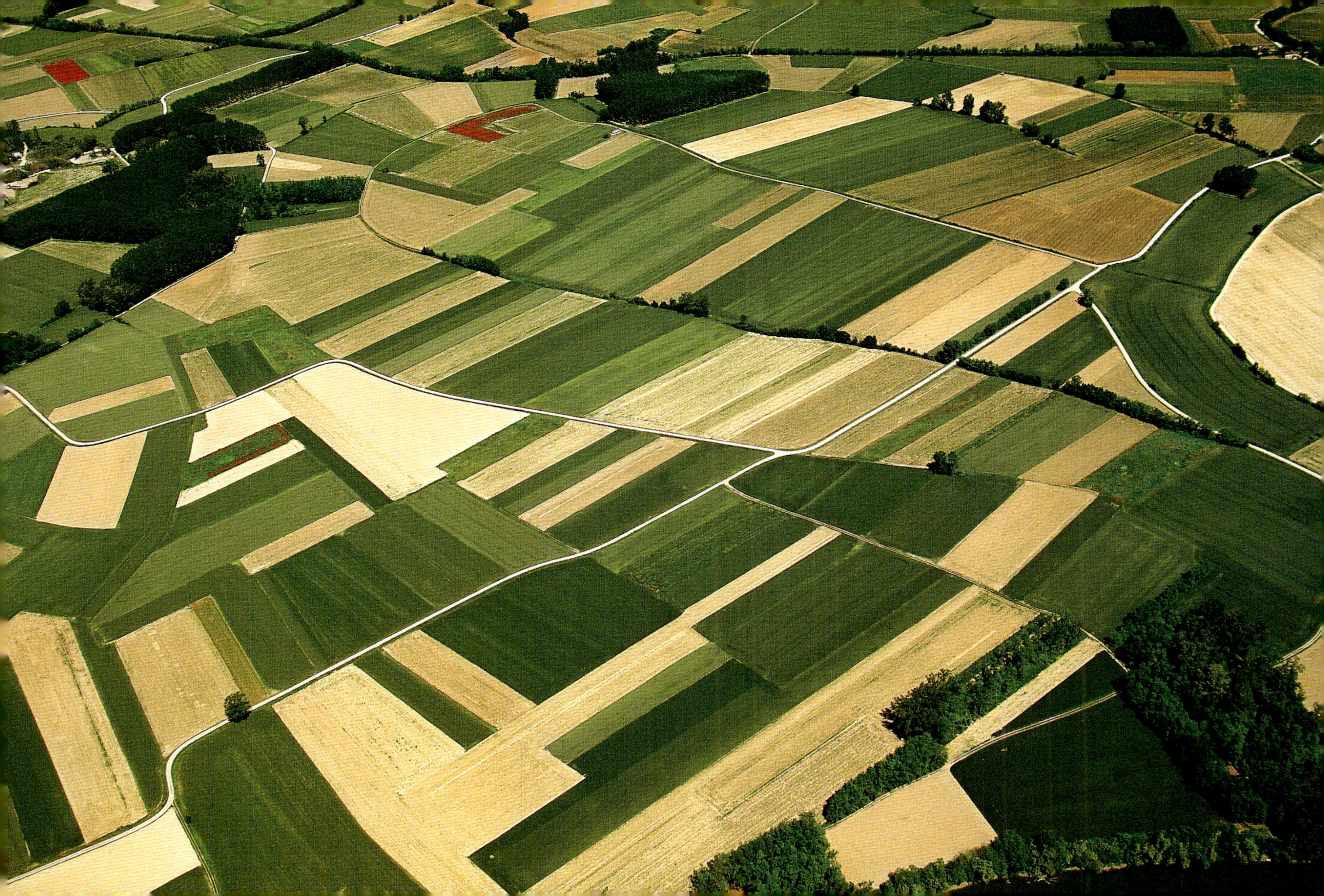

The Padano Plain, in terms of its geography, should perhaps be divided into three quite distinct parts: the real plain itself, carved through by the Po River and all its tributaries (mostly flowing in from the left); the plain located in the Veneto and Friuli regions, crossed by the Adige, Tagliamento, Isonzo and Piave rivers which all flow directly into the Adriatic Sea; and finally the plain in the Emilia-Romagna region, taking in the course of the rivers Reno, Rubicon and a number of others that also debouch along the Adriatic coastline. Shut in by the ring of the Alps to the north and by the Apennines to the south, the Po Valley, which in appearance might seem quite flat, in fact conceals a very different reality, in that beneath all the masses of sediment deposited by rivers is a crowded concentration of the mountain systems extending down from the Alps and the Apennines. We can therefore argue that the Po Valley is really a mountainous depression that has filled up with sediments which have made it absolutely flat, while falling gently away toward the Adriatic Sea where parts of this territorial complex extend even below sea level. Gravel of varying densities and, underneath, sand, mud and ever finer silt have formed the composition of the soil down to a considerable depth, stripping it away from the mountains and carrying it all down to the bottom of the valley via the river currents, eventually reaching the sea. It can be said without fear of contradiction that every grain of sand on the Adriatic shoreline is in fact a tiny fragment of Monviso, Monte Rosa, Monte Bianco, the Dolomites or the mountains in the Tuscan-Emilian Apennines. Held firmly in the grip of the mountains, exposed to the often cold and unforgiving winds coming from the east, this great plain has nevertheless over thousands of years offered man land which is fertile and easily cultivable, blessed with an abundance of water and every other convenience. Here man has reached levels of agricultural productivity worthy of the *Guinness Book of Records*: the production figures per acre of grain and rice are amongst the highest in the world and the environment has inevitably felt the stress that humankind has been imposing on it over the centuries, after having stripped away the original covering of vegetation. At one time, in fact, the Po Valley was covered by a single, immense forest dominated by broad-leaf hardwood trees suited to the cold, damp climate such as bay-oaks, durmasts, alders, willows and poplars, all trees that have survived only in limited, protected areas located principally along the banks of the rivers where they have not been replaced

24 left Rows of vines as far as the eye can see, protected by anti-hail nets: this is the summer landscape that one sees in the low-lying countryside around Cuneo.

24 right The area around Vercelli is at the center of an agricultural zone dedicated almost exclusively to the cultivation of rice.

25 Straddling the border between the provinces of Alessandria and Asti is the area known as Montferrat, a succession of hills that mark the southern limits of the Po Valley.

27 At the center of the rural traditions found in the Po River plain is the *cascina*: a courtyard surrounded by typical two- and three-story homesteads and their haylofts, while other outbuildings house the farm machinery.

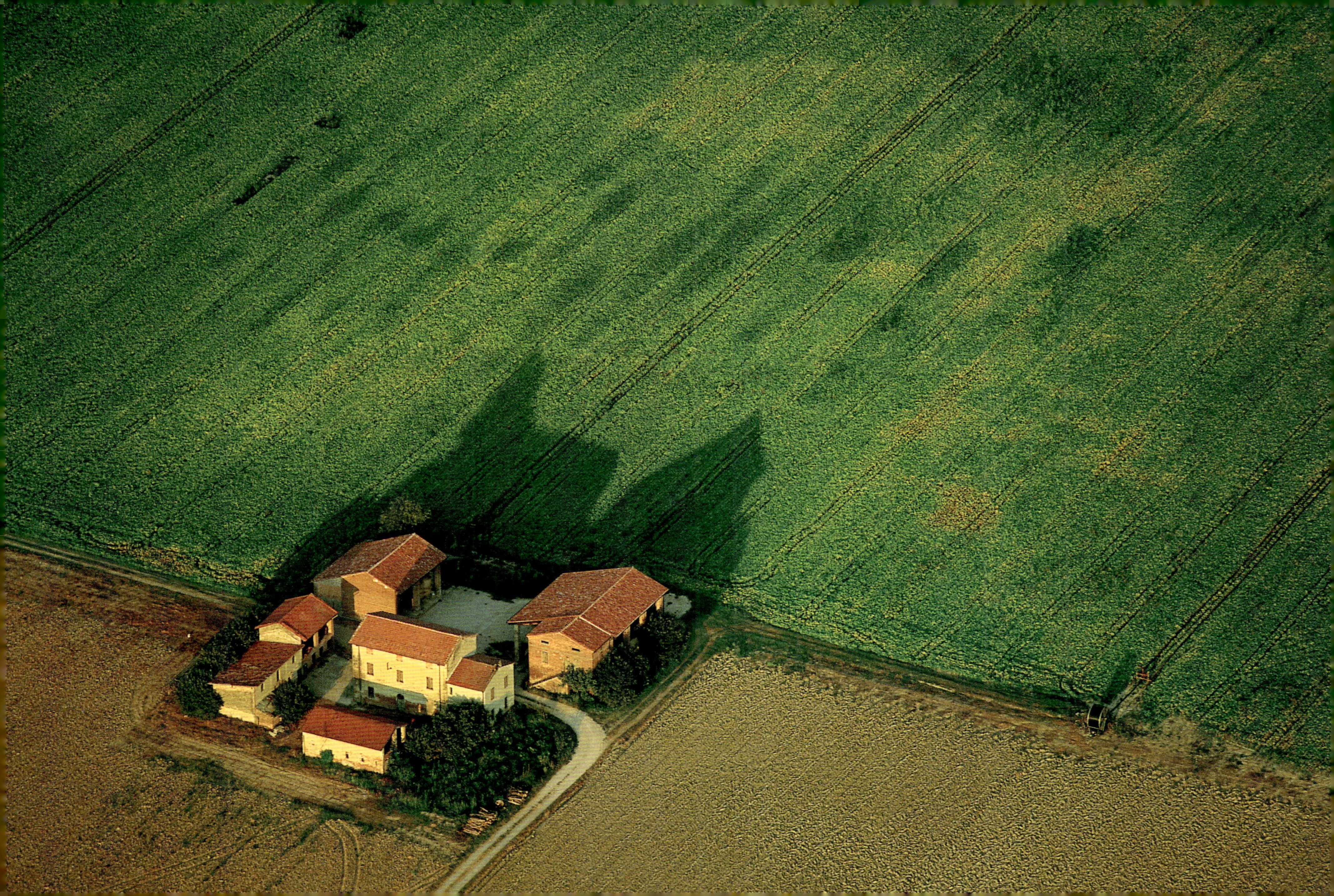

by carefully laid-out plantations of poplars. The disappearance of this woodland cover and the spread of urban centers have led in many instances to the lowering of the water table, a phenomenon that has been rendered even more dramatic by the extraction of water both for irrigation and industrial purposes as well as by the pollution caused by chemical products poured over the crops which, because of their exceptional productivity, are vulnerable to harmful organisms and need intensive doses of fertilizers. In this way the countryside of the Po Valley has become a standardized countryside, composed of squared-off fields, perfectly straight roads, and urban centers laid out according to a geometrical plan. In order to rediscover the fascination of the countryside of the past, one needs to go right to the extremities of the great river valleys, whether it be toward the north or to the south, to the east or the west; there one can find once again the hedges, the rows of trees and shrubs, the canals bordered by lines of reeds and willows. There the great farm complexes rise like castles from the flat surroundings of the fields and assume once again the status of old days: the only settlements in a countryside made up entirely of fields. Further to the east, where the Po Valley becomes the Veneto-Friuli Plain, the country takes on a look that is even more ancient. The rivers flow more freely, meandering between the crops as they leave wide flood plains and great deposits of gravel such as the great pebbly bed of the Tagliamento River that can be seen from far away. In the ordered textures of the cultivated fields, small natural biotopes, wooded and

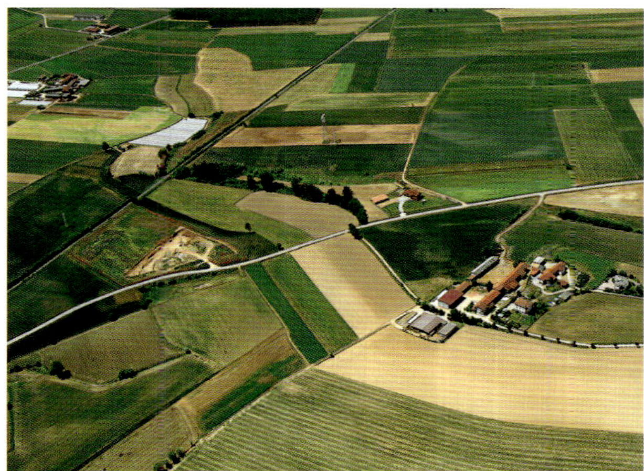

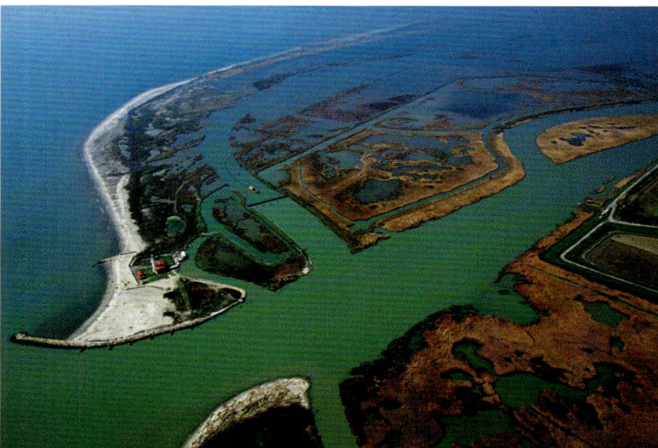

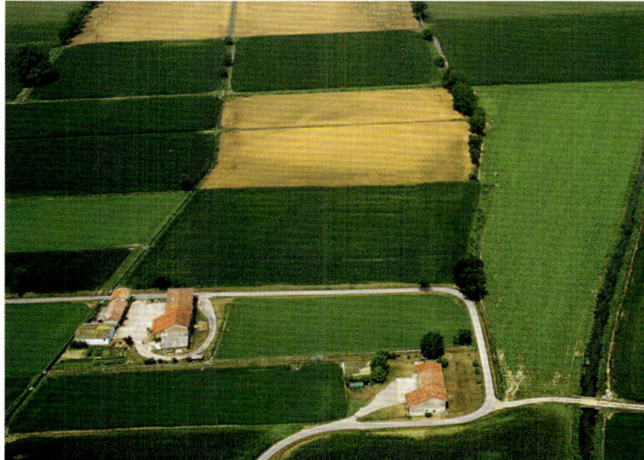

28 left To the south and to the north of the Tanaro River, in the Cuneo area, the land is laid out geometrically in neat plots where cereals and vegetables are grown.

marshy, make their appearance, opening up like greenish-blue buds in the ordered world built by man for the cultivation of corn, rice, grain, vegetables, grapes and alfalfa for dairy farming. The Po Valley is a paradise for the people who live there but who nevertheless have to put up with the conditions imposed by their great and all too frequent enemy: the fog, which slows everything down and renders life difficult for everyone, town dwellers and country folk alike. It is a treacherous blanket which, in the cold winter days, wraps itself like a white shroud around humans and animals, houses and trees, fields and rivers, roads and railways and completely blots out the countryside. It becomes difficult to move around: the safest means of transport always remains the train and even the river traffic has to slow down. The boats that ply their trade on the river between Cremona and Mantua, or even lower down as far as the estuary, have to rely on radar. At one time this equipment did not exist and the traffic on this great river, whether of barges or ferries, had to be interrupted if the visibility was not adequate. Today the traffic never stops, unless of course the water level is too low. In the Po River, between Cremona and Mantua, approximately three million tons of mixed cargo are regularly transported each year. Each barge, driven by powerful engines, can carry the equivalent of about fifty trucks complete with trailers, and is crewed by a captain, a pilot and a cook – this latter being a key figure since these barges become in fact homes in motion. There is no time to get bored and there's no lowering one's guard: a bit of low water or an obstacle in the way and the damage is done! There are also specially qualified individuals whose job is to check the water levels and reveal the presence of threatening areas of low water. A system of white and red lights is used to direct the navigation on the Po, on this great river that is not just a watery road convenient for transporting merchandise of all shapes and sizes but is also the creator of a landscape of land and water, with rows of poplars and sandy banks where birds stop over for the winter and where people go sunbathe in summer. Along the approximately 375 miles (600 km) of its course, the river crosses a large number of Italian regions and wherever it goes, in Piedmont as in Lombardy, in Emilia as well as the Veneto, the people that live alongside it look on it as a very great friend, at times perhaps a little disrespectful and even hostile, but always still a great friend. Sometimes raging, when the water level becomes dangerously high and the banks have difficulty containing the fury of the waters which hurl themselves against the road- and railway-bridge piers, and at other times severely low in water, when the flow becomes slow and murky, leaving great glistening beds of gravel exposed and the banks bare, the Po shows all the signs of suffering from the ills that afflict the rivers of all the industrialized regions of Italy and of the world. Notwithstanding the pollution, the elimination of the vegetation along the banks, and the drawing off of the water for agricultural and industrial purposes, the Po still continues to be Italy's greatest

28 center The sandy islands characteristic of the Po Delta between Chioggia and Comacchio appear as strange designs in the brackish waters.

28 right The ordered fields of cereals and the farmsteads are all an integral part of this aerial view of the Lombard plain to the east of Milan.

river, its longest, the richest in terms of water volume, and the most navigable. It is approximately 388 miles (625 km) from its source, at the foot of Monviso, down to the spectacular estuary on the Adriatic, one of the most important in all of Europe from a wildlife point of view and the equal, if not superior, to those of the Rhône in France or the Danube on the Black Sea. A flight over the mouth of the Po is to discover a unique landscape, set in a universe of geometrical lines, partly the result of the arbitrary meanderings of the river currents as they wind like twisting serpents in search of the way to the sea, and also in part due to the masterful, centuries-old consolidation and canalization techniques with which man has built up the embankments and created man-made valleys for the fishing – an ancient activity, as demonstrated by the discovery of superb mosaics dating from Roman times that depict scenes of fishermen and of the fish that were to be found in these waters in the period of the Roman Empire. Many settlements on the sandbanks and small islands of the delta have been constructed with materials selected from the vegetation which grows around the boundaries of this immense world of brackish water. This is the result of necessity since, in the Po Delta, there are no large trees to be found, no stones available, and no clay for making bricks; consequently to build houses people use reeds, willow branches and any other materials that can be found in the lagoon. They are nevertheless quite complete as homesteads, with everything from the chimneypot to the veranda to a landing place for small boats. These little homes sprout out of the reed thickets like mushrooms and amaze us by the perfection with which they have been built by the inhabitants of the lagoon. Such is the world of the lagoon: a geometry of banks and channels which mark the limits of a changing world that adapts itself to the whims of the weather, on occasion giving up space to humankind, and at other times taking it back again; a world which at one time was put on the same level as an enemy to be liquidated because it was mistakenly believed to be unhealthy, unproductive and hostile to humankind. Of all the many reasons for which it is little by little becoming accepted that these marshy environments must at all costs be preserved (motives which also include economic considerations – fishing for eels is very much more profitable than growing potatoes!) – one of the principal js the defense of biodiversity, ensuring the continued existence of a wide range of animal and plant species which live in, and rely on, these moist zones. Approximately one half of all the 500 species of birds living in Europe are dependent to some degree or other on lakes, rivers and marshlands; also huge are the families of water plants that constitute a world of their own in terms of their variety, their elegance and their ability to survive in a difficult and changing environment that is baking hot in summer and gripped by ice during the winter.

31 The fishing methods and equipment used in the Venetian lagoon are extremely varied and include nets, dredging machines, traps, hooks, gathering equipment and harpoons. A rough survey identified 25 so-called "arts," as these historic methods with their varieties of equipment are known. Of these arts, 17 are still in use.

32-33 At the end of the summer, with the cereal crop fields south of the Po have become wide expanses of stubble punctuated with bales of hay.

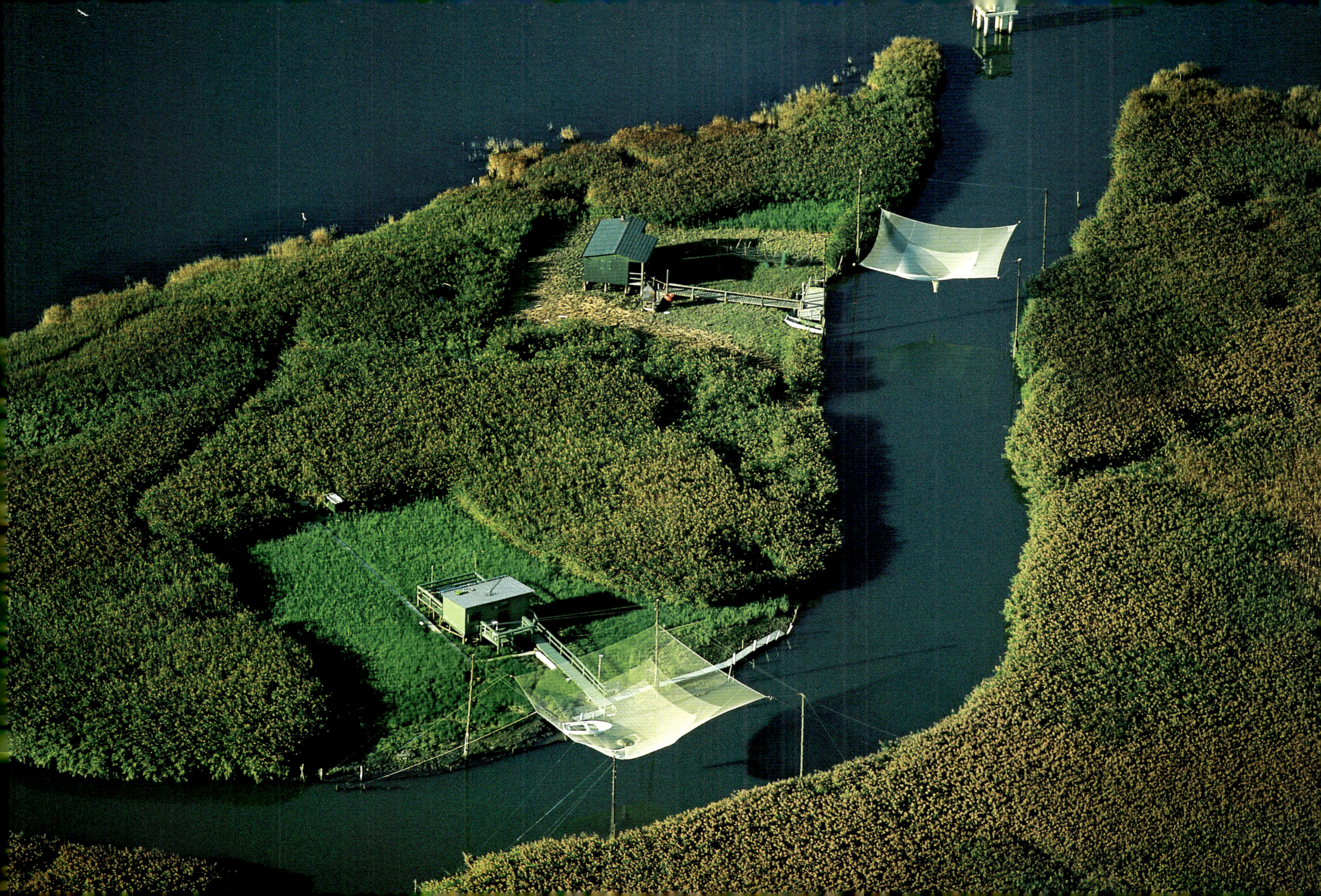

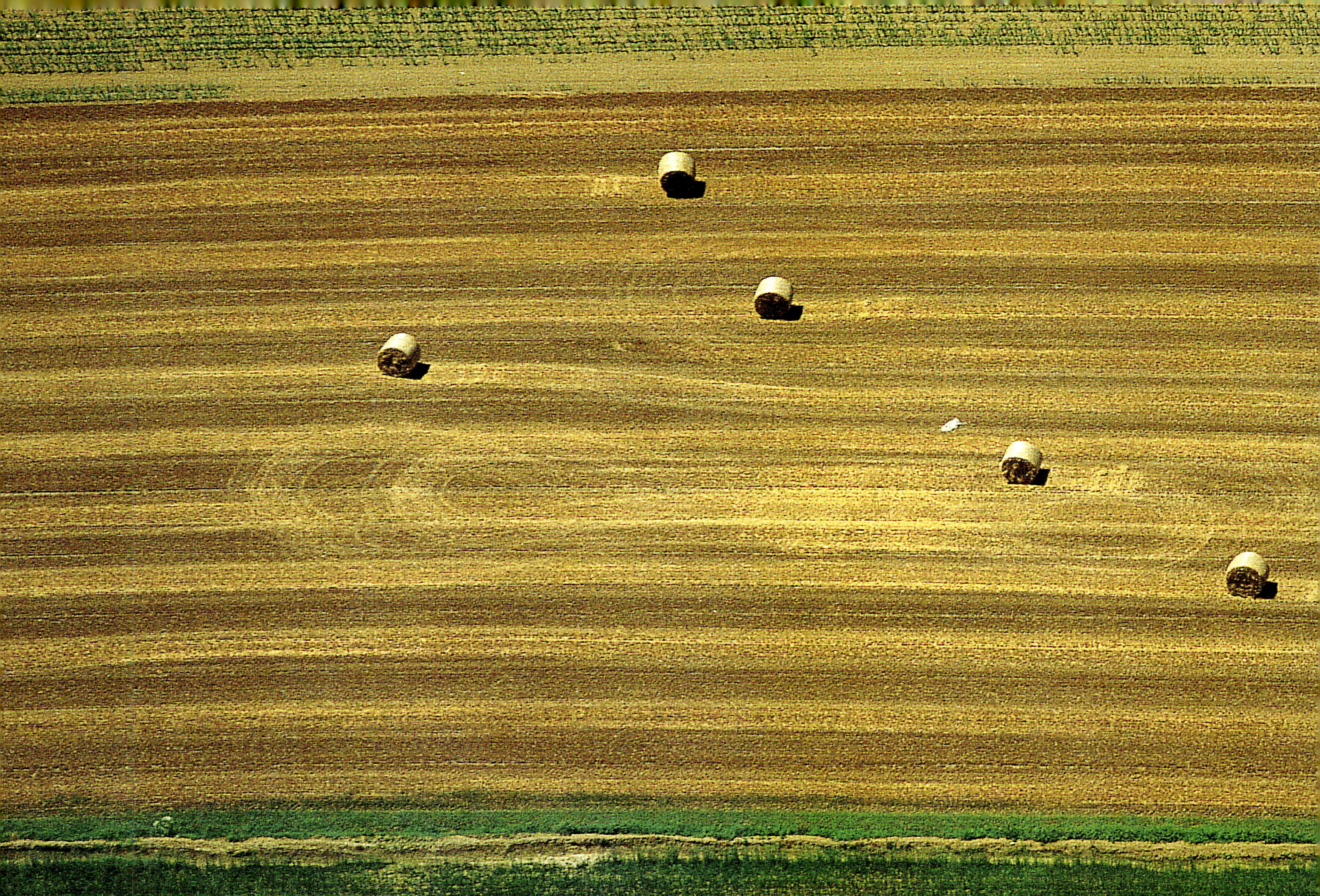

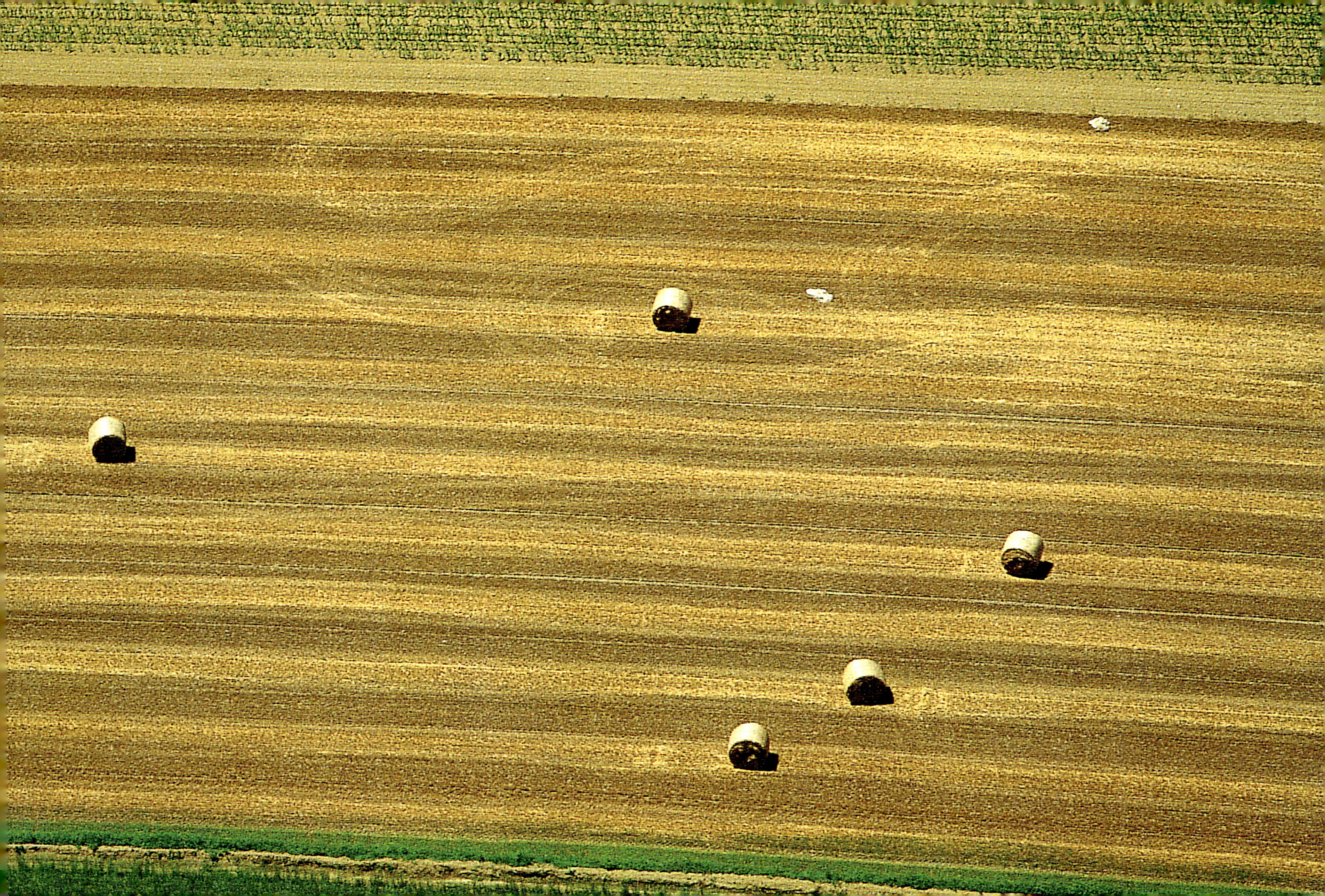

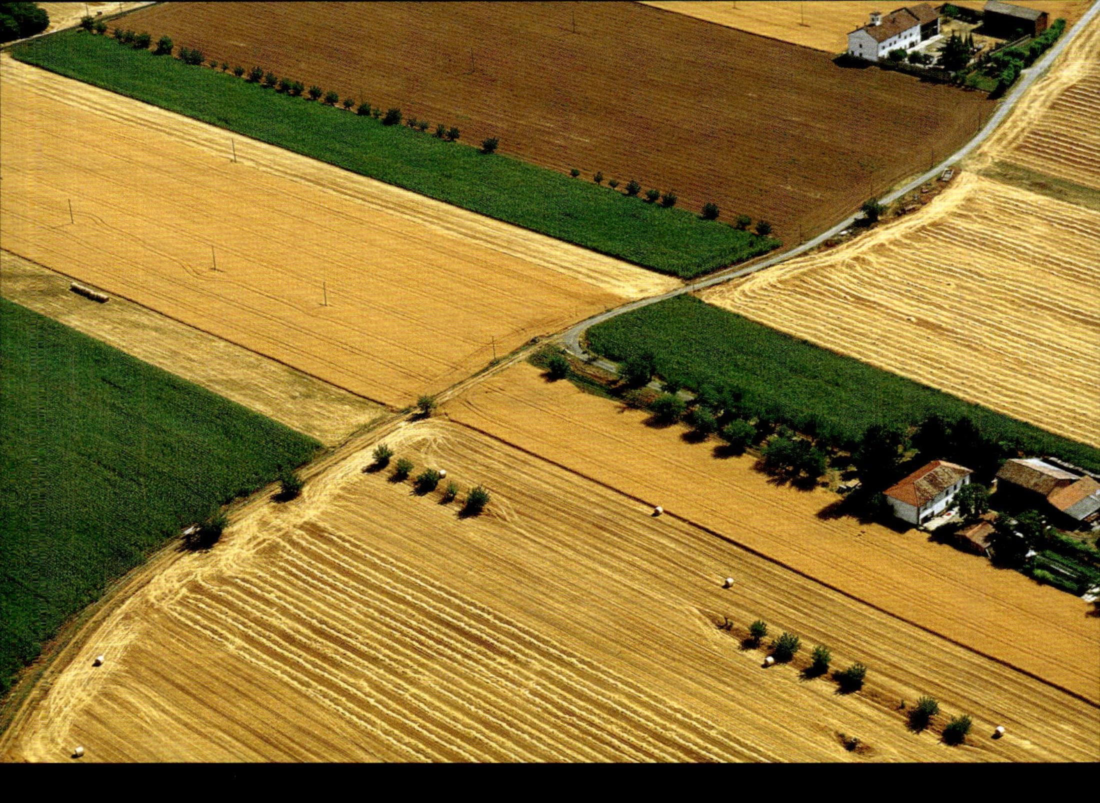

34 and 35 The countryside between Novi Ligure and Tortona (Alessandria), especially in summer, is reminiscent of a modern painting: the fields are geometrically shaped and well-ordered, contrasting the warm colors of the freshly cut stubble with the intense green of the crops that are still ripening. Several farmsteads stand out in the general panorama, a legacy of a rural world on the brink of extinction.

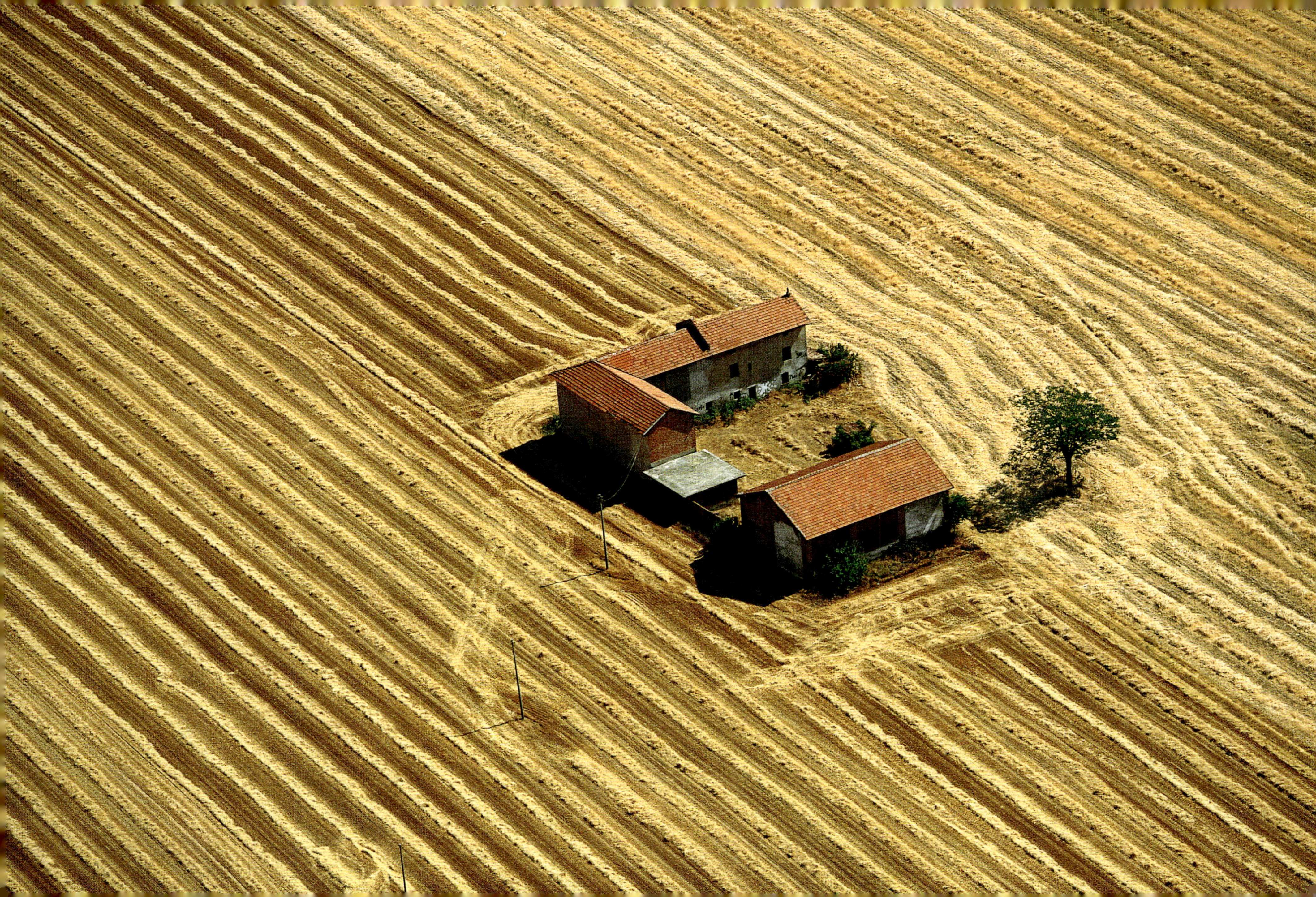

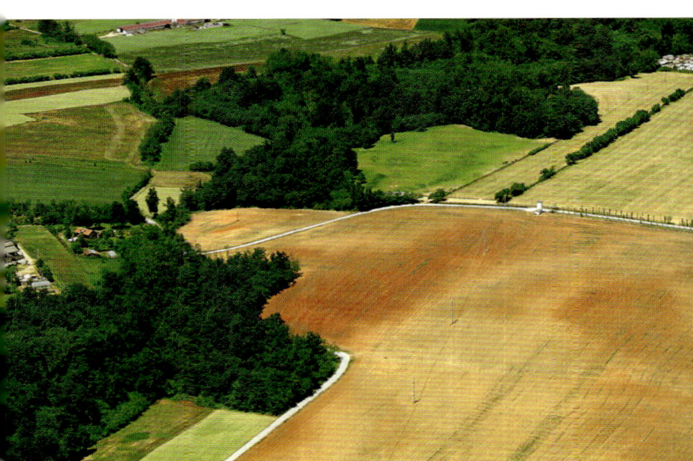

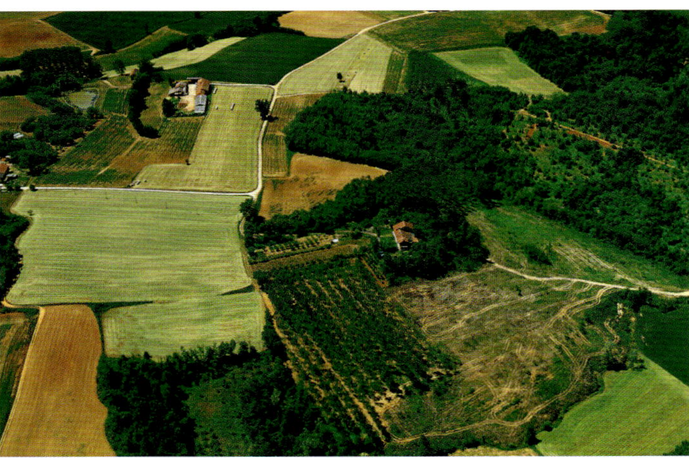

36 The western Piedmont countryside follows the underlying geological structure of the territory: the nearer one gets to the Alps, the more the plains begin to show gentle undulations that develop into the regular hill systems prevalent in the Langhe and Canavese regions. Whereas the land in the plains was intensively cultivated, the rising ground becomes more irregular and checkered with coppices.

37 In the countryside around Acqui, where the Montferrat and Langhe regions border the lower slopes of Liguria's Apennine mountains, the plains give way to the hilly lands where the famous wine is the area's chief product.

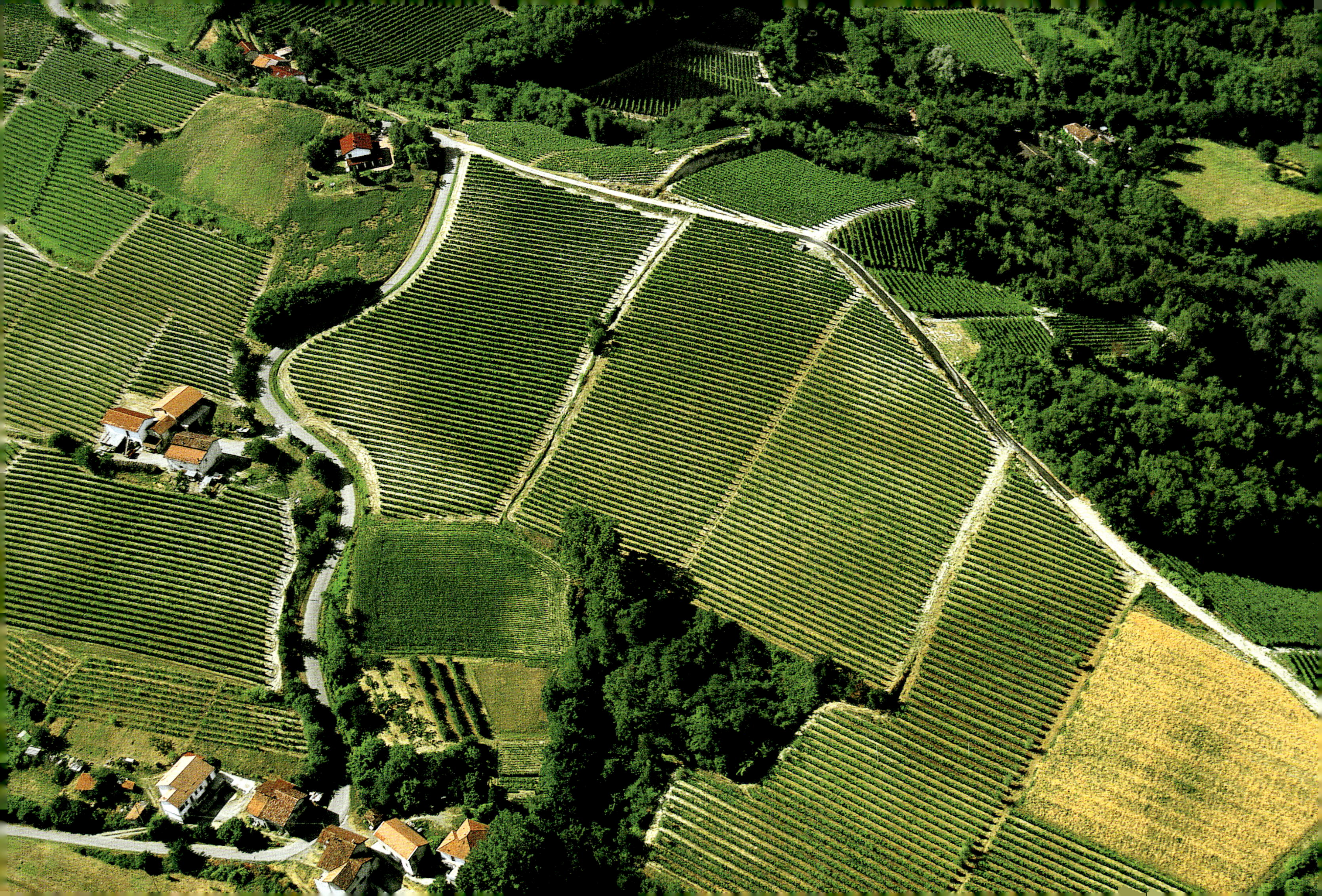

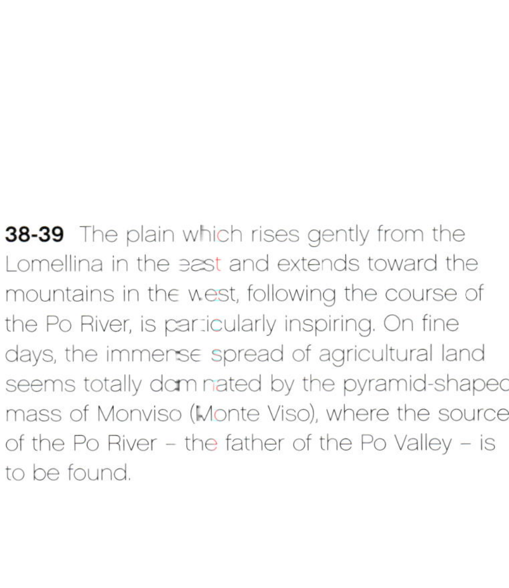

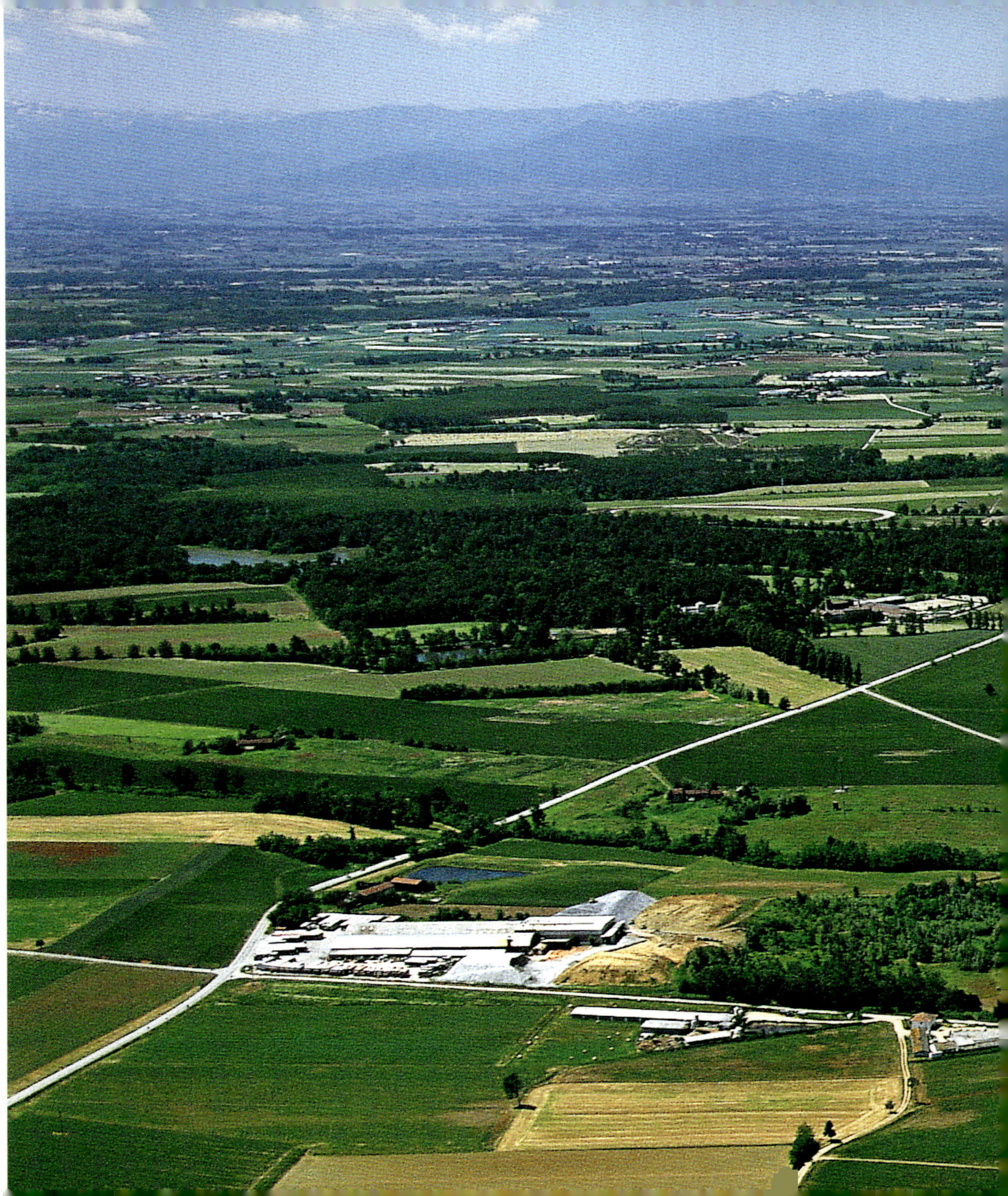

38-39 The plain which rises gently from the Lomellina in the east and extends toward the mountains in the west, following the course of the Po River, is particularly inspiring. On fine days, the immense spread of agricultural land seems totally dominated by the pyramid-shaped mass of Monviso (Monte Viso), where the source of the Po River – the father of the Po Valley – is to be found.

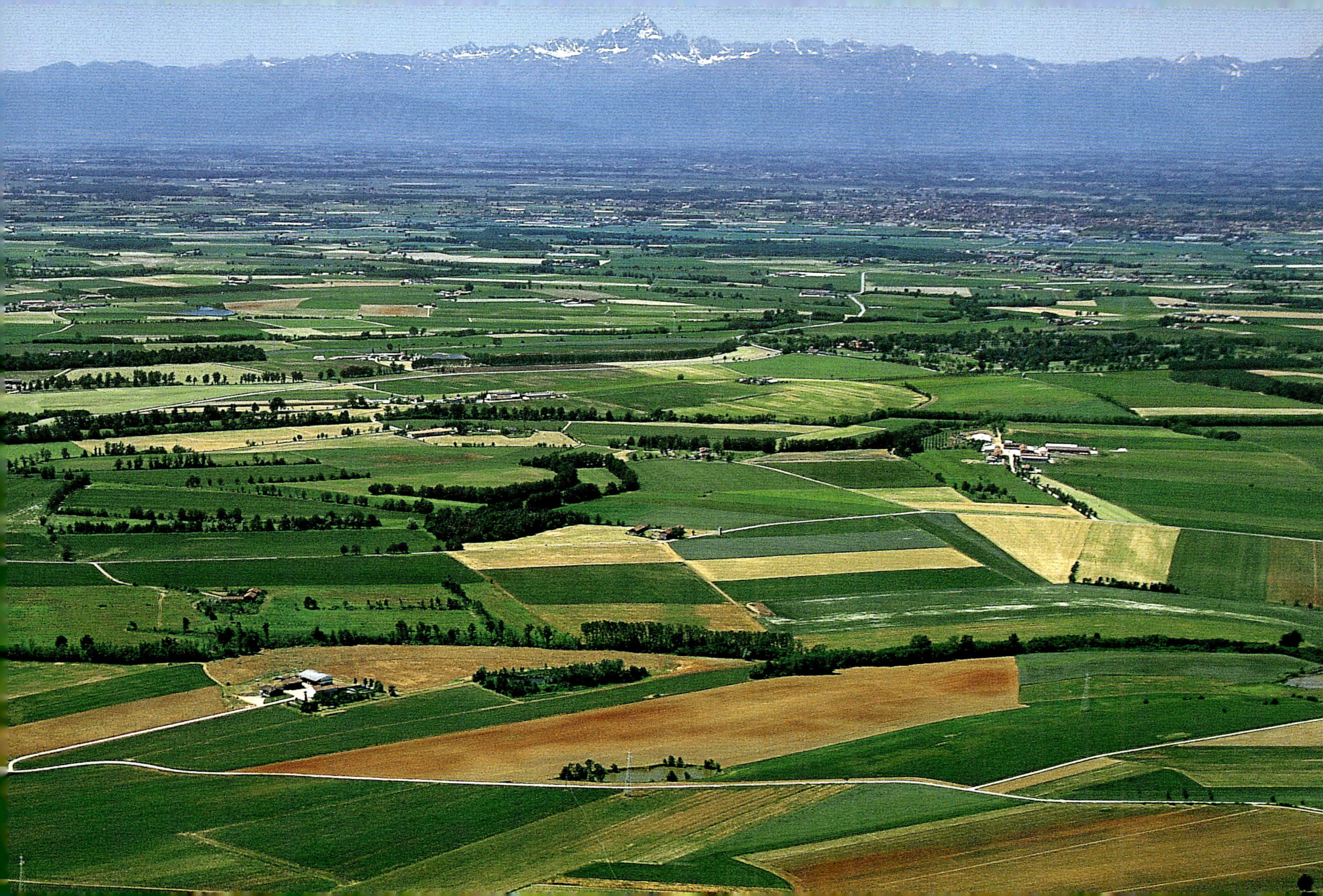

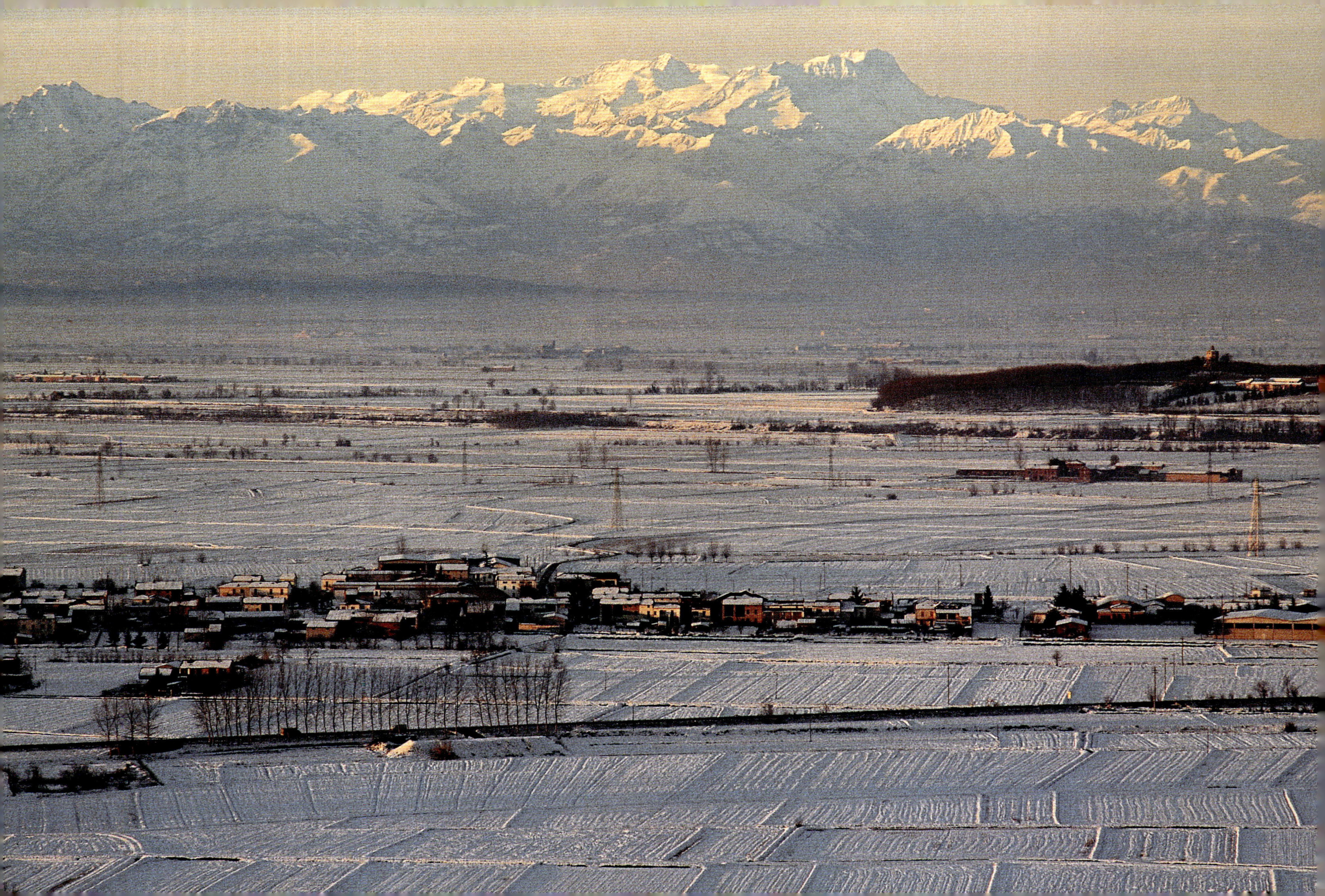

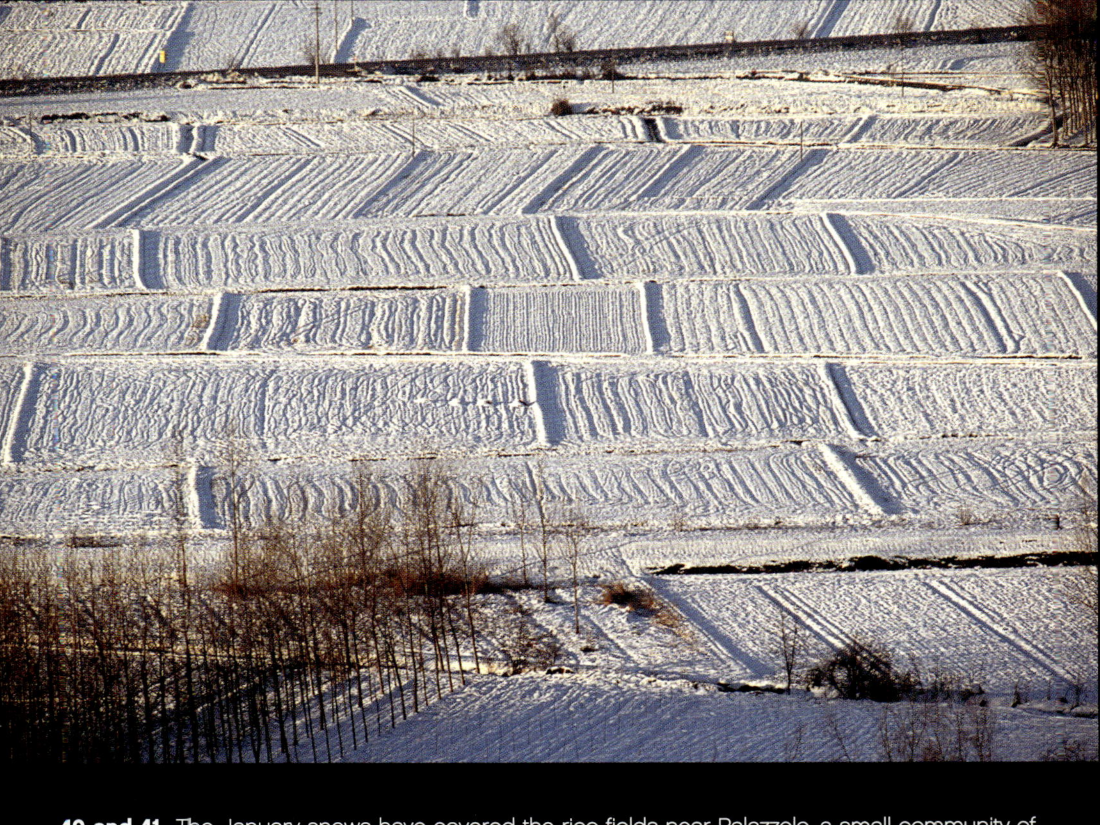

40 and 41 The January snows have covered the rice fields near Palazzolo, a small community of the lower Vercelli area. In the background, Monte Rosa's immense mass dominates; it seems to be much nearer because of the clear light.

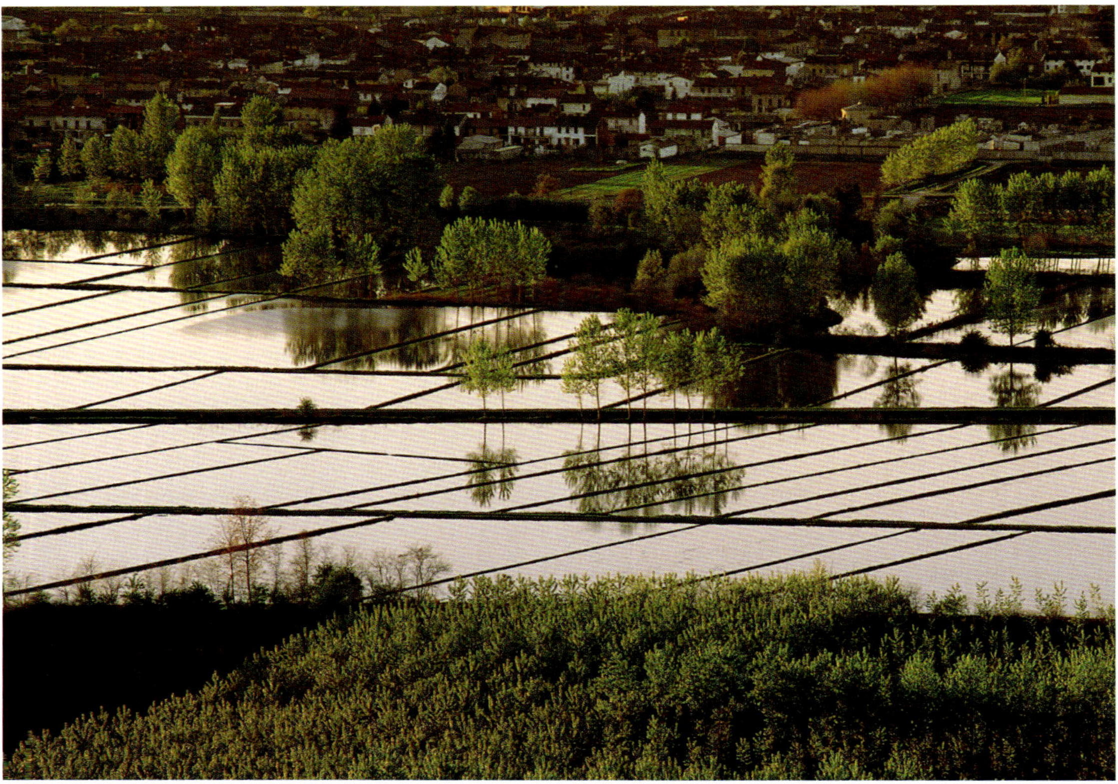

42 Early spring gives the rice-fields a new look: the water, flowing in from a centuries-old irrigation system, transforms the fields into watery mirror-like expanses that, in this part of the Po Valley, have become known as "the checkered sea."

43 Little by little, as the warmer season progresses, the Vercelli area rice fields show further changes: the shoots develop and the fields take on hues of green and turquoise, bringing this idyllic setting to life. The farm in the center of the picture is a *grangia*, a type of rustic building erected in the period when the Cistercian monastic order flourished. The *grangia* was designed as a self-sufficient center of production, and today is still a central element in the rice-growing economy of this part of Piedmont.

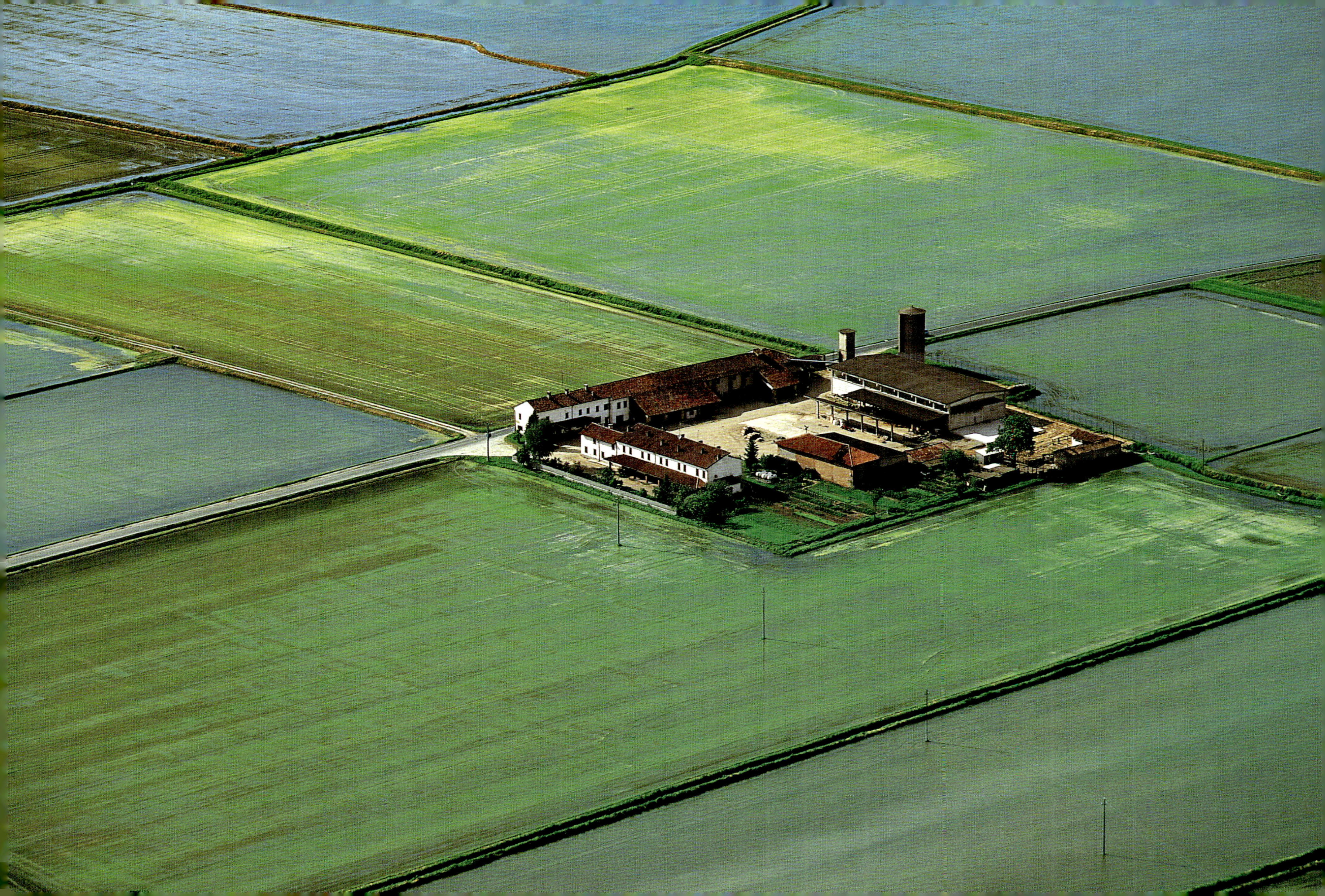

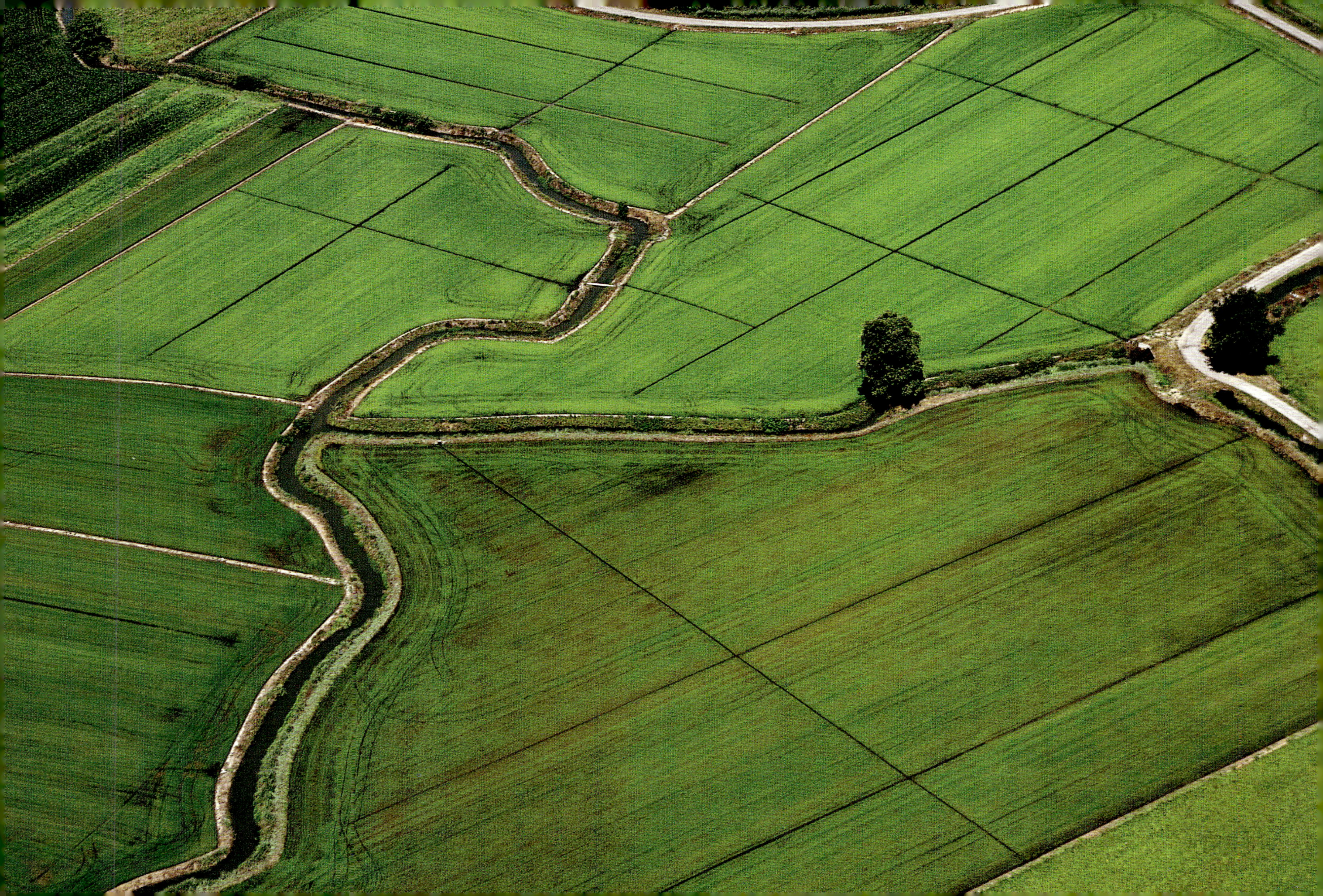

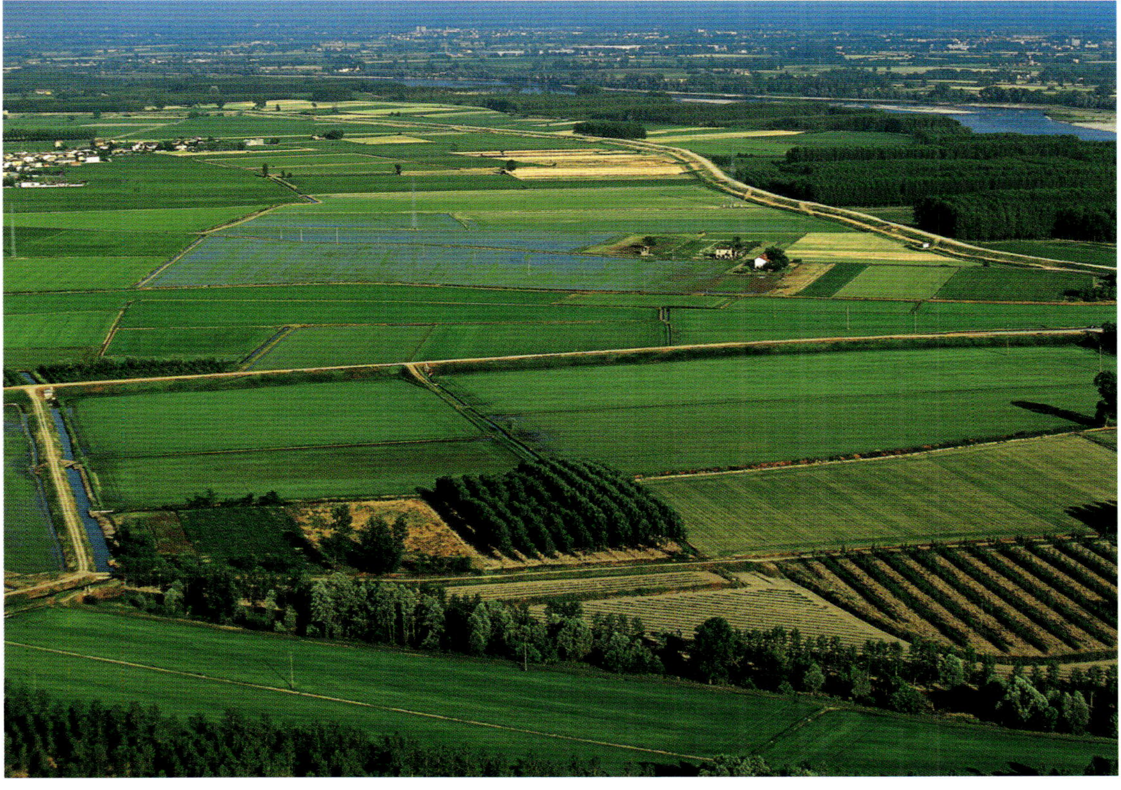

44 and 45 Over the centuries the lands given over to the cultivation of rice have been greatly increased and now extend from the Vercelli area (in the west) as far as the Mantua region (in the east). The crop's profitability and the region's soil (rich in clay and therefore impermeable) have combined to promote the adoption of high-quality rice cultures, widely valued in foreign markets. These photographs, taken in early summer, show the rice-fields just when they are greening up and, seen from above, are reminiscent of gentle grassy fields.

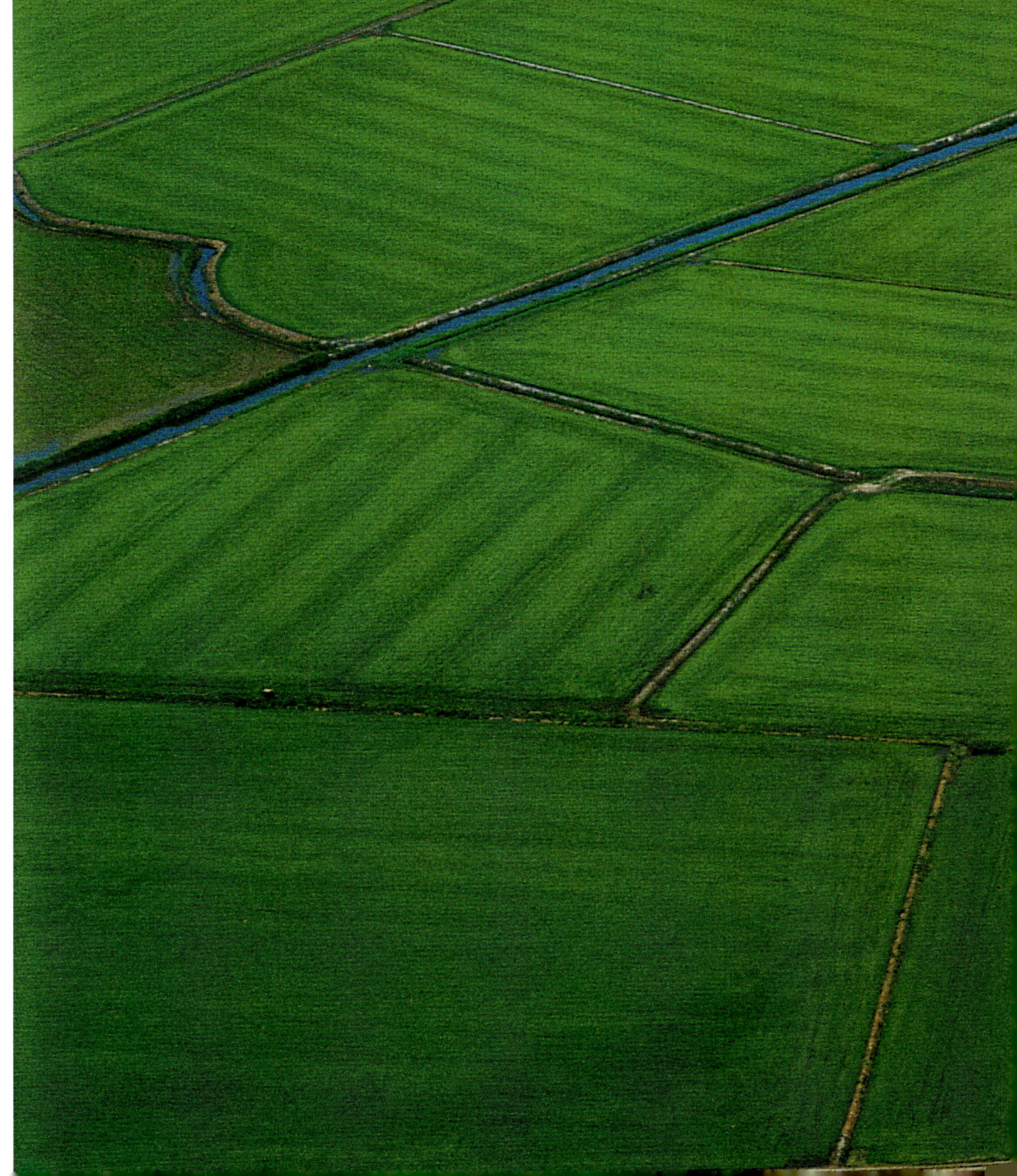

46-47 The Lomellina area is at the very heart of a territory known as the "rice triangle," which straddles the provinces of Vercelli, Novara and Pavia. Thanks to the soil's heavy clay content and to the water brought to the area by a canal network headed by the Cavour Canal, this part of the Po Valley is under very intense cultivation and is one of the world's mostly highly productive areas.

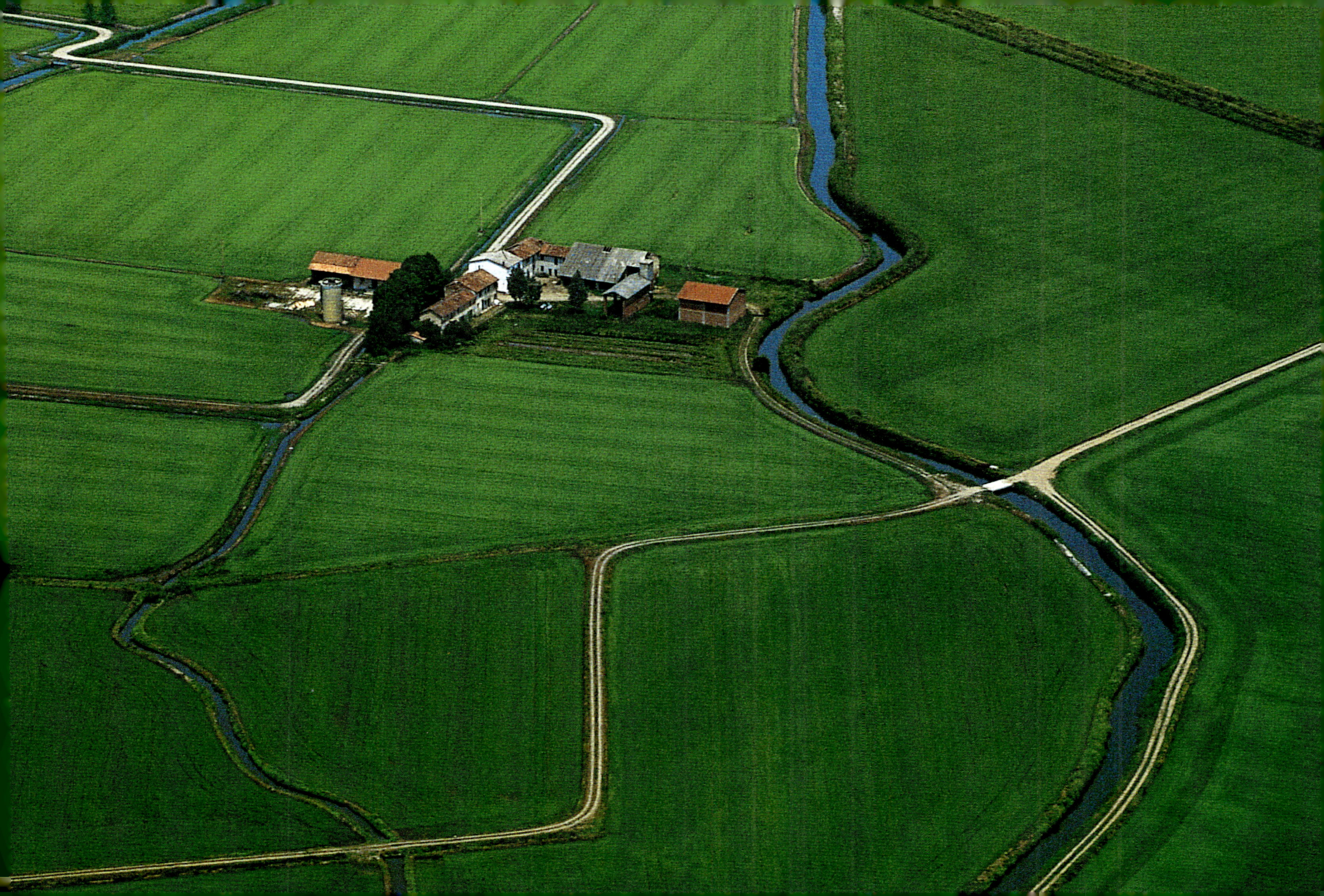

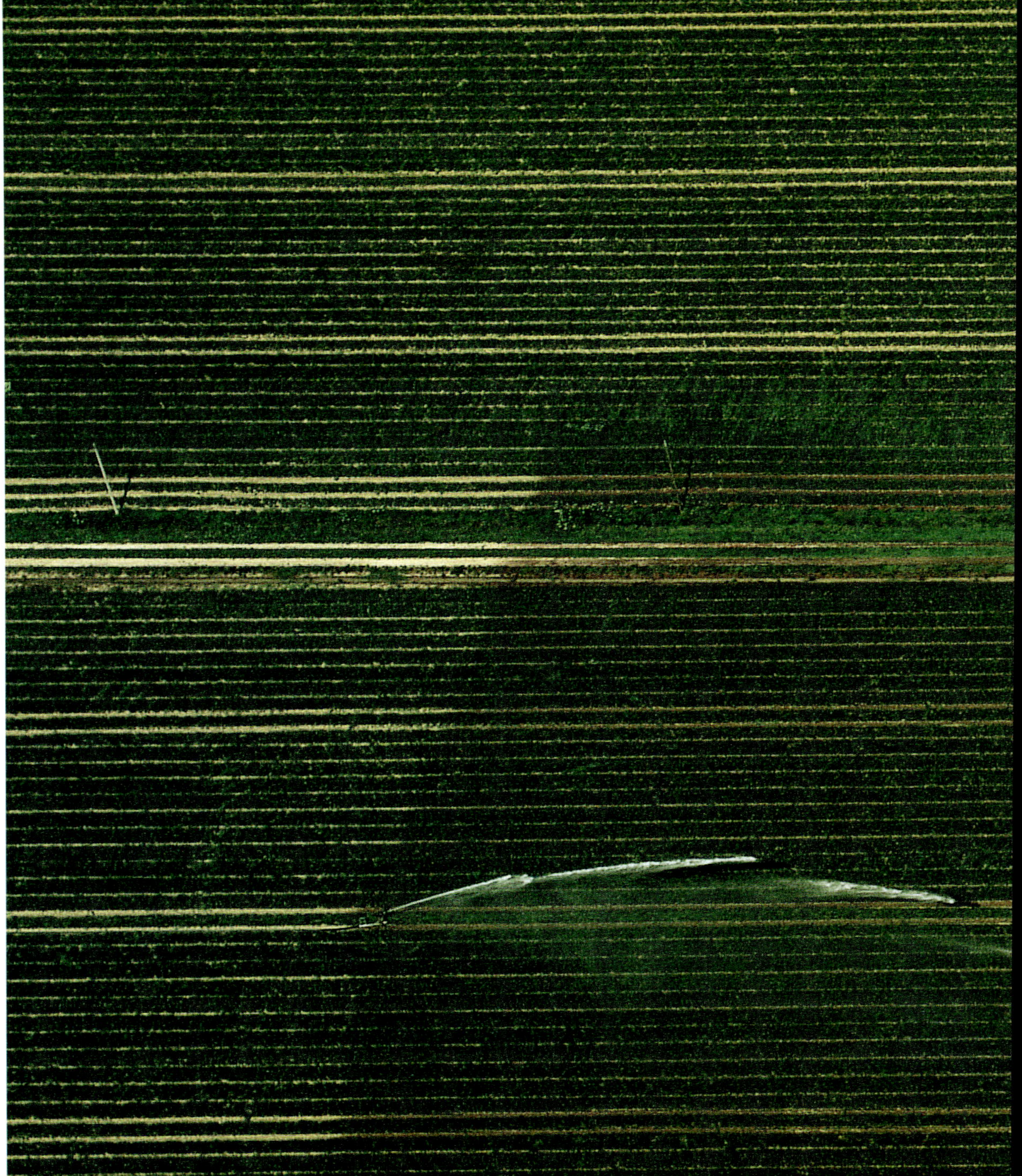

48-49 The jet of water the sprinkler has thrown in a half moon arc looks like a brush-stroke on a canvas painted in summer colors; the Emilian countryside, as seen from the skies, offers a succession of these little scenes of rural life, lost in time.

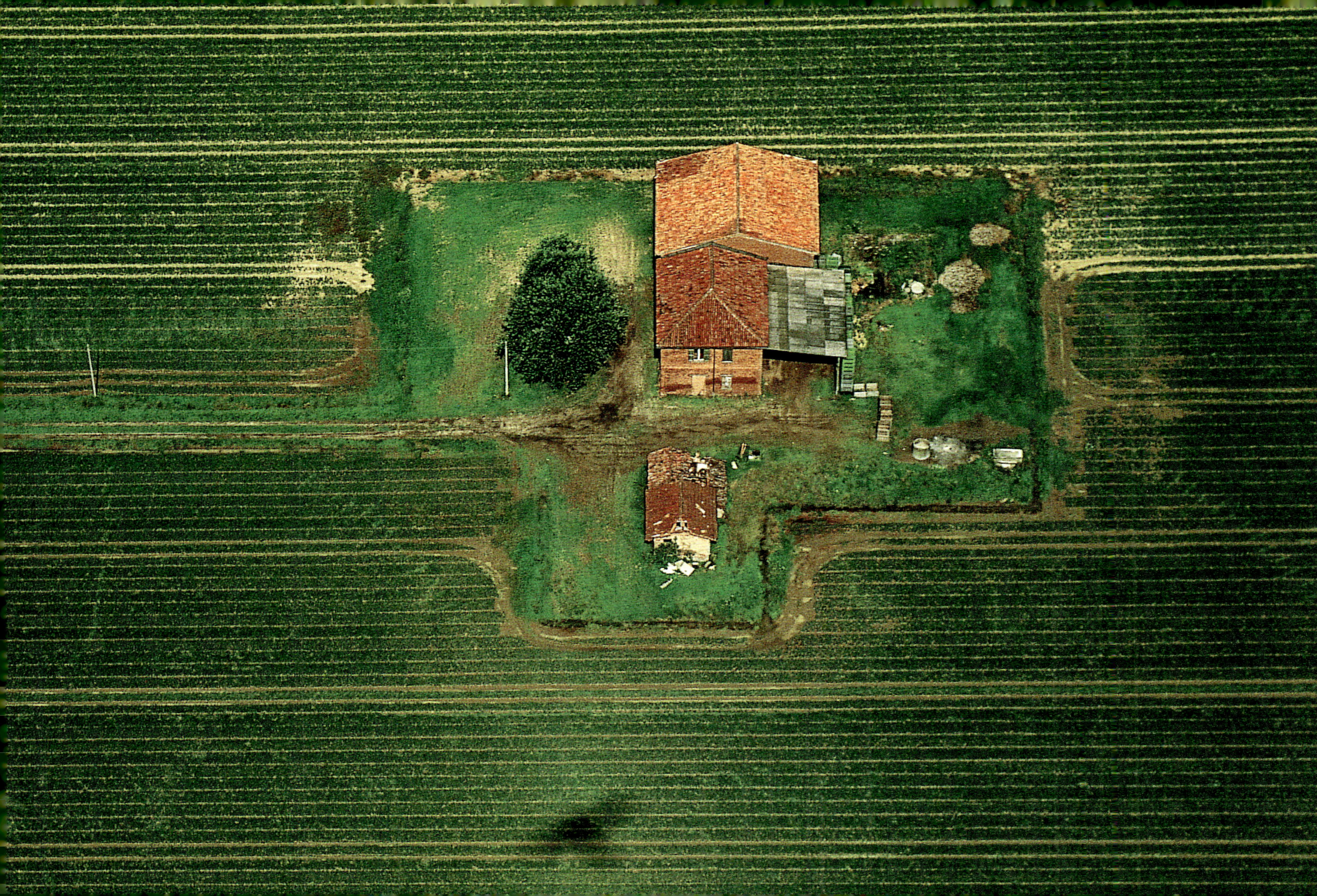

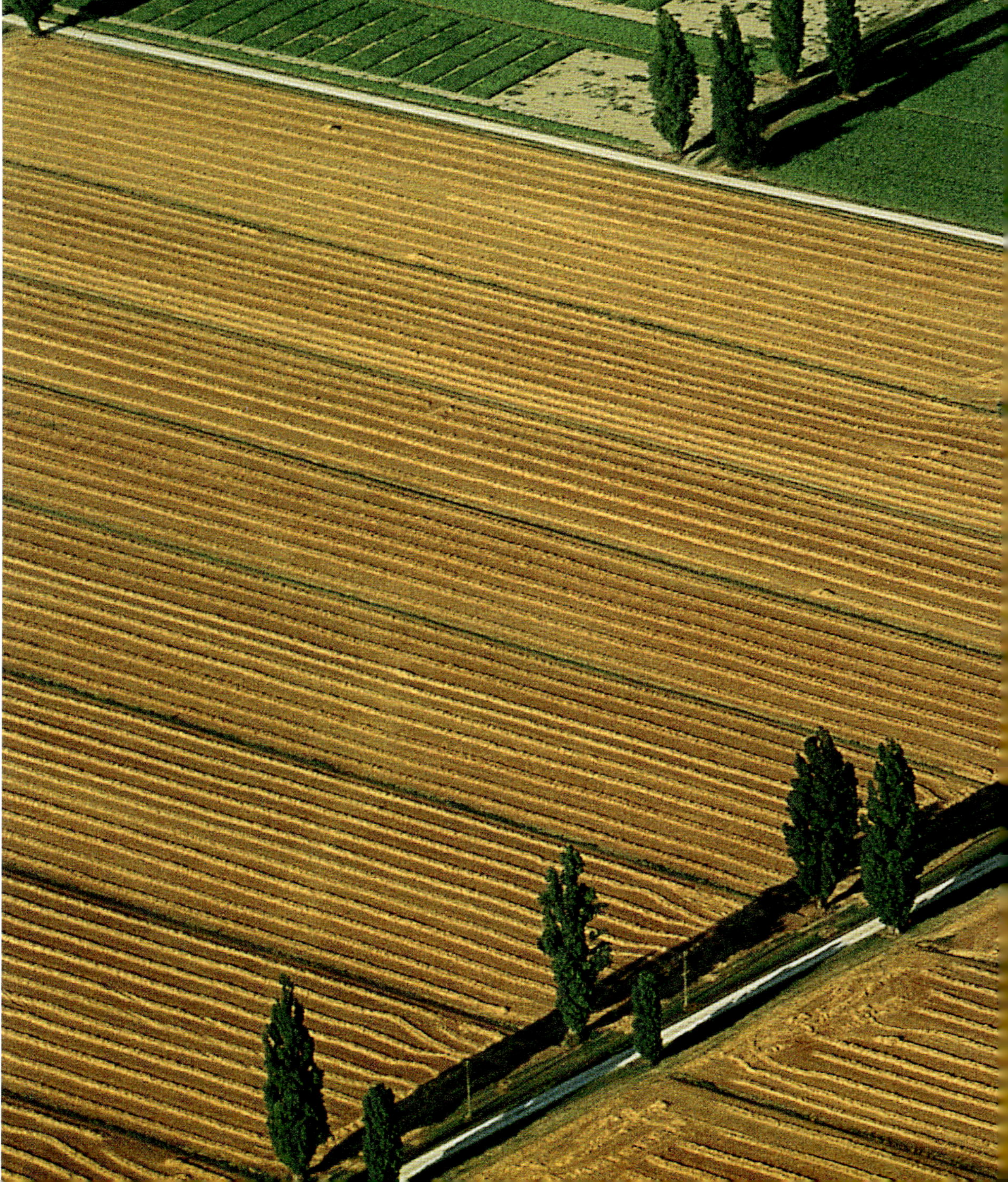

50-51 The grain is ripe and the rectangular plots in this tract of the Ferrara landscape are now long strips of golden yellow. The still verdant areas of cultivation indicate the presence of either vegetables or soya, this latter being a leguminous crop often grown in the Po Valley to ensure a restorative rotation in land use.

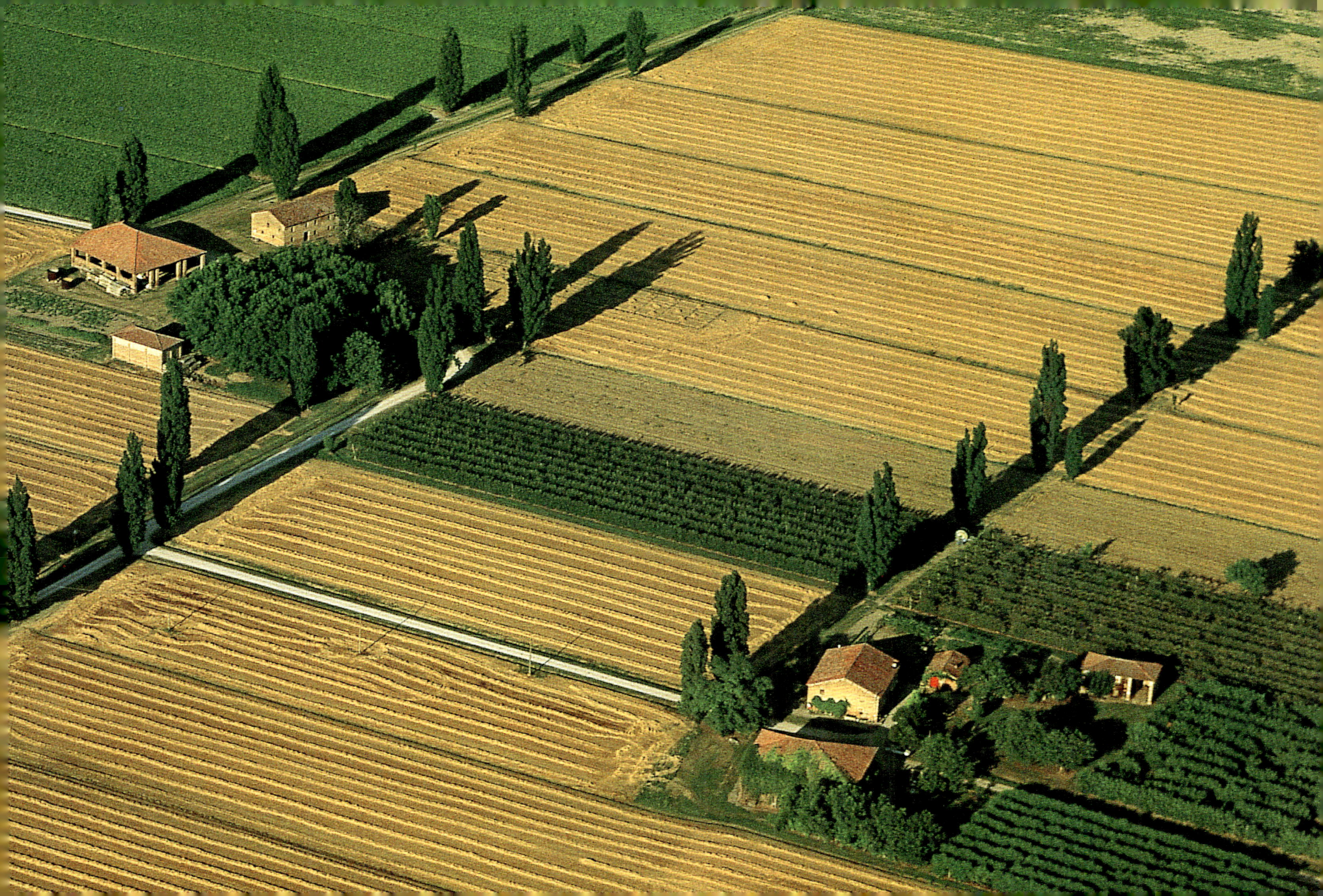

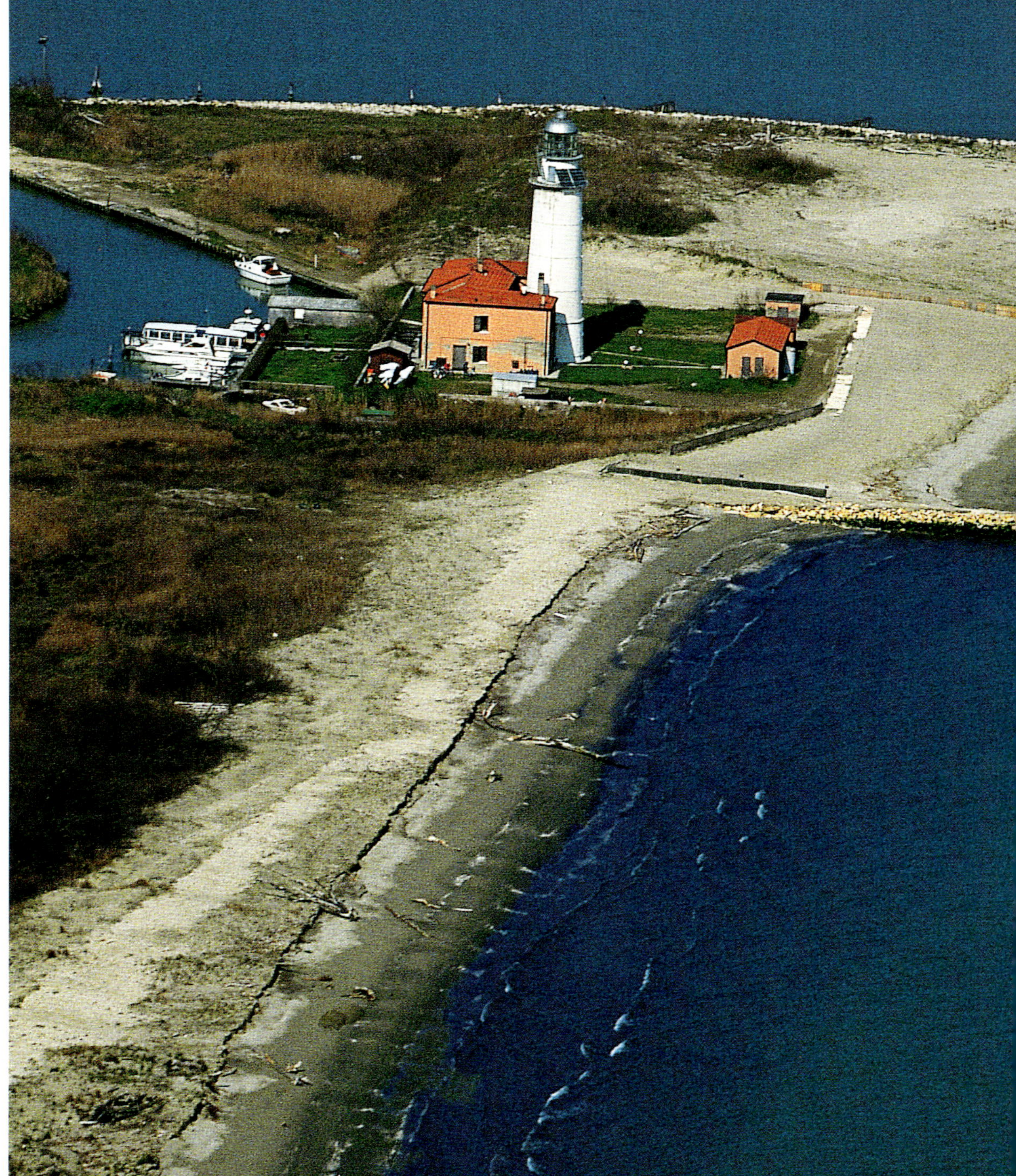

52-53 Two aircraft are circling one of the numerous lighthouses located around the islets in the Po Delta, on the border between the Veneto and Emilia regions. The delta, which still occupies a very considerable expanse of territory, is all that remains of what was once a much larger area of marshland known as the Padusa Valley which, in ancient times, extended much farther north and south of the Po.

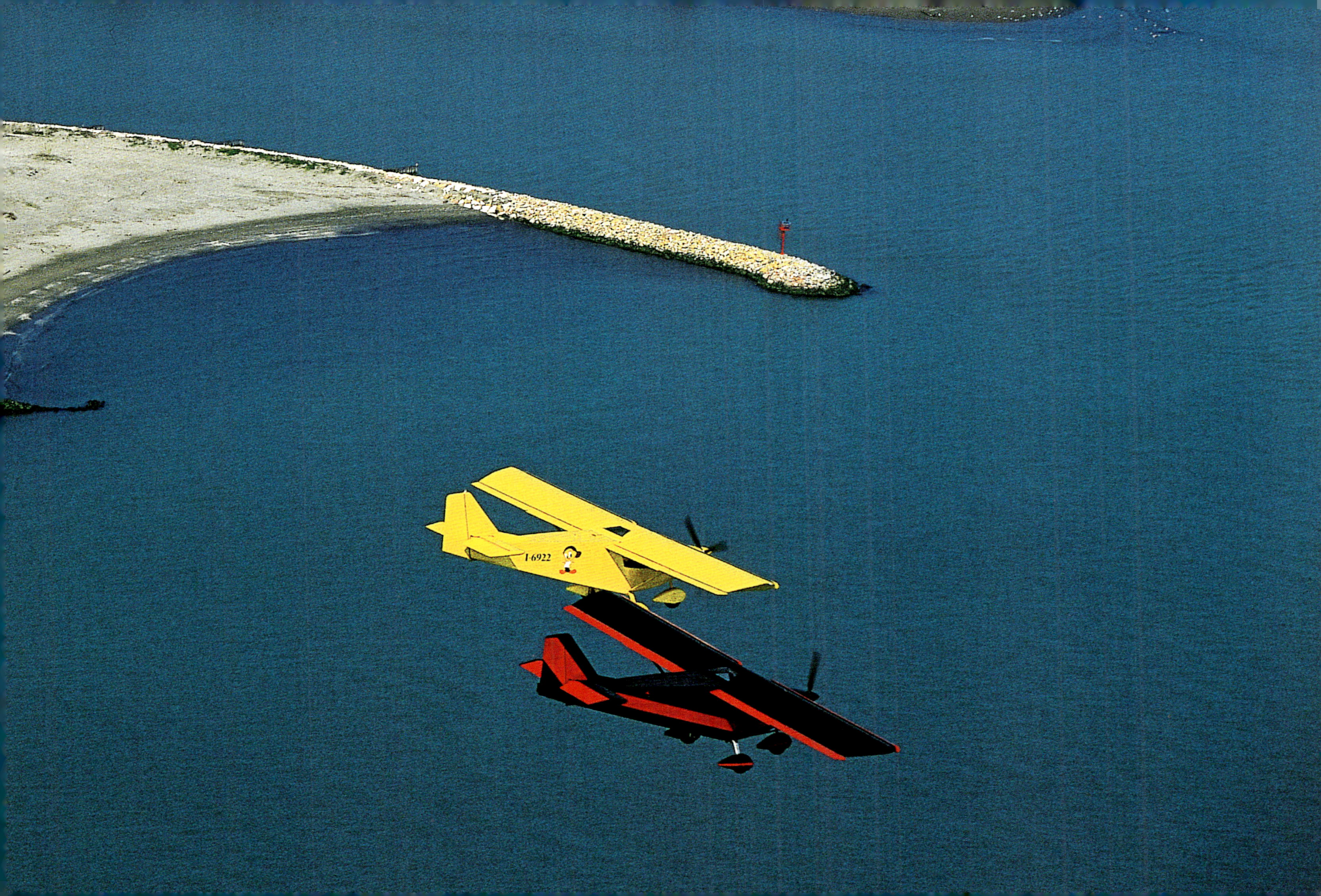
I-6922

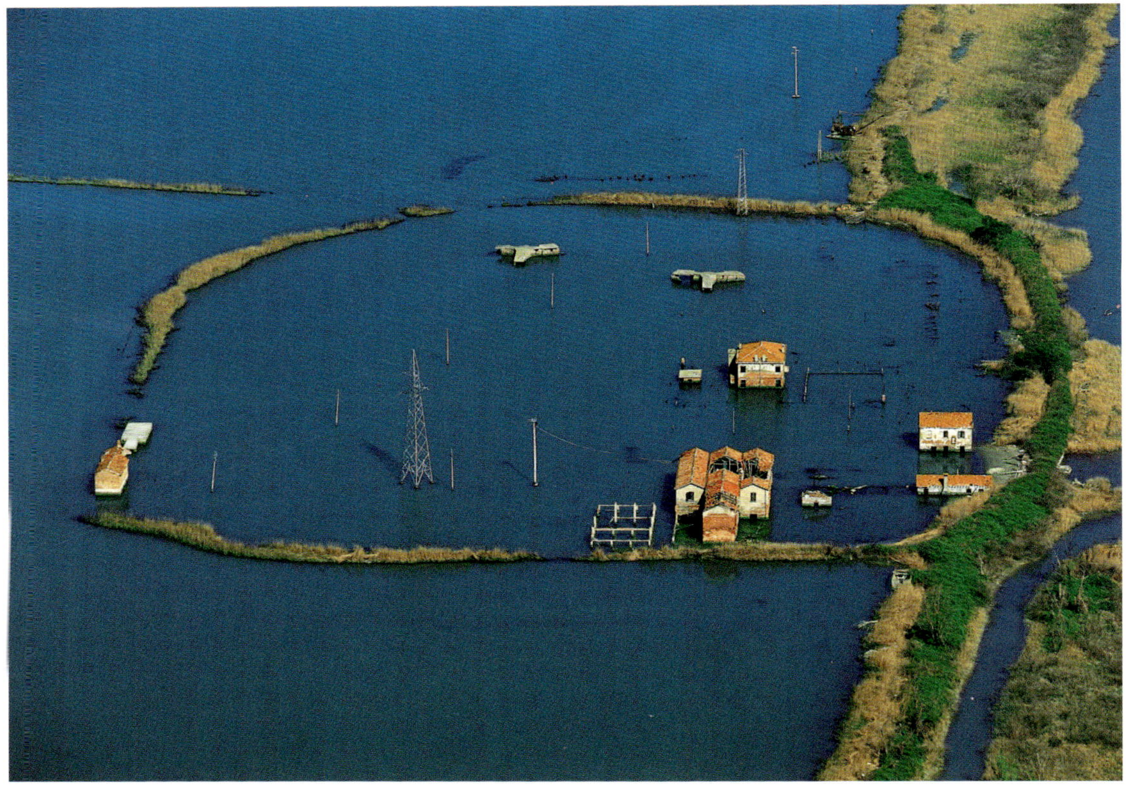

54 and 55 The Po Delta Park is the largest expanse of protected wetlands in Italy. The flora and fauna are notably varied and include as many as 1000 different species. The wildlife is particularly diverse with more than 400 species, including mammals, reptiles, amphibians and fish. Because of its historic and nature-related relevance, UNESCO has added the Po Delta to its list of World Heritage Sites.

56-57 Natural and man-made channels crisscross the Chioggia Lagoon (Venice) and join in forming this maze of land and water controlled by sluices vital for the management of fishing, one of the major resources of the local economy.

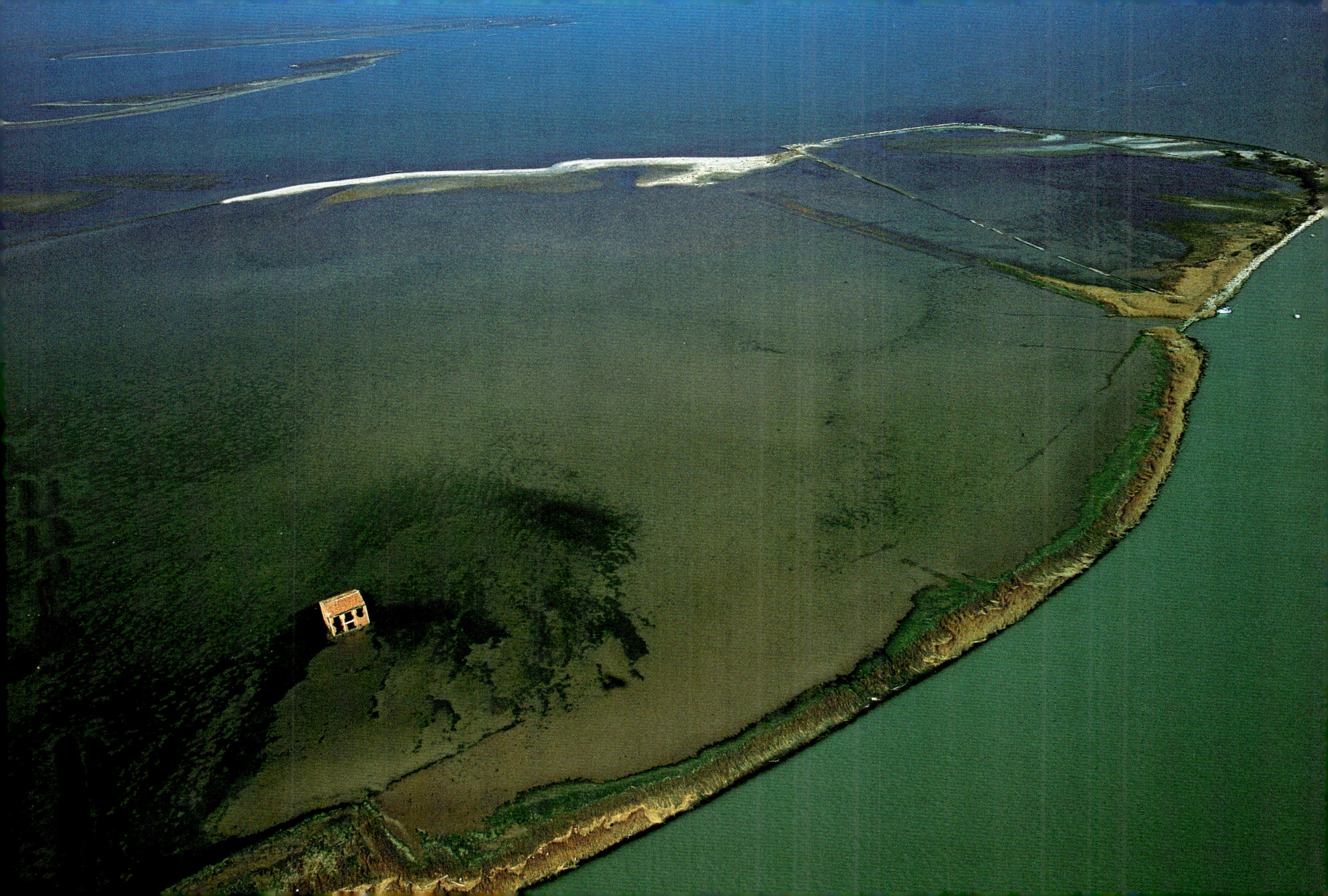

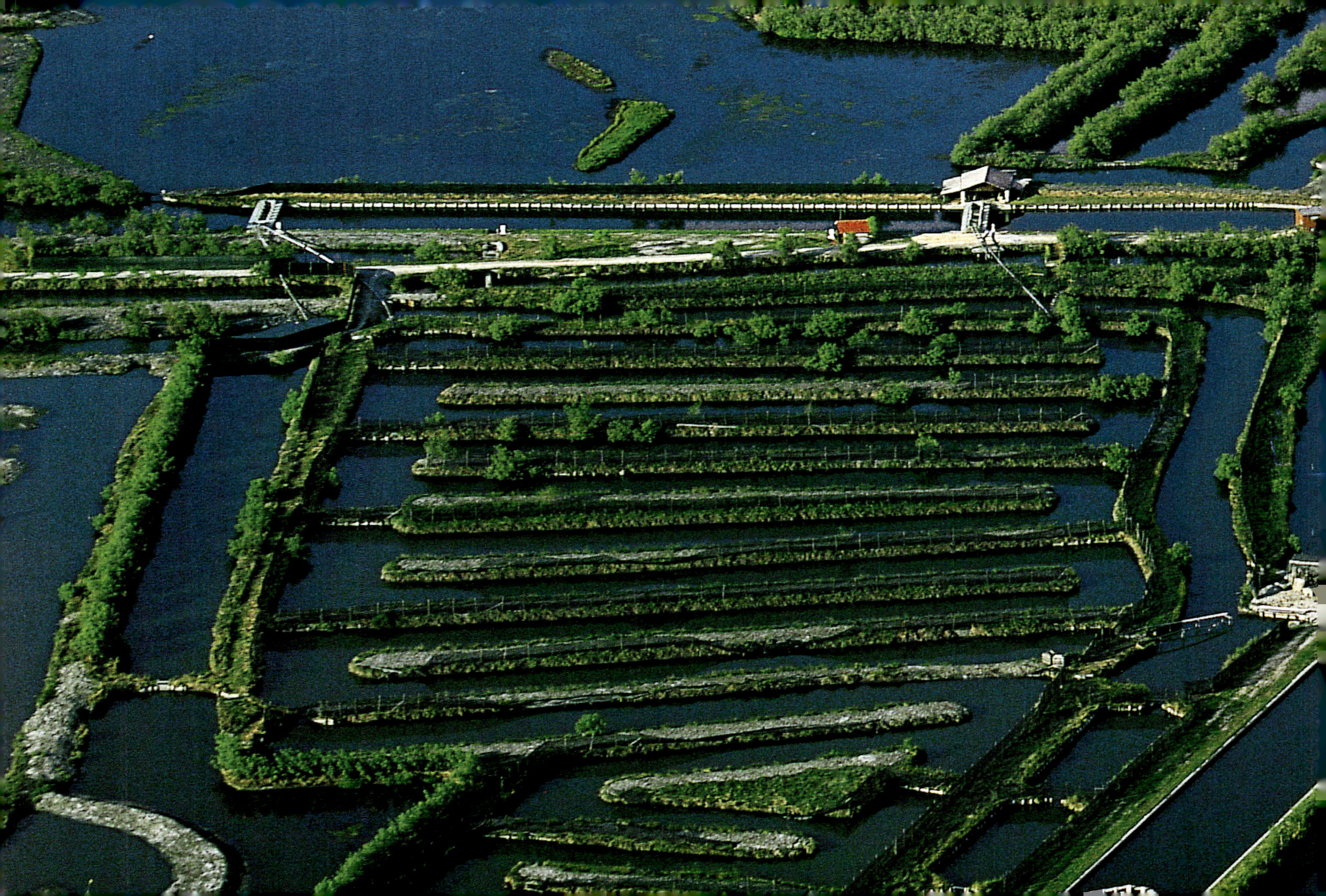

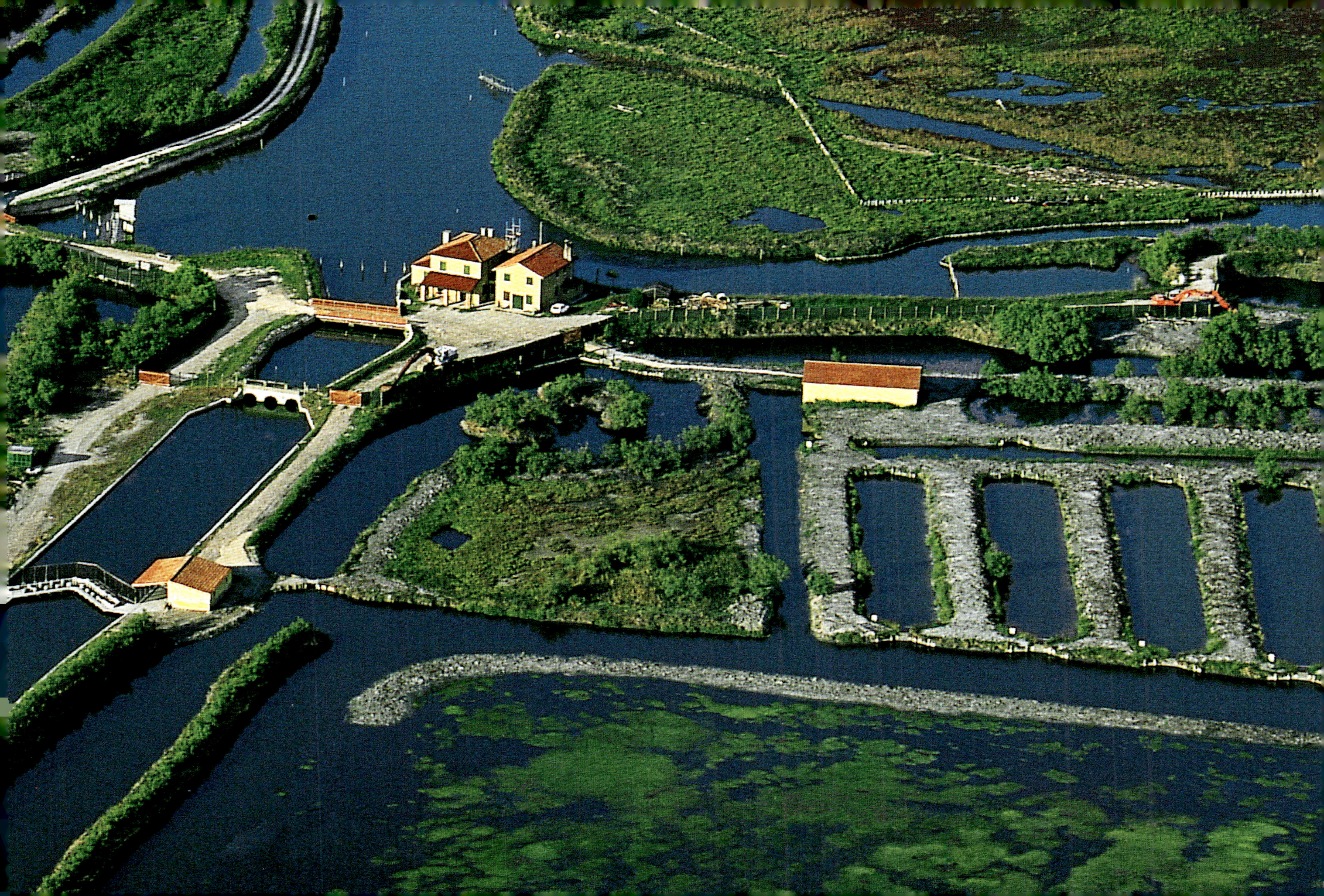

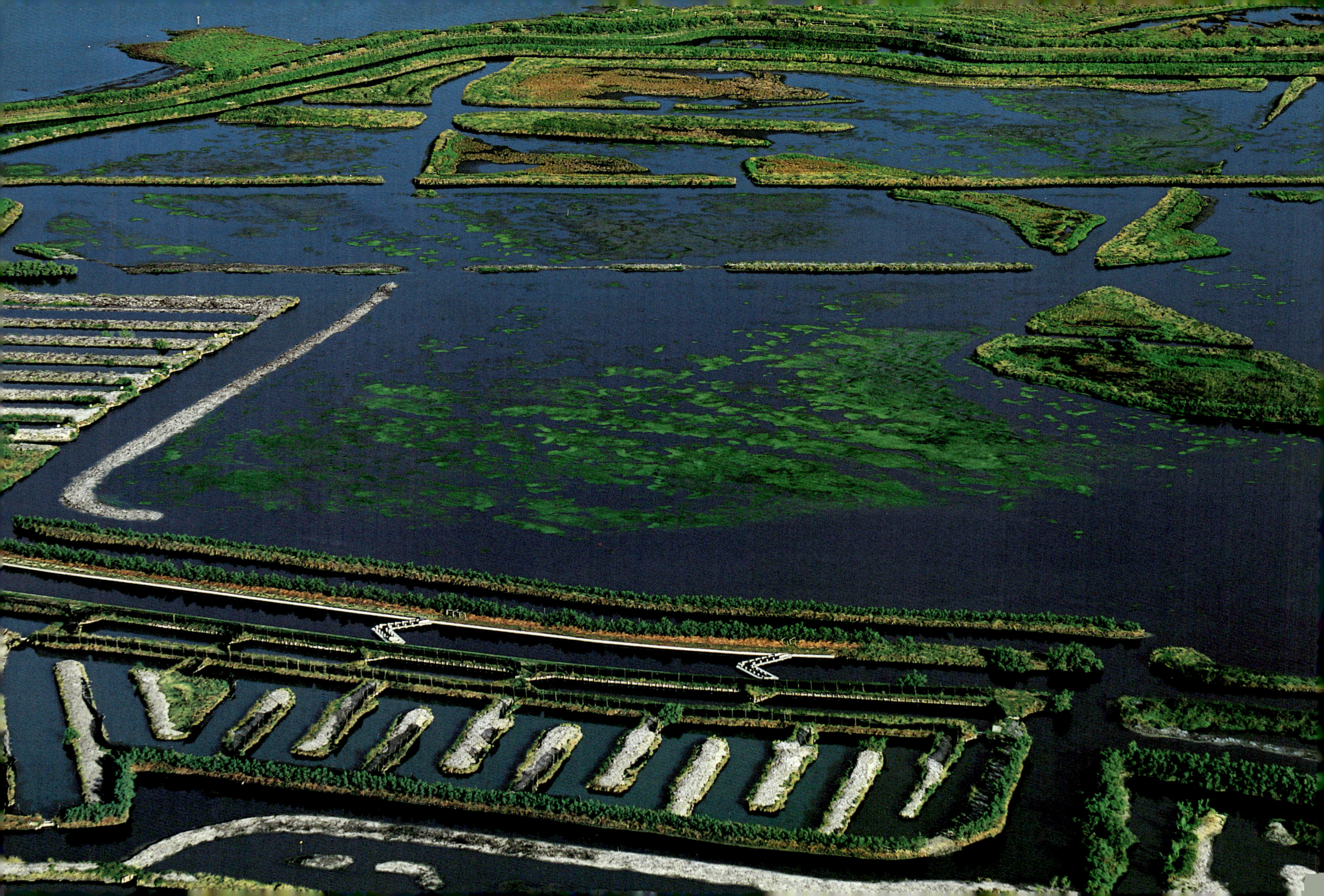

58 The Venetian Lagoon represents a complex ecosystem rich in its variety and habitats, where over the centuries the handiwork of humankind has had a heavy impact, modifying the watercourses by digging out channels and erecting barriers. One of the most unusual results of these modifications to the environment are the fish reserves, expanses of salt water given over to fish farming and controlled by means of a series of sluices known as *chiaviche*.

59 Channels and sandbanks define the limits of the marshy waters of the Valli di Comacchio. Situated within Emilia-Romagna, in the provinces of Ravenna and Ferrara, they extend over 27,180 acres (11,000 hectares) from Comacchio as far as the Reno River, taking in the *Valli* of Lido di Magnavacca, Fossa di Porto, Campo and Fattibello.

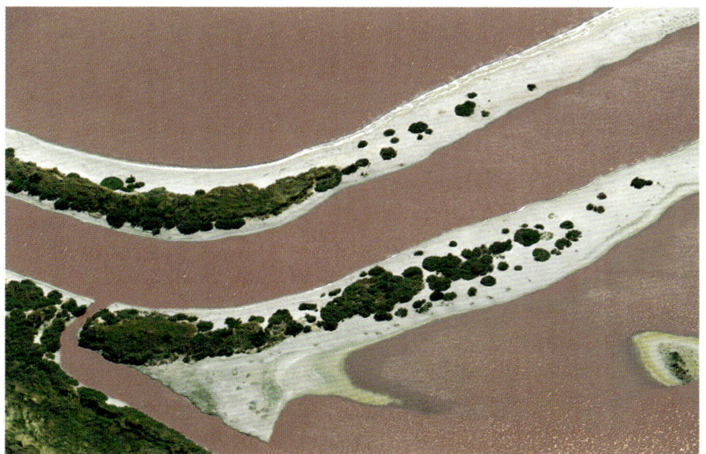

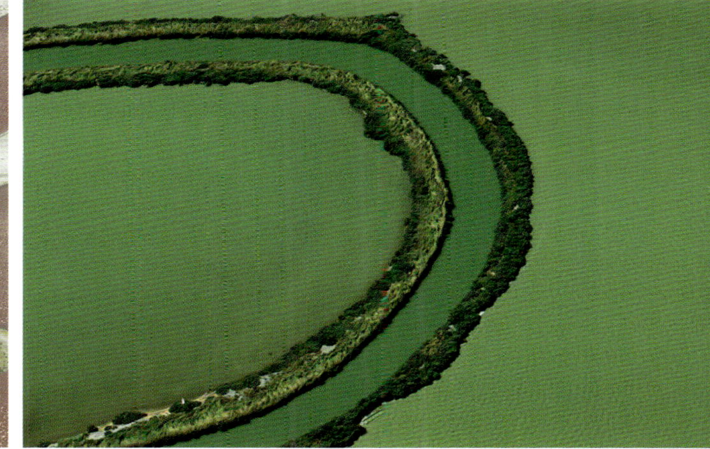

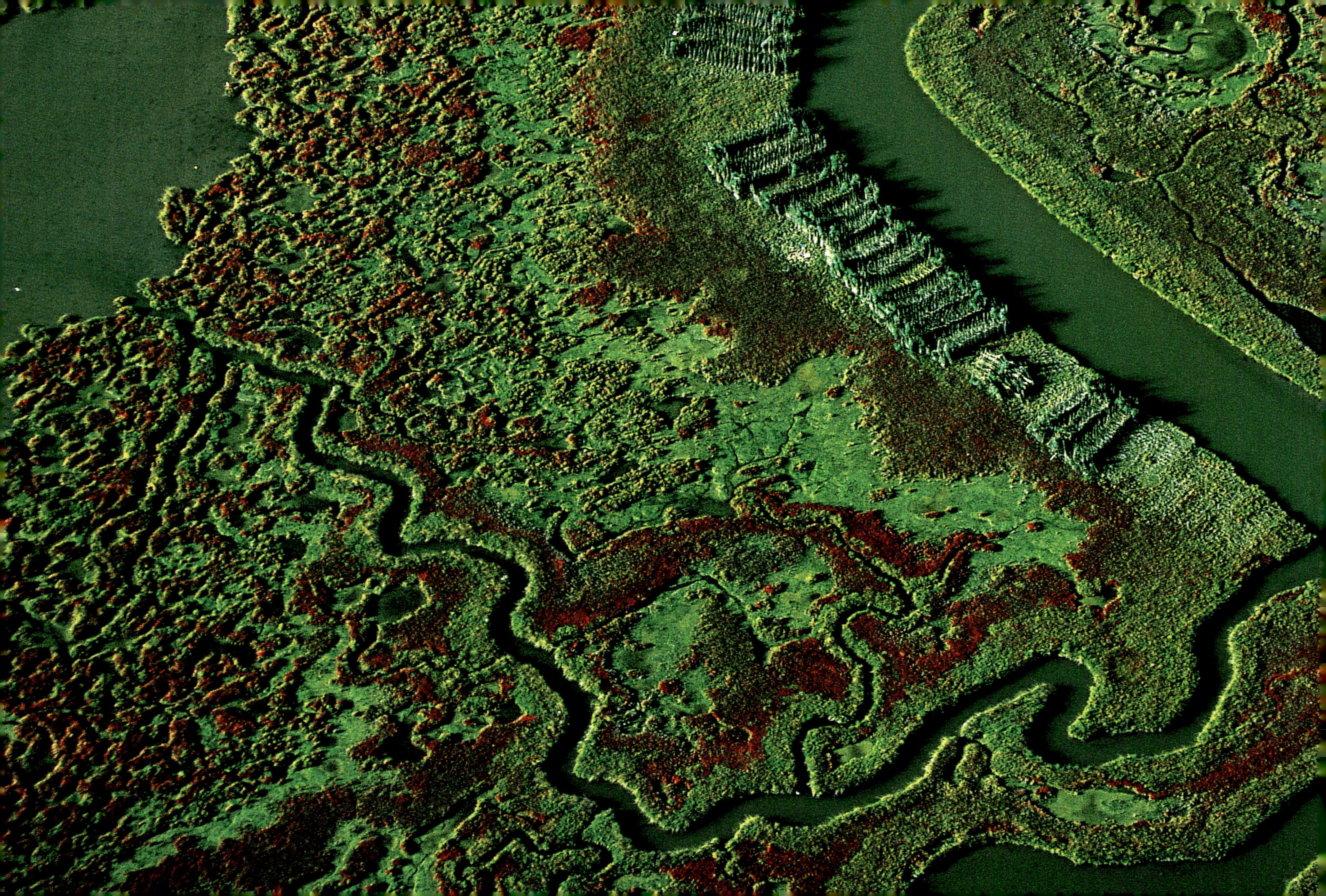

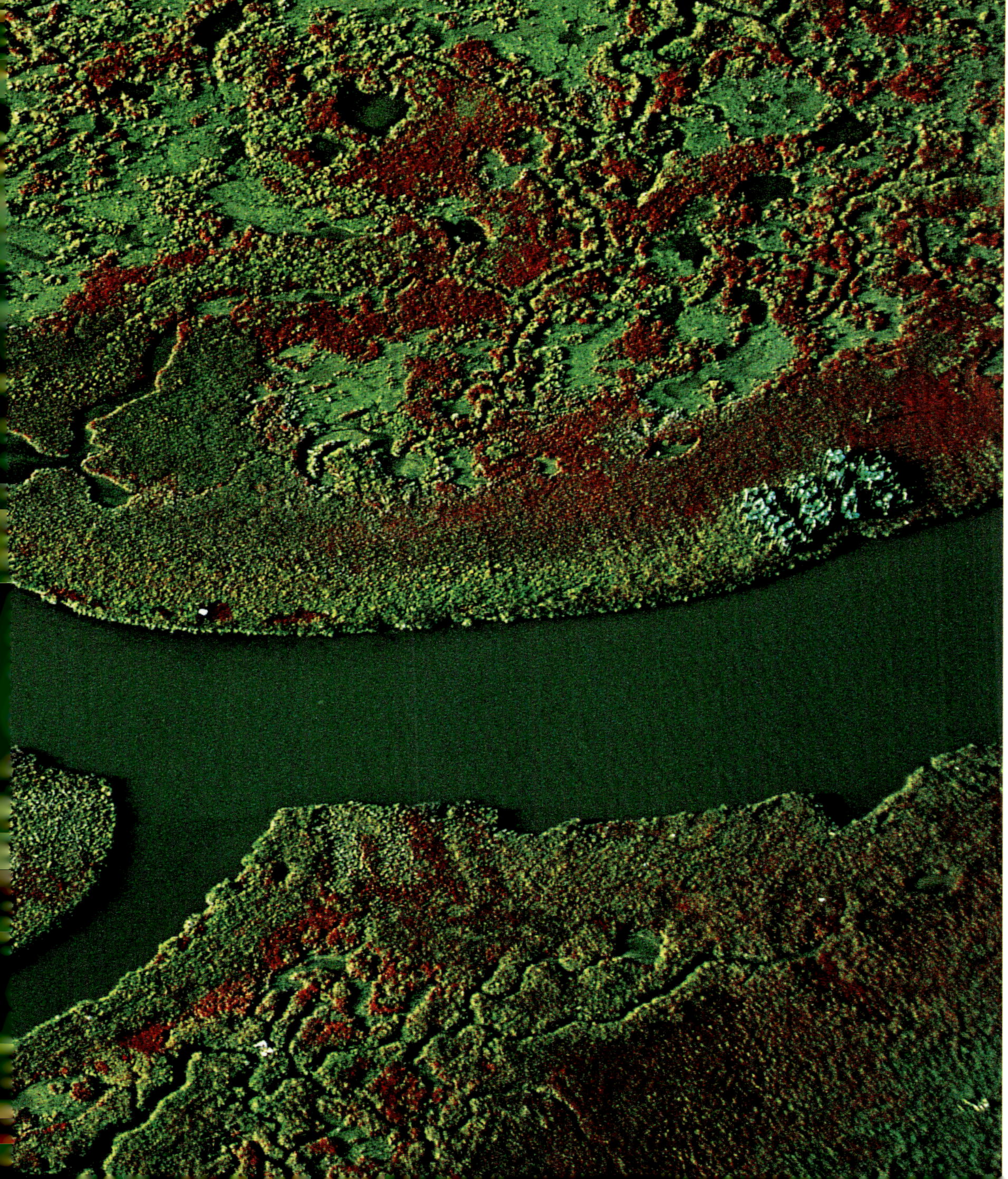

60-61 The capillary ramifications of the sweet waters, mixed in with their salty equivalents, combine to create quite extraordinary landscape effects, which are clearly visible from above. About 80 percent of the Venetian Lagoon is covered by mud flats and saltwater marshes.

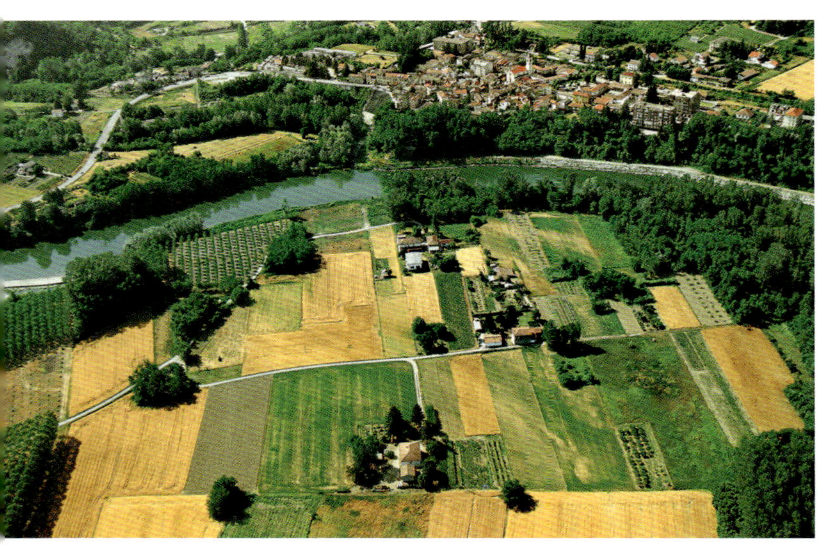

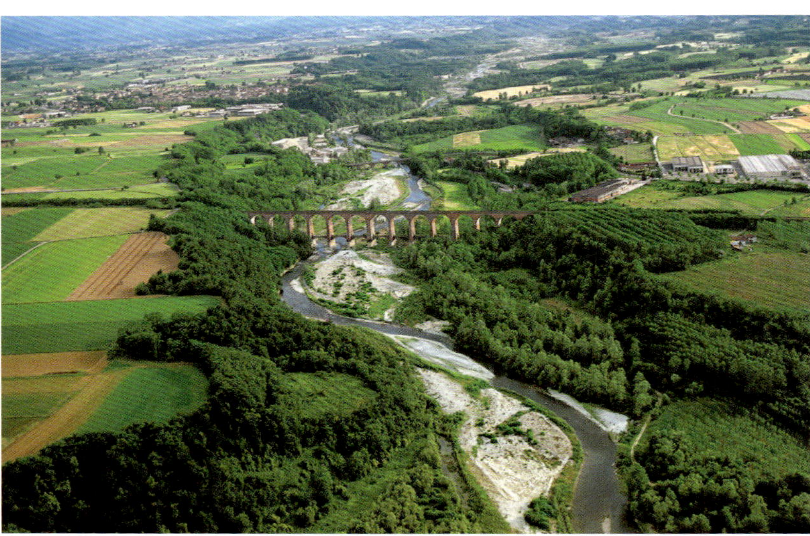

RIVERS

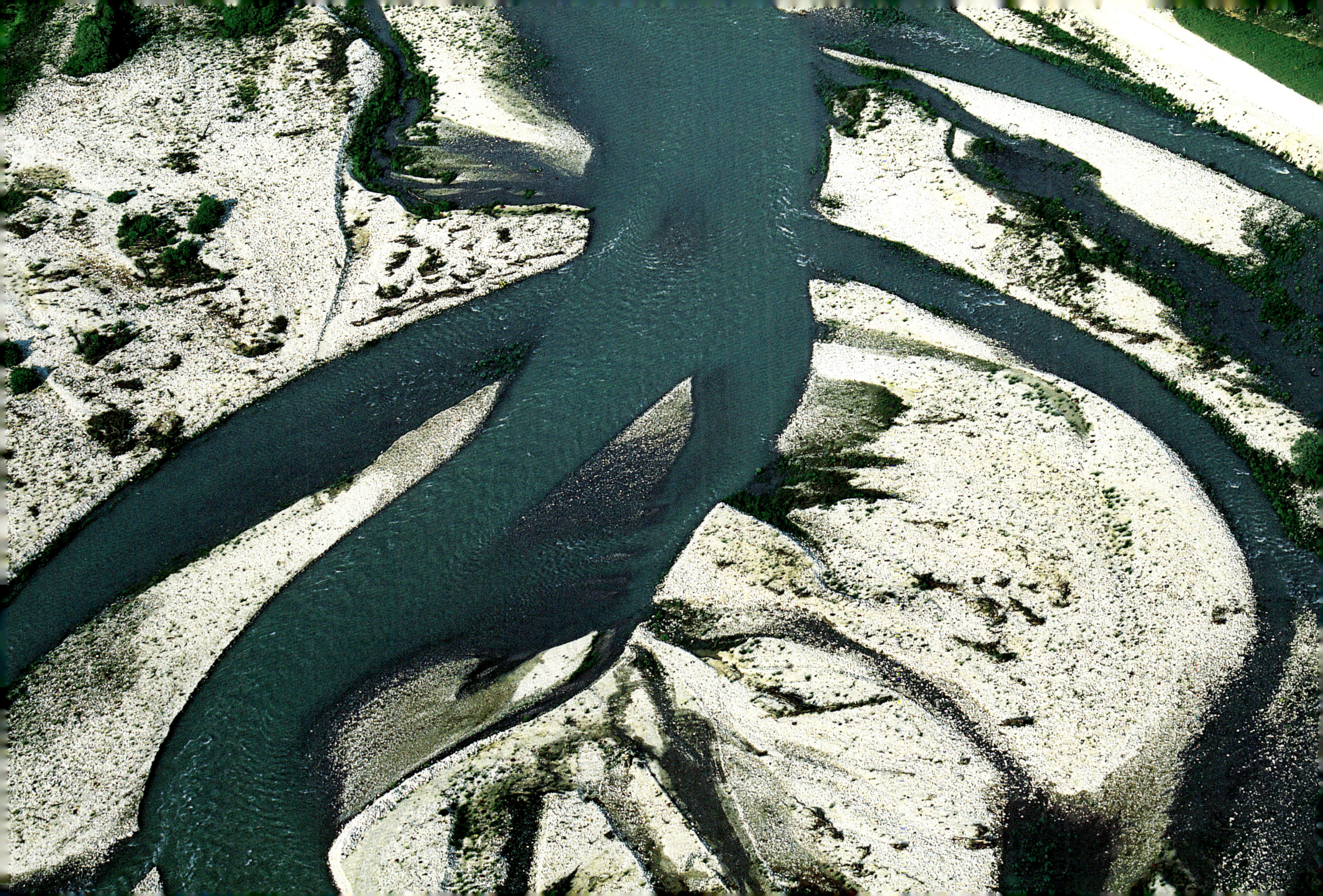

It is quite common in Italy to find people still living in close contact with a river that has resources to offer, sometimes quite unexpected and highly unusual: for example the reeds that grow along its banks. It is a particularly pleasing sight in winter when these reeds, turned a light brown color, creak in the wind as they receive visits from flights of small birds searching for seeds and for the insects that are nesting in the stems. The canes that grow along the banks of the river are extremely useful and important, since they can be used in the construction of huts, trellises, shelters for fishermen and surface coverings; even in the coldest of winter days, men still go out to collect them. What is needed is a magic wand to restore the Ticino River to its primitive splendor. But it may not need a real dose of magic because, of the things that are genuinely beautiful, many examples can still be found: the mills, the embankments, the great walls and the sturdy bridges, seen under the golden rays of sunset and against the background of a snow-laden range of mountains. Equally attractive is a different river located in Lombardy, the Mincio, which flows past Mantua, the splendid city which is famous as the birthplace of Virgil. This is a city that is devoted to its river, the source of water for the surrounding countryside and also for providing the driving force for its watermills and power plants. The Adige valley splits the chain of the Alps in two, separating the Central and Western Alps from those to the east. This was a severance rendered even more durable and irreversible by the presence of a complex network of road and rail infrastructures linking Italy to central Europe, passing through Trentino and Veneto regions. In the upper reaches of the river in the Upper Adige and Trentino regions, the woodlands come down almost as far as the river banks, spreading around the little glades dedicated to the gathering of hay or the cultivation of modest quantities of agricultural produce; this is the land of the little wooden shacks called *masi*, still lived in today. Then, when the valley starts to open out and the mountains of precious porphyry retreat back from the banks of the river, the geometric layouts of well planned urban centers begin to make their appearance, first smaller communities and then larger towns such as Bolzano and Trento, to be followed by industrial estates and then the carefully laid out orchards of apple trees, white with blossom in spring, green in summer, and red and yellow in the season when the fruit ripens and the leaves take on warm-colored hues. The mountains which look down over the valley along certain stretches of the river are among the most beautiful in all Italy. The Adige reaches Verona when its course is at its fullest, flowing lazily by while allowing itself to be admired by this splendid city's riverside roadway. The water courses of the peninsular should perhaps be

62 left Near Acqui, the Bormida River slides away between gently rising hills, toward the city of Alessandria.

62 right The Stura di Demonte is the major tributary of the Tanaro River, which it joins just after Fossano (Cuneo).

63 The Po river runs right across the Po Valley, widening as it passes the flatter sections and forming these playful patterns of water and sand.

65 In its mountain stretch, the Stura look very like a wild torrent, as can be seen from this photograph taken near Vinadio (Cuneo).

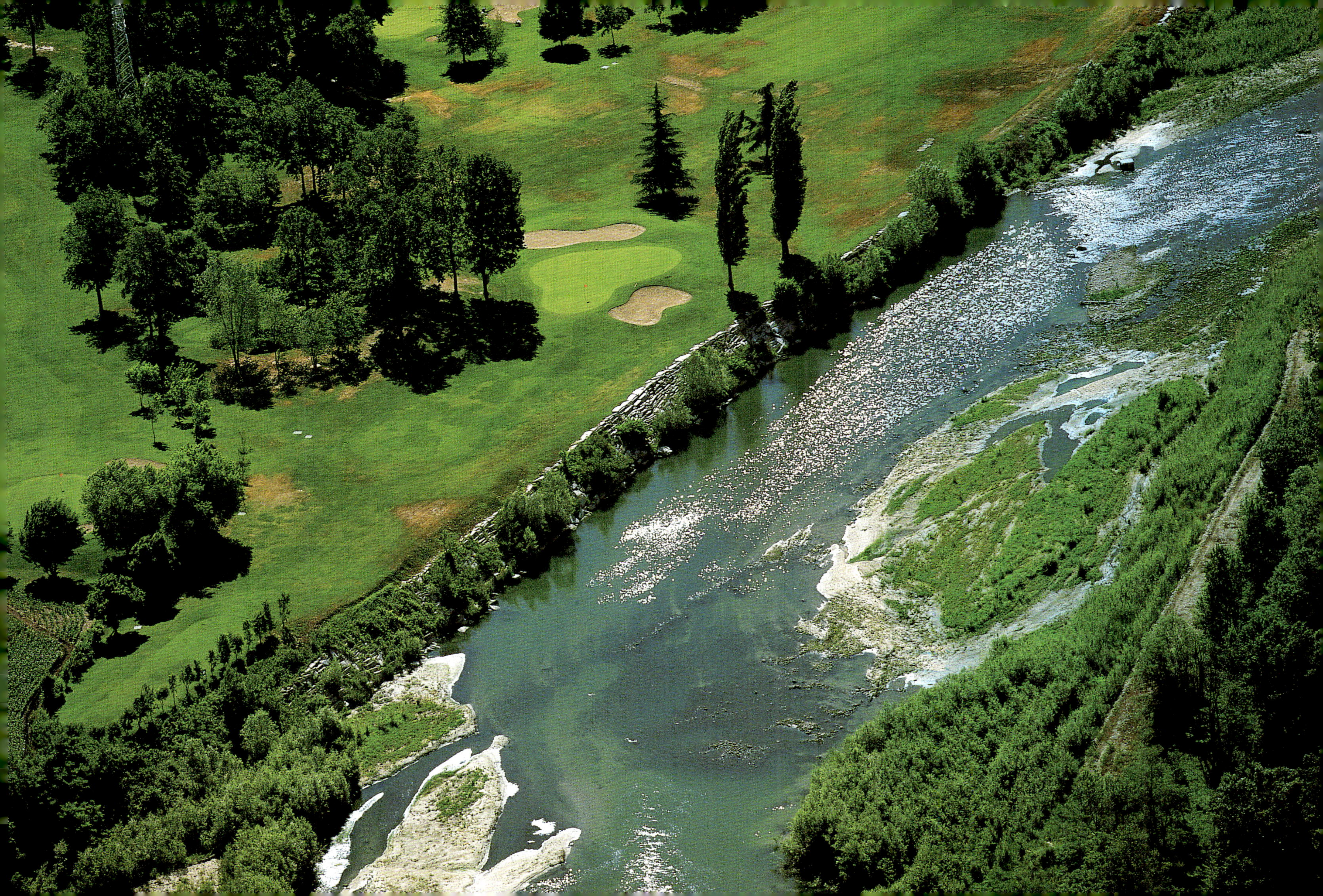

more fairly described as enlarged mountain torrents. When the rains come, the waters take on the color of the earth that they have stripped away from the mountains and hillsides of the Apennine Range. The Arno is a typical example of a river with all the characteristics of a mountain torrent: it rises on Mt Falterona and heads off in the direction of Florence, revealing all its tight meanders in among the hills of Tuscany. It arrives in Florence as a river already mature but not too much so; it has been truly memorable when in spate, and proved tragically so when it devastated this city of great art, probably facilitated by the actions of man in stripping away the tree coverage on the slopes of the hydrographic basin, thus preventing the woods from holding back the fury of the rains which for days were to hammer down on the upper reaches of the river. In its lower part the course of the river crosses a level flood plain known as the *Valdarno inferiore*, which is surrounded by higher ground of modest elevation, predominantly given over to the cultivation of the olive and the vine but also with some residual forest areas of oak, hornbeam, manna-ash, and maple. The countryside bordering the river looks like a well-ordered chessboard of tiny plots of land with a number of farmhouses and scattered settlements; the marshlands which at one time characterized the final stretch of the river are no longer to be found. This part of Tuscany is one of the most densely populated areas of Italy largely because of the fertility brought with the sediment deposited by the river and its tributaries, extending to the plains around Pisa and the beaches of the Tyrrhenian Sea lined

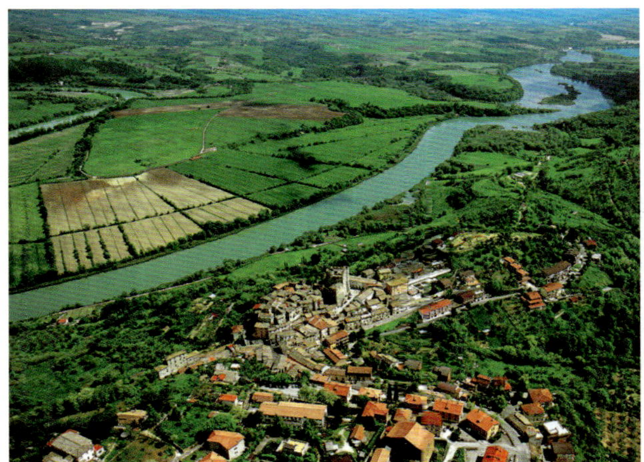

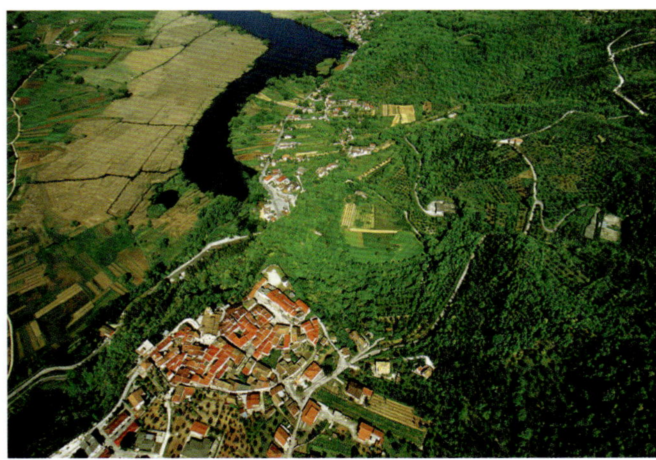

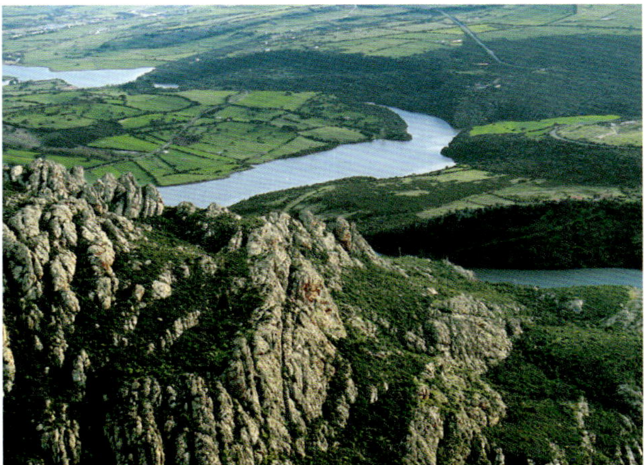

66 left The Tiber takes good care of several important natural treasures found along its banks. The Tiber-Farfa Regional Natural Reserve, shown here in a photograph taken near Nazzano (Rome), was created specifically to protect this patrimony of extensive bights and meanders that offer a home to a considerable variety of animal species.

with well-maintained and salubrious pine forests. A great deal has been spoken and written about the Tiber: poems, reports, bad things and good. A Roman could never speak badly of the river: for better or worse, it is the third river of Italy and is undoubtedly the most important because of its role in the history of the country. There is a time of the year when it seems to be almost beautiful, when at the end of winter and the beginning of spring its waters are swollen with the contribution from the snows of the Apennines as they come to terms with the thaw; at this time its color is practically blue. During the rest of the year the waters are brown because of the mass of mud that is carried down toward its mouth, or even green due to the masses of single-cell seaweeds which make the water look like an organic broth which, by the way, is not necessarily a bad thing for wildlife. The Tiber is a fine river, and is in fact much improved and richer in life today than it was thirty years ago, above all in the stretch flowing between Lazio and Umbria. Here, before starting on its last journey toward its destination in the Tyrrhenian Sea, the river lingers with a series of gentle meanders down a green corridor in the valley dominated by the severe mass of Orvieto with its elegant cathedral, its characteristic mediaeval town center, and its many small craft workshops. Within a stone's throw of Orvieto stands the town of Civita di Bagnoregio, quite separate but having in common exactly the same precarious situation of instability on top of a rock. This is a town which some have persisted in regarding as dead but which in reality is bursting with life and initiative. It is a spectacular town built on tuff, seemingly balanced on high ground made up of clay and sandstone, now so eroded as to seem almost perched on a platform facing a highly uncertain future. Visiting the region known for its ravines is like making a jump back into the past to rediscover a landscape which has conditioned the lifestyles of its people to such an extent as to settle the destiny of an entire populous community. It is a surreal setting, a background for a western movie. For as far as the eye can see the hills seem to have been cut about and wounded, as if flayed by the hand of a giant. It is a fantasy landscape from which mankind seems to have been excluded But this, of course, is not possible. The people are certainly there and have colonized this area of crumbling and unstable countryside as well, digging grottoes and tunnels out of the clay to make corridors, dining rooms and bedrooms, workshops and studios where, for centuries past, an entire population has lived, labored, suffered and probably even celebrated. Certainly these gullies have caused a great deal of suffering, but these surroundings still make an impression with their colors, their shapes, their forms. This is a countryside of villages poised on cliff tops, of vast views over surrounding valleys. It is a landscape that has undoubtedly left its mark on the peoples who have lived there. The rain continues to fall on the ravines, and will carry away yet more particles of clay so that the following day the environment will have changed, imperceptibly, but still

66 center The Rio Carpello is part of the Lake Posta Fibreno Natural Reserve (Frosinone), one Italy's most important environmental oases.

66 right The Flumendosa, Sardinia's second largest river after the Tirso, rises from springs located in the Gennargentu massif.

changed. This is a changeable countryside carrying the marks of time, which men see from a distance but then perhaps look at again with a touch of nostalgia. Italy's third largest river flows without hindrance between twin rows of poplars, willows and alders which, with their dense crests of emerald green foliage stretching out over the water, seem almost to wrap the river in their embrace, so much so that whoever ventures out in a canoe has the sensation of finding himself in one of the leafy tunnels of a forest of one of the great rivers of Africa or the Amazon Basin. Once the season of heavy rains has passed, during which time the river shows its worst side by dragging along tree trunks and, unfortunately, rubbish of all shapes and colors in great swirls of mud, the late spring sees the Tiber take on a quite different aspect and become rich in fish: chub, bleak, grey mullet, tench, eel and carp for the most part, but other types are also to be found including the catfish which is of American origin and unknown to our wildlife until its introduction back in time. Between Tuscany, Lazio and Umbria, thanks to two dams constructed by the energy corporation Enel, the river forms two artificial lakes. Lake Corbara has crystal clear waters rich in fish, this being the realm of the pike, the perch and the grebe. Then there is Lake Alviano, 1235 acres (500 hectares) of fens, marshes and flooded woodlands, inhabited by a vast population of birds: from the herons, where all of the eight species to be found in Europe can be seen, to the ducks, from the falcons to the snipes. When passing through Rome, between Castel Giubileo and Magliana, the river travels between two rows of poplars and willows and, in the center, becomes hemmed in by two massive retaining walls made up of blocks of marble. At certain times one gets the impression that the city and river together form part of just a single ecosystem which, given a modicum of commitment, could confer a countless number of benefits to its two-legged residents as well. The very last stretch of the Tiber breaks out into the Roman countryside which surrounds the great metropolis of Rome, as ever in continuous expansion. This shows an uninterrupted flow of gentle rises and falls and small valleys that separate the higher ground of the interior, up against the Apennines or the volcanic mountains, from the coastal areas that are generally low-lying, sandy and often marshy. At the center is the meandering course of the Tiber, which at this point has practically reached its maturity, its route being marked by a dense screen of ash trees, English oaks, elms, poplars and elders while all around, exposed to the sun that is rarely lacking in these parts, can be seen meadows, small spreads of holm-oaks and phillyreas, forests of Turkey oaks and durmasts and enormous cork-oaks standing alone. Wherever one directs one's gaze one cannot fail to identify, in a marvelous mingling of the new with the old, of man with nature, the evidences of a human landscape.

69 The Allaro is an important river in the heart of Aspromonte, in Calabria. It is often in spate and gives its name to the valley in which it flows, the Stilaro-Allaro Valley. Like all such rivers, the Allaro is not very long, has a characteristically pebbly bed, becomes a veritable torrent in winter, but is completely dry for the rest of the year.

70-71 The Stura di Demonte River carries a particularly large volume of water, so large as to exceed that of the Tanaro itself, where the two rivers merge. This picture was taken in summer near Cherasco (Cuneo), when the water level was low.

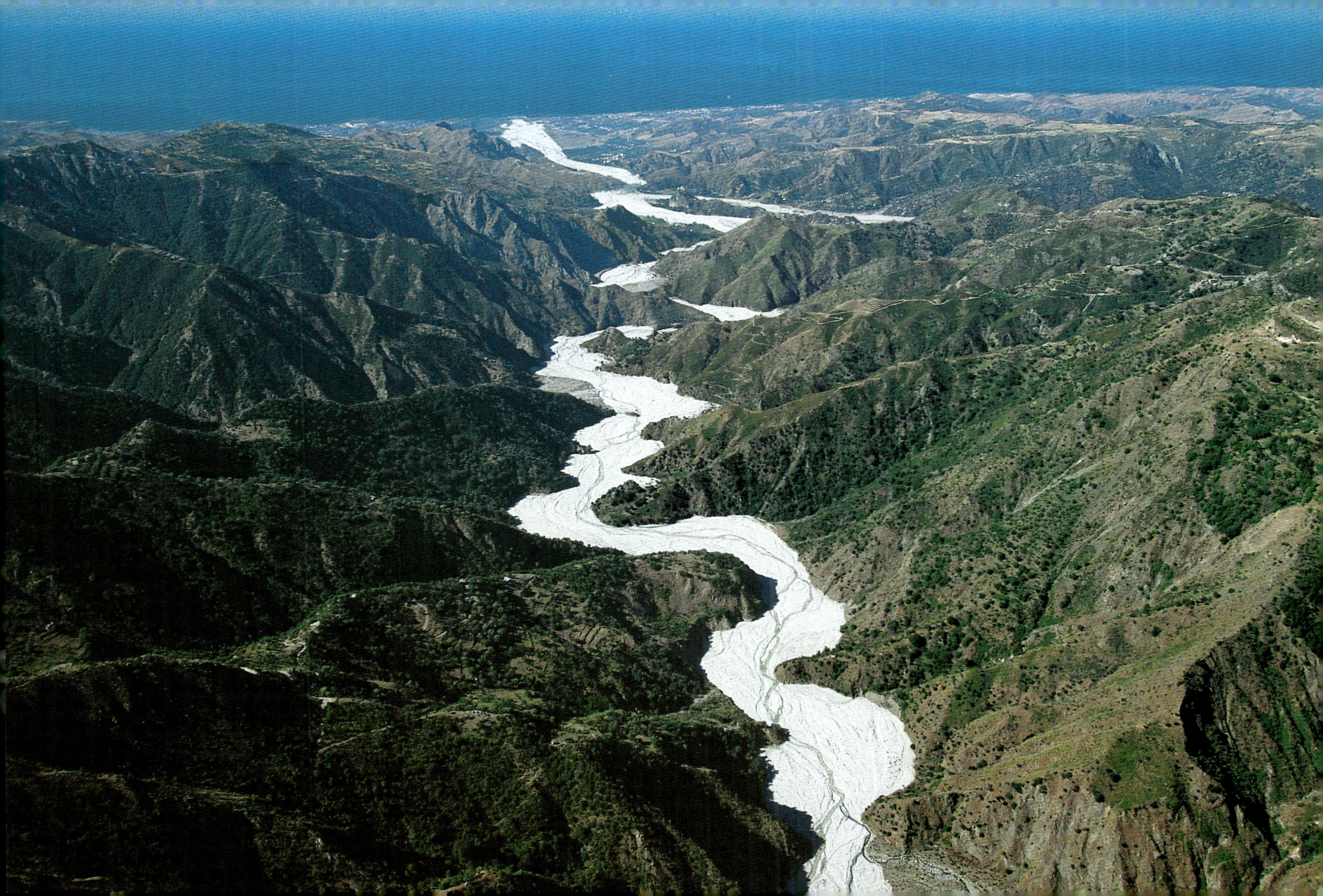

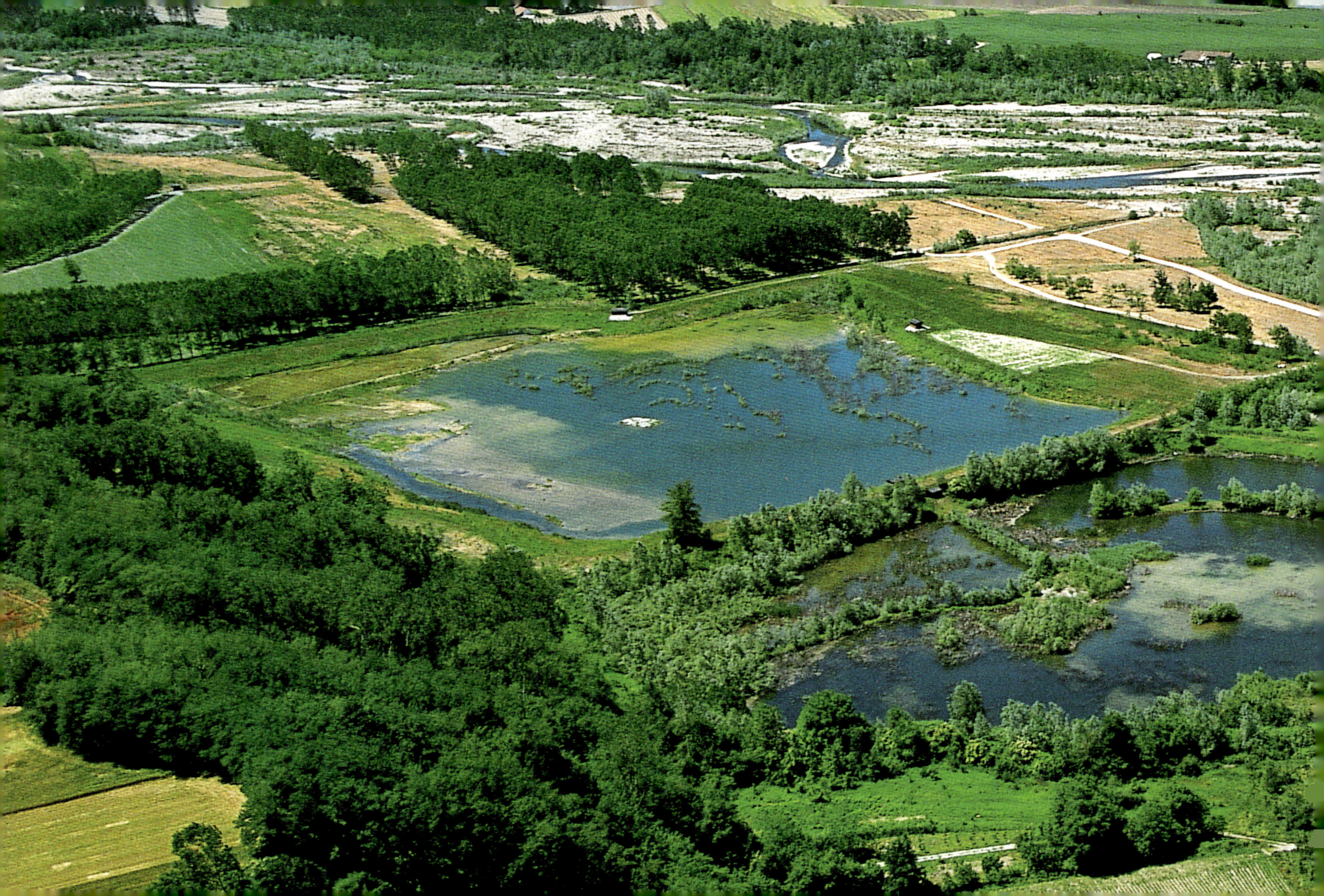

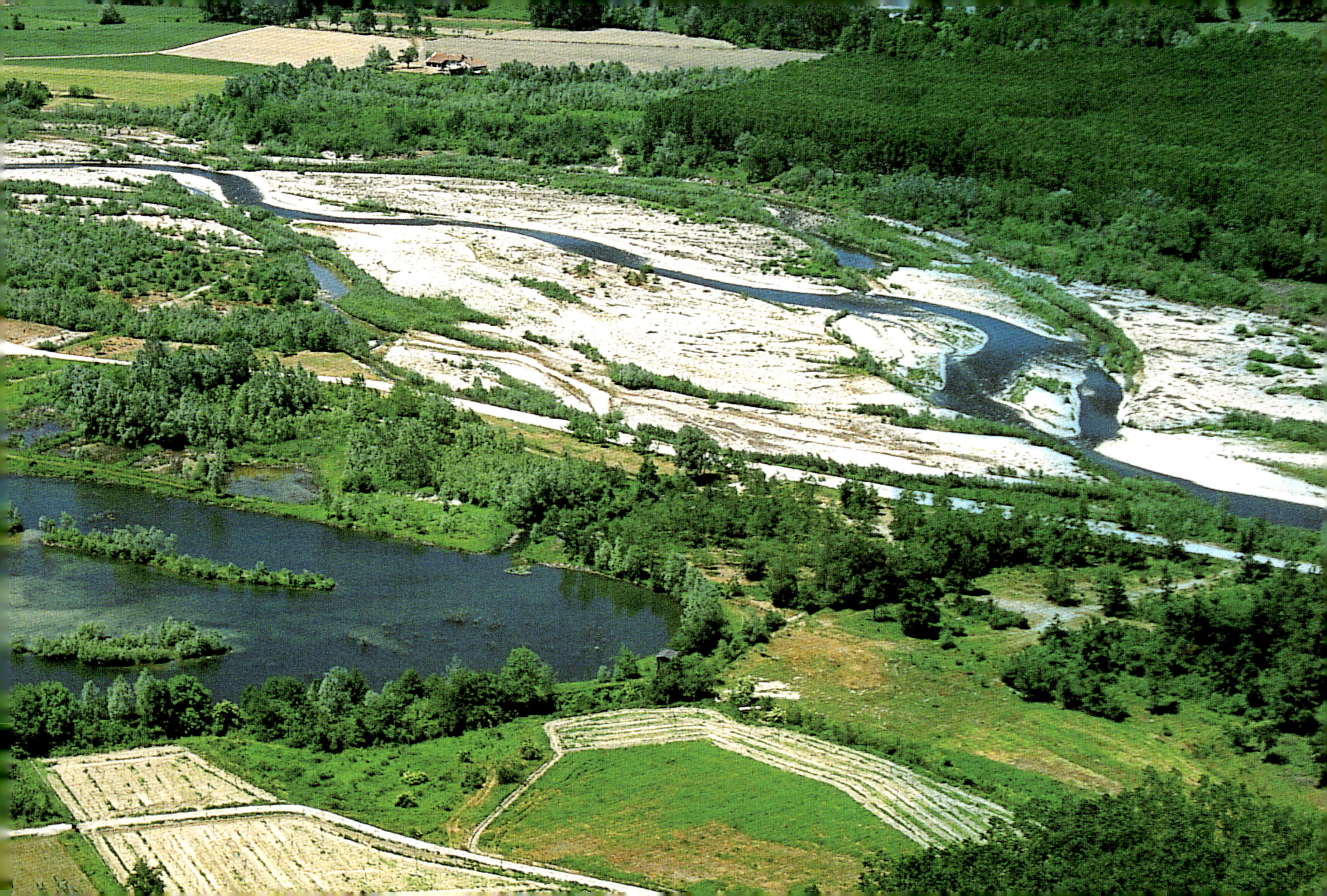

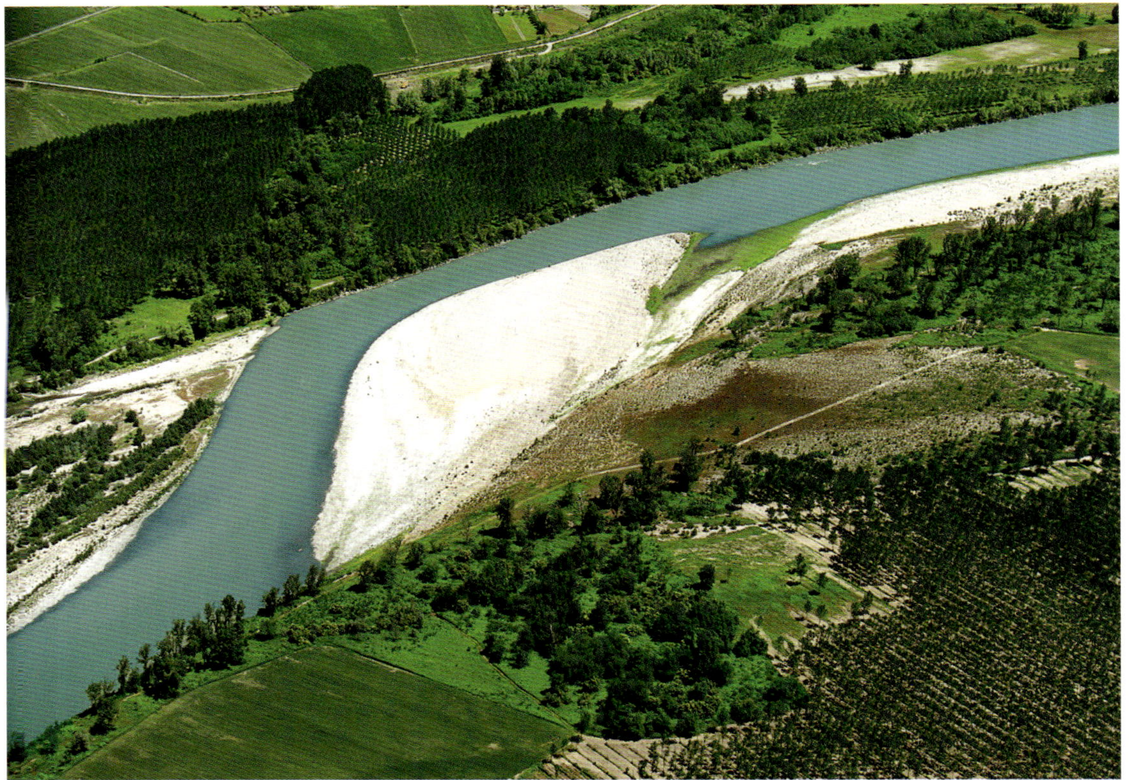

72 and 73 The Po River, with its 405 miles (652 km), is Italy's longest river as well as that with the largest basin. Since ancient times and long thereafter, it was navigable and used as a "highway" by the barges that carried merchandise from the Adriatic ports. The volume of water increases as the river progresses down the valley and the number of inflowing tributaries grows: comparatively modest in Piedmont (to the left, near Crescentino), the volume has already built up in Lombardy (to the right, near Pavia).

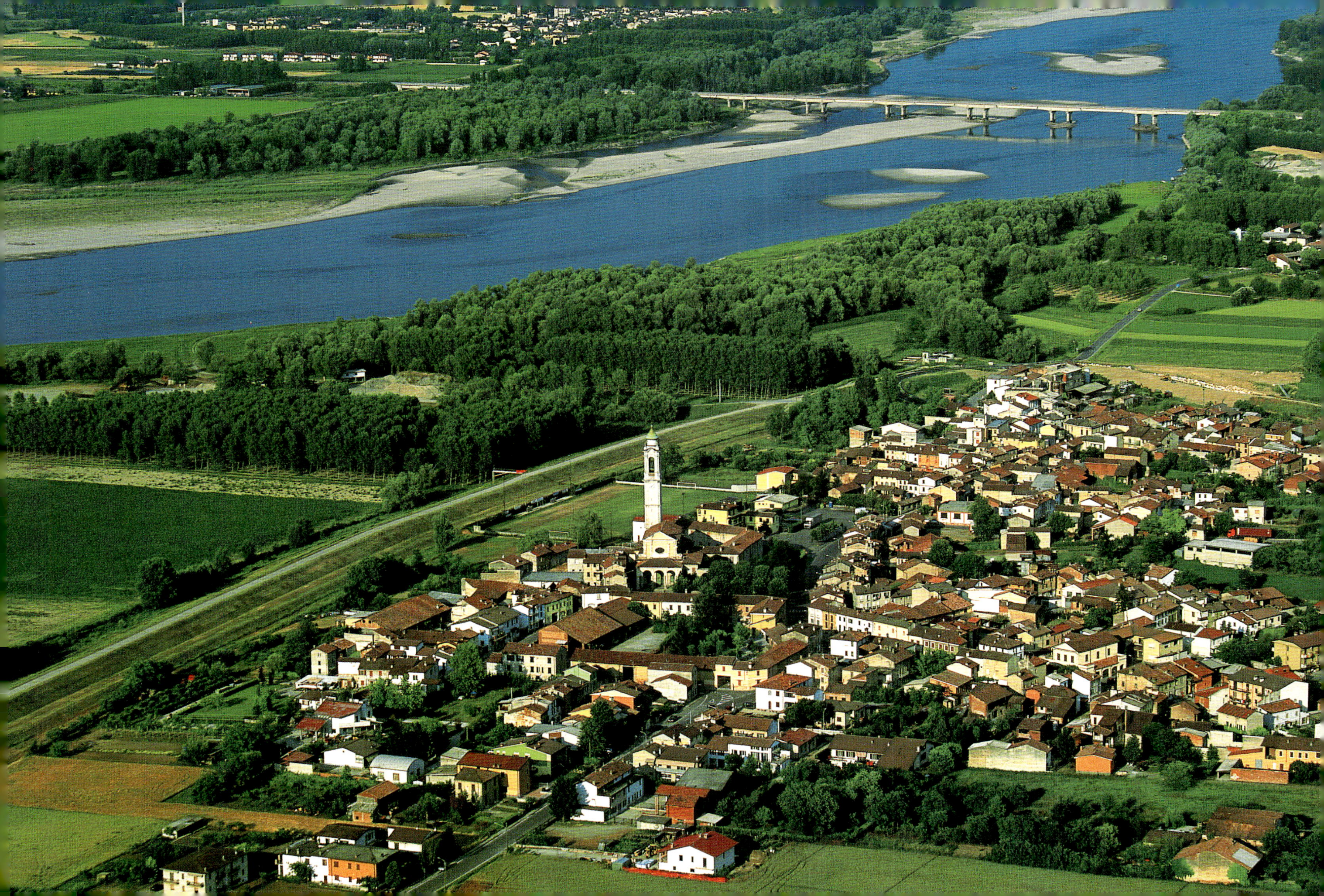

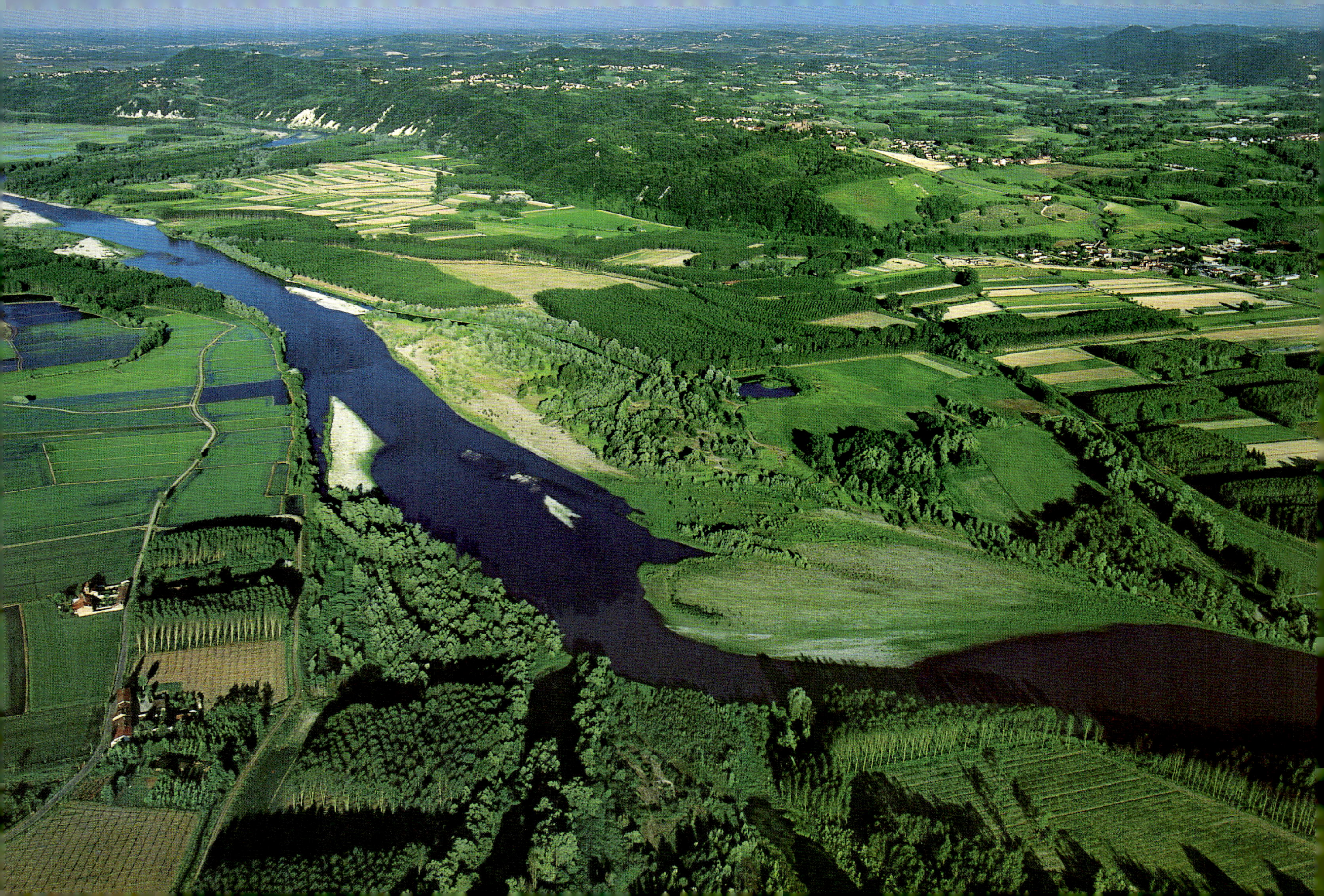

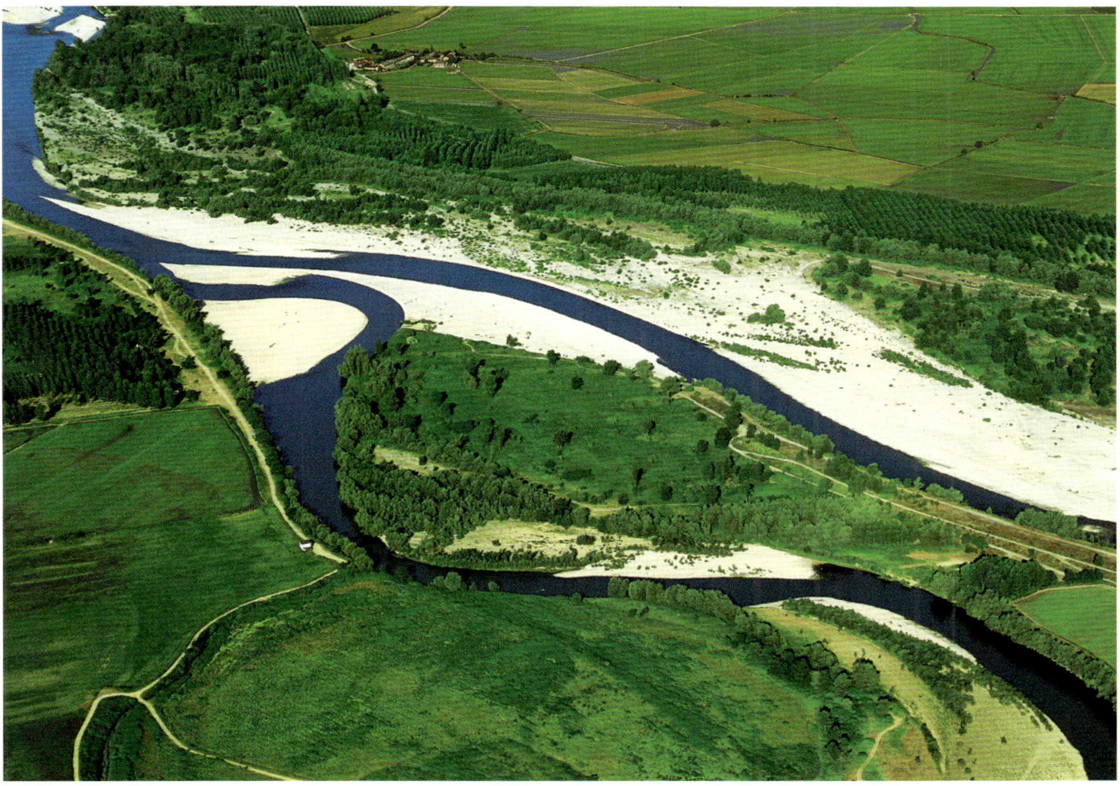

74 The source waters of the Po are to be found on Monviso, 12,600 ft (3841 m), and are increased by numerous other tributaries still in this mountain stage. By the time the Po reaches the plain (the photograph was taken near Chivasso) it has already acquired a bed that at its wider points is about 650 ft (200 m) in breadth, with a quite considerable flow of water.

75 The Sesia River is one of the Po's principal tributaries. It flows in from the north after a course of some 85 miles (138 km), which begins in the higher reaches of the Monte Rosa massif.

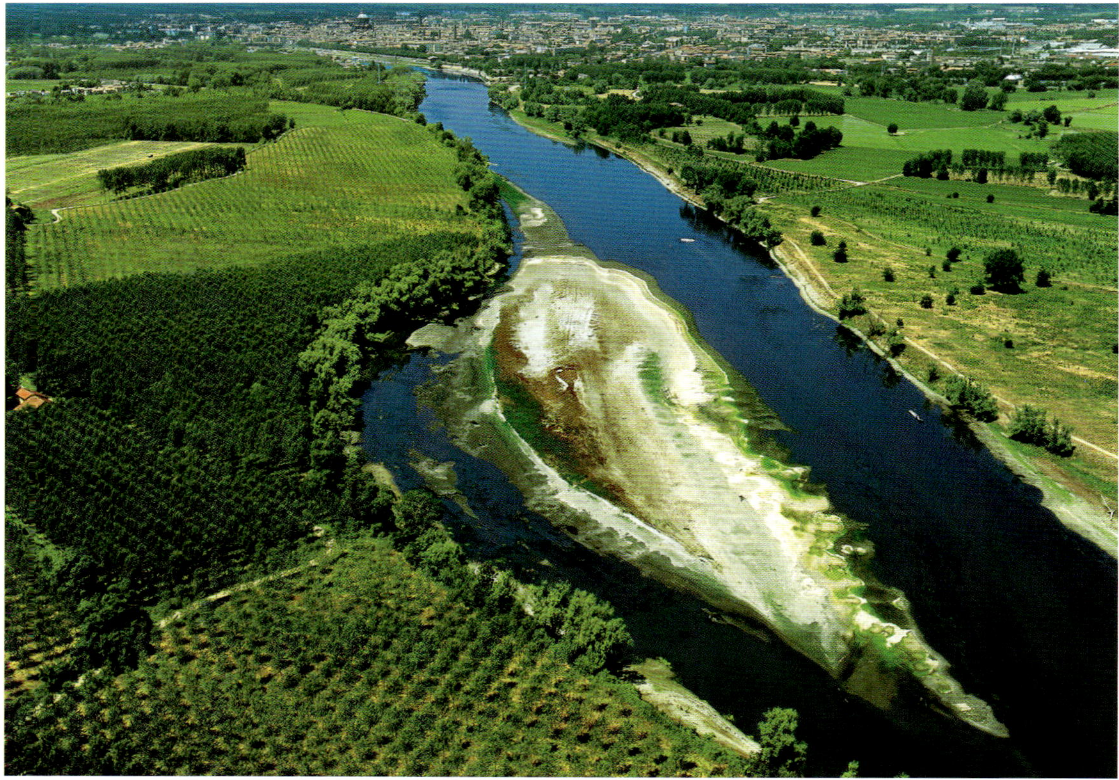

76 and 77 The Ticino River rises in the Nufenen Pass in Switzerland, empties into Lake Maggiore, and then leaves it again with a much increased volume of water to follow once more its course toward the Po Valley. Here it just brushes the Lomellina area and, after passing through Vigevano and Pavia, it flows into the Po from the left within the territory of Linarolo. Typical of the flatter sections of the river bed are the *zatteroni* or "rafts," which are small, sandy islets like those shown in the photographs. The *zatteroni* emerge in summer or when the water flow is otherwise at a minimum.

78-79 Because of its volume, the Ticino River is of great importance both for irrigation and as a source of electrical energy. But the river is especially appreciated by students of nature for the richness of its habitats, which enjoy the protection of two nature reserves.

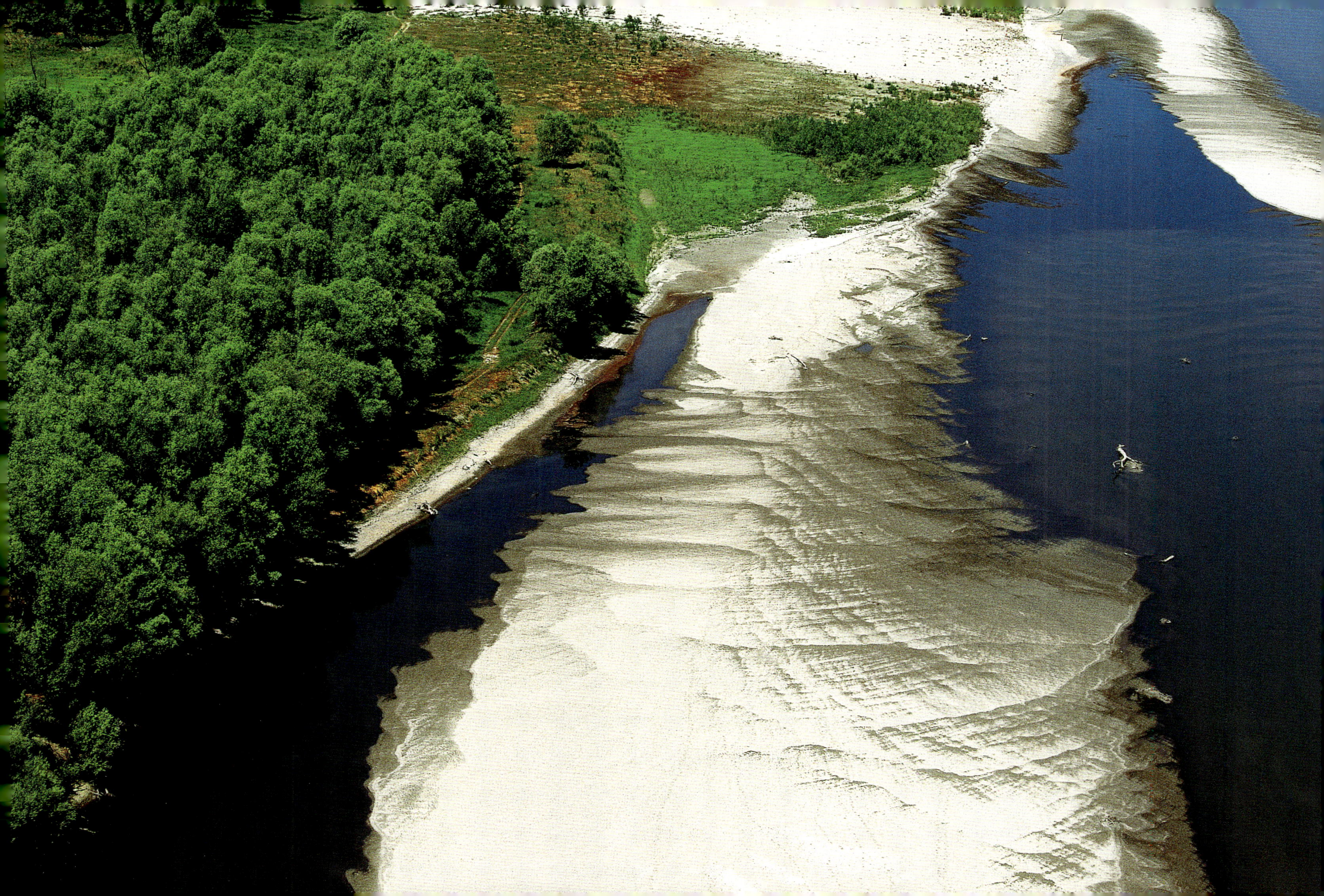

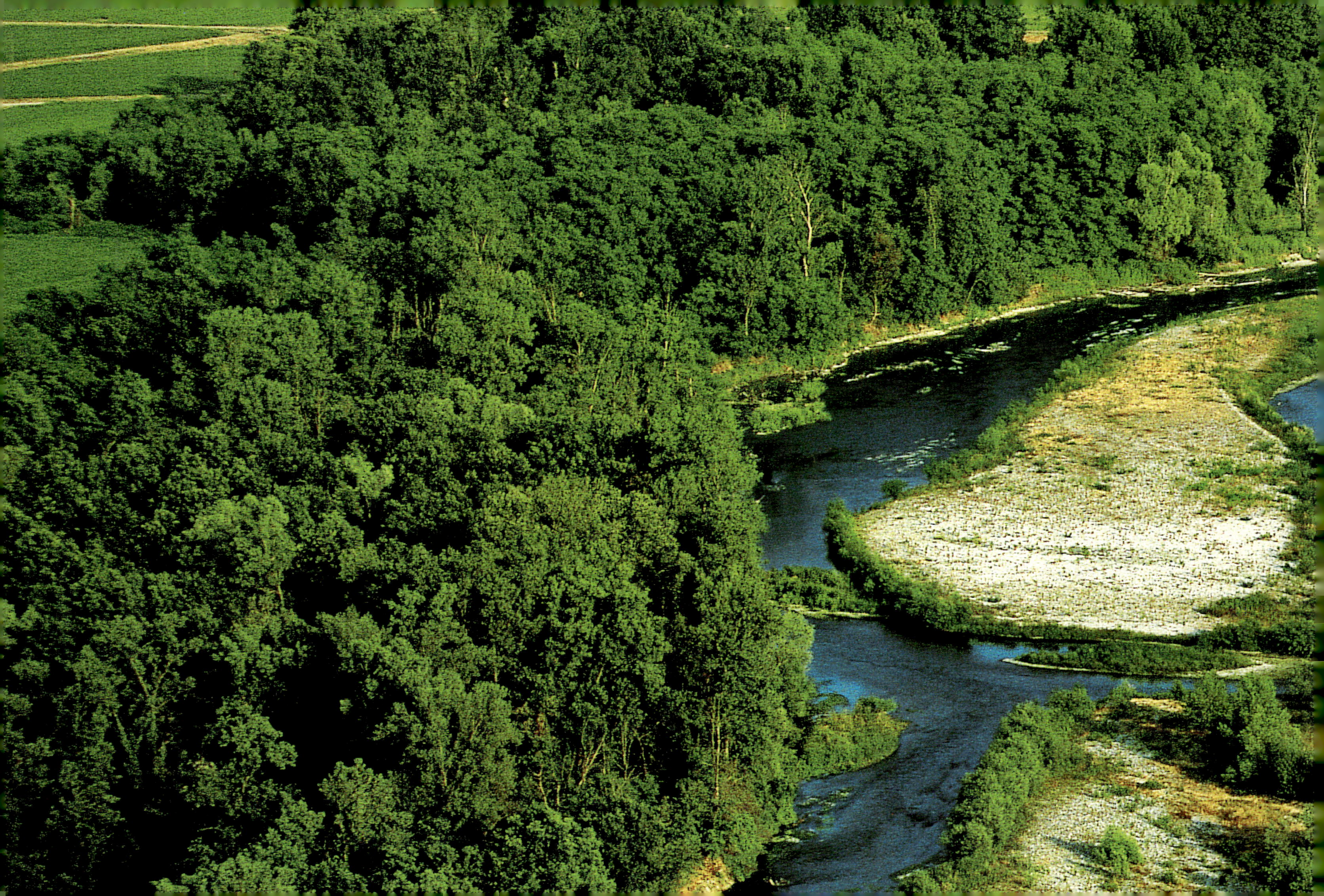

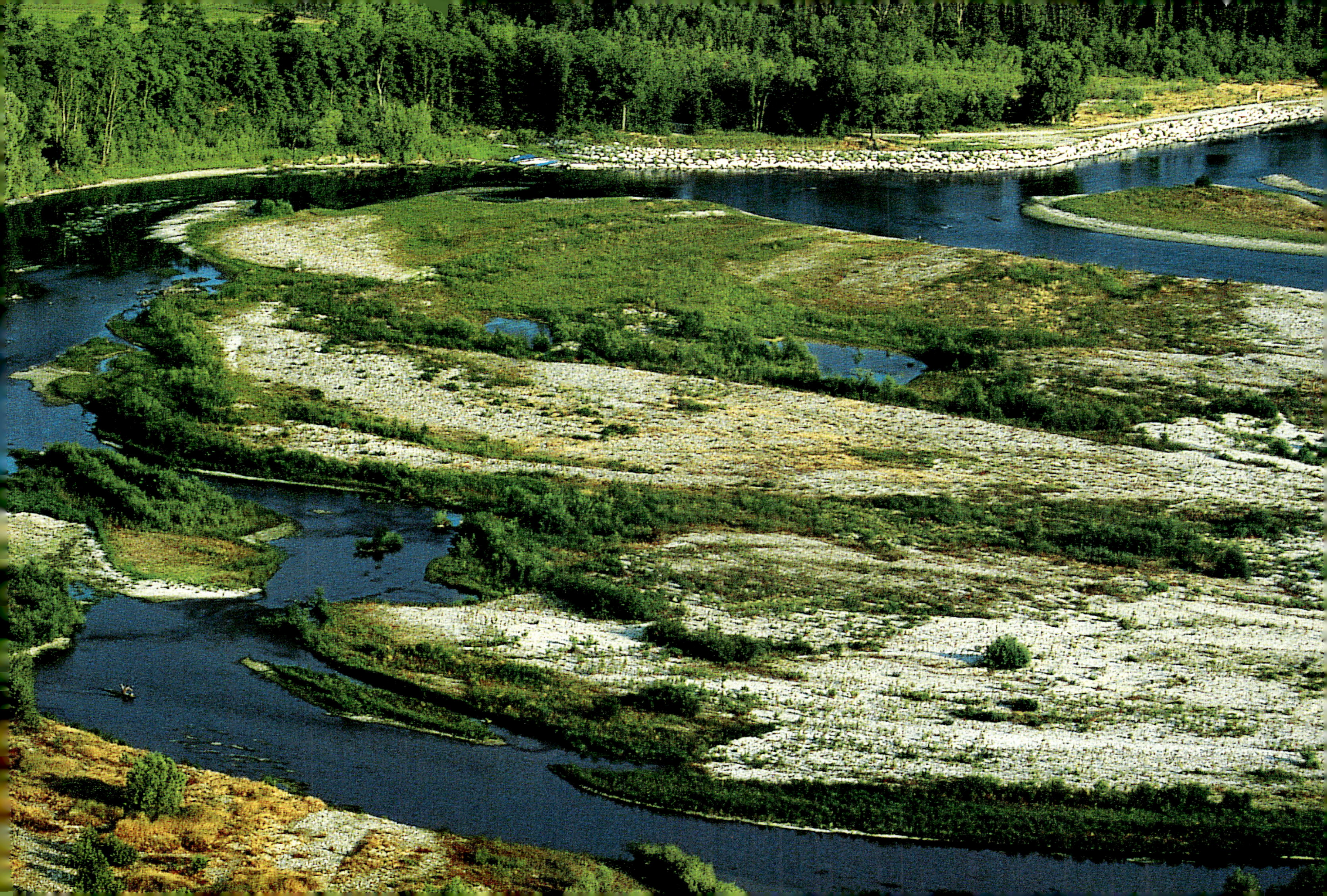

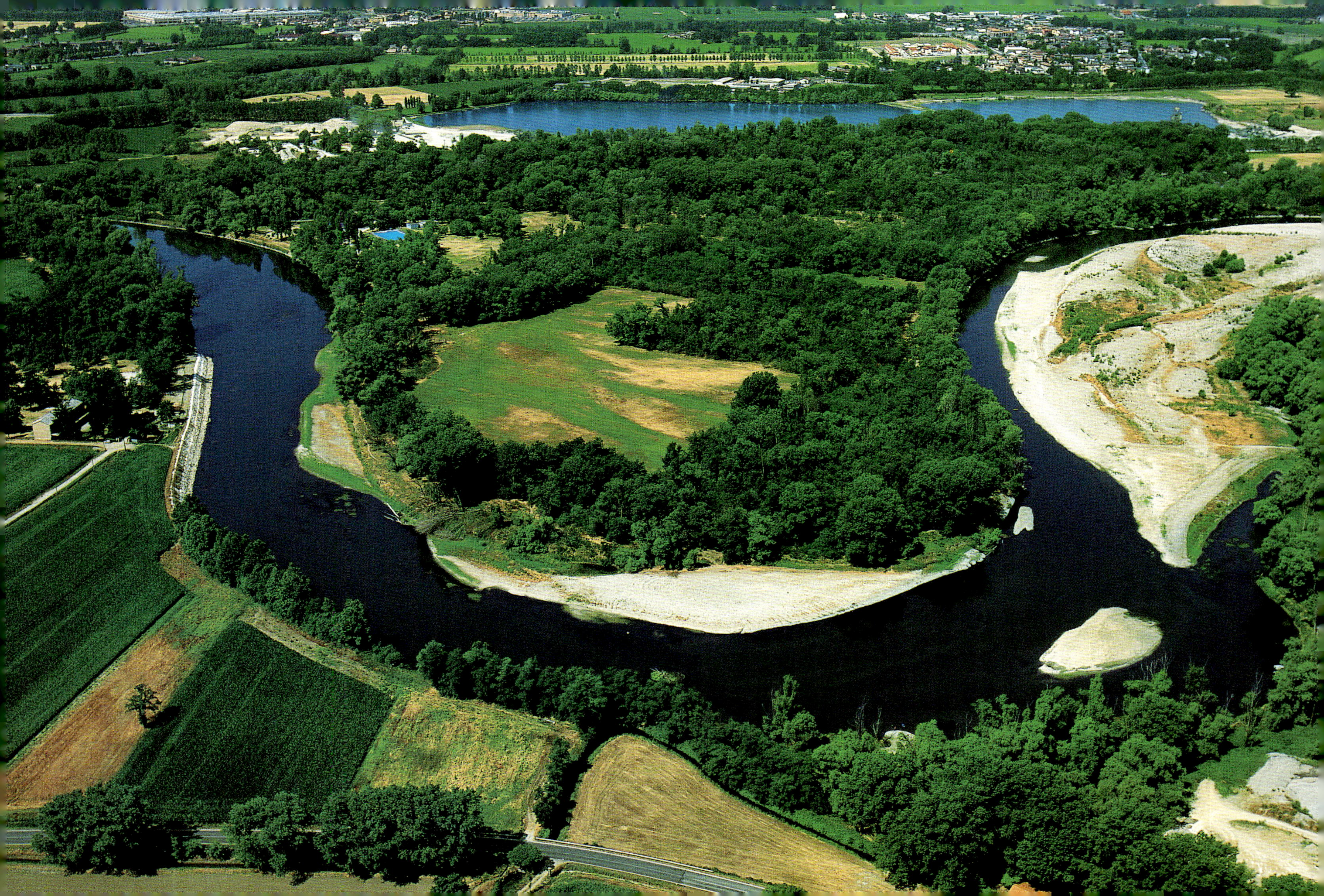

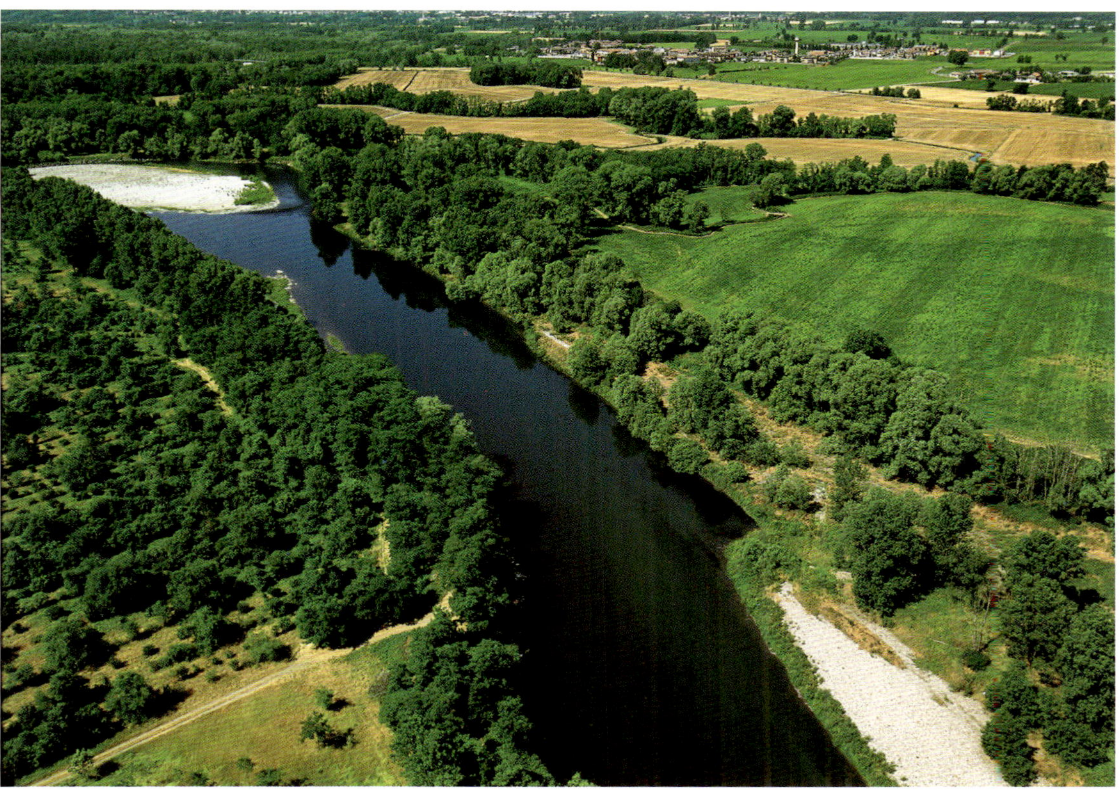

80 and 81 Of all the rivers that empty into the Po, one of the most frequently cited is the Adda, shown here passing near Lodi. This is the longest of all the Po's tributaries, 194 miles (313 km) and is Italy's fourth longest river after the Po, the Adige and the Tiber. It has served as a natural military barrier and its banks have witnessed a number of episodes that form part of Italy's history.

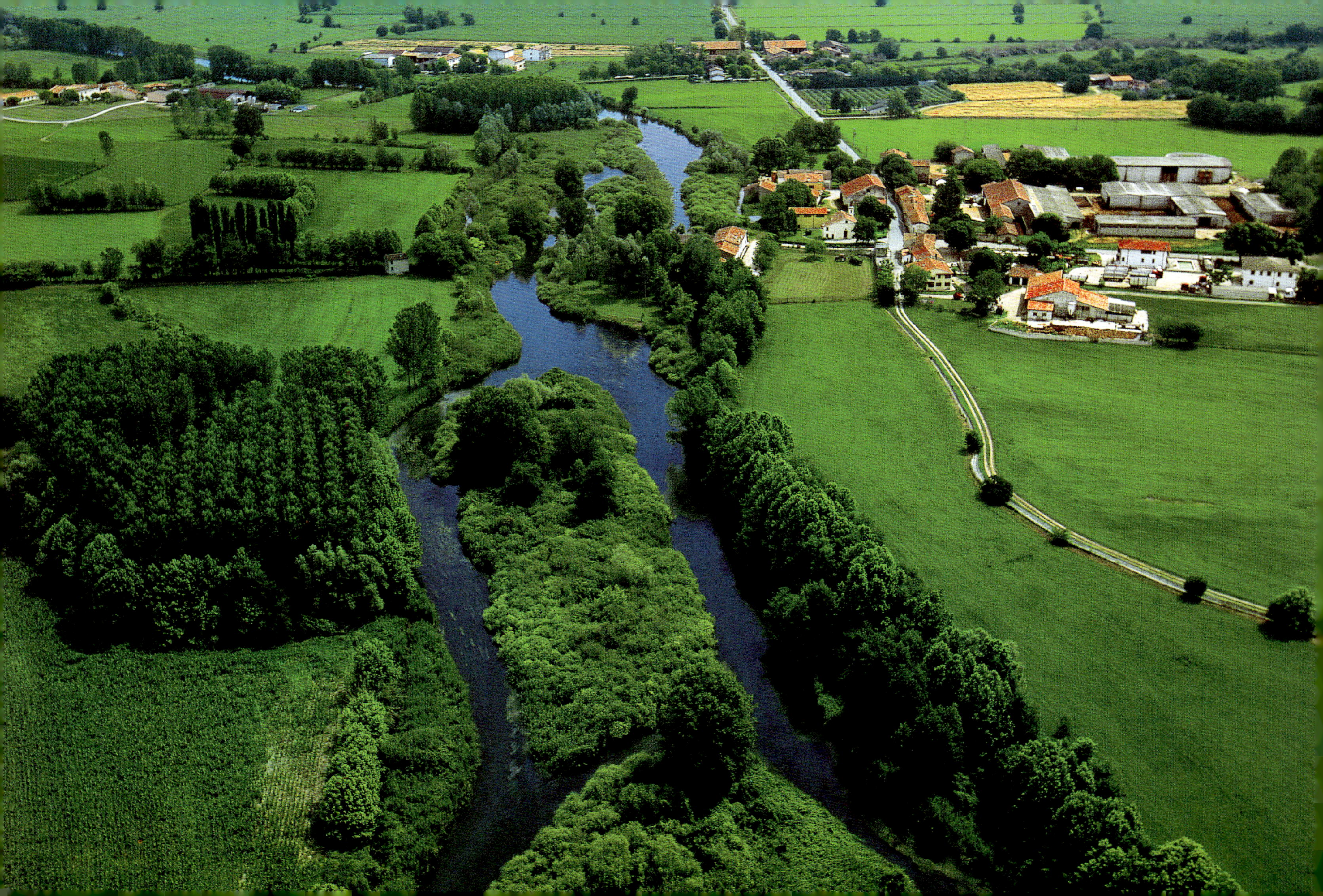

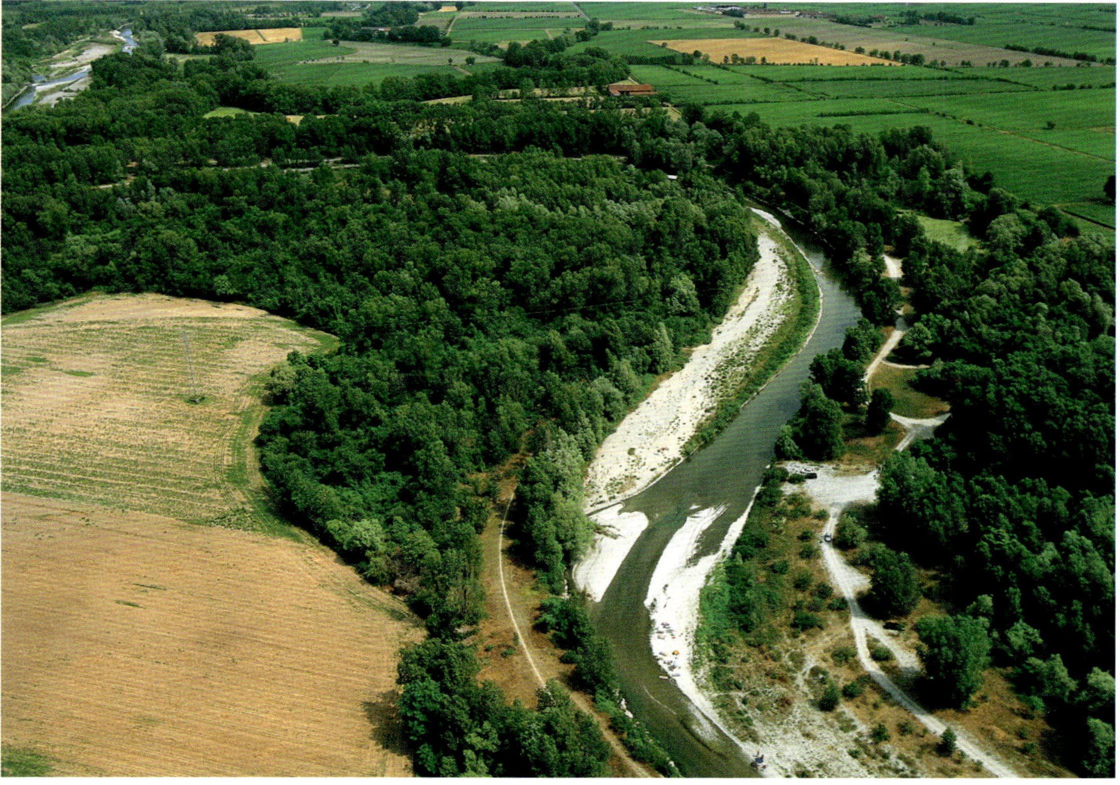

82 The Mincio River is made up of two distinct parts: the Sarca before entering Lake Garda and the Mincio when leaving it. In reality, they could equally well be considered as two separate rivers in view of their totally different characteristics (one a torrent, the other placid and wide) and in terms of their water quality. The Mincio, when passing through the area around Mantua (see photo), is protected by its nature reserve status.

83 The Oglio (the photograph was taken near Soncino (Cremona) is the Po's second longest tributary (174 miles/280 km), and one of the most attractive from a landscape point of view. In addition, two nature reserves have been created along its banks.

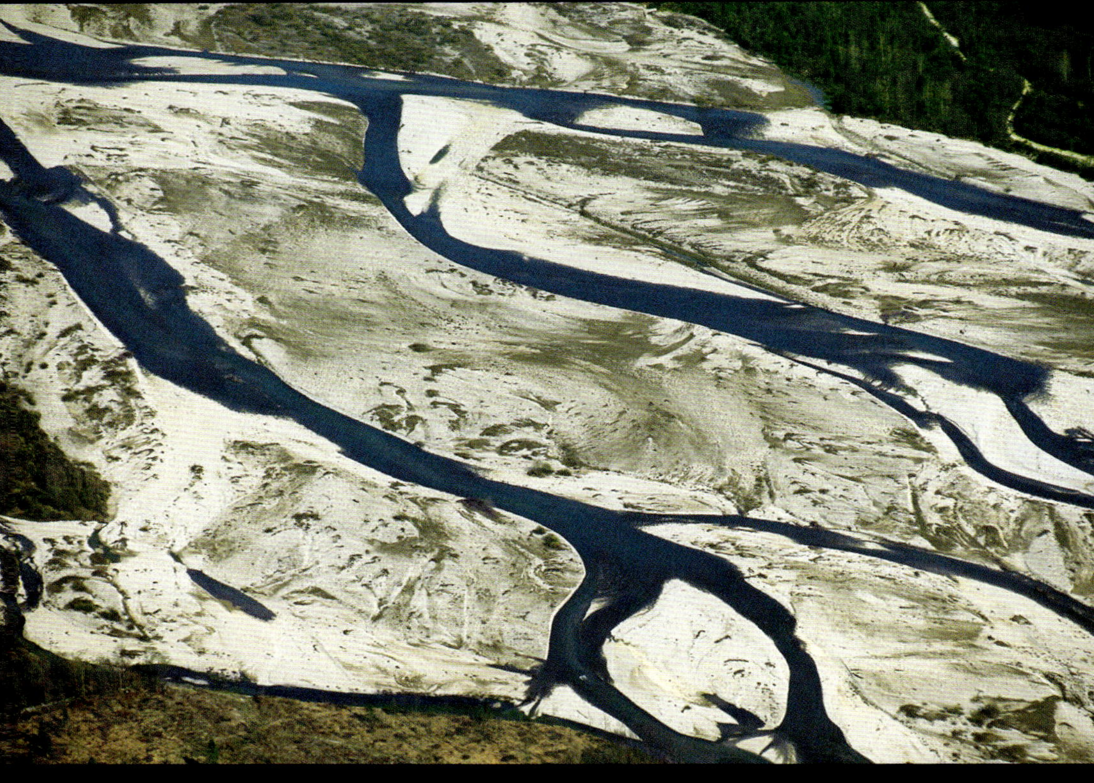

84 and 85 The Piave River owes much of its fame to its military iconography, which records it as one of the most important and legendary trenches of World War I. Today, however, this Veneto region river is seen with a completely different eye: its course in the mountains is a torrent, passing through truly awesome surroundings such as the Orrido dell'Acquatona, and it offers a vast variety of settings. In the ones shown here (to the east of Montebelluna), the riverbed can be several miles wide. However, in its last stretch, the Piave has been practically forced into a channel, following interventions by Venice, which shifted the Piave's course to the east to protect the Venetian Lagoon.

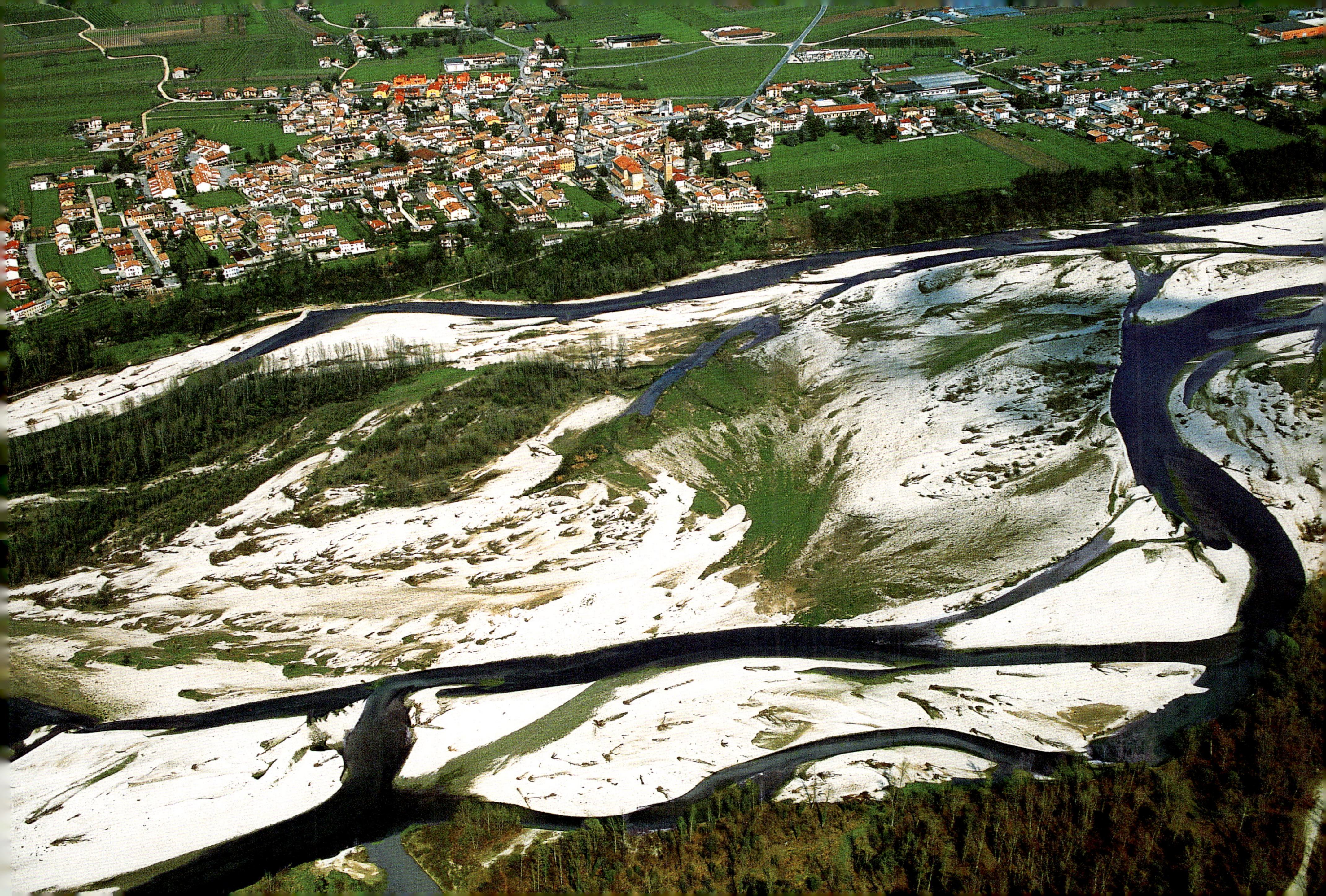

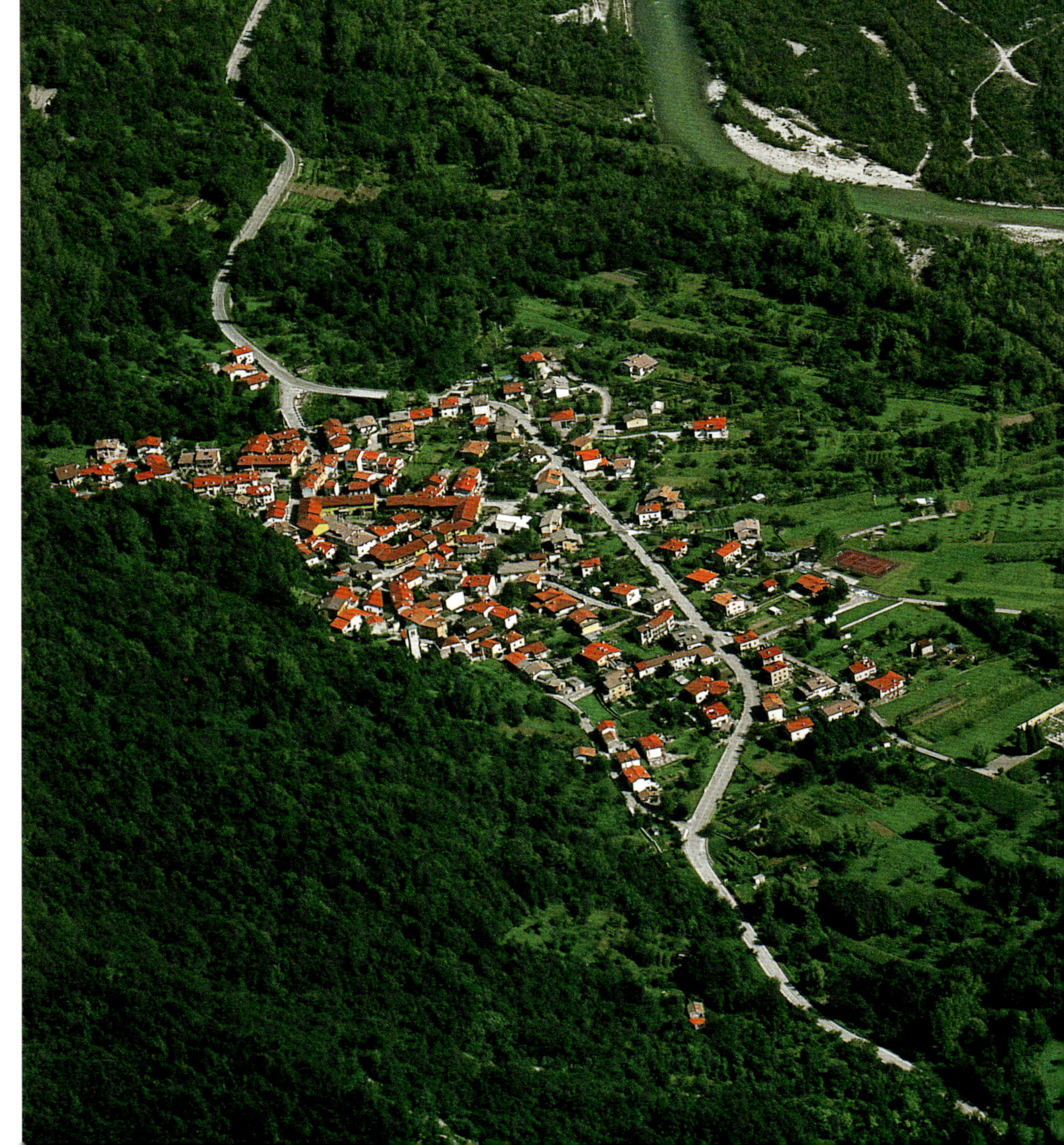

86-87 The Tagliamento rises in the mountains along the border between the Veneto and Friuli regions. Where it crosses the flat plain (as shown in the illustration near Spilimbergo) it can be up to 1.8 miles (3 km) wide, branching out into a number of separate channels. Its gravelly bed is extremely pervious and consequently absorbs all of its own water supply, thus offering this unusually striking spectacle.

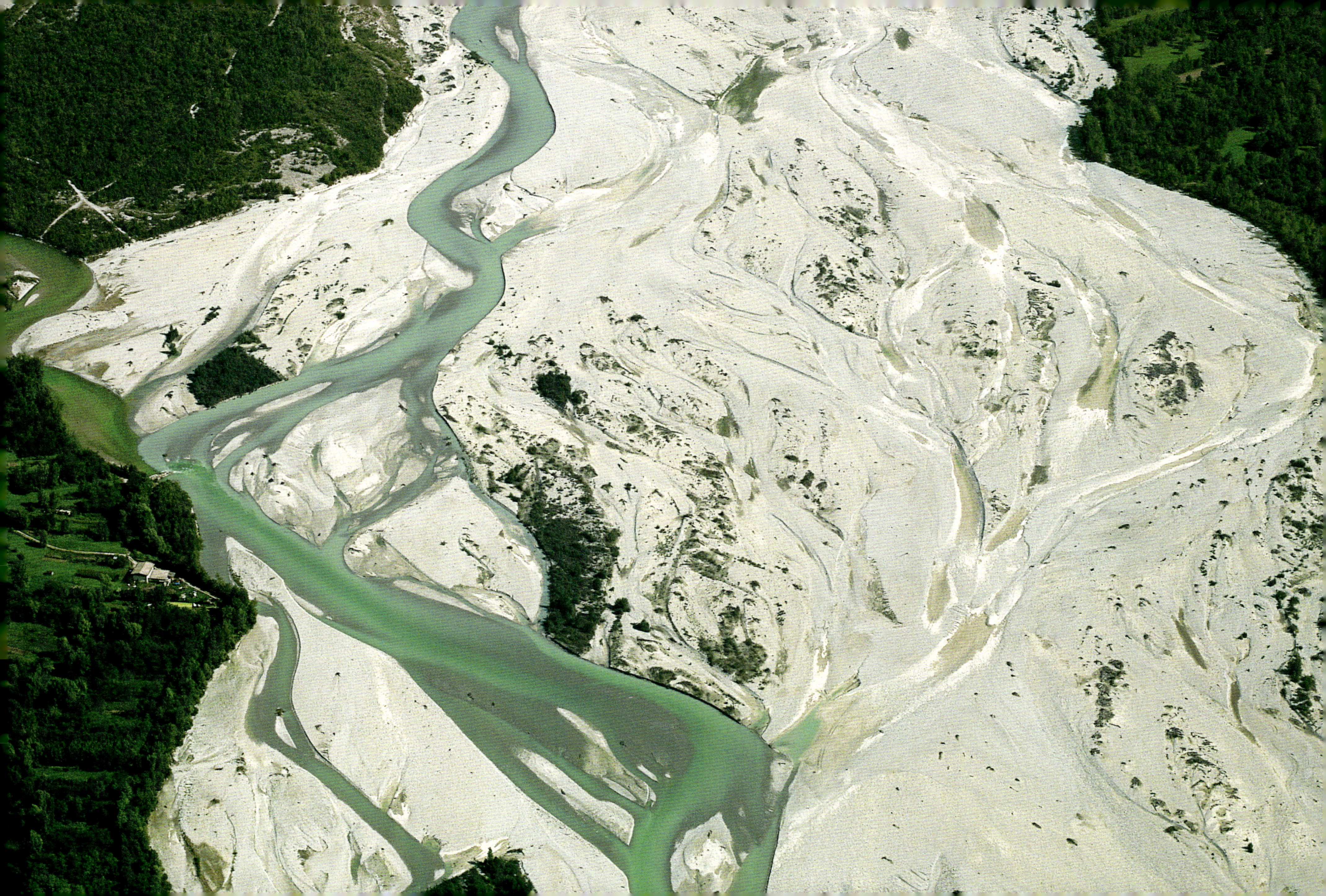

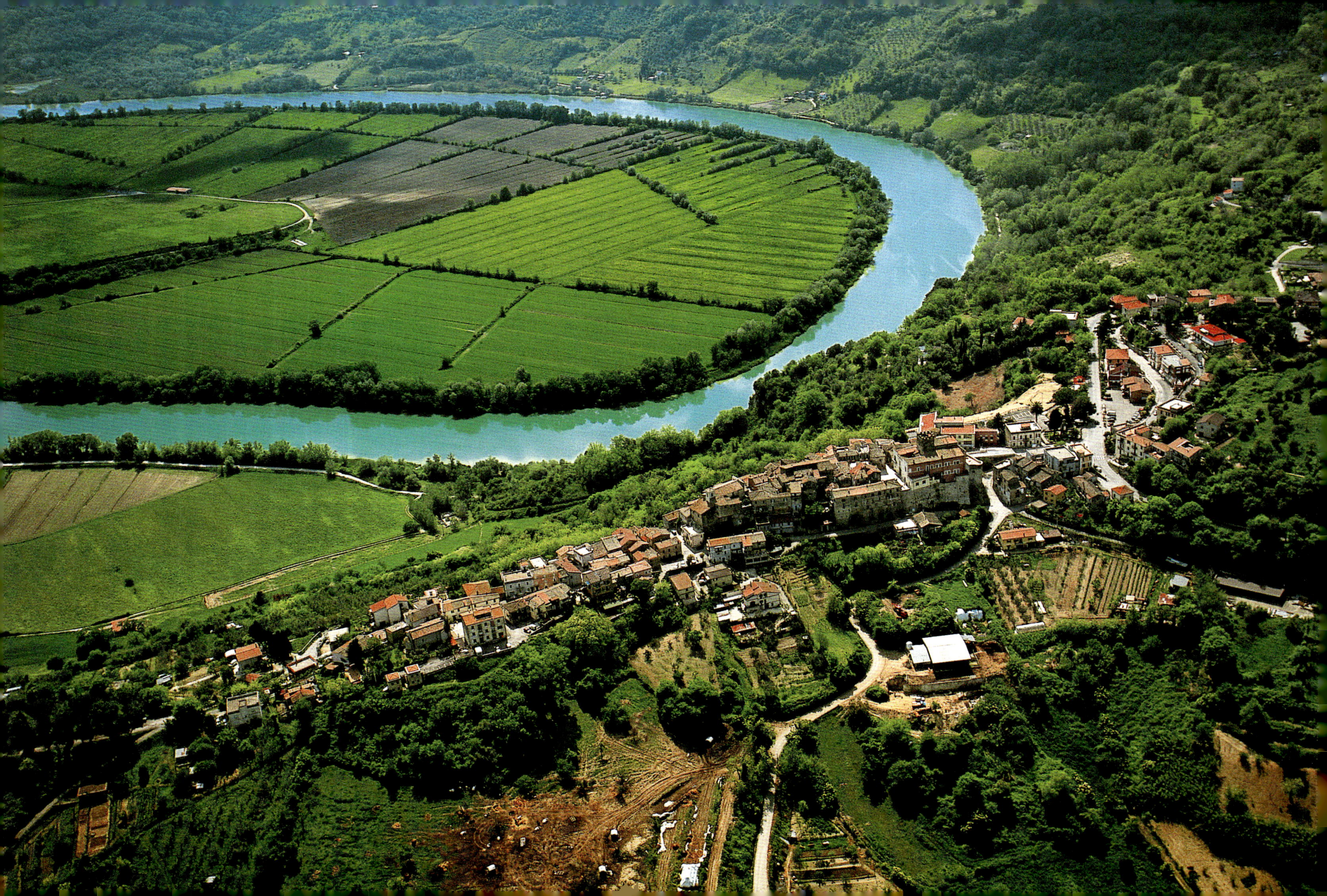

88 The Tiber is Italy's third longest river and is notable for the stretch in Rome, which was founded along its banks. Overall, the Tiber follows an extremely tortuous and scenically fascinating course, particularly above the Eternal City, as can be seen in this photograph taken near Torrita Tiberina.

89 The Tiber rises at Mt Fumaiolo; after a brief stretch on Tuscan territory, it pushes on into the Roman countryside (the pictures show respectively Filaccino and Nazzano) and passes through Rome, before debouching into the Tyrrhenian Sea at Fiumicino through one of the delta's two mouths.

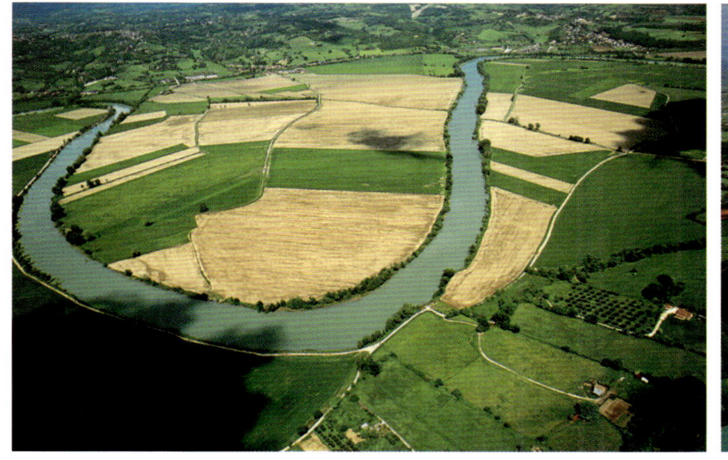

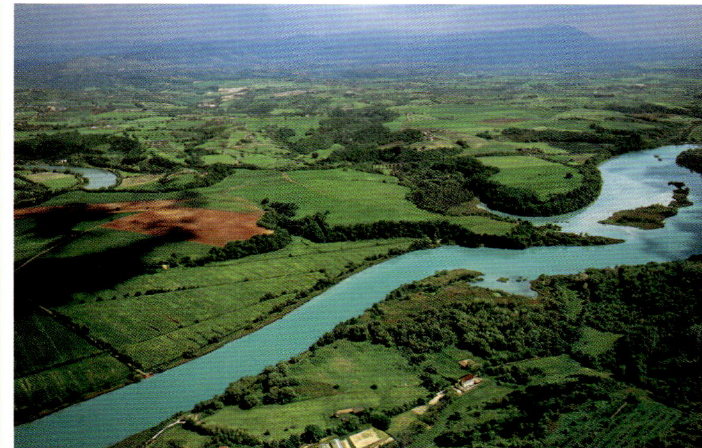

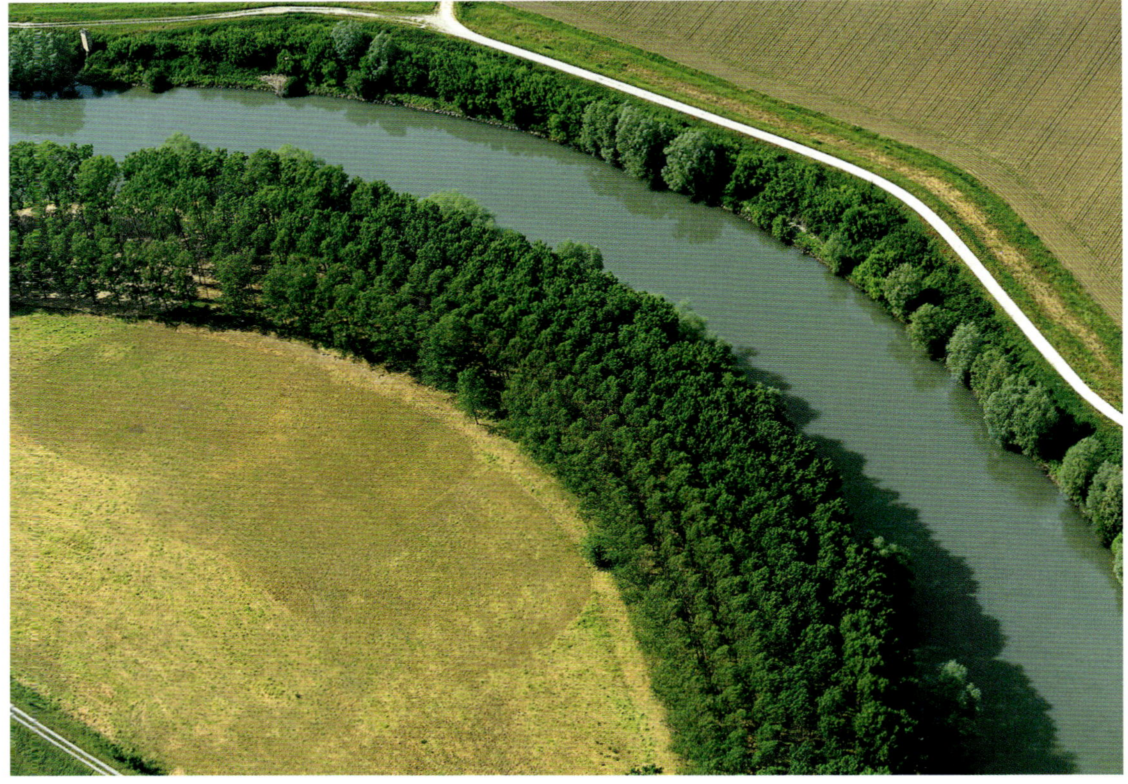

90 and 91 Central Italy's rivers all have their sources in the Apennine ridge, which lacks the glaciers needed to supply really large rivers. The rivers, particularly those emptying into the Adriatic, are all short and decidedly seasonal; their flow is subject to wide variations according to the seasons. The two rivers in the illustration (to the left the Tronto, located in the Marche region, and to the right the Sangro, in the Abruzzo territory) both have relatively narrow beds, enjoy a rich supply of water only in the spring, and are obviously extensively exploited to irrigate crops.

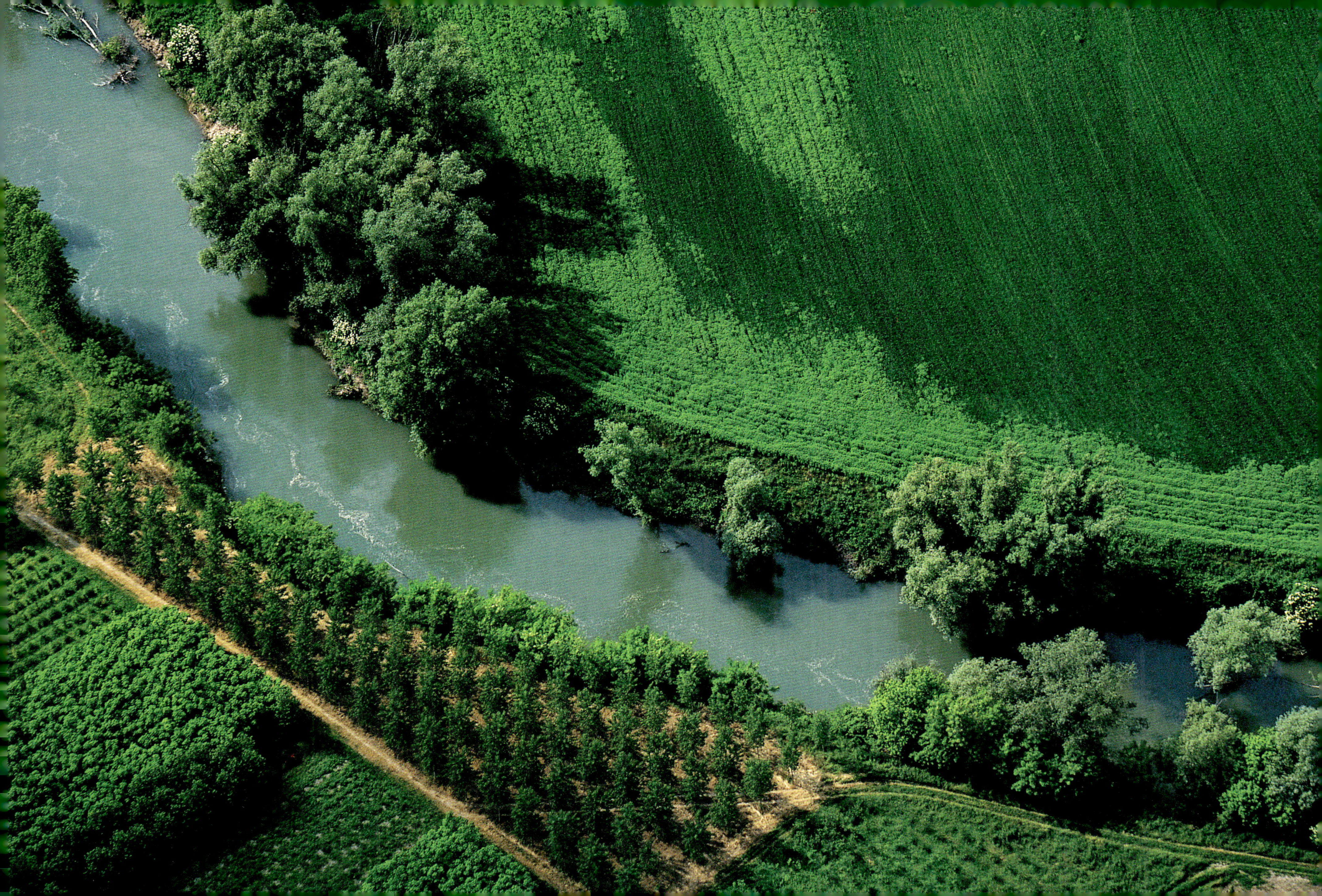

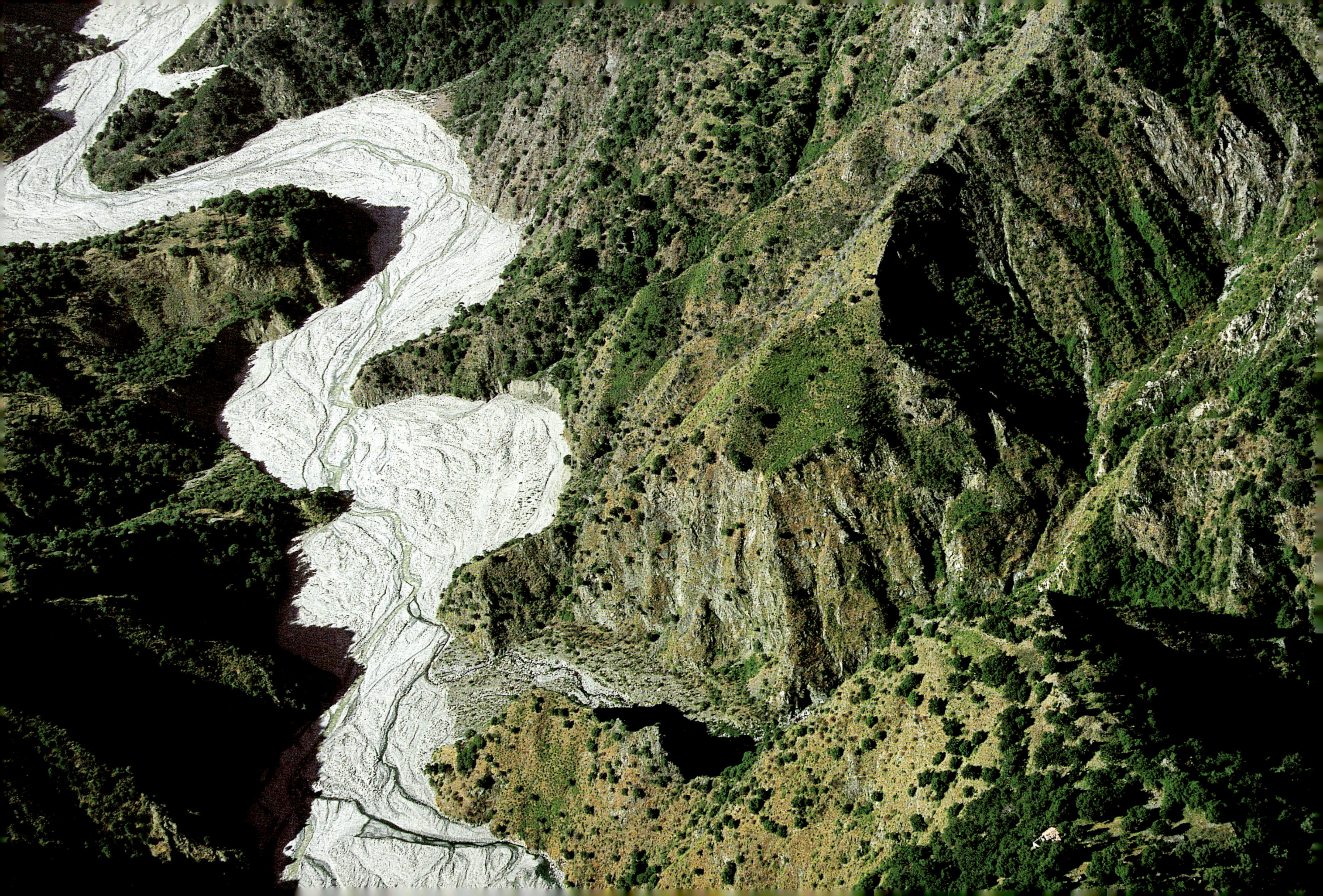

92 The Stilaro (the Elleporo of ancient times), is a Calabrian river that, together with its twin the Allora, gives its name to the entire valley through which it flows. It traverses the Aspromonte area and takes in a number of lesser water courses, including the ones like the Folea, the Ficara and the Ruggiero torrents and again, the Mulinelle torrent, all of which often pass through narrow gorges which give rise to numerous waterfalls, the highest of which is the Cascata del Marmarico in the Folea gorge.

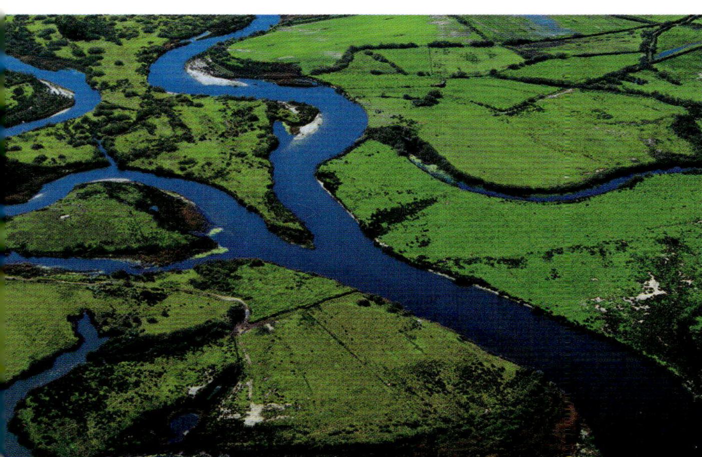

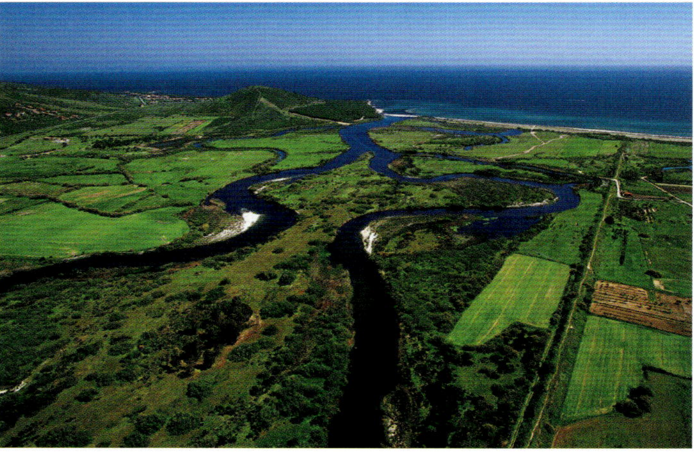

94 and 95 The Rio Posada typifies Sardinia's north-eastern coast. It rises in the Punta Latari but is blocked off about 6 miles (10 km) from the sea to form Lake Concas, from where it then flows on to the Tyrrhenian Sea near Posada with a unique many-branched estuary. This particular part of the Posada area, at one time somewhat boggy, is now fertile agricultural land, even though in the neighboring ponds known as Tundu and Lungu traces of the original watery surroundings still exist.

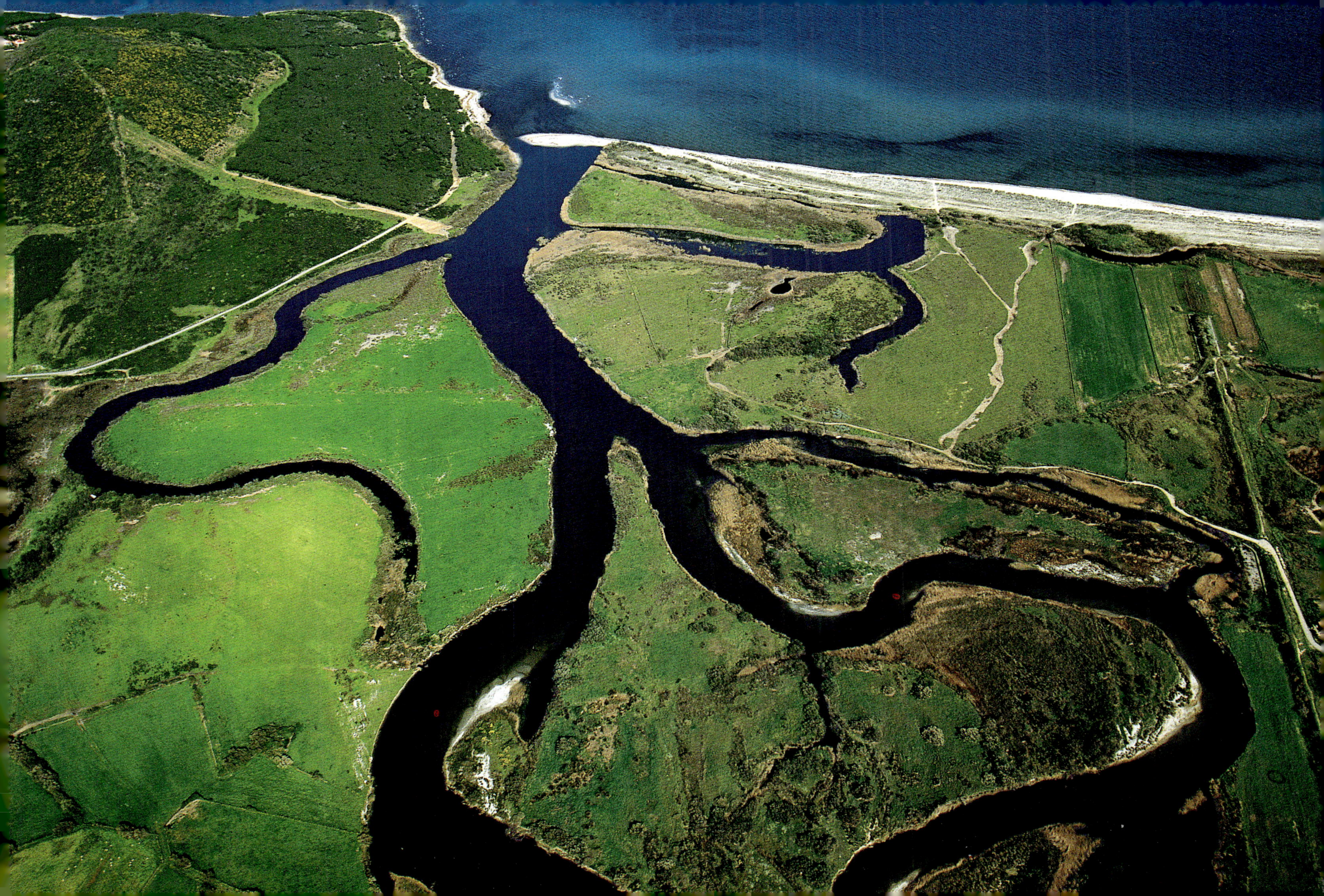

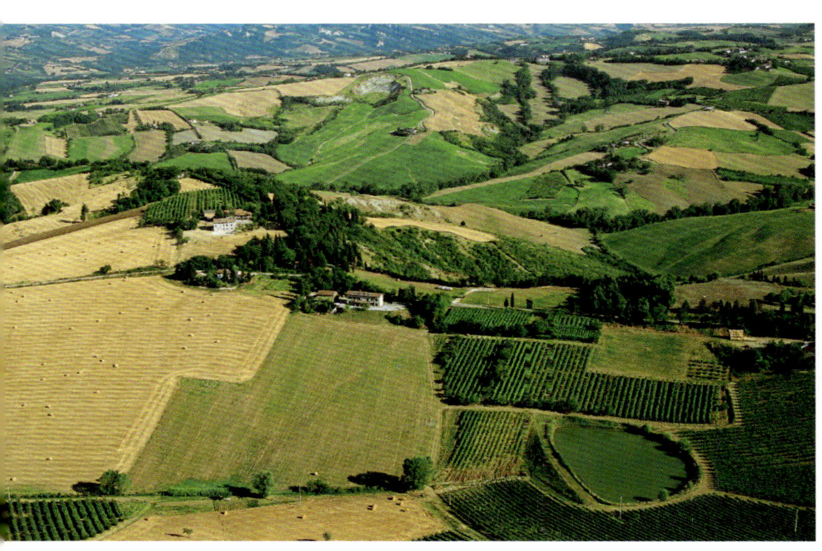

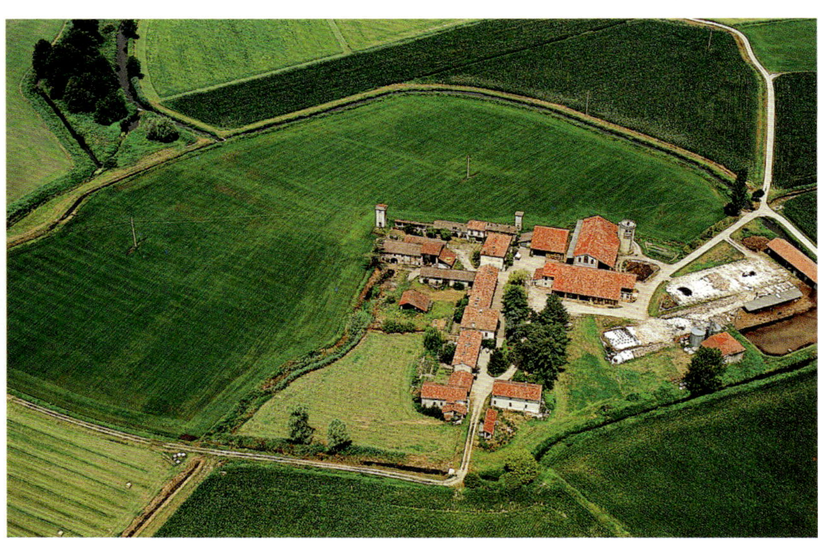

LANDSCAPES OF THE CENTER AND THE NORTH

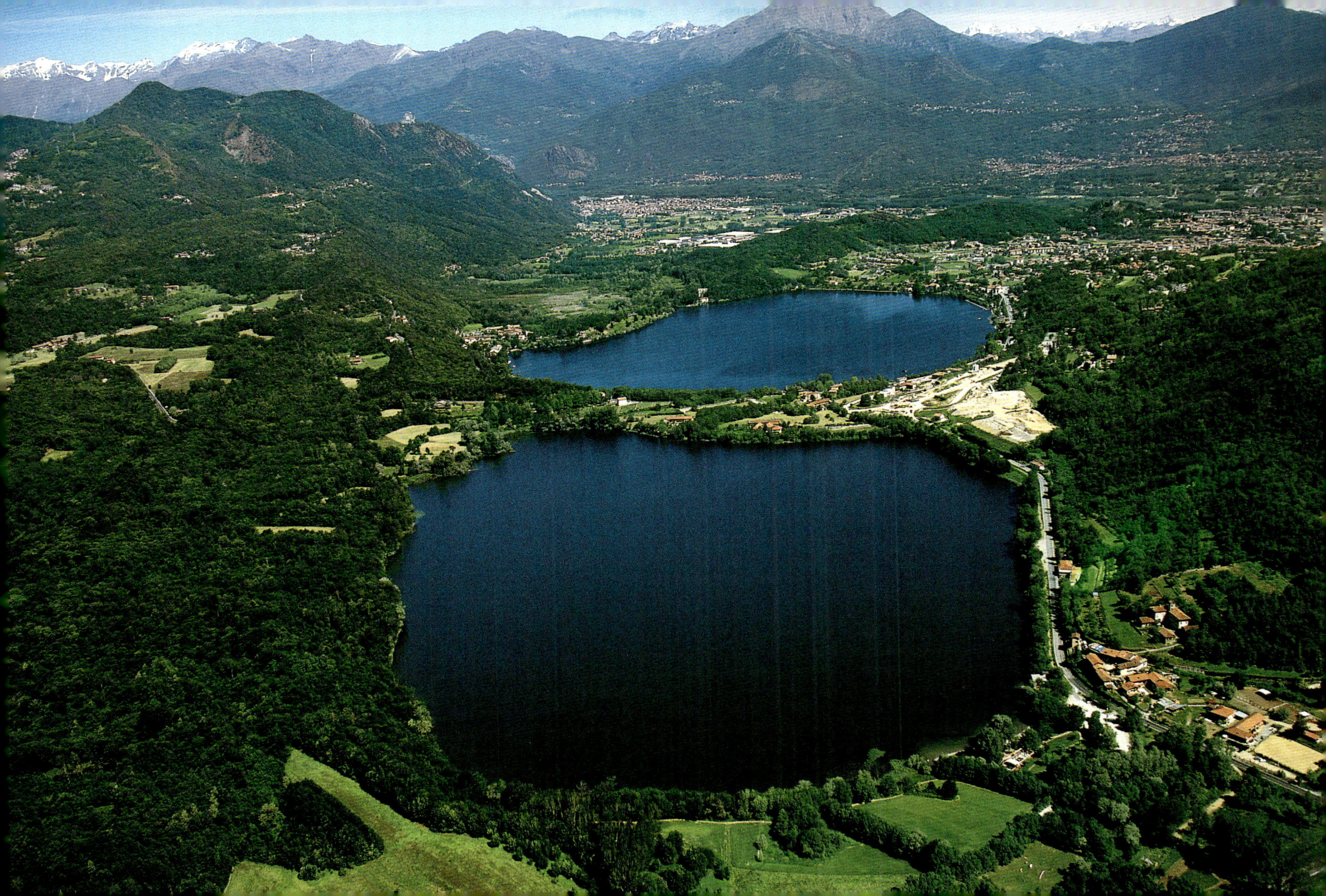

Every region has its story and that of the Langhe can be subdivided into three distinct sections: the first age, which brought about the formation of rocks at the bottom of an ancient sea, from grains transforming to sediment which became increasingly compact over millions of years. The second age occurred when titanic forces pushed up the bottom of the sea with the rest of the Po Valley, and shaking off the primeval water, the ancient sediments touched the sky and became hills and mountains. The third era is marked by the effects of time and the work of humankind. They smoothed the coarse soil and covered it with woods and fields, pastures and towns.

However, this work only had a partial effect, because the Langhe still remains a partly rough hilly region with a series of hills separated by narrow valleys plowed through by whirling streams. The land has been famous since the Ancient Roman times because of its exquisite products, such as the white truffle which grows amid the grey and azure marls dominated by the impressive structures of the distant Apennines and the great Monviso peak of the Alps, which stand out almost like a royal crown enclosing a wonderful landscape of fields and woods, punctuated by innumerable small towns. The phenomenon of the abandonment of cultivation is also visible here, especially in the upper part of the Langhe where agriculture was always a risk because of the sloping nature of the land. Once, a living could be made out of the small fields surrounded by woods, but today these efforts are not properly rewarded and the fields have been abandoned and reduced to *gerbido*, that is, back to their wild state with ever-growing weeds and shrubs. Humankind draws back and little by little, nature, on tiptoe, regains its former estate.

The story is different when it comes to Montferrat, a region devoted to producing high-quality wines which are famous all over the world and are fortified by the fertile soil of the hills of the area, divided into a series of hydrographic basins situated next to each other. Montferrat soil is made of yellowish sands and ash-colored clays and has a soft consistency on which external agents have worked with ease, to such an extent that the deep and narrow valleys look like cuts made by a knife blade on a soft cake. Sheltered towns are found around the castles on top of the hills. These castles were the first inhabited places

96 left The countryside of Meldola, a few miles from Forlì, is a hilly area, particularly fertile and rich in water – and therefore in crops.

96 right The farmhouses in the Mantuan area are the icon of Northern Italy's traditional and unique rural landscape.

97 A wildlife sanctuary protects the Avigliana lakes, two small circular basins of morainic origin, located in the town and municipality with the same name, in the province of Turin. They are called respectively Big Lake and Small Lake.

99 Lake Candia, in the Canavese area (Turin) is a well-known wildlife sanctuary just a few steps from the Alps.

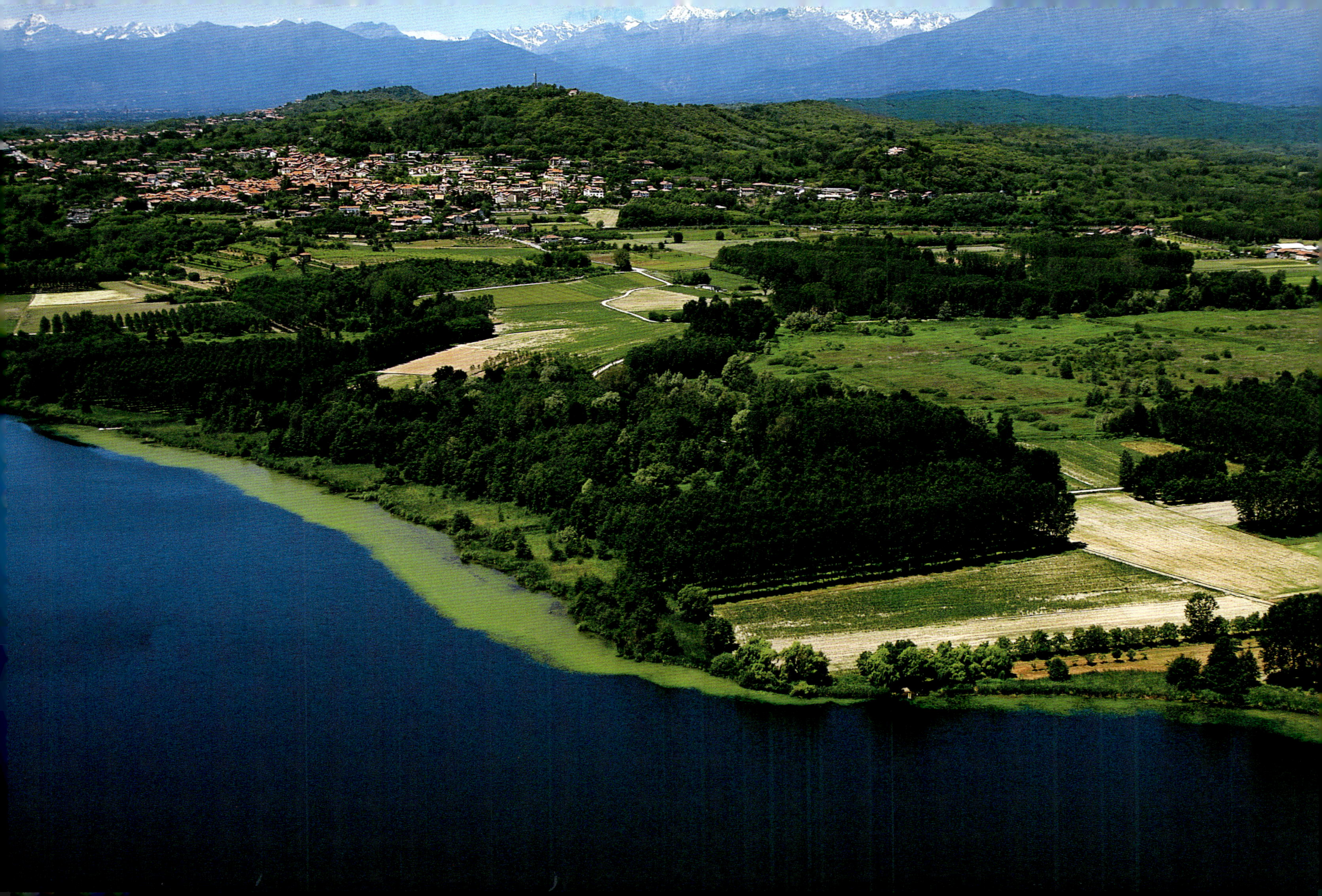

of this region, which covers the Po and Tanaro rivers, the Liguria Alps and the northern Apennines. Castelletto Merli, Odalengo, Moncalvo are the names of the pretty little towns which have an important place in the history of Italian wine production, and have left an indelible mark on one of the most striking, hilly landscapes of Italy, thanks to the characteristic geometric lines of their vineyards.

Moving toward the south of Italy, in the southern part of Tuscany the hilly landscape changes radically, yet its main calling remains that of grape-growing, an activity pursued since ancient times. This is as ancient as the heritage of Etruscan and Roman civilizations which is still seen today along the beautiful Via Cassia, the Roman road which starts from Rome, goes north through the Tuscan landscape and ends in Siena, passing through the realm of the ancient Etruscan populations, across a sweet, harmonious countryside made mostly of volcanic reliefs, rich with blue lakes crowned by harsh woods of oak and hornbeam, and with splashing streams among shiny pebbles and damp fronds of black maidenhair fern. The prevailing feature of this territory is the volcanic rock called tuff: light and porous, its color ranges from dark ocher to reddish shades, depending on the variety. Tuff is so easy to work with that it was the main stone the Etruscan and Romans used in the past to build most of the cities in Upper Lazio; it is still the

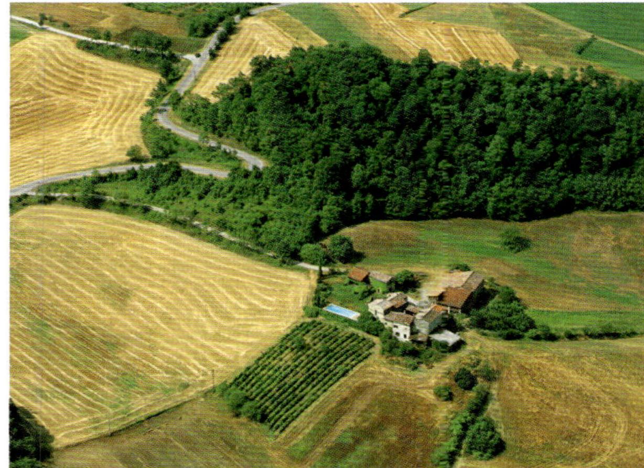

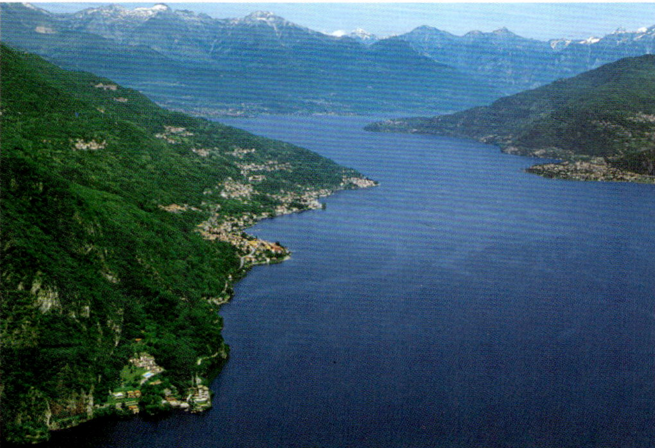

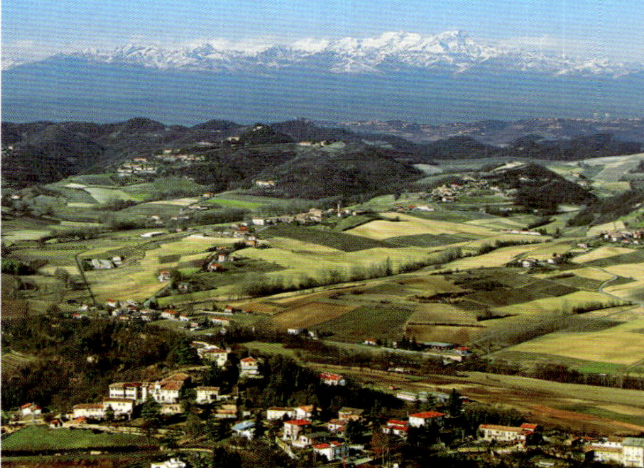

100 left The Tuscan-Emilian Apennines offer several views like this, belonging to Sassuolo (Modena): although the crops – especially cereals and vines – are rather widespread, the original woody bush is still quite thick.

dominant material used in this area. This rock is the result of the eruption of the volcanic complexes of the Sabatini, Volsini and Cimini mountain chains.

The most beautiful tuff creations are the Etruscan necropolises, the cities of the dead which must be visited in religious silence because this is where one of the greatest civilizations of the Mediterranean flourished, soon taken over by the rustic Romans, who copied and absorbed from them as much as possible. Just as beautiful are the towns of medieval origin, usually sheltered on hilltops, sometimes in absurd positions such as those which rise out of the tuff peaks and are a part of the rock itself. These tuff formations divide, as though cut by a knife blade, the valleys carved out by the streams.

Enclosed within Siena, Florence and Arezzo, the hilly Chianti region extends over about 98,850 acres (40,000 hectares); it is famous the world over for its wine production. The region is also known for its landscape, which is a harmonious mixture of natural elements such as woods and little streams, and human creations such as well-ordered vineyards, small wheat fields, beautiful rural houses and villages which are characteristically sheltered on hilltops. Known today as "Chiantishire" for its significant foreign – especially English – population, who have chosen it as a second home, if not their primary residence. Since the Middle Ages, Chianti has been a land of exceptional grapes and fantastic wines, as well as a long-time region of dispute between Siena and Florence: a dispute which was resolved when Florence defeated Siena was in 1555.

With the production area of Chianti wine administratively identified as the territory bordered by Siena, Val d'Elsa, the Chianti hills and Florence, the fame of Chianti is related not only to fine wine making, but also to a gentle landscape where the hills seem softened by the effects of time and the work of humankind. For once, man did not impose his domain on the land, but adapted his work to the course of the woods and the streams by creating terraced areas to make space for olive trees and vineyards, and narrow avenues flanked by old oak and fierce cypress trees.

The landscape of the Marche is still like that of the paintings of Raphael and other great Renaissance artists who were able to portray the composure and depth of a luminous landscape where the hills and mountain ranges appear like waves of the sea, becoming increasingly azure until imperceptible in the distance.

100 center The Lario, better known as Lake Como, is a lake of glacial origin and is the third largest basin in Italy. It is shared by the provinces of Como and Lecco.

100 right Montferrat is an interprovincial territory which extends to the south of the Po, in the Piedmontese zone around Alessandria and Asti. The Moncalvo area, seen in the picture, is the heart of Barbera and Grignolino, with wines produced from the grapes picked near this town.

Enclosed by the Adriatic Sea, Emilia-Romagna, Tuscany, Umbria, Lazio and Abruzzo, the Marche region is dominated by the Apennines, which are chalky formations in the Sibylline Mountains and transform into sandy marl formations in the Montefeltro area. The towns, often sheltered on hilltops, offer an expansive panorama and on the clearest days, the eye can see as far as the peaks of the Sibylline Mountains profiling the sky and catch a glimpse of the Dalmatian coast on the other side of the Adriatic Sea.

In summer, the Marche countryside takes on amazingly vibrant colors: the yellow of the already mature harvest, the green of the woods and the thousand tones and shades of the hedges, the buttery white clouds at the horizon, the light blue sky – all mix together better than any artist would know how to represent. It is the landscape of a painter, but also the land of an active and hard-working population that gave the nation the splendor of the great Renaissance courts and the culture of the universities of Urbino, Macerata and Camerino, among the oldest in Europe.

Camerino is a city full of students and teachers, many of whom are young; they come from all parts of Italy. It is therefore one of the few towns where one can forget that our society is getting older. The city stretches over a hill enclosed by a strong wall, and is surrounded by hills with sprinkling of rural houses. On one side, these hills slope down toward Castelraimondo and Matelica, on the other side they rise up to become mountains, in the direction of Foligno or, more south, of Sibillini. From the *rocca* of Camerino, which used to belong to the Borgia family, we can admire the profile of the distant mountains which fade into the blue of the sky. In summer, the sky is the background for flocks of swifts; they flash by, chasing each other, chirping and slicing the air with their knife-like wings. Big white clouds like cauliflowers seem to have erupted from the distant hills as if an invisible volcano had emitted steam clouds and pure white ash into the air.

As all the Apennines, also those of the Marche have long suffered from the deforestation activities of humankind, hungry for wood and pastures for sheep. The resulting landscape is definitely beautiful, but absolutely devoid of woods, as Vittorio Marchesoni, the illustrious botanist who taught in Camerino in the 1950s, used to point out.

103 The Colline Metallifere (the "Metallic Hills"), located at the end of the Tuscan-Emilian Apennines, owe their name to the fact that the soil is very rich in minerals, extracted since ancient times, especially during the Etruscan age.

104-105 Entering the Val d'Aosta we can enjoy the wonderful view of hills planted with vines, producing fine DOC wines.

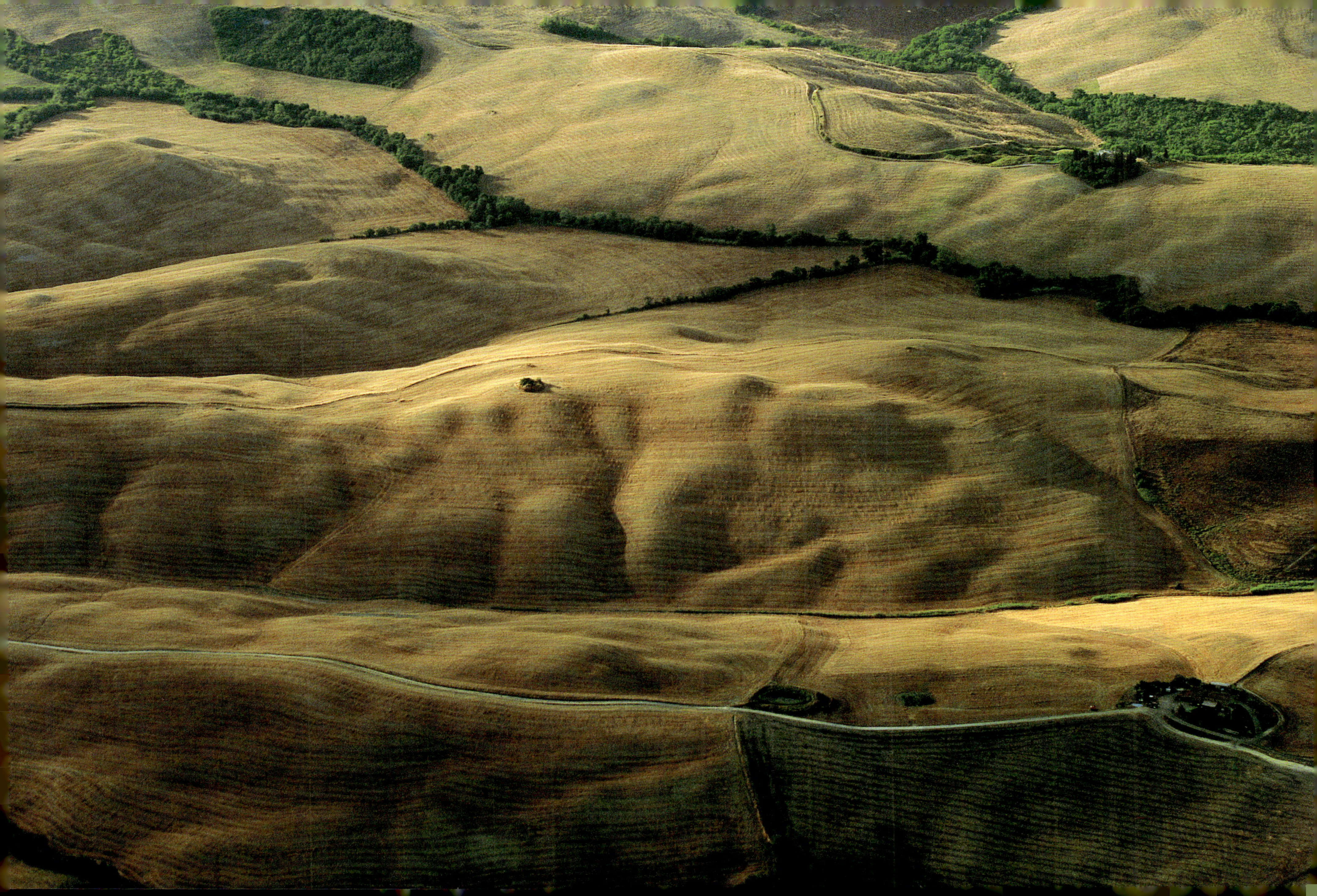

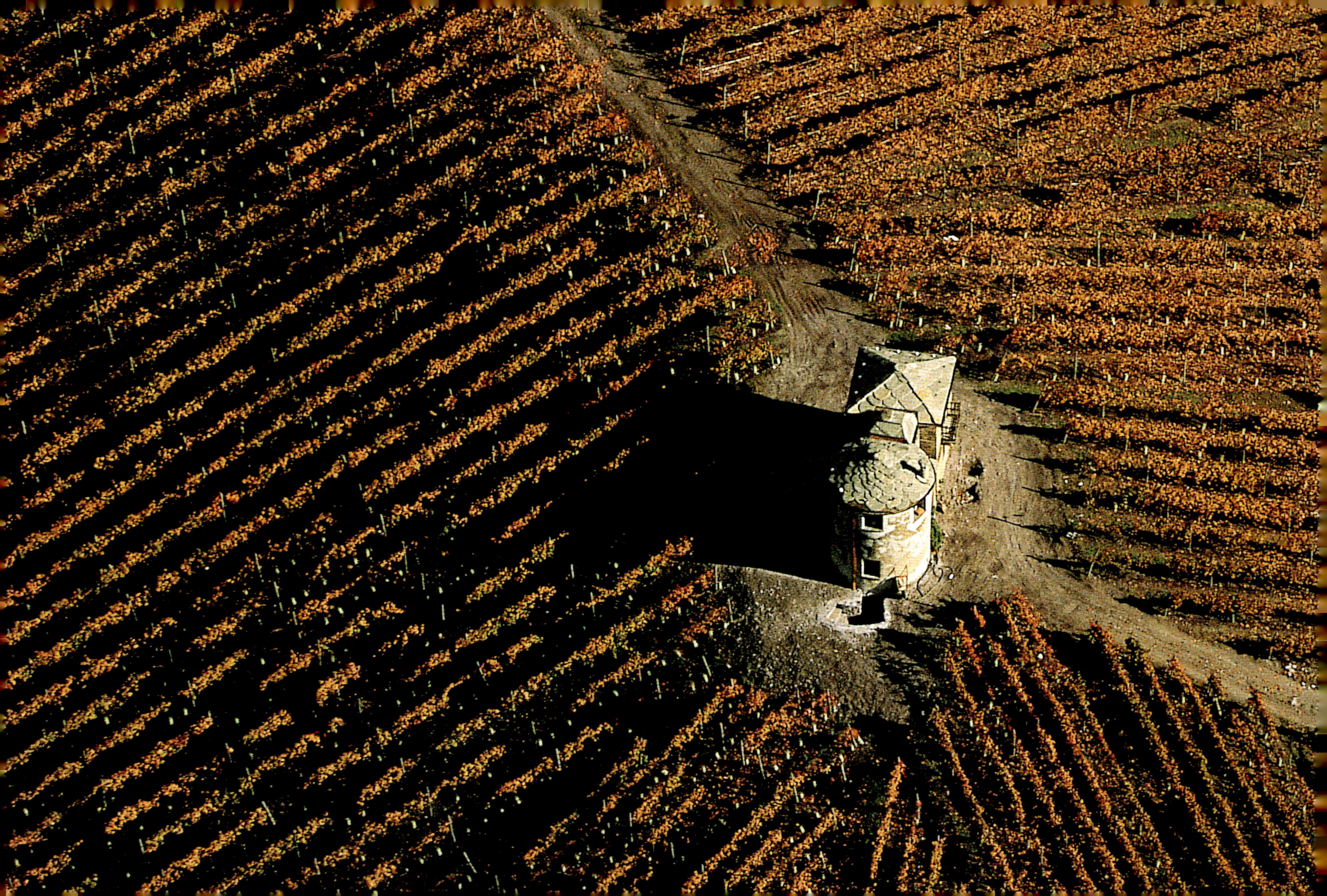

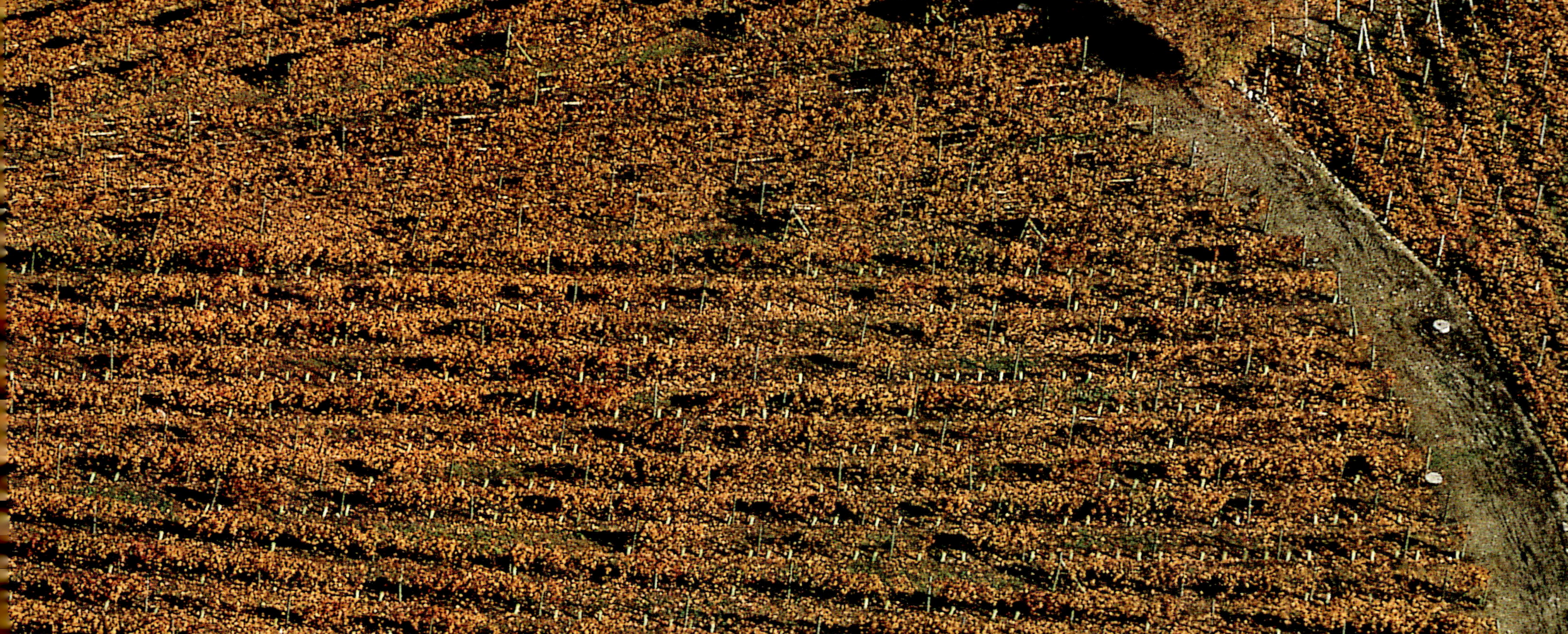

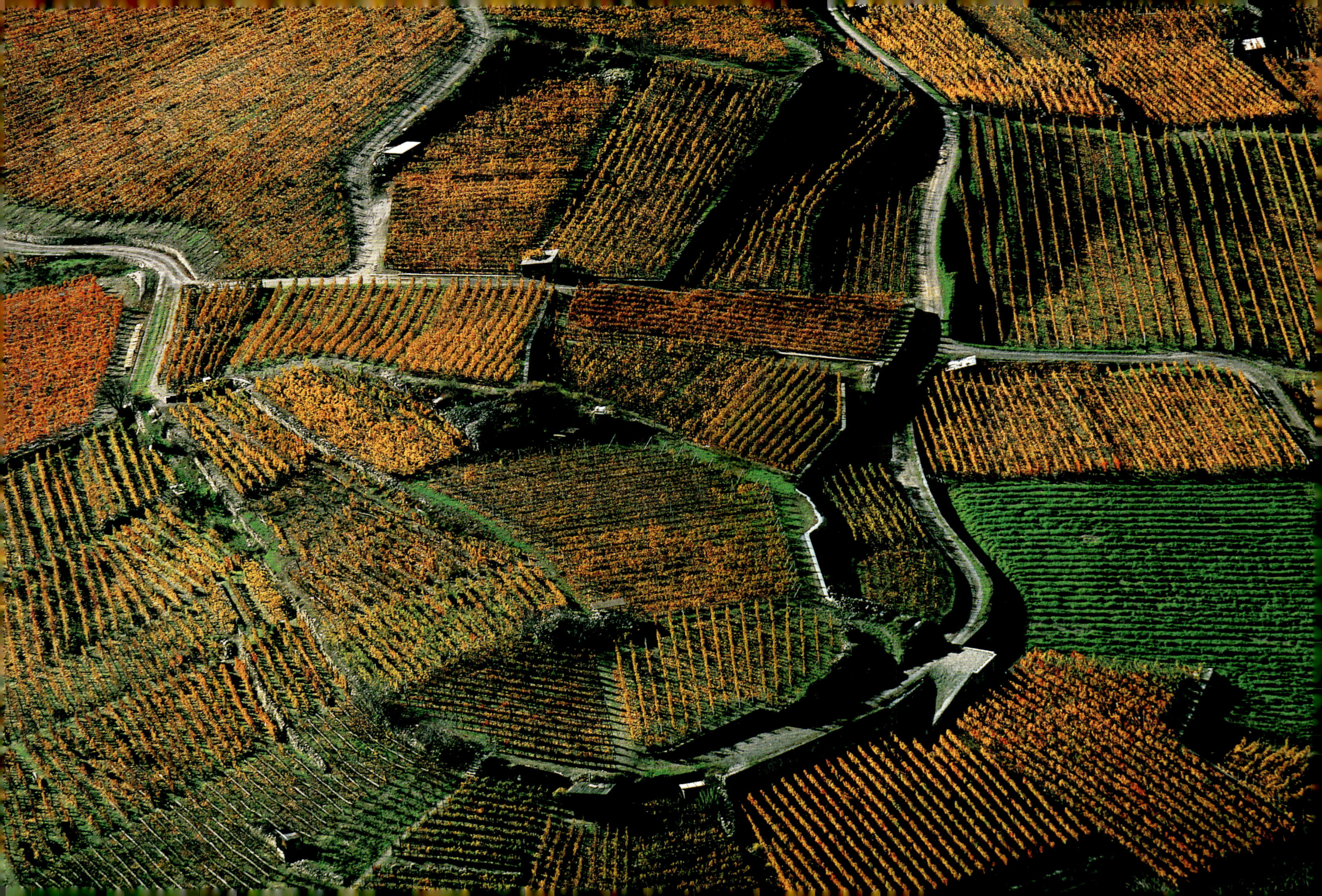

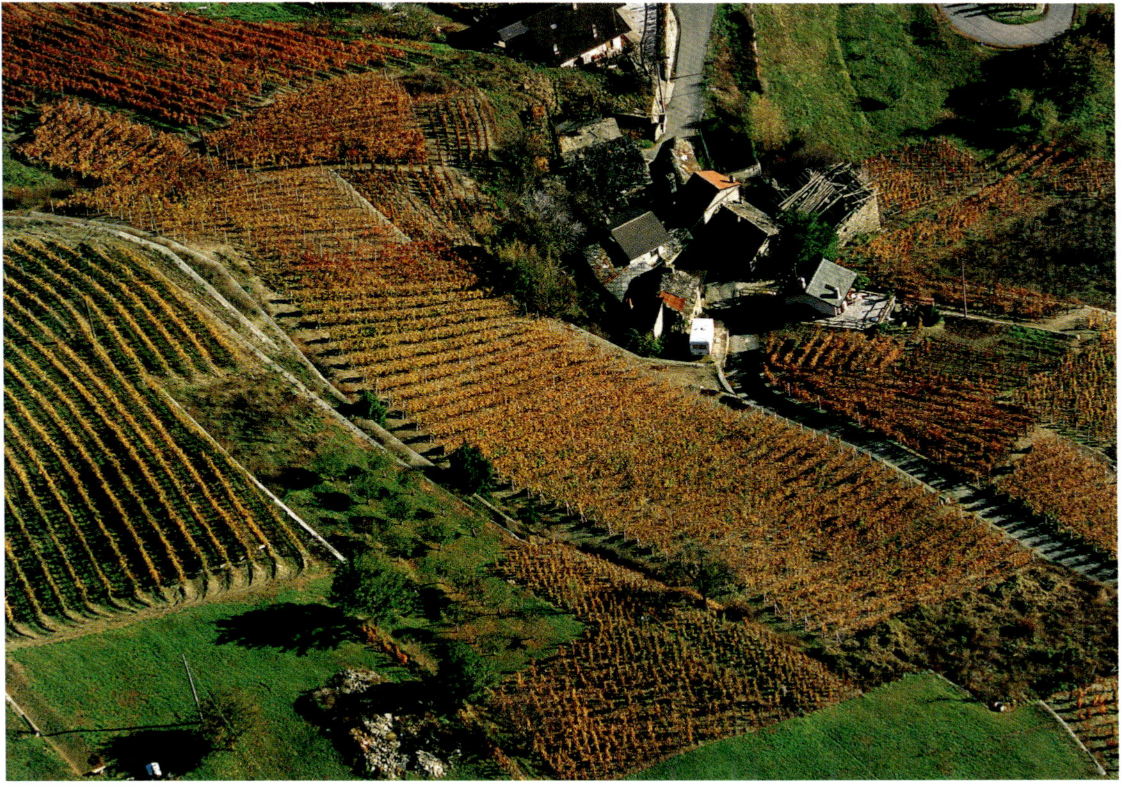

106 and 107 The vine-growing territory of the Val d'Aosta coincides almost entirely with the sides of the central valley, crossed by the Dora Baltea, which run from Pont-Saint-Martin to Morgex, concerning mainly the sunny southwestern side. In the 20th century the vine-growing area of the Val d'Aosta decreased so sharply that it now barely totals 1235 acres (500 hectares); many farmers have chosen to grow more profitable crops and consequently some fine and well-known type of vine, like the Donnas, Muscat de Chambave, Clairet de Chambave, Enfer d'Arvier, Malvoisie de Nus, Malvoisie d'Aoste, Torrette de Saint-Pierre, might be disappearing.

109 The Langhe region is home to a group of rather steep hills, located in the valleys created by the rivers of southwest Piedmont; they rise between the Tanaro River, the Ligurian Apennines and the Bormida River. The average height is c. 1805 ft (c. 550 m) but this also depends on the configuration of the land. The prevailing crops are clearly grapes and hazelnuts, which also give the name to the Langa where they are grown. Among the most famous, the Barolo Langa (in the picture), the Barbaresco Langa, the Asti Langa, and the hazelnut Langa.

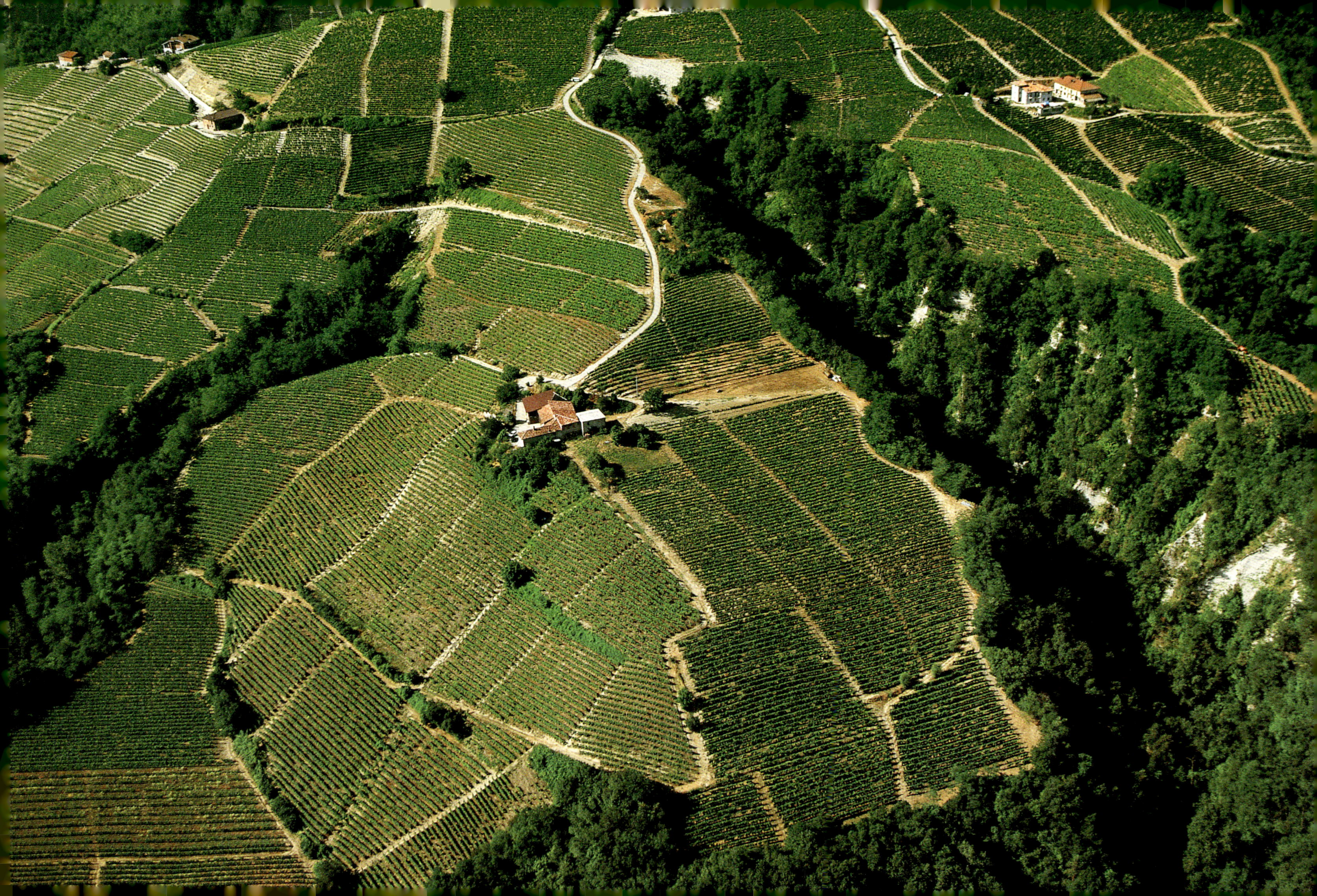

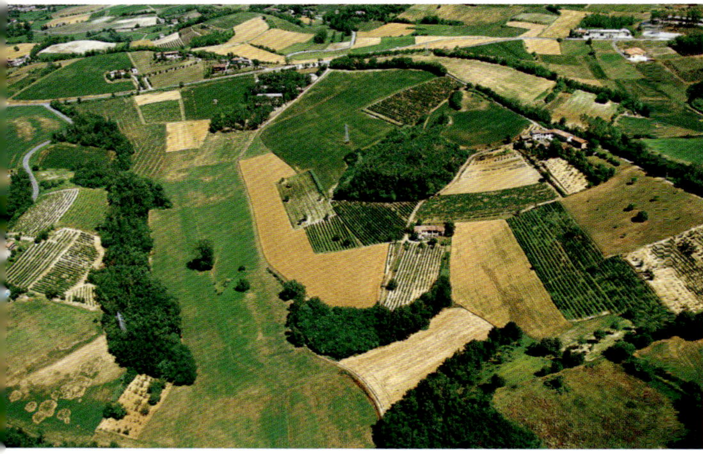

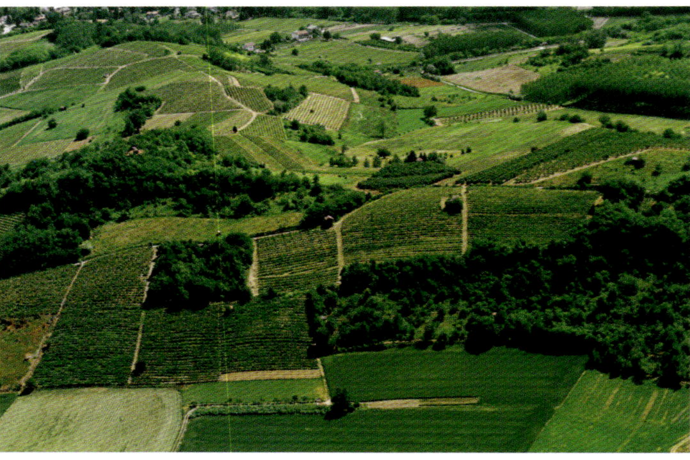

110 Montferrat, a hilly region planted with vines, is administratively divided into the areas of Alessandria and Asti. The first, to the north, takes the name of Montferrat Casalese (in the picture) and it is the heart of the DOC Barbera wine.

111 The southwestern part of the Alto Monferrato, on the left side of the Bormida River, offers a view of gentle undulating hills. It is the area around Acqui Terme, famous for its thermal springs since the Roman age.

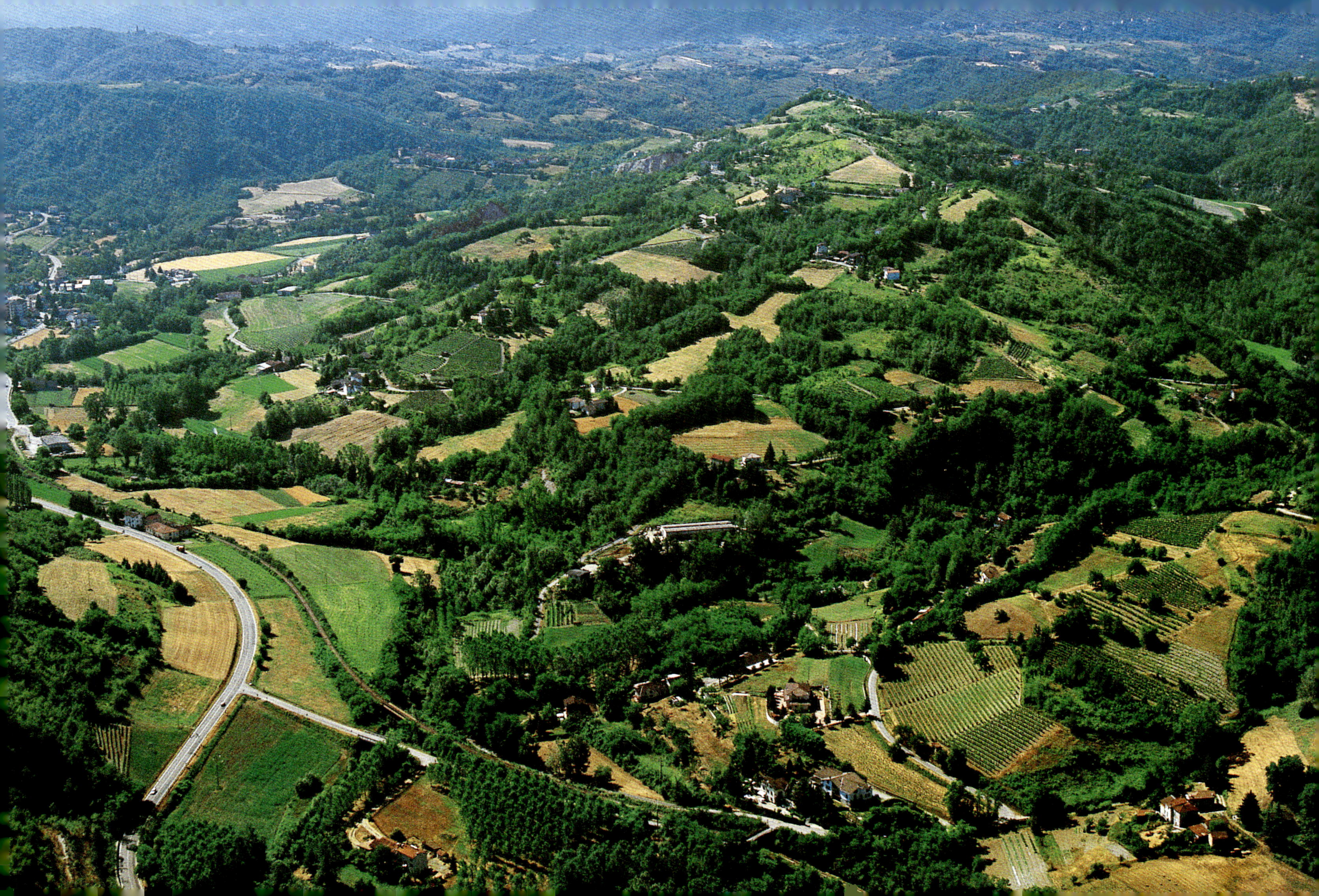

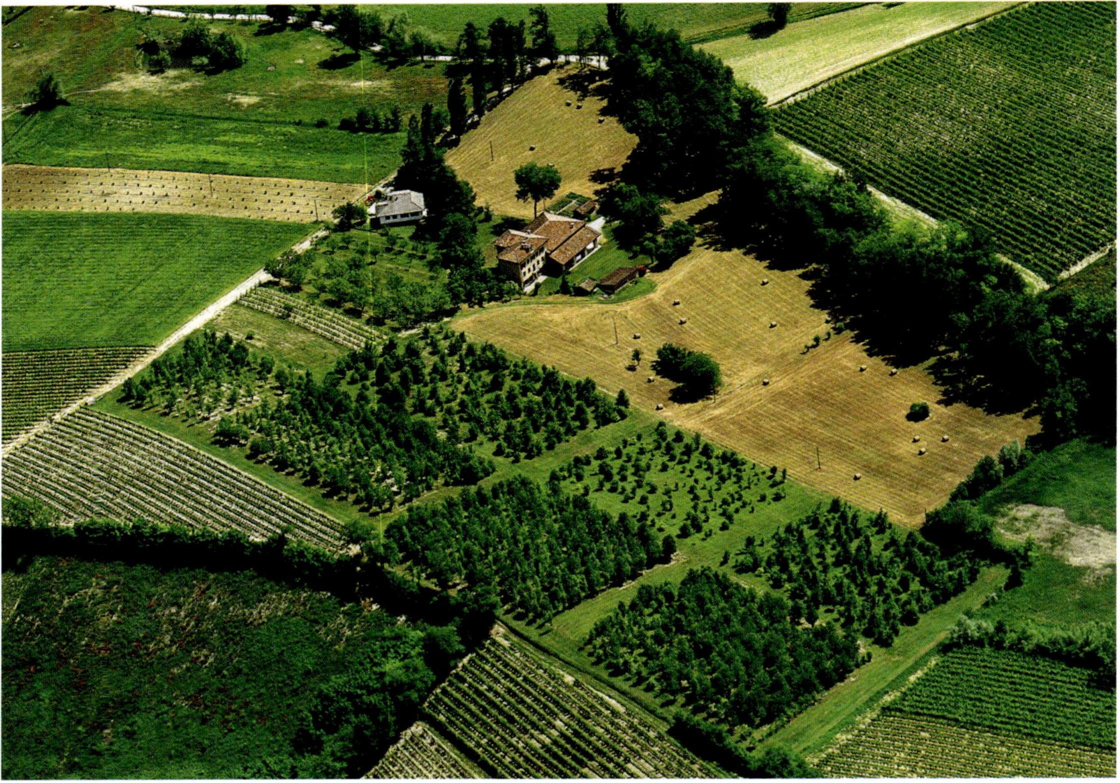

112 The hills of Montferrat near Asti are well-known for their agricultural production: vines, which provide the finest grapes, hazelnuts and fruit – not to mention cattle breeding and truffle hunting. Therefore, at the center of Montferrat landscapes we once again see the farmhouse, usually on top of the hills and strategically located to allow for the cultivation of the different crops.

113 The southwestern zone of Alto Monferrato coincides with the historic region of Oltregiogo, on the edge of Scrivia Valley's left side. Near the town of Novi Ligure, toward the northern slopes of the Ligurian Apennines, a series of wavy hills, mostly planted with vines and partially still wooded, softens the landscape.

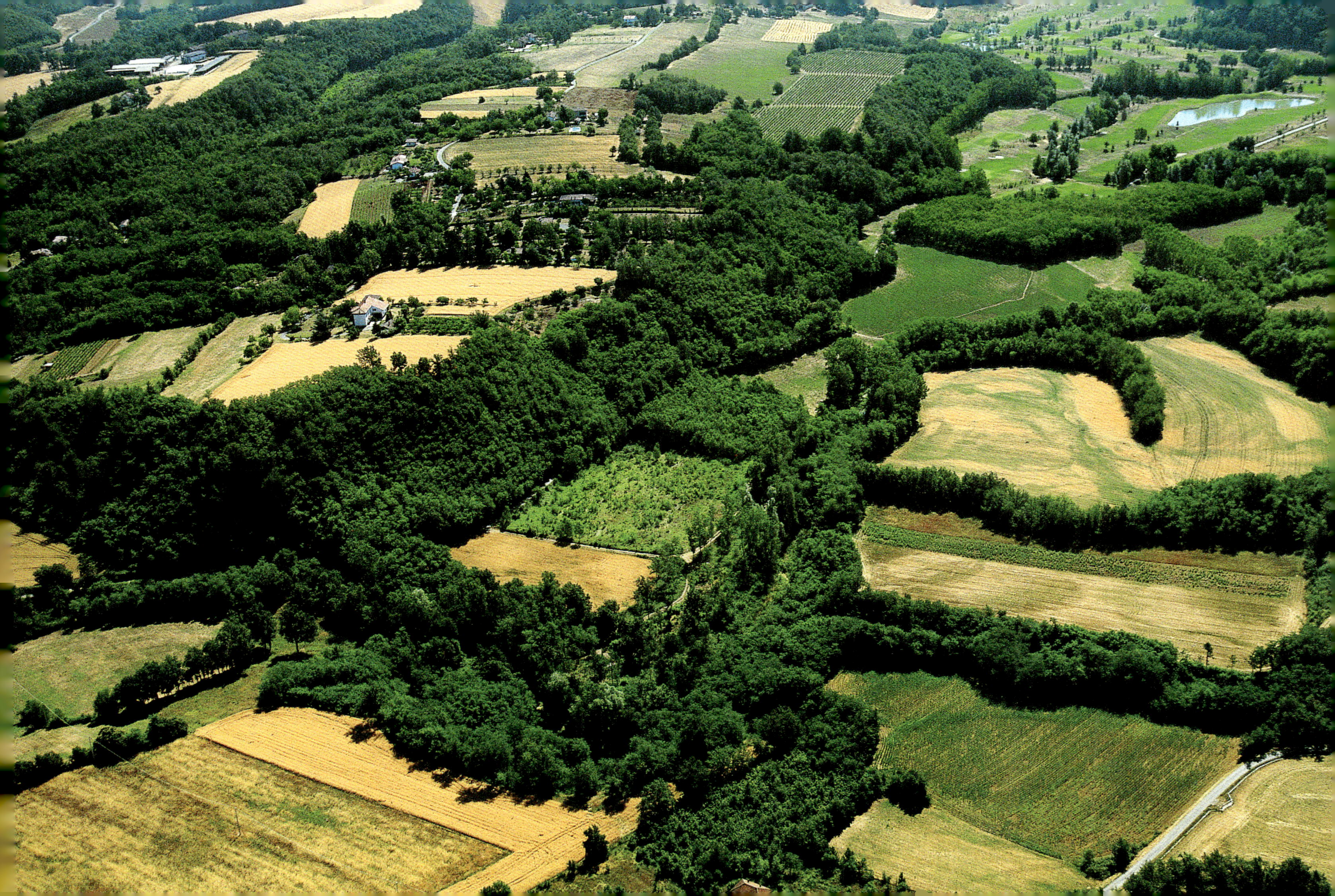

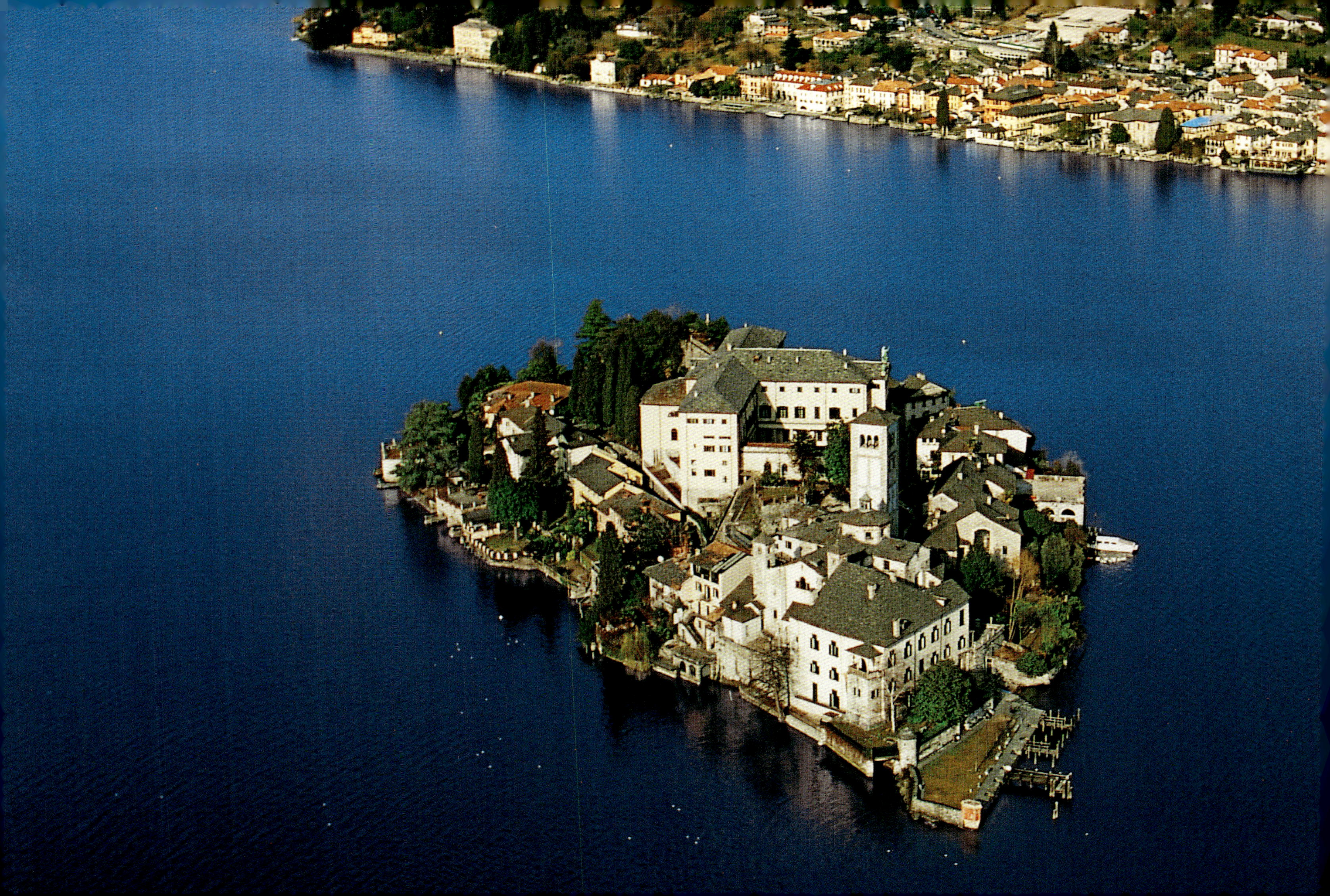

114-115 Lake Orta is perhaps the most exemplary among the Alpine lakes that enhance northern Italy. It is small, surrounded by mountains, and has its sources in the southern front of the Simplon glacier. However, contrary to other Alpine lakes, which have outflows to the south, the waters of the Lake Orta flow out of the lake to the north. In the middle of the lake's blue water, set like a jewel, is San Giulio Island, portrayed in the picture.

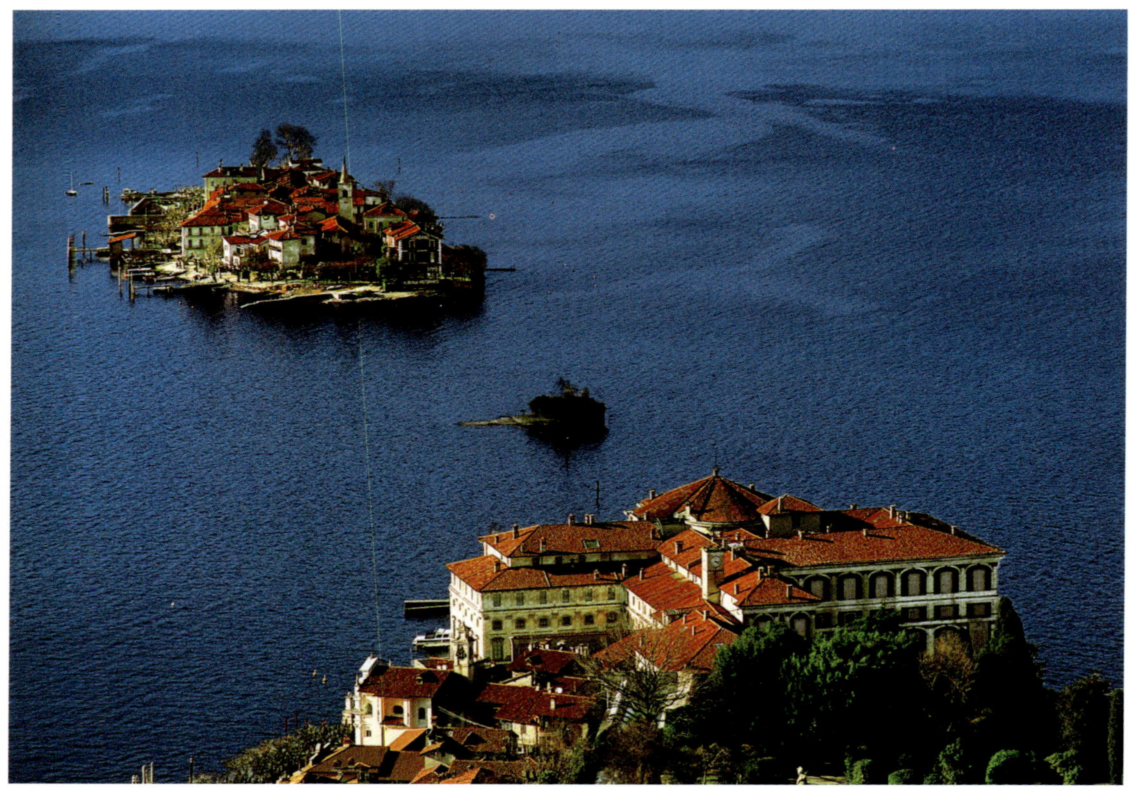

116 Lake Maggiore (or Verbano) is one of the main Alpine lakes and the second largest basin in Italy. Its waters extend into Ticino Canton and the provinces of Varese, Verbano-Cusio-Ossola and Novara. The picture portrays Isola Bella, one of the so-called Borromean Islands, on which stands the Palazzo Borromeo, located on the island's northwestern coast.

117 Isola dei Pescatori (Fishermen's Island), also known as Isola Superiore, is the only Borromean Island in Lake Maggiore that has been continuously inhabited – in this case for at least 700 years.

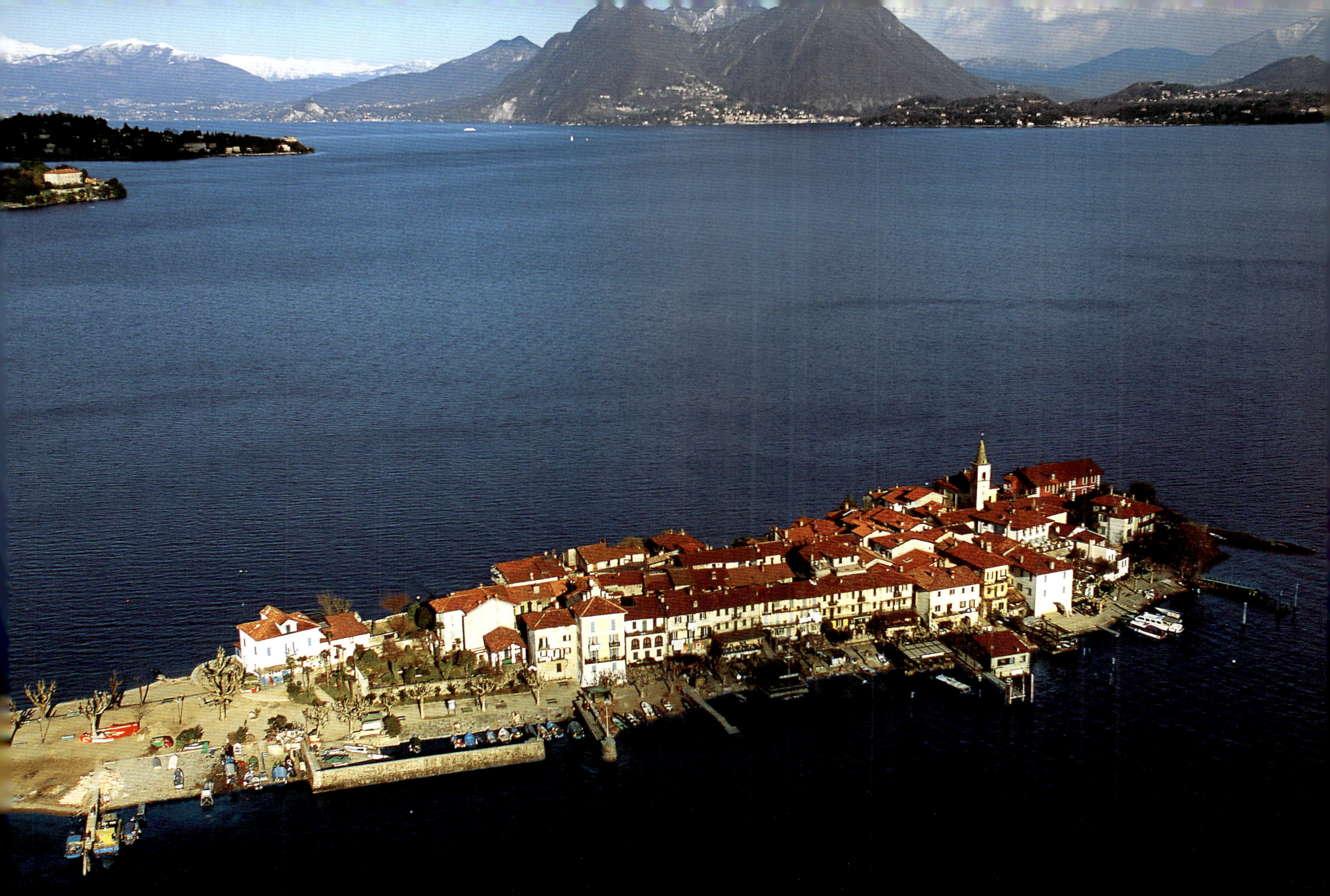

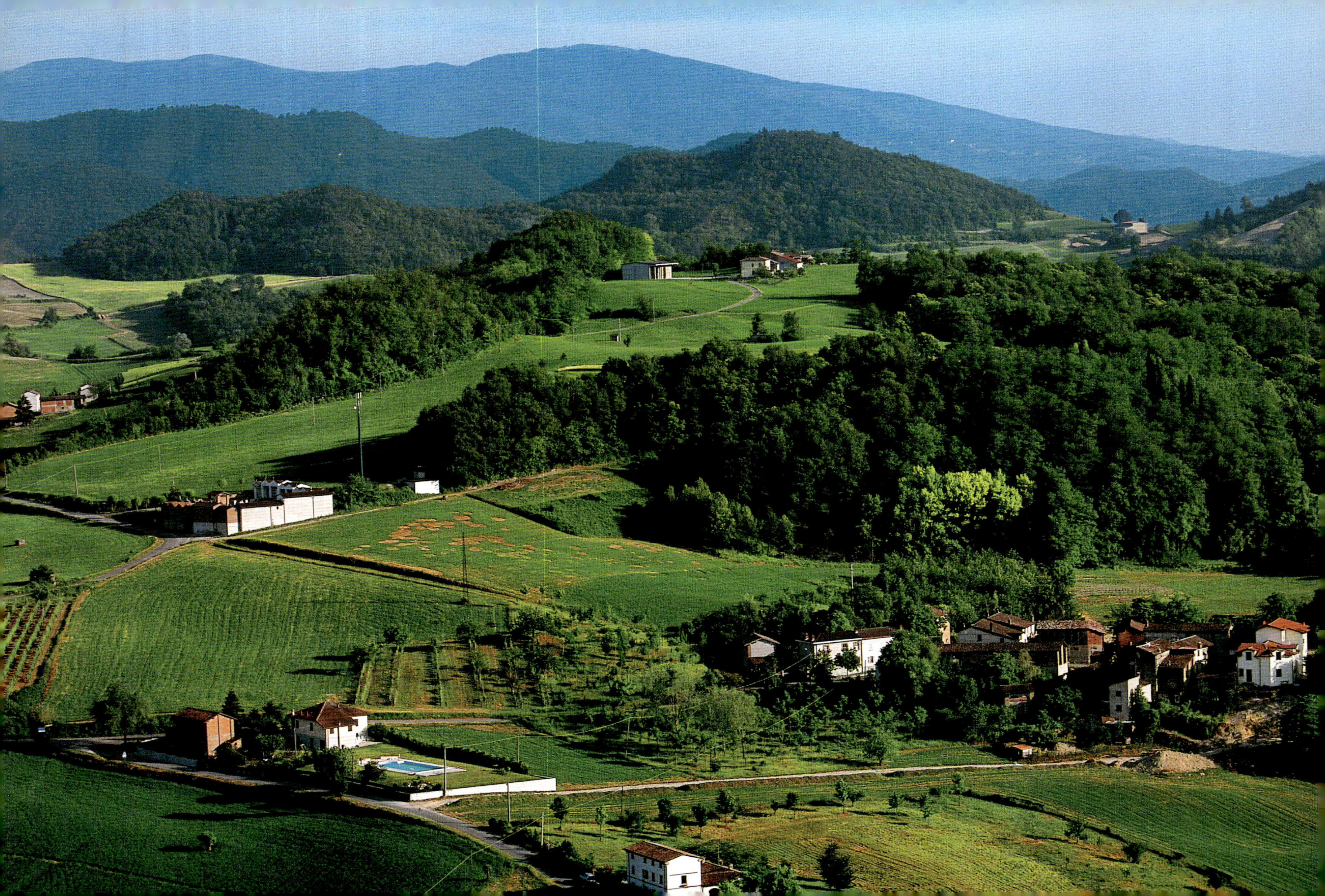

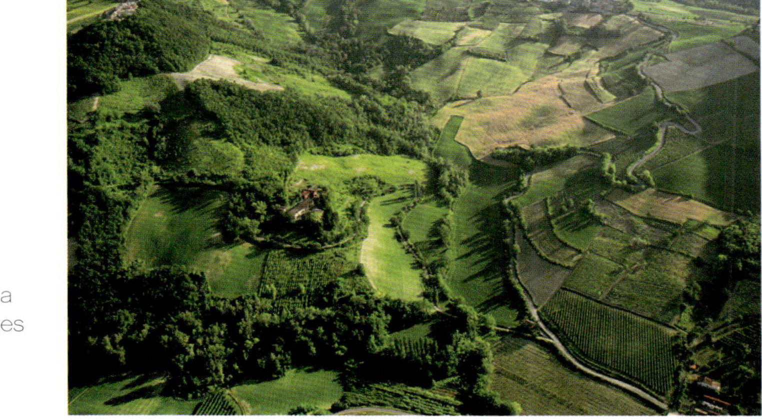

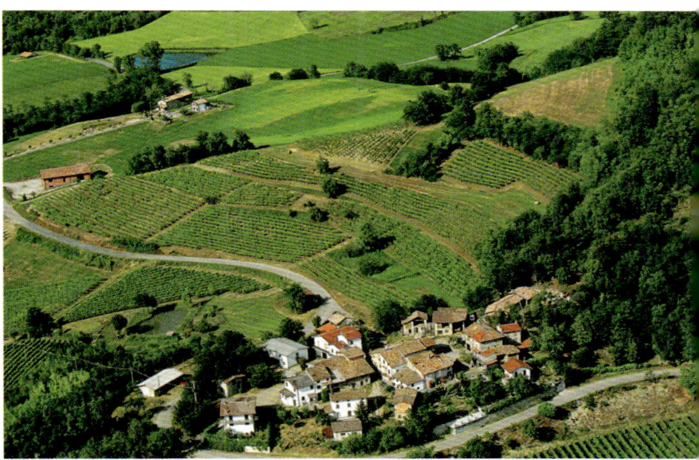

118 and 119 The Oltrepò Pavese occupies a triangular portion of Lombardy's territory south of the River Po. It is a primarily hilly area, mainly planted with vines, whose grapes yield the well-known Bonarda wine, but there is also a small flat area along the Po and a mountainous zone, at the southern vertex of the "triangle."

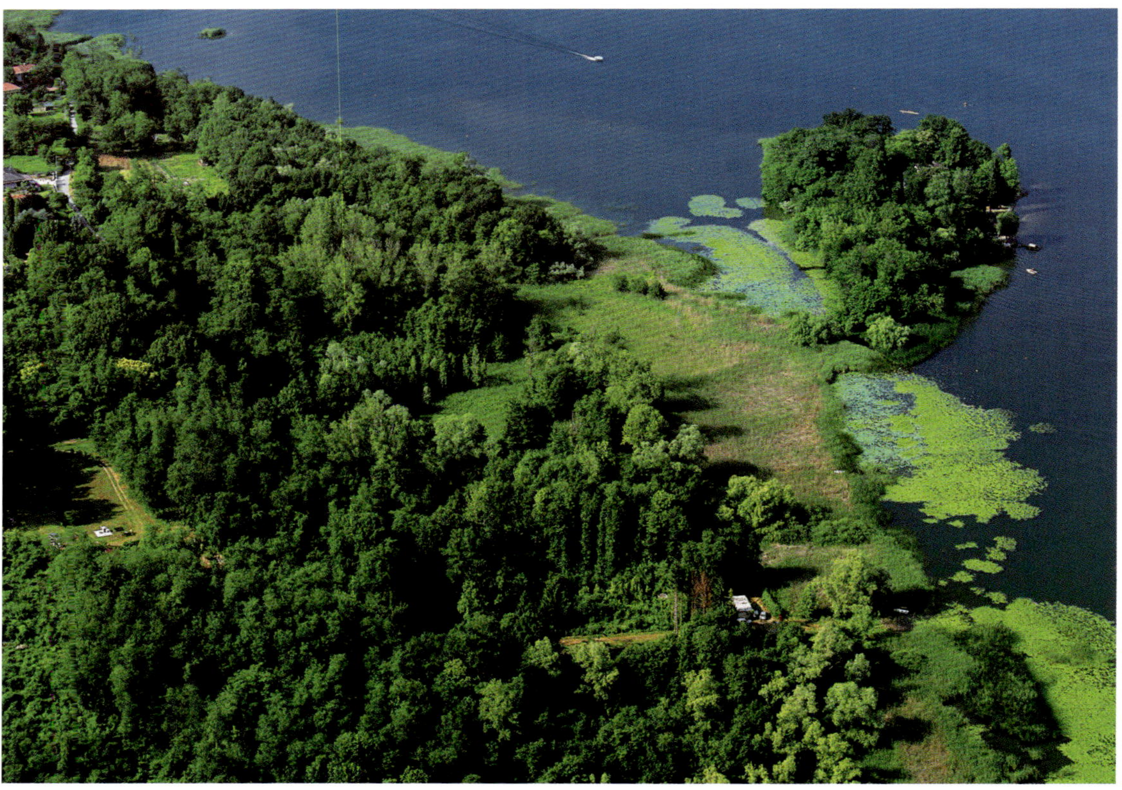

120 Lake Varese rose from the Varese Prealps approximately 15,000 years ago, when the Verbano glacier created the large basin where today the city and its lake exist. In 1863, along the lakeshores, where swimming is not allowed, some remains of the ancient lake-dwellings were found.

121 Lake Lugano (also called Lake Ceresio) is an Alpine lake in Ticino Canton, in the Varese and Como provinces. The lake section shown here is in the canton; the town is Porlezza.

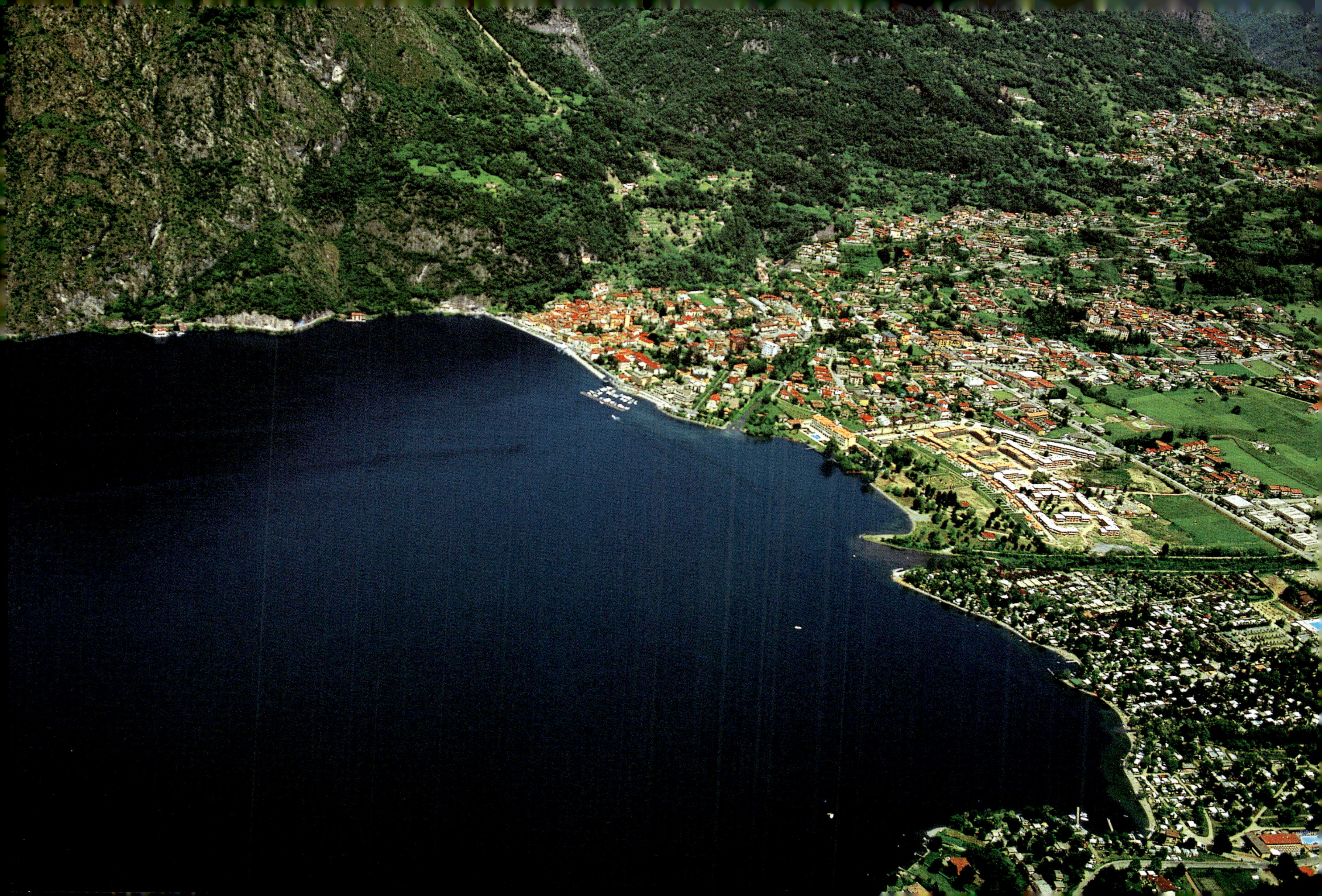

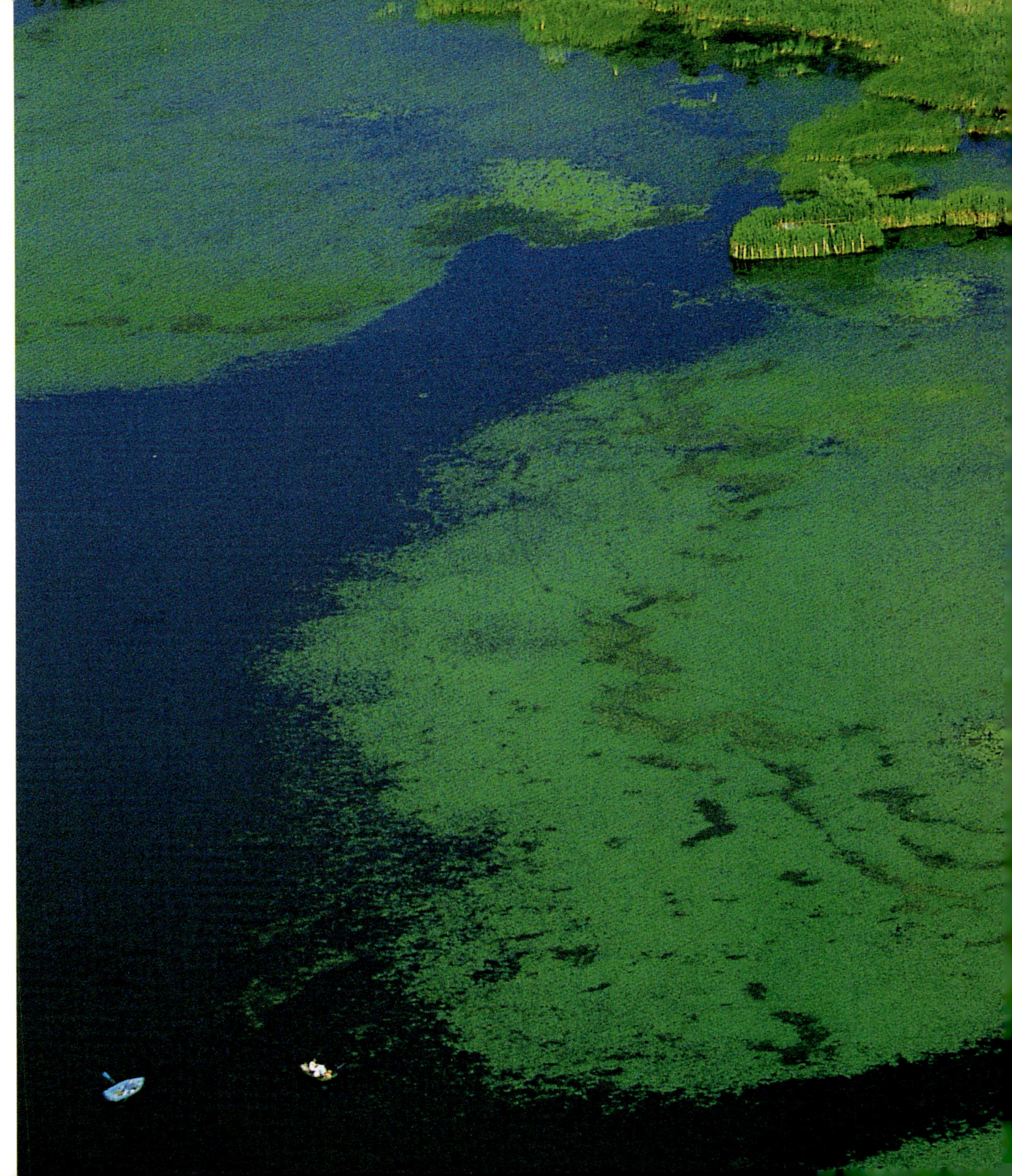

122-123 Lake Varese occupies only part of the large basin created in ancient times by the receding Verbano glacier. This is why the whole Varese area is sprinkled with marshes, peat-bogs and stretches of clear water, with large canebrakes, willows trees and alders.

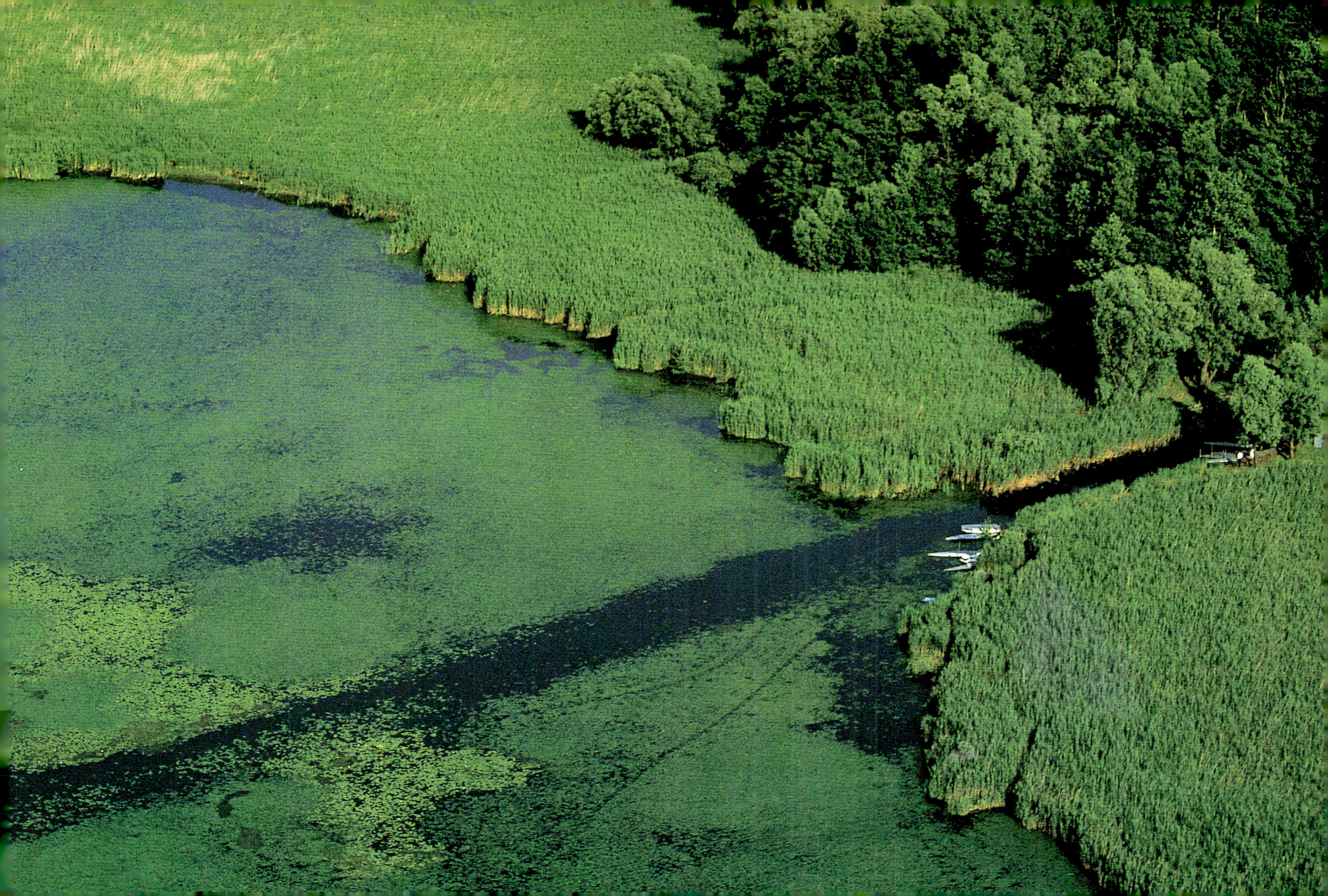

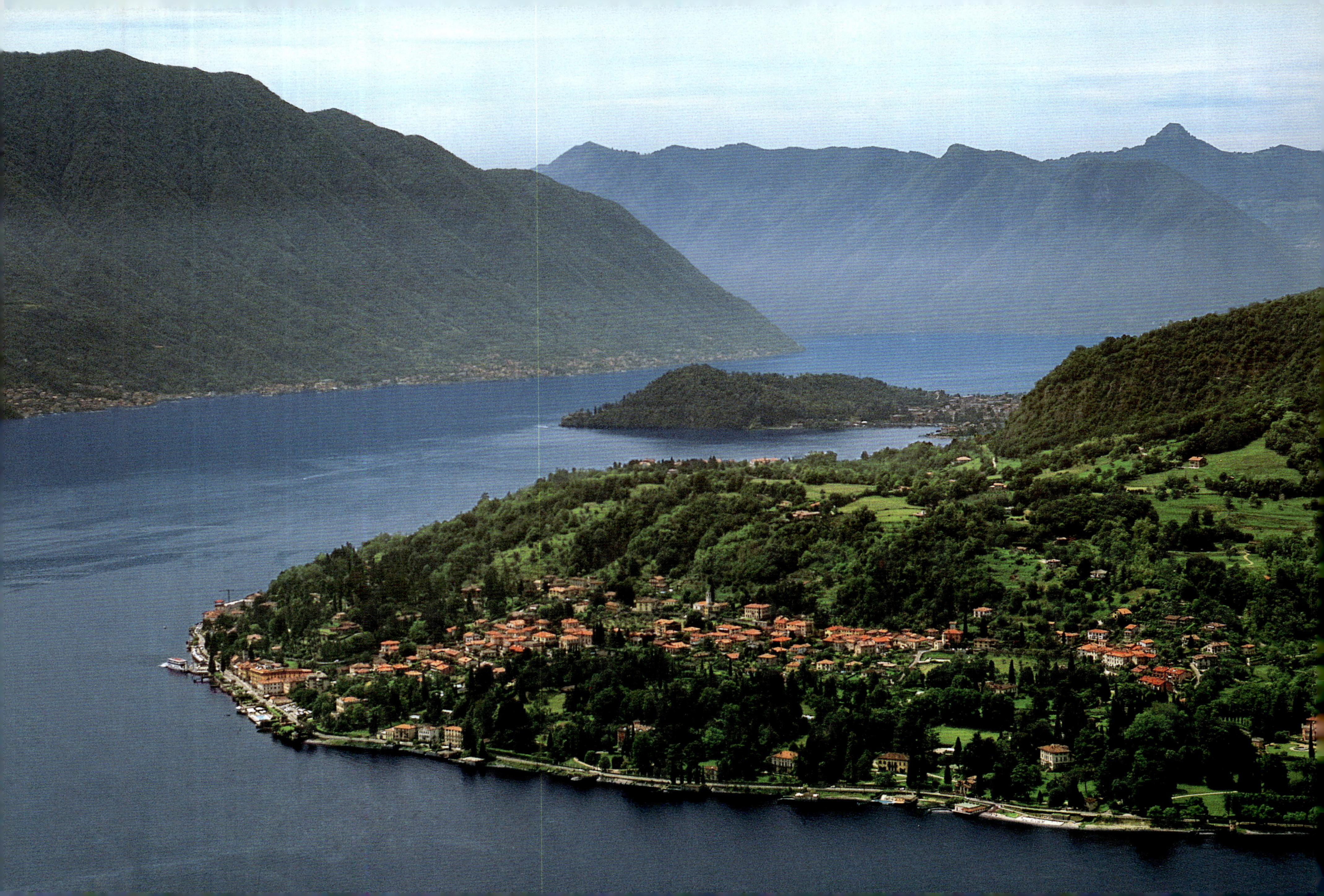

124 Lake Como (also called Lake Lario) has a typical reversed "Y" shape. The picture was taken exactly from the point where the two southern arms merge to form a single northern arm. The small village in the foreground is Griante, while in the background is the green promontory of Lenno.

125 left Punta Balbianello and the villa of the same name occupy the end of the Lenno promontory in the arm of Lake Como that belongs to Como province.

125 right Bellagio is one of Lake Como's most popular visitor attractions. The beautiful area portrayed here is where the three arms of the lake merge.

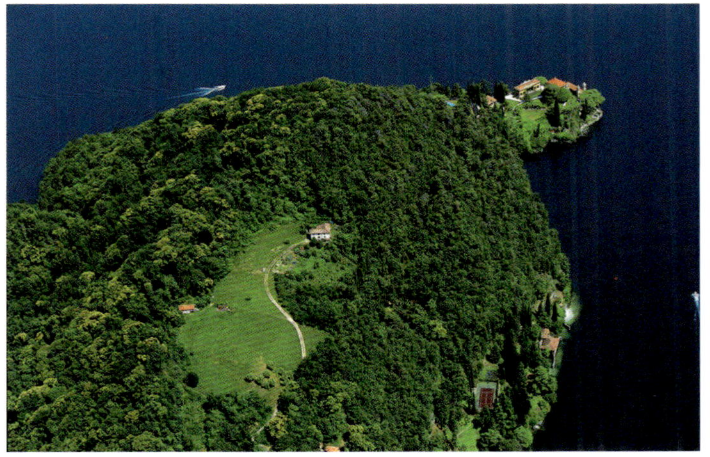

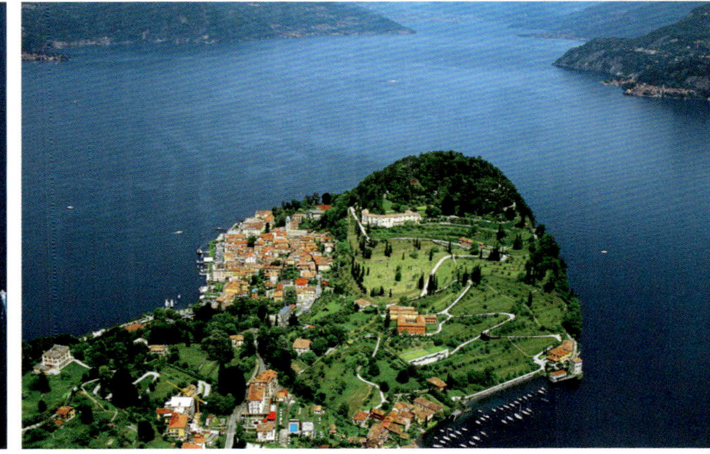

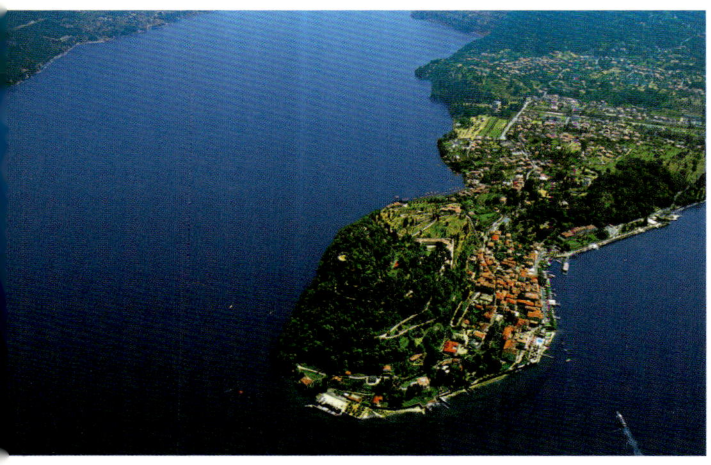

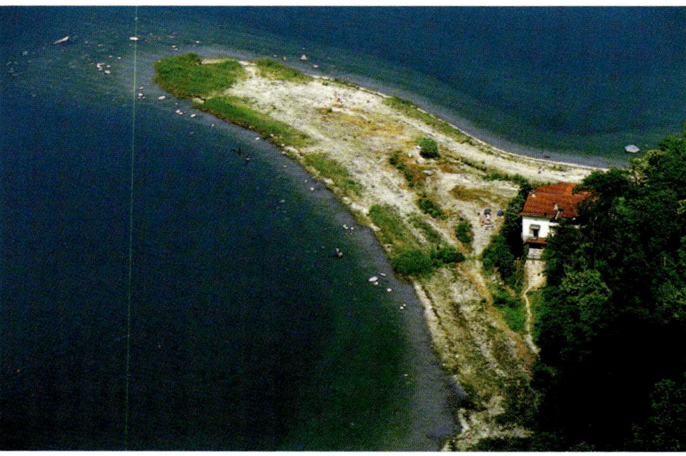

126 left In this picture, part of Bellagio stands out, a sort of promontory situated where the arms of Lake Como merge.

126 right At the north end of Lake Como, where the waters of the Mera and Adda rivers enter the lake, the shores look wilder, and when the water level is not high, small shore areas like this one surface.

127 A half-moon of houses, seemingly flattened over the lake by the looming mountain. This is the small village of Dervio, overlooking the eastern side of the Alto Lario (Upper Lake Como). All around are dense woods of oak and chestnut trees typical of the lower mountains and hills.

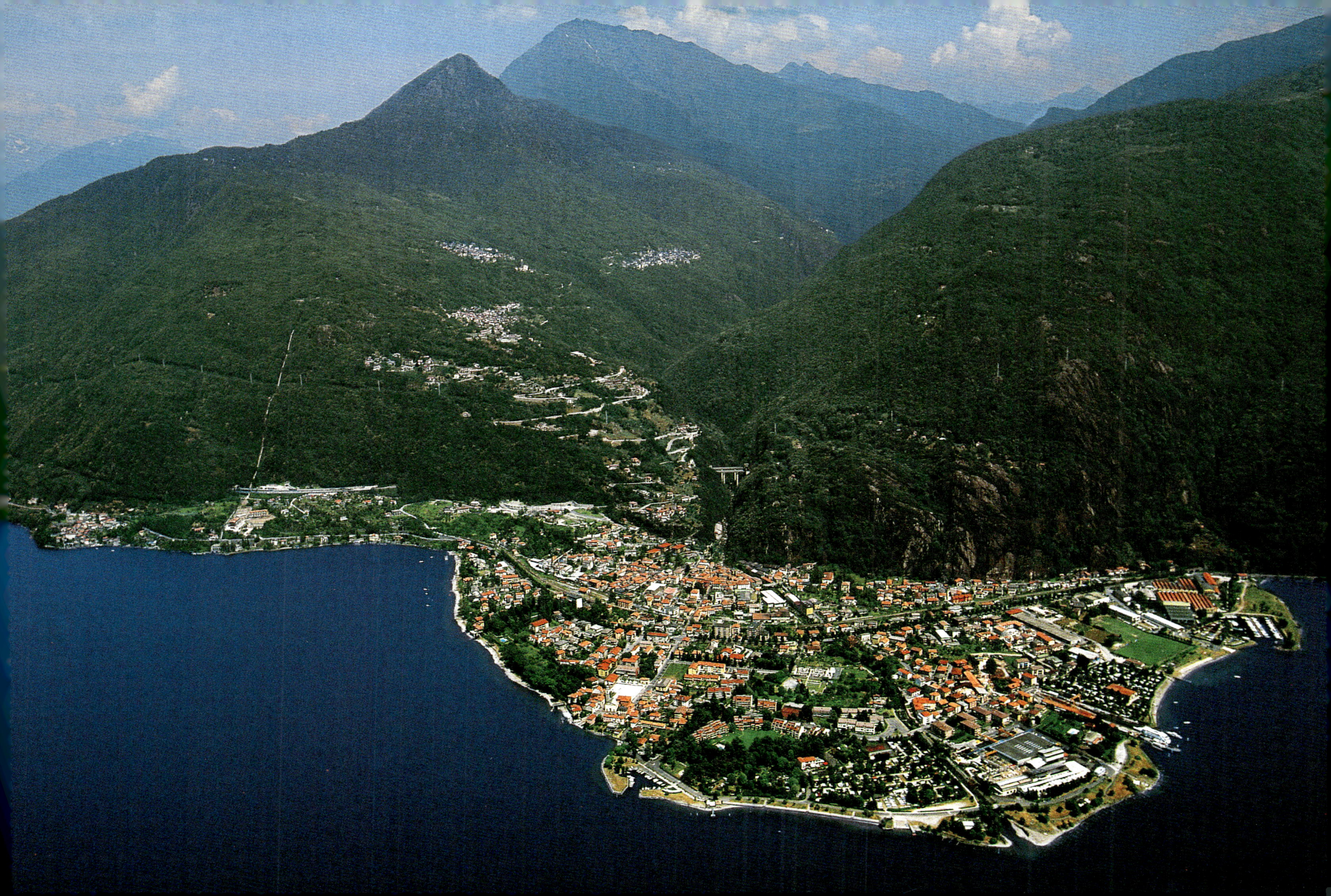

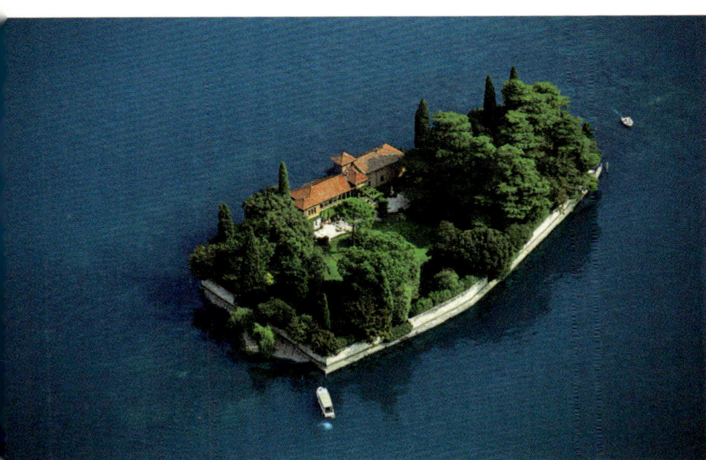

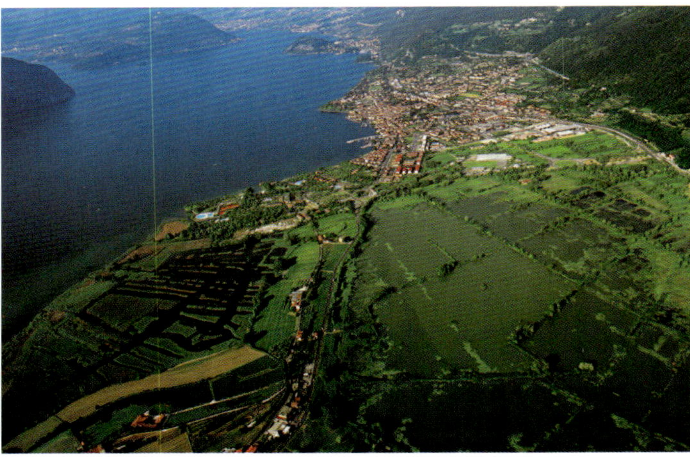

128 left The small island of San Paolo, in the middle of Lake Iseo, is home to the monastery of the same name. Once the monks moved to this island, the buildings and the island itself became private property.

128 right The small village of Iseo stands on the lakeside that belongs to Brescia province. This area has been inhabited since prehistory, as shown by the pile dwellings found here.

129 South of Iseo is the Torbiera peat bog, a sanctuary that has no equal in Europe. The landscape is picturesque, with its scattering of small stretches of water, and basins resulting from the excavation of the clay.

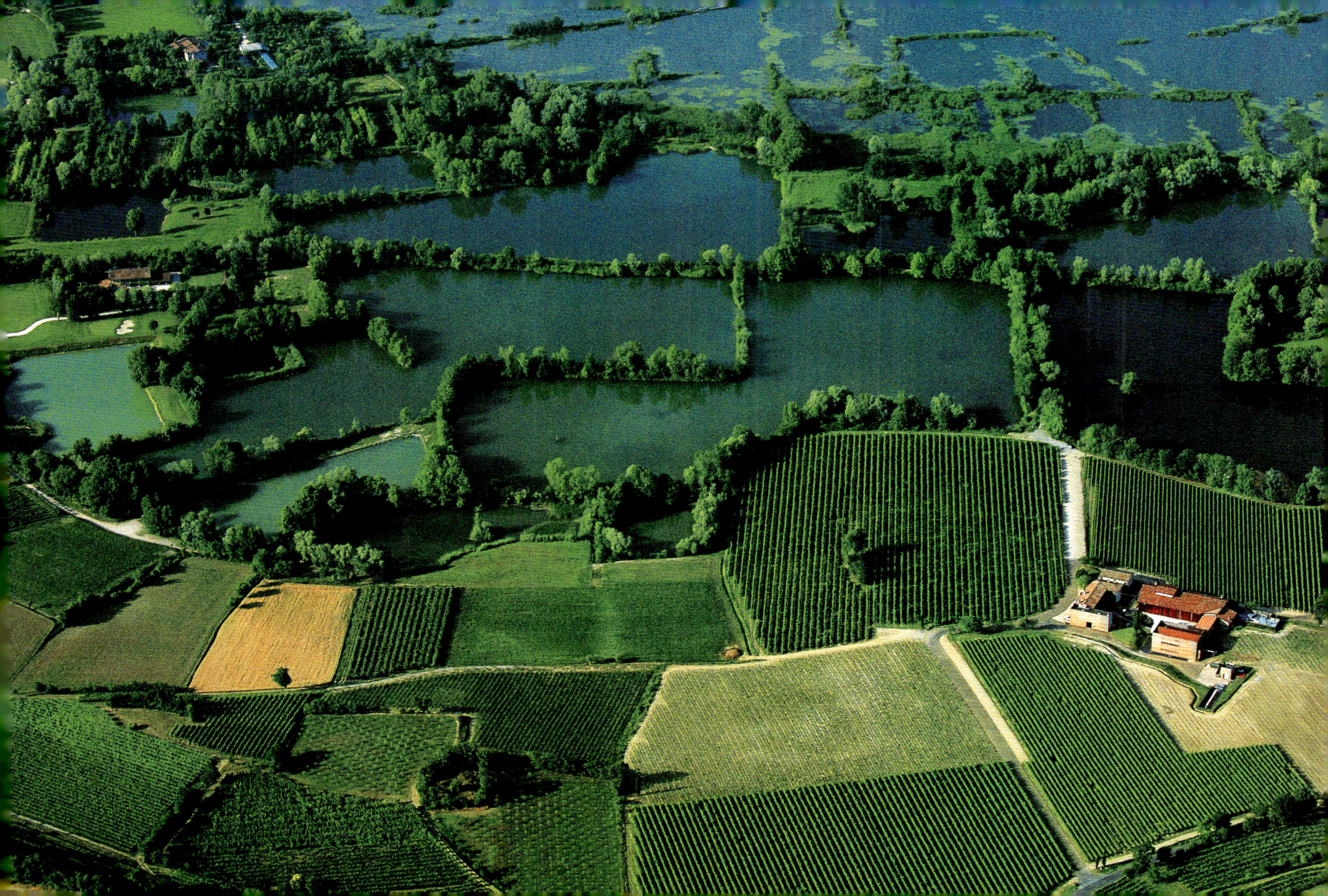

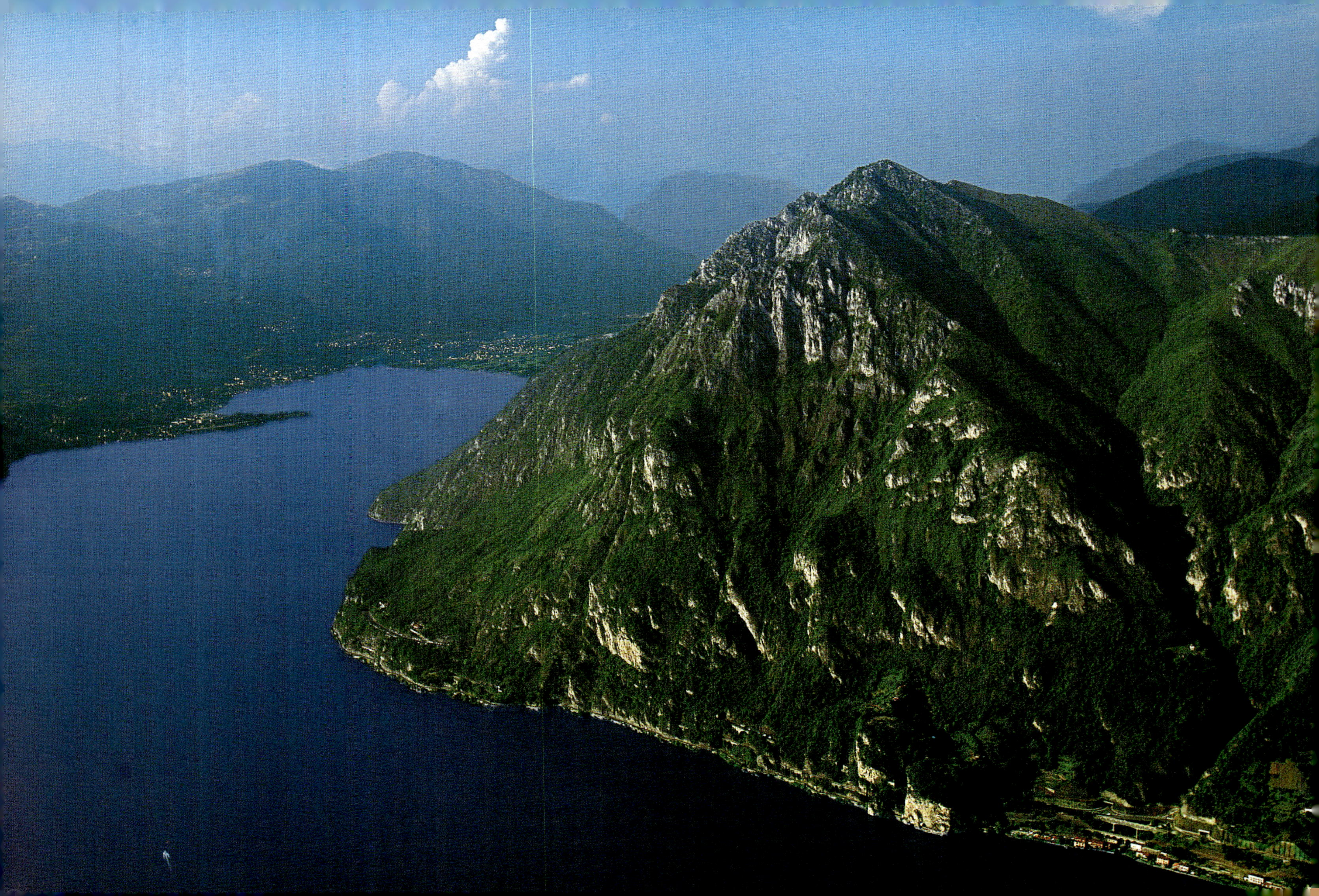

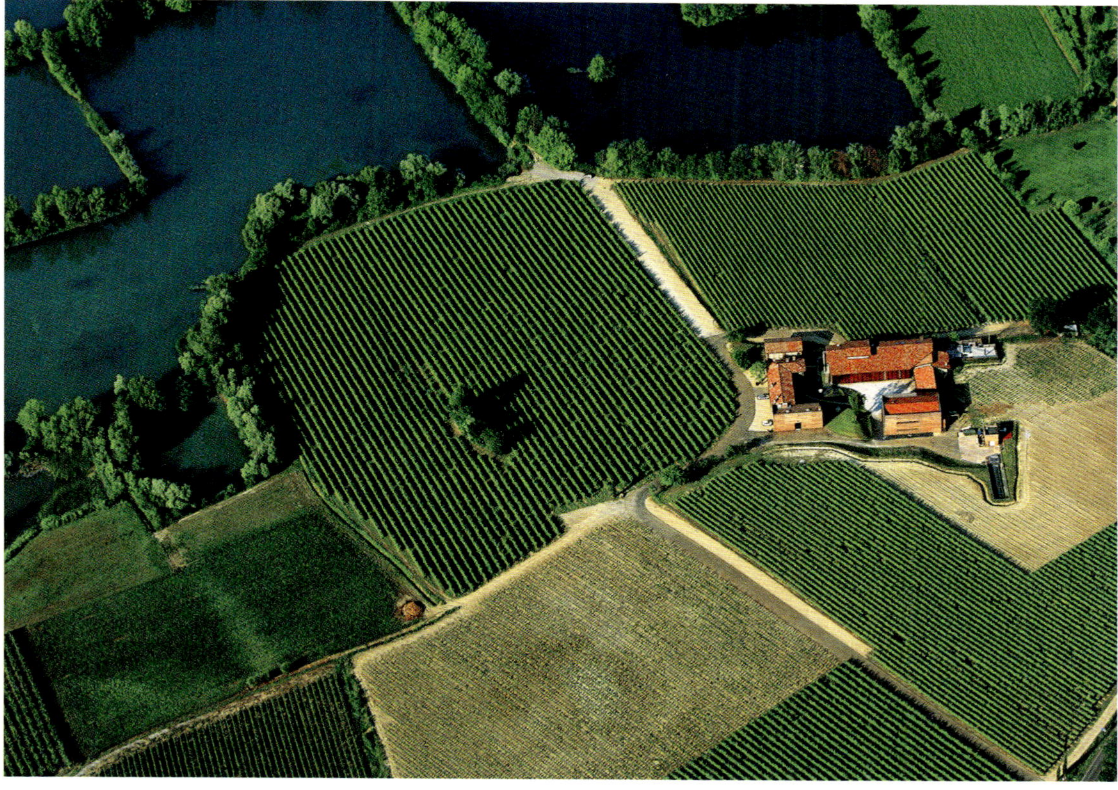

130 Corna Trentapassi (c. 4095 ft/1248 m), also known as Punta di Vignole, is an isolated mountain overlooking Lake Iseo between Marone and Pisogne; it offers wonderful views over the lake and the surrounding countryside.

131 South of Lake Iseo extends the Franciacorta, a hilly zone well known both for its mild landscape and for the production of wine, particularly *spumante*. The scenery is visibly affected by this activity: the hills are methodically structured and "combed" in rows; the lots are small and geometrical.

132-133 The Tremosine plateau, on Lake Garda's western side, sinks sharply in the water with a sort of cliff: it is the result of a geological phenomenon which reached its peak 5 million years ago when the Adamello Massif was formed.

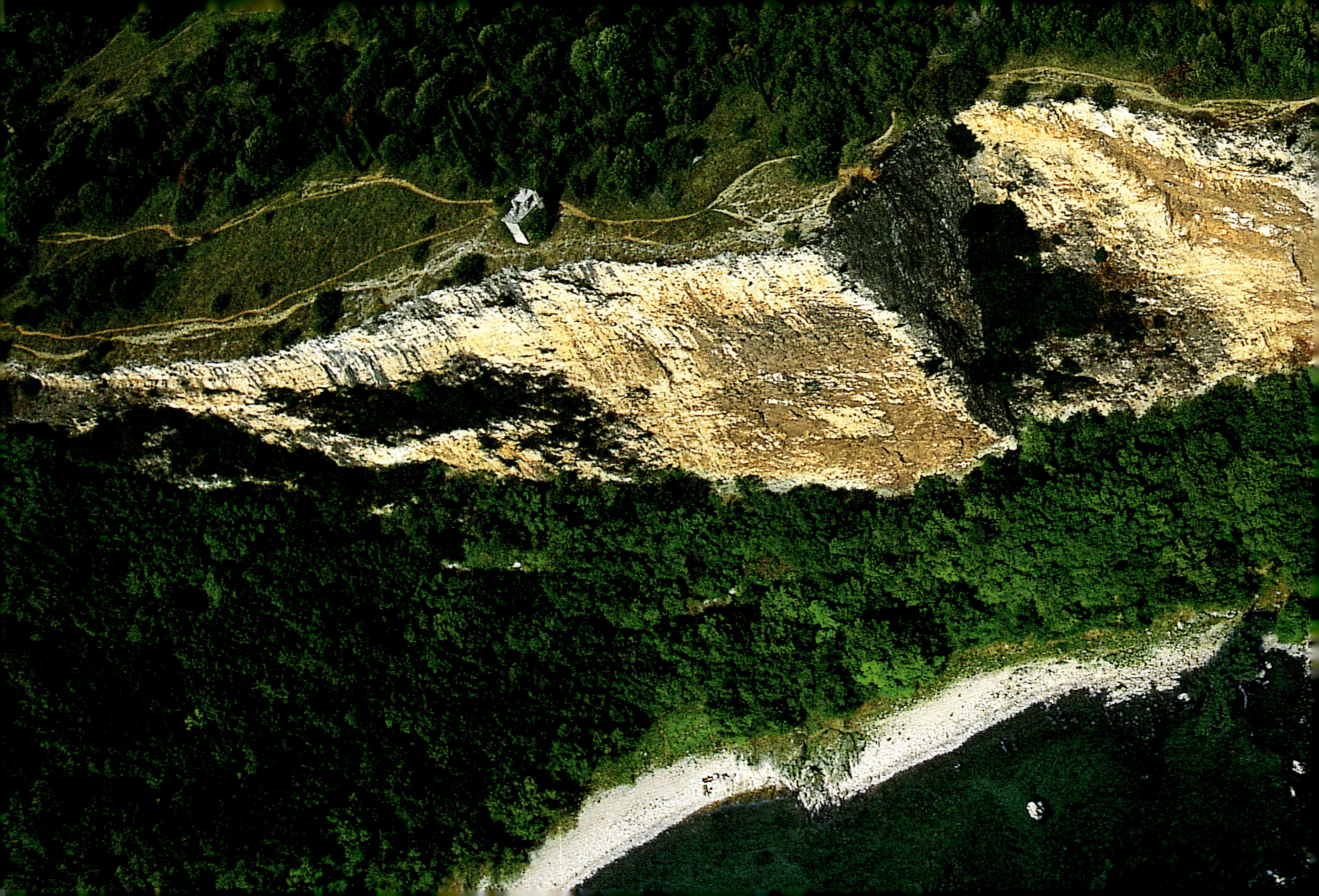

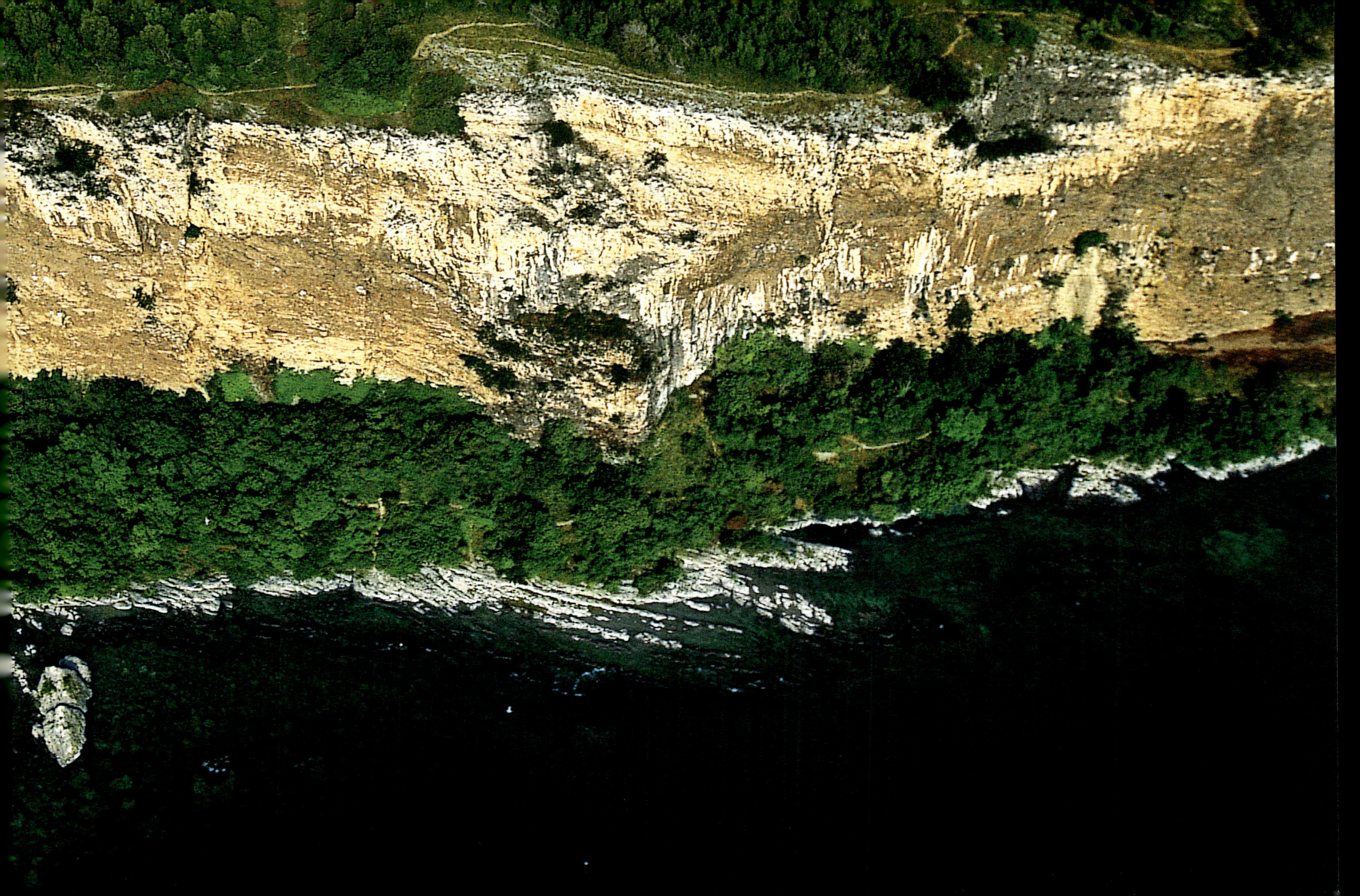

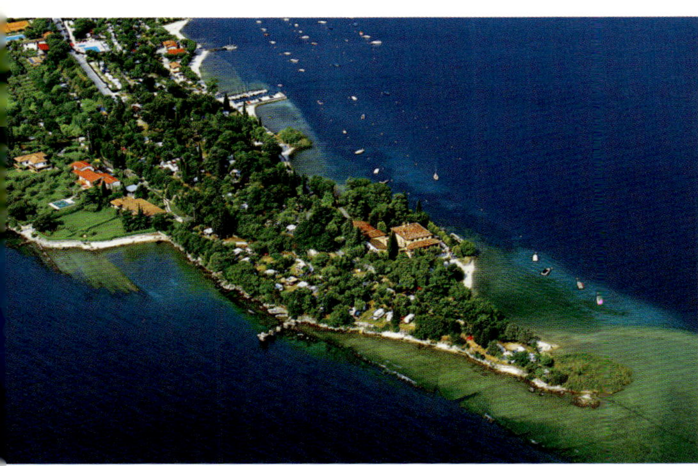

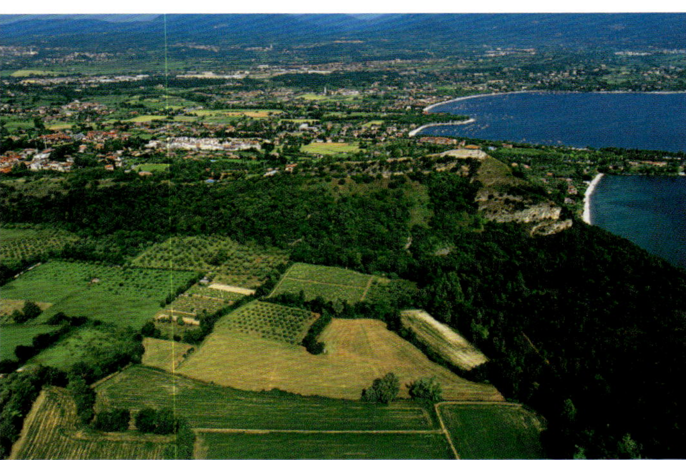

134 left Punta San Biagio extends toward Isola dei Conigli (Rabbit Island) (not shown), from the southwestern side of Lake Garda. When the water level is low, it is possible to reach the island on foot.

134 right Seen here are Punta San Biagio and the small village of San Felice del Benaco, photographed from Rocca di Manerba.

135 The town of Salò overlooks the gulf of the same name in Lake Garda; it is closed to the west and to the south by morainic hills and to the north by Mt San Bartolomeo. Salò's history and environmental beauty make it a popular visitor attraction.

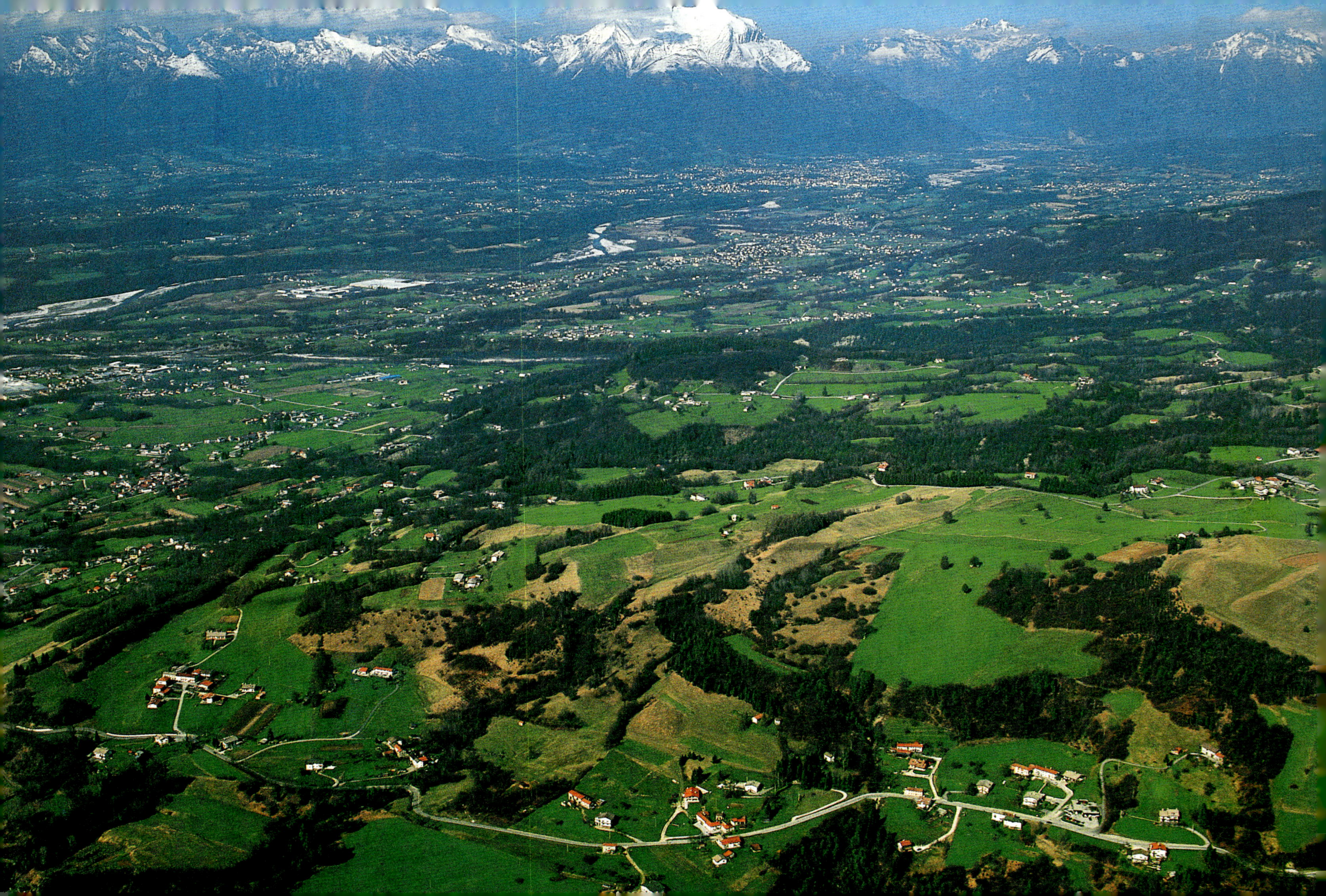

136 The landscape around Vittorio Veneto (Treviso), on the slopes of the Treviso Prealps, is definitely beautiful: there was a prehistoric glacier here; it left a legacy of numerous morainic hills, portrayed in the picture.

137 left Like Vittorio Veneto, Asolo (Treviso) is as well located on the slopes of a morainic group known as Venetian Prealps.

137 right The hills preceding the Carnic Prealps, in the Friuli region, are famous for their fine white wines, appreciated all over the world.

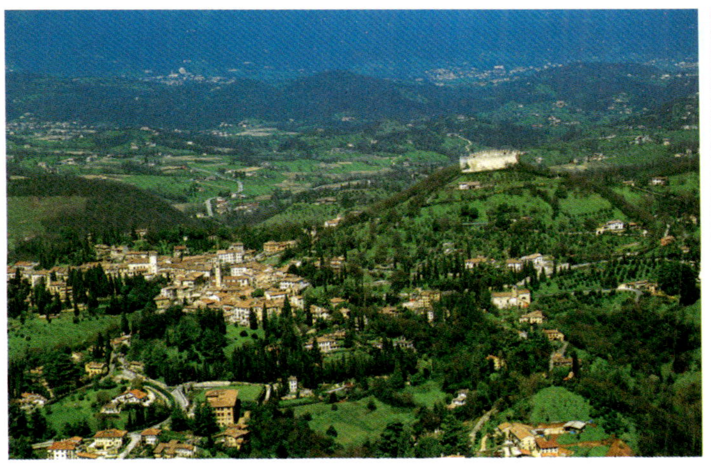

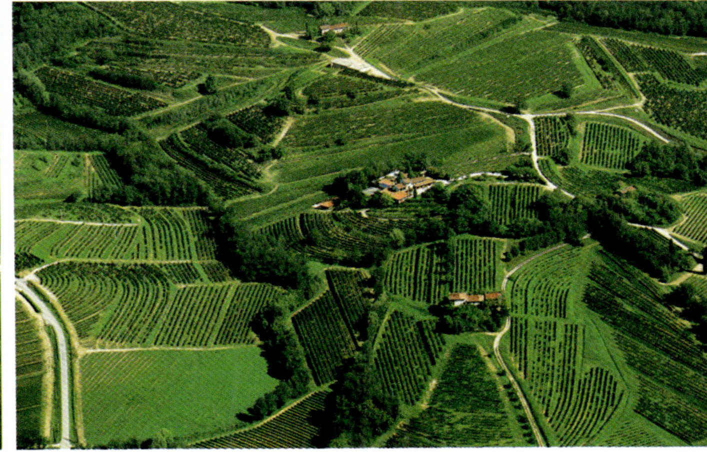

139 The countryside of Livinallongo, a Ladin valley formed by the upper reaches of the Cordévole stream (Belluno), still exhibits the characteristic features of the Trentino Prealps: slight grass-clad slopes, dotted with thick conifer woods and by a series of small farmhouses, today mostly rented to visitors.

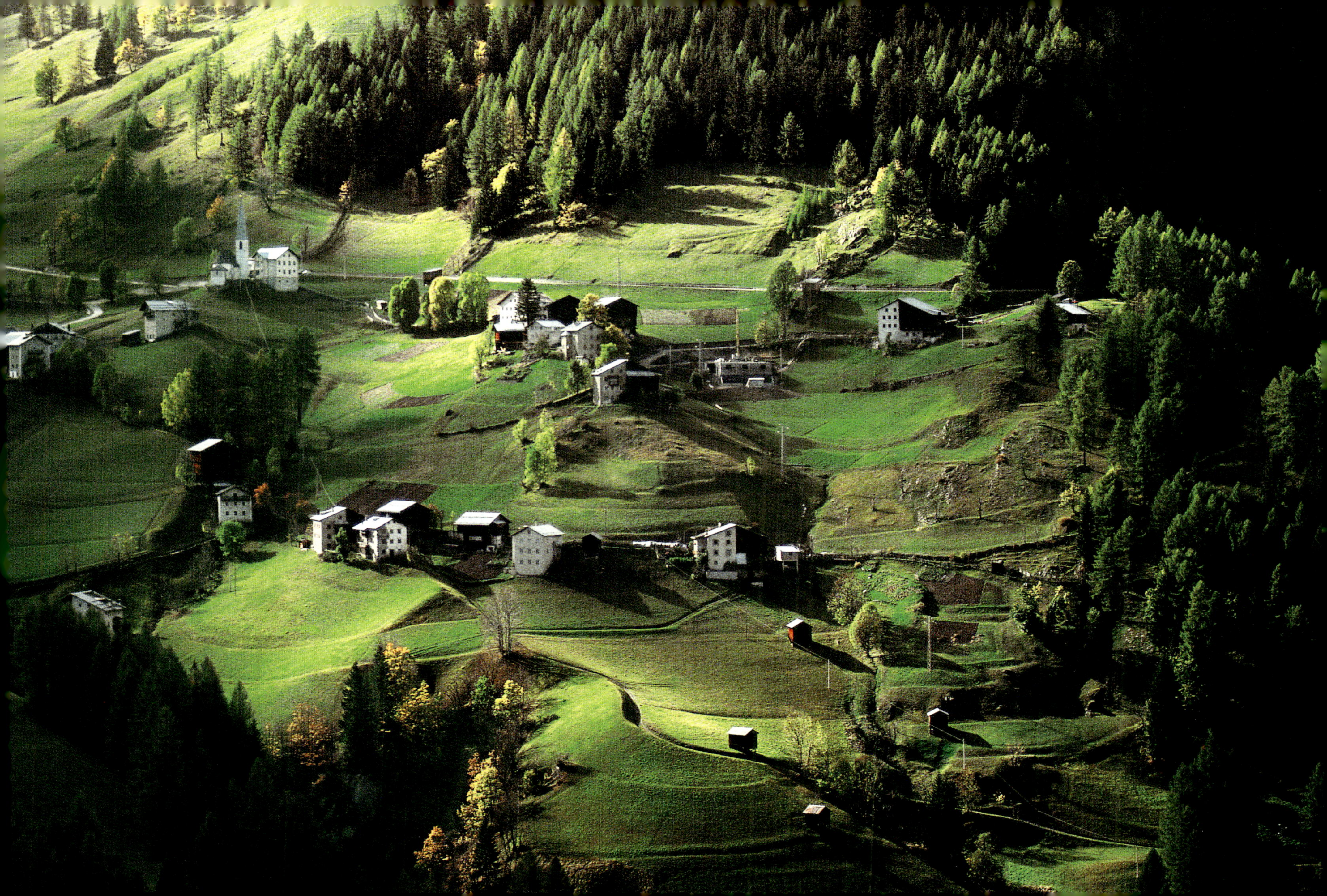

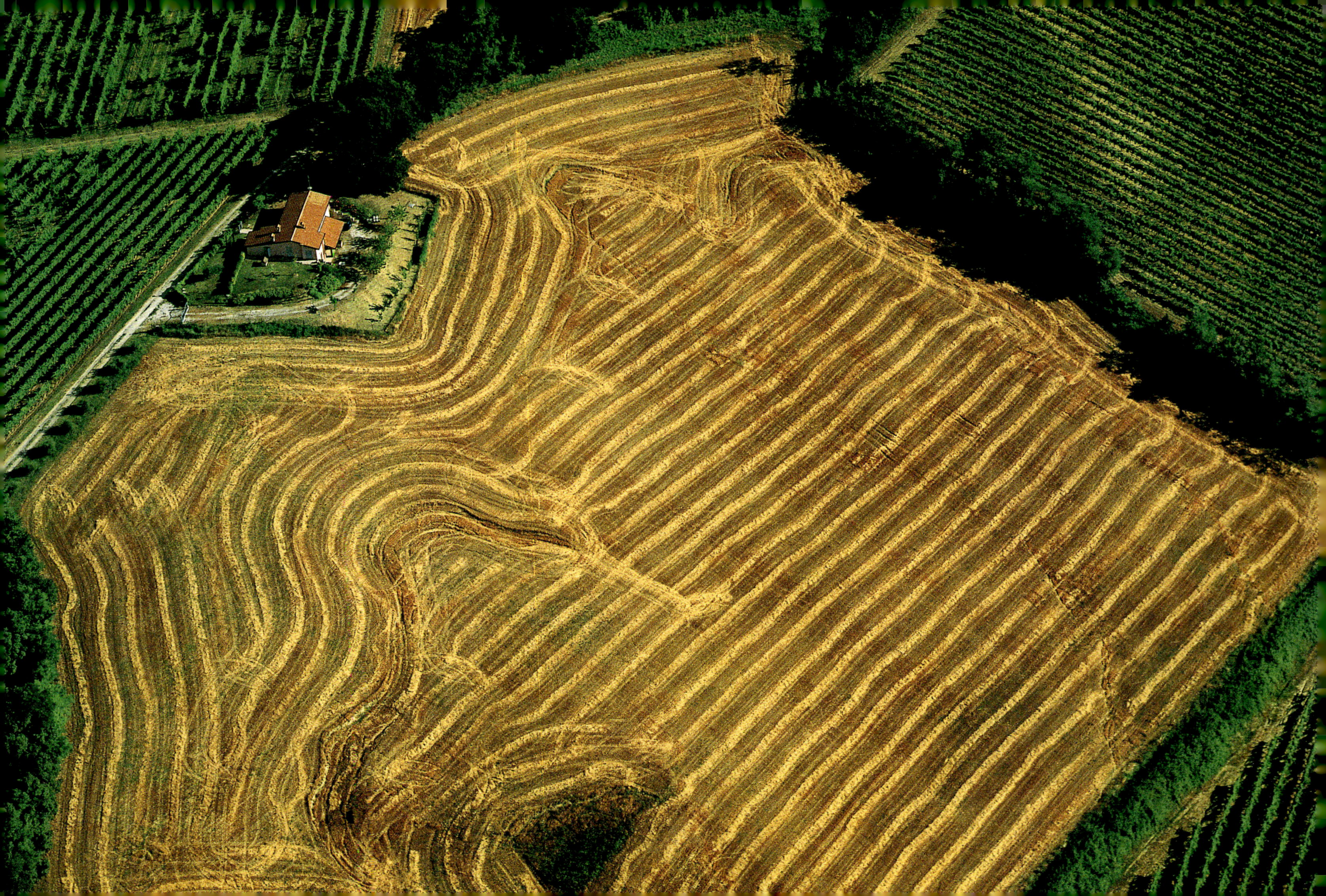

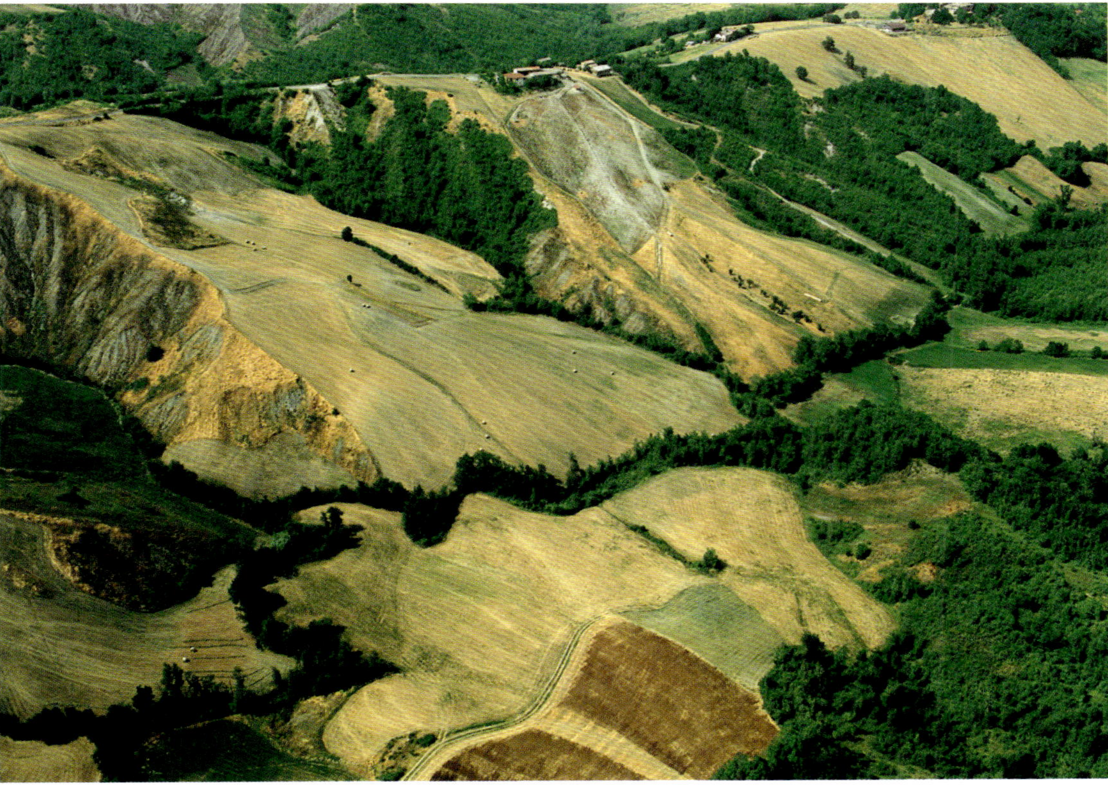

140 The hills in the Parma area mirror the area's intensive agricultural exploitation: cereal fields coexist with plots planted with vines, whose grapes produce the famous Lambrusco.

141 In the Reggio Emilia Preapennines, between Terrachiara and Canossa, tilled and untilled lands alternate; part of the dense forest that once covered all the territory around Reggio Emilia still survives.

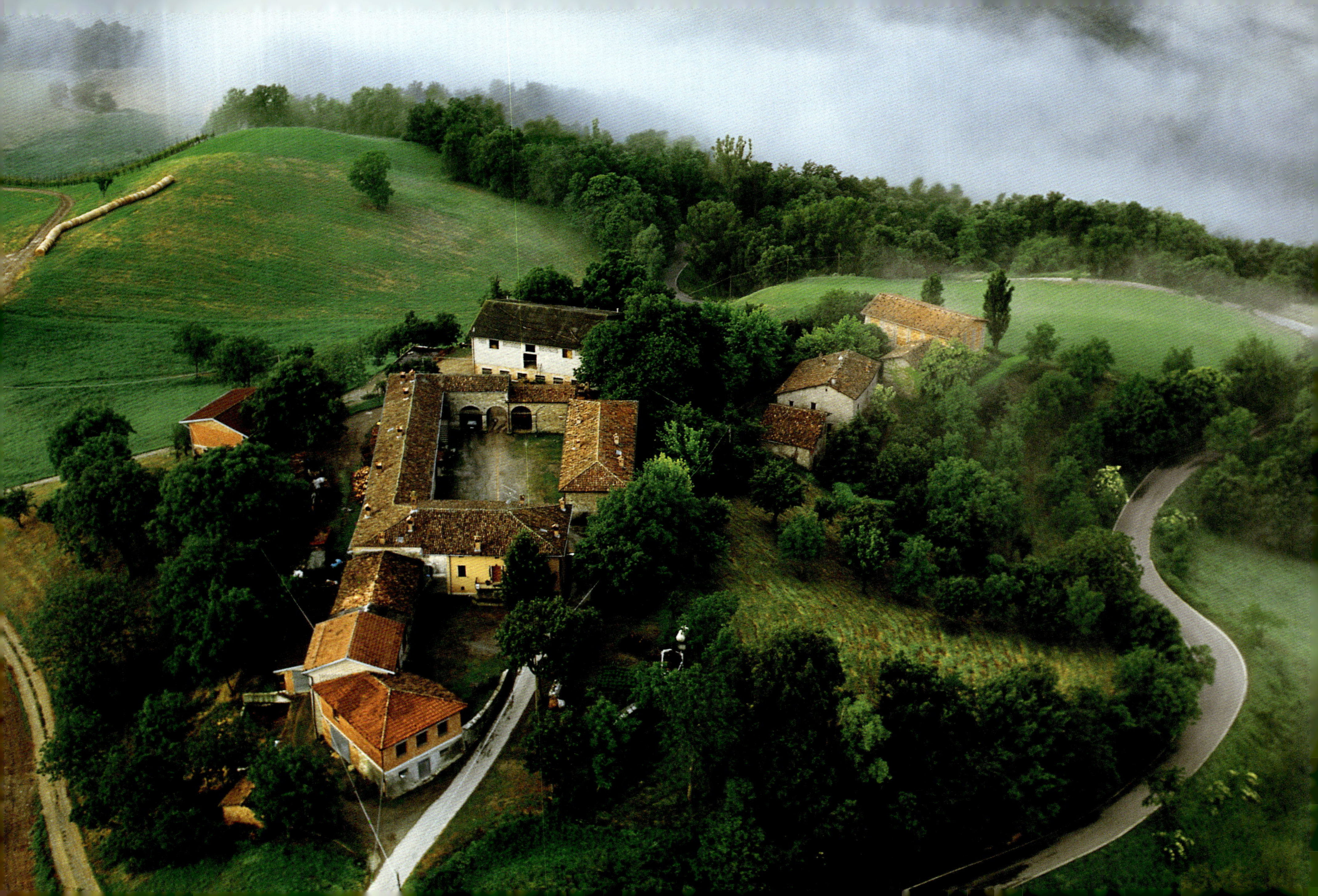

142 and 143 left Two restored farmhouses, now used only as residences, stand on the hills around Reggio Emilia. Over the last two decades many people have moved from the cities and the small villages of the plain to the Apennine slopes, bringing these sites back to life.

143 right The Reggio Emilia Preapennines still offer views like this, where the wooded bush extends toward the mountain slopes and the clouds seem to rise from the trees.

144-145 Low clouds on a humid late summer day. in the countryside around the Reno River Valley (Bologna), time seems to have stopped.

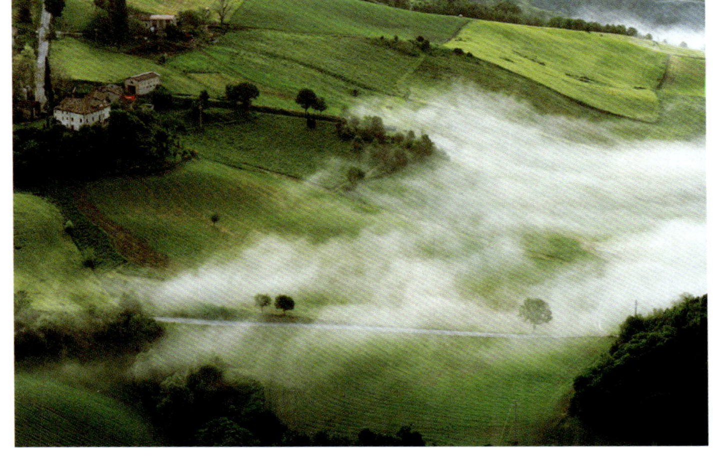

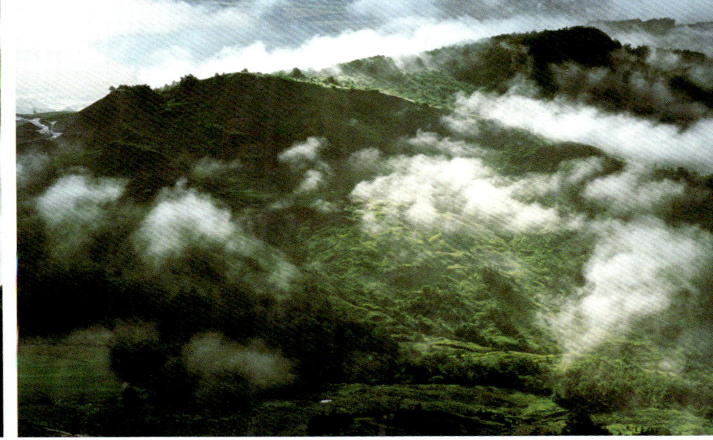

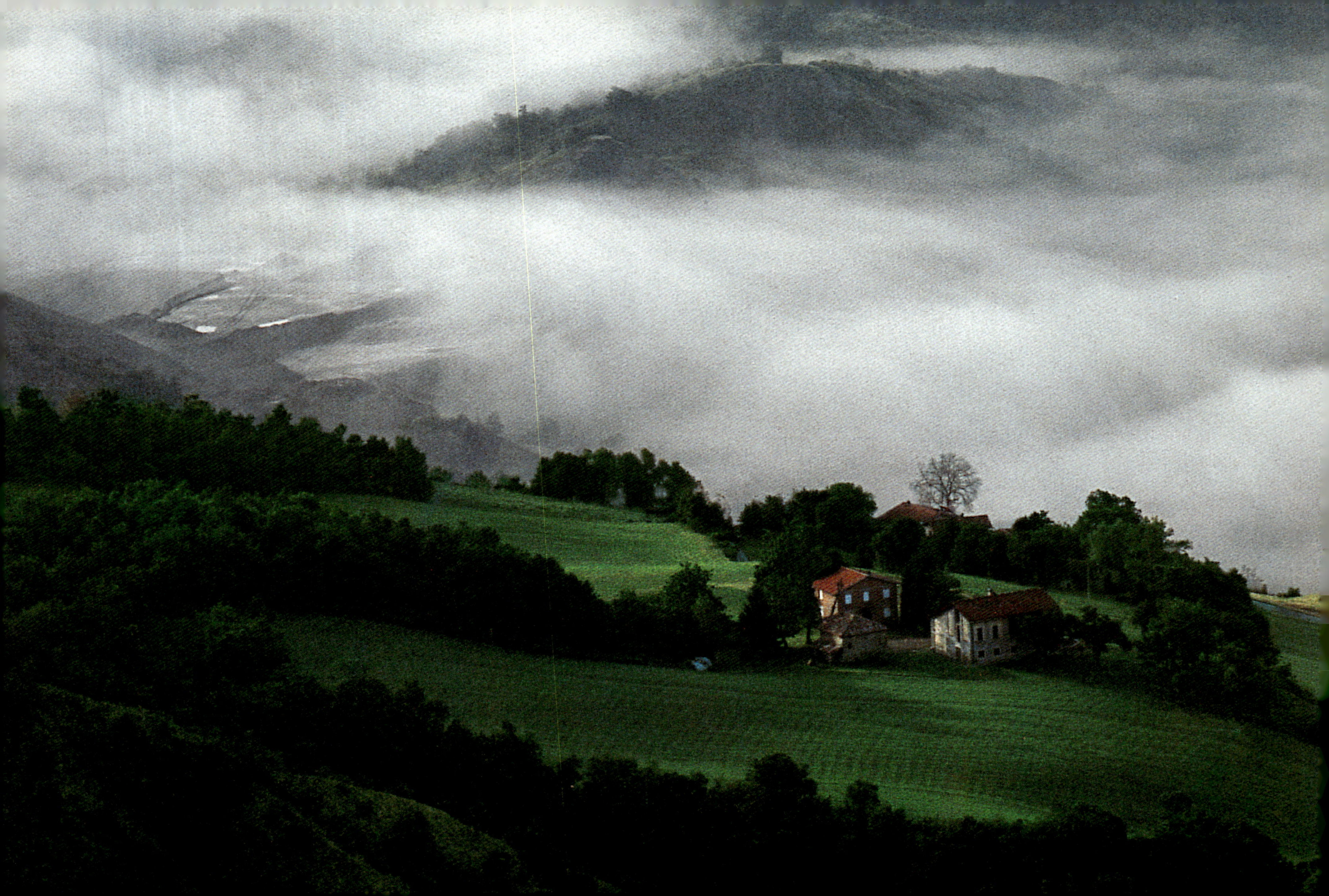

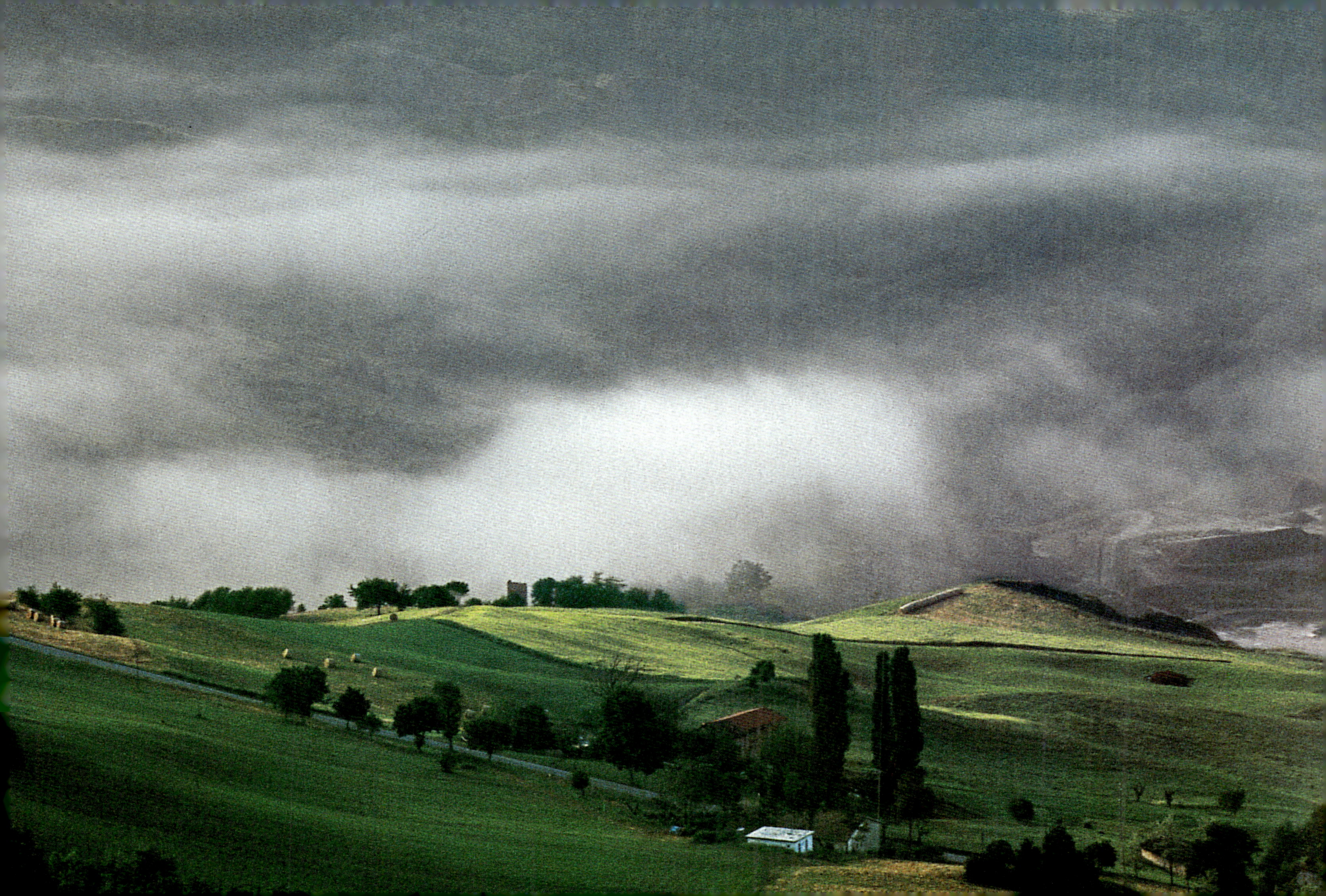

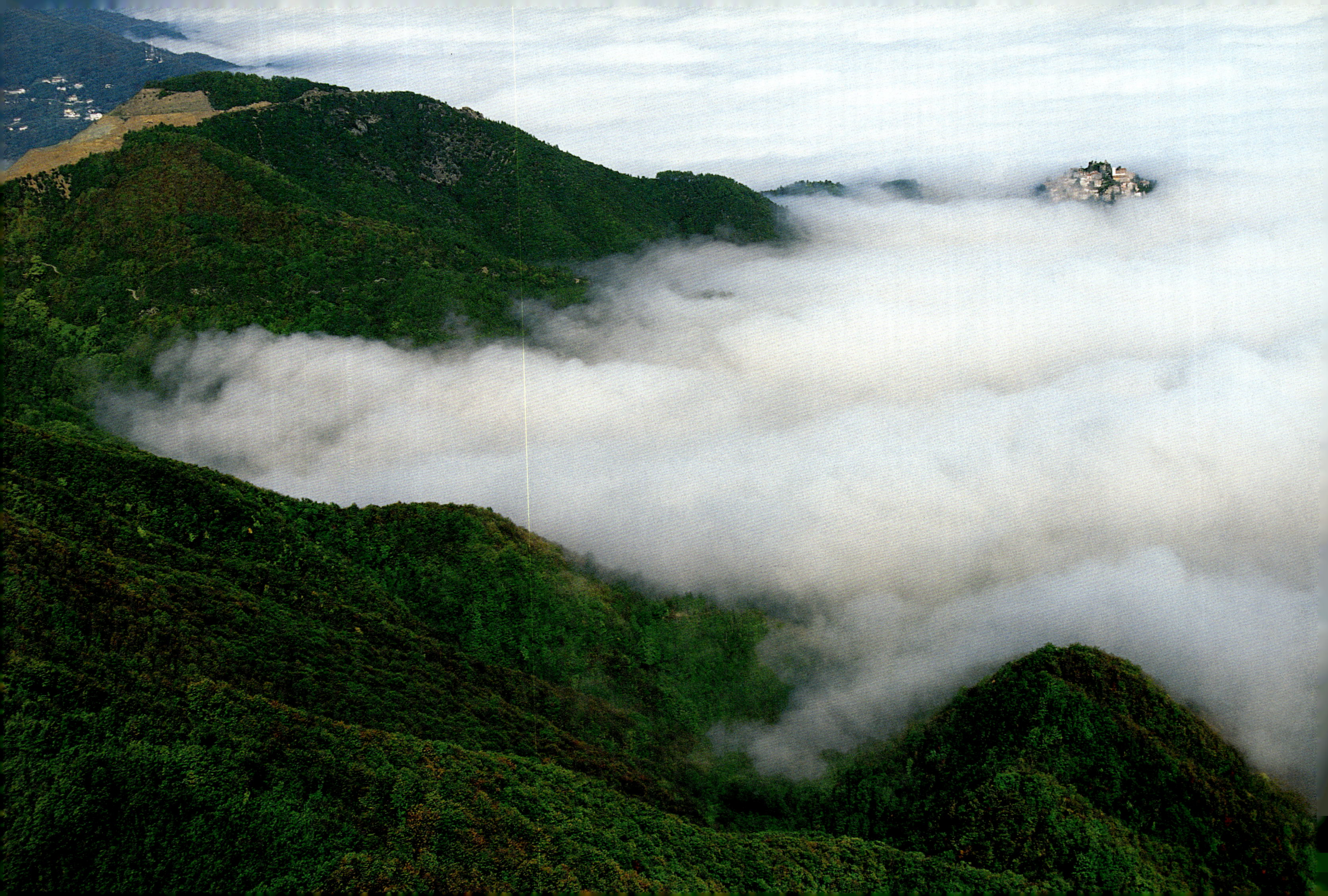

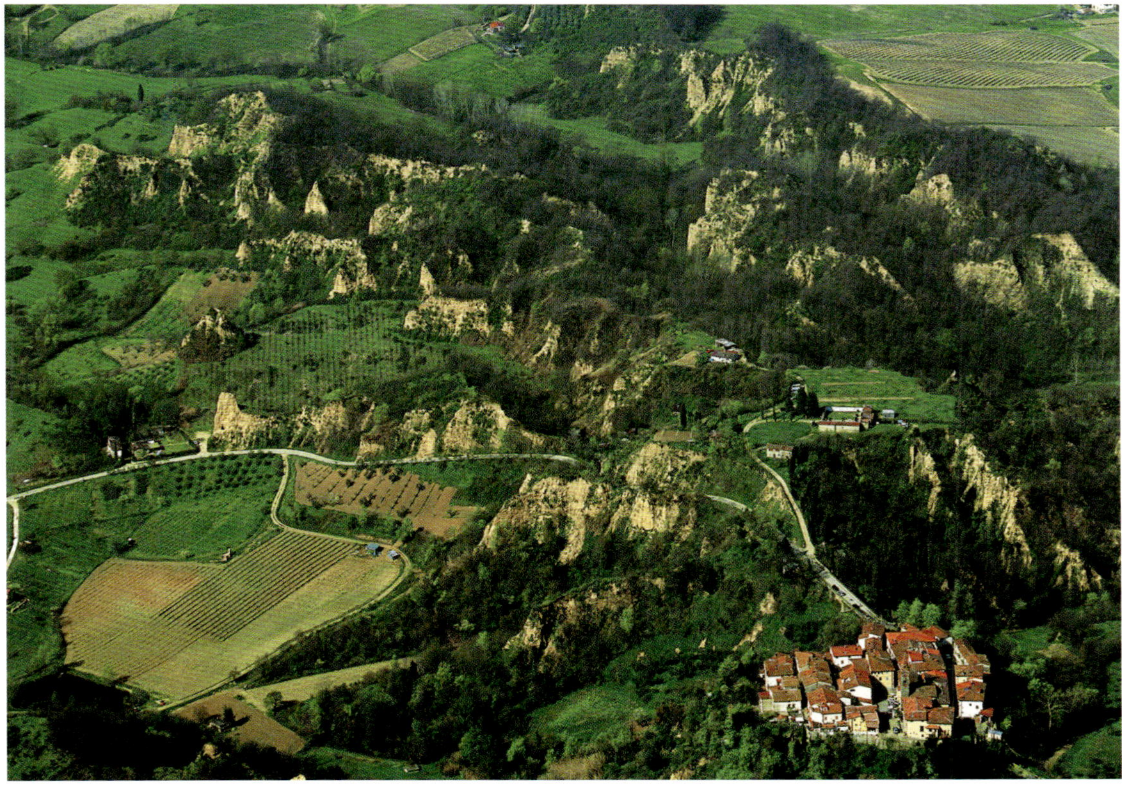

146 Autumn on the alp of Catenaia, in the Casentino, is a palette of colors on which lies a blanket of clouds.

147 The Valdarno, to the east of Florence, is a casket of amazing sceneries: among the most spectacular shapes are the Balze, pinnacles and rocky spires which once fascinated Leonardo da Vinci.

148-149 The Crete, situated to the southeast of the city of Siena, are typical barren hills, where gullies and *biancanas* alternate in a picturesque way, forming this weird landscape where the only vertical elements are the rows of cypresses.

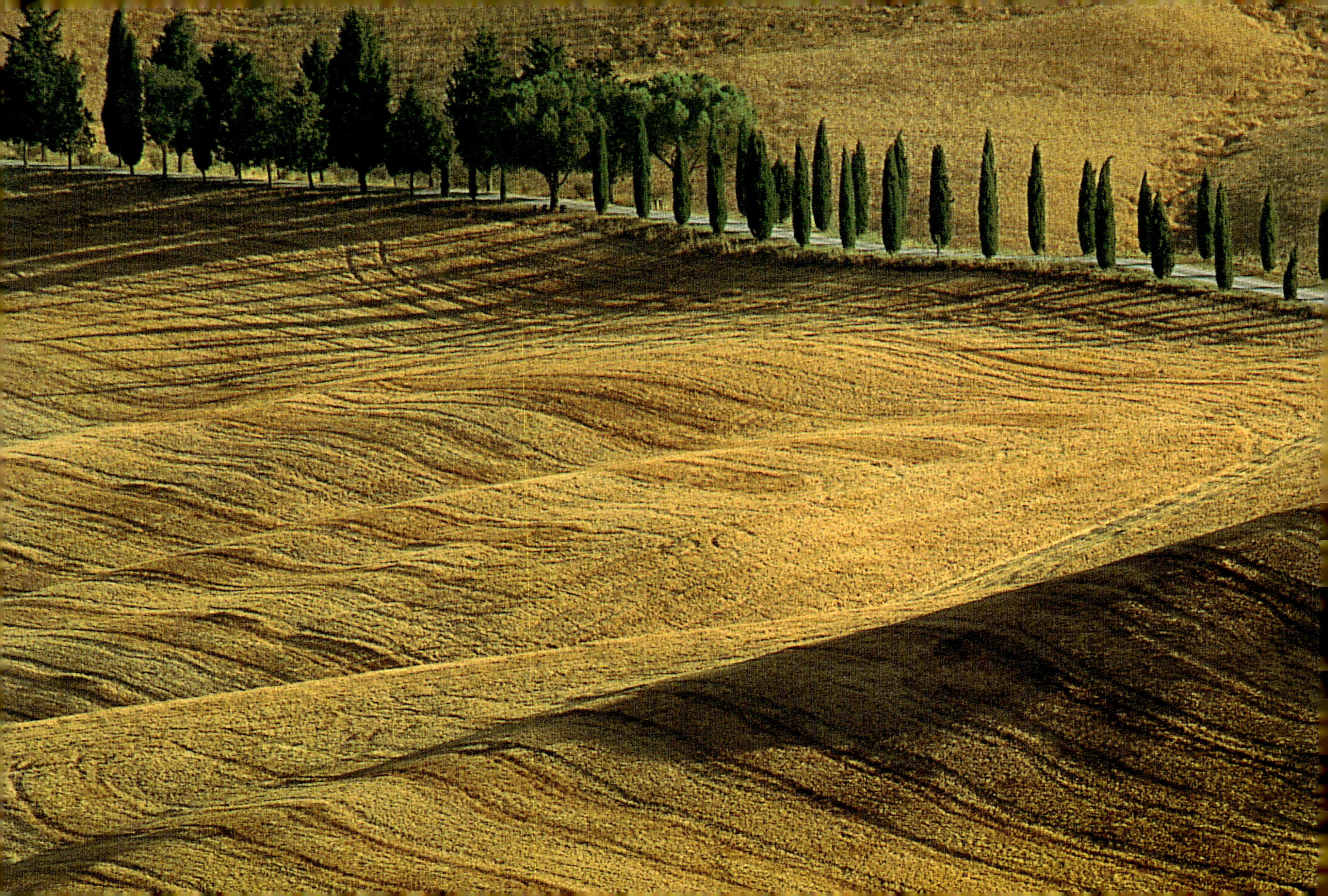

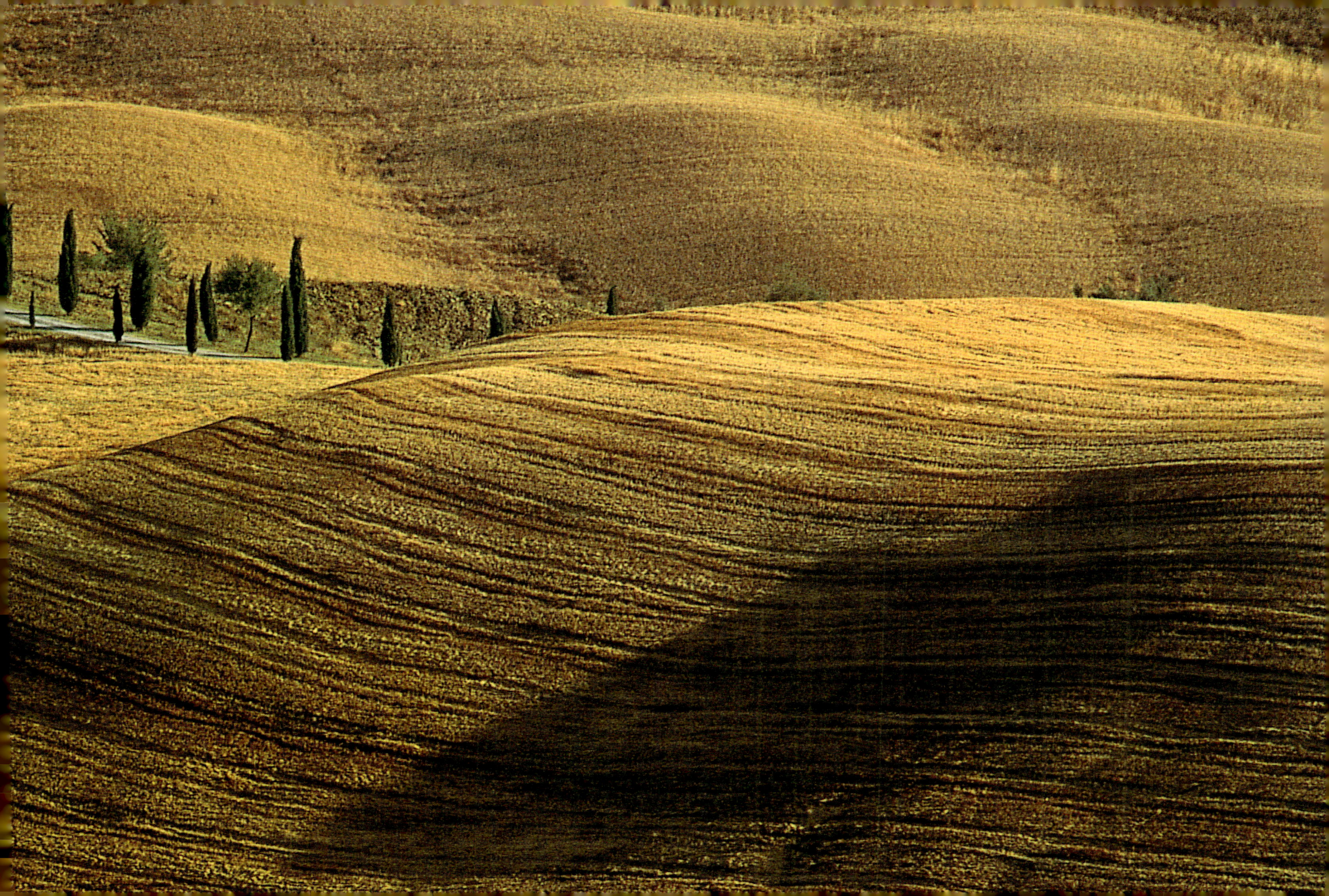

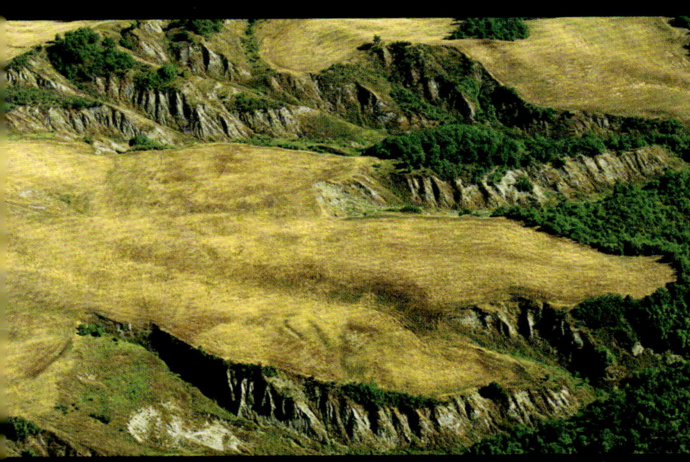

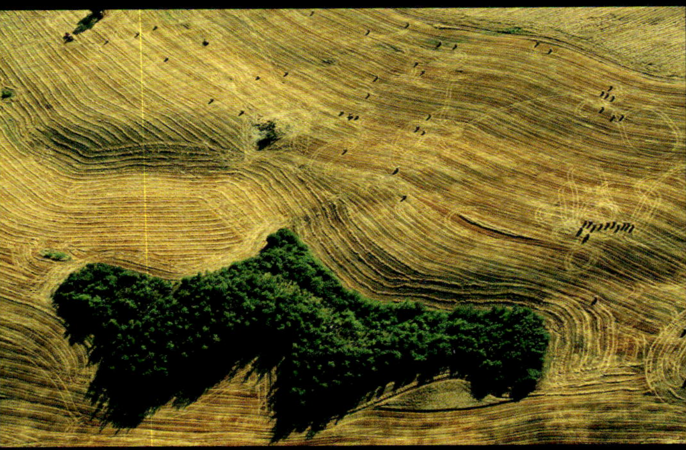

150 left Impressive erosive phenomena hollowed out the hills near Sarteano, in the picture, on a plateau between the Val d'Orcia and the Valdichiana (Siena).

150 right and 151 The Colline Metallifere are Tuscany's biggest group of hills; they extend over four provinces (Florence, Siena, Pisa and Livorno) and until the last century they were considered a precious source of minerals. Today they are more appreciated for their natural beauty and the scenery they offer.

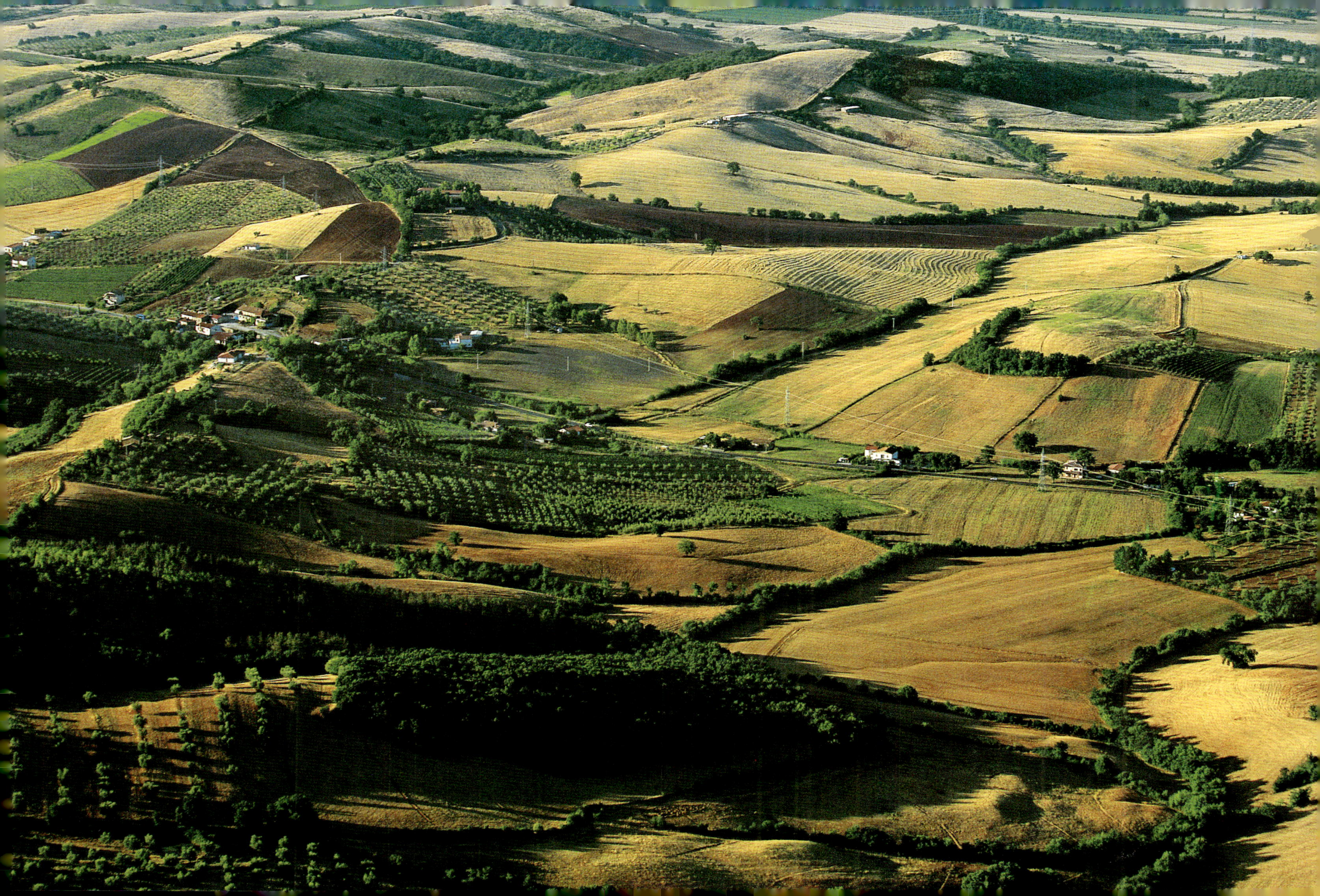

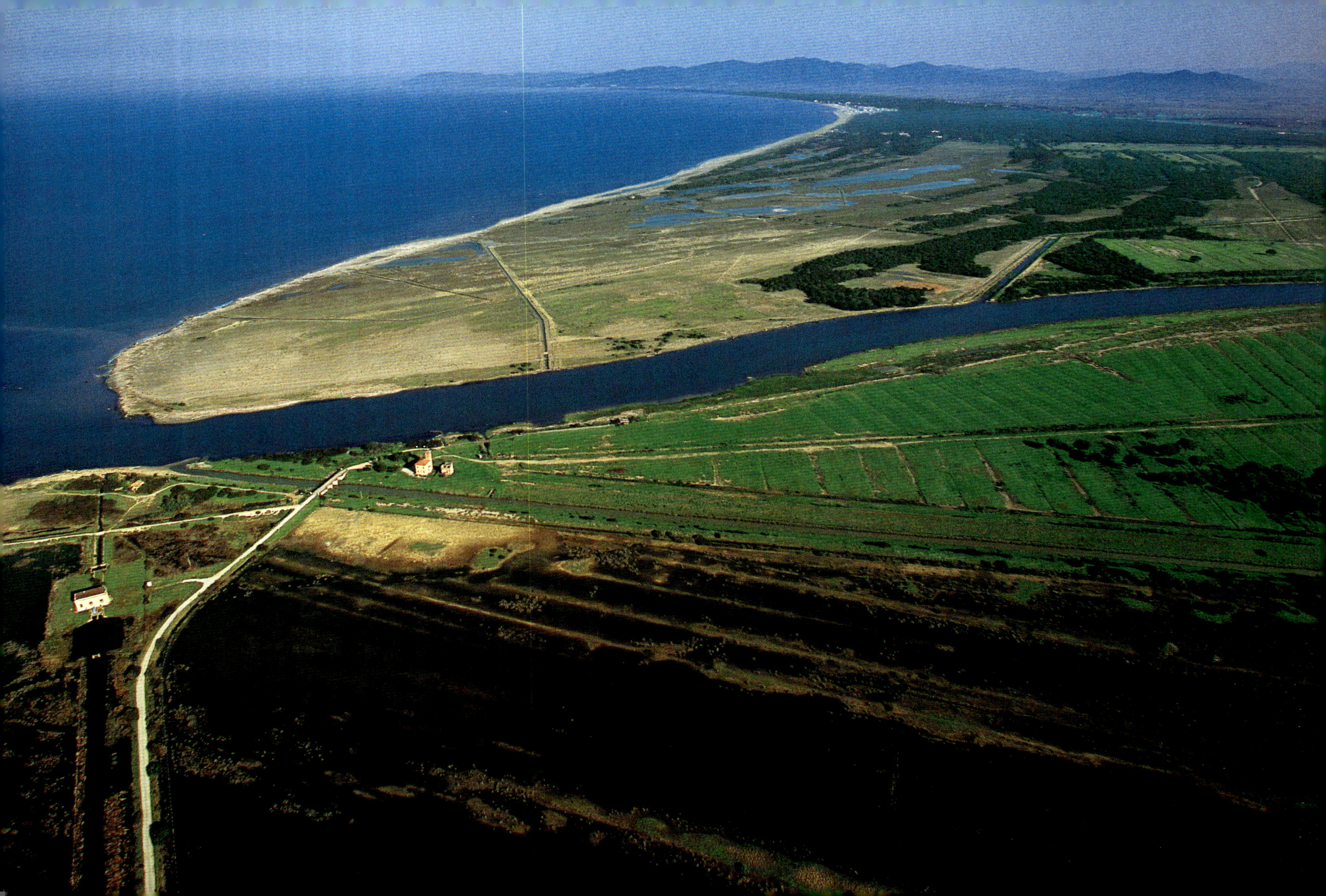

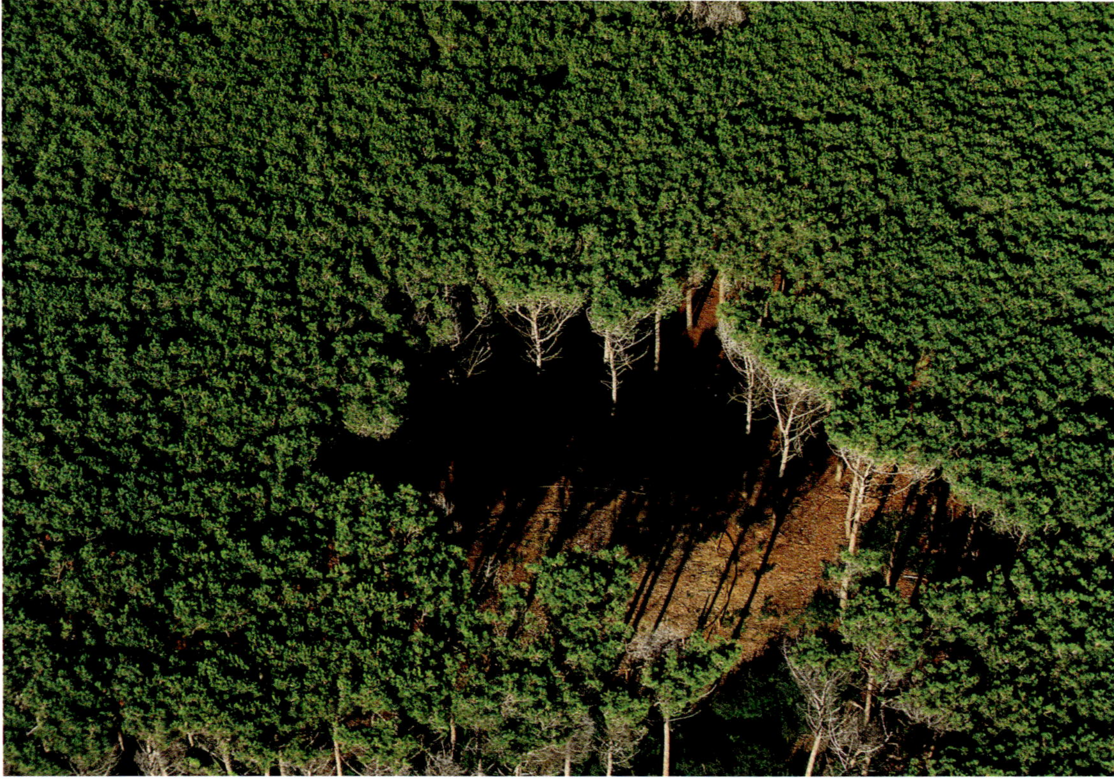

152 The mouth of the Ombrone, in the heart of the Maremma, creates a rich and unique environment where the Parco dell'Uccellina was founded. A sanctuary for endangered pecies and a locality loved by tourists from allover the world, this part of the region could provide the perfect picture postcard, showing all of Tuscany's qualities and beauties.

153 A rift in the thick forest of cluster pines reveals there could be a spring of water: we are in the Parco dell'Uccellina, the heart of the Maremma, around Grosseto.

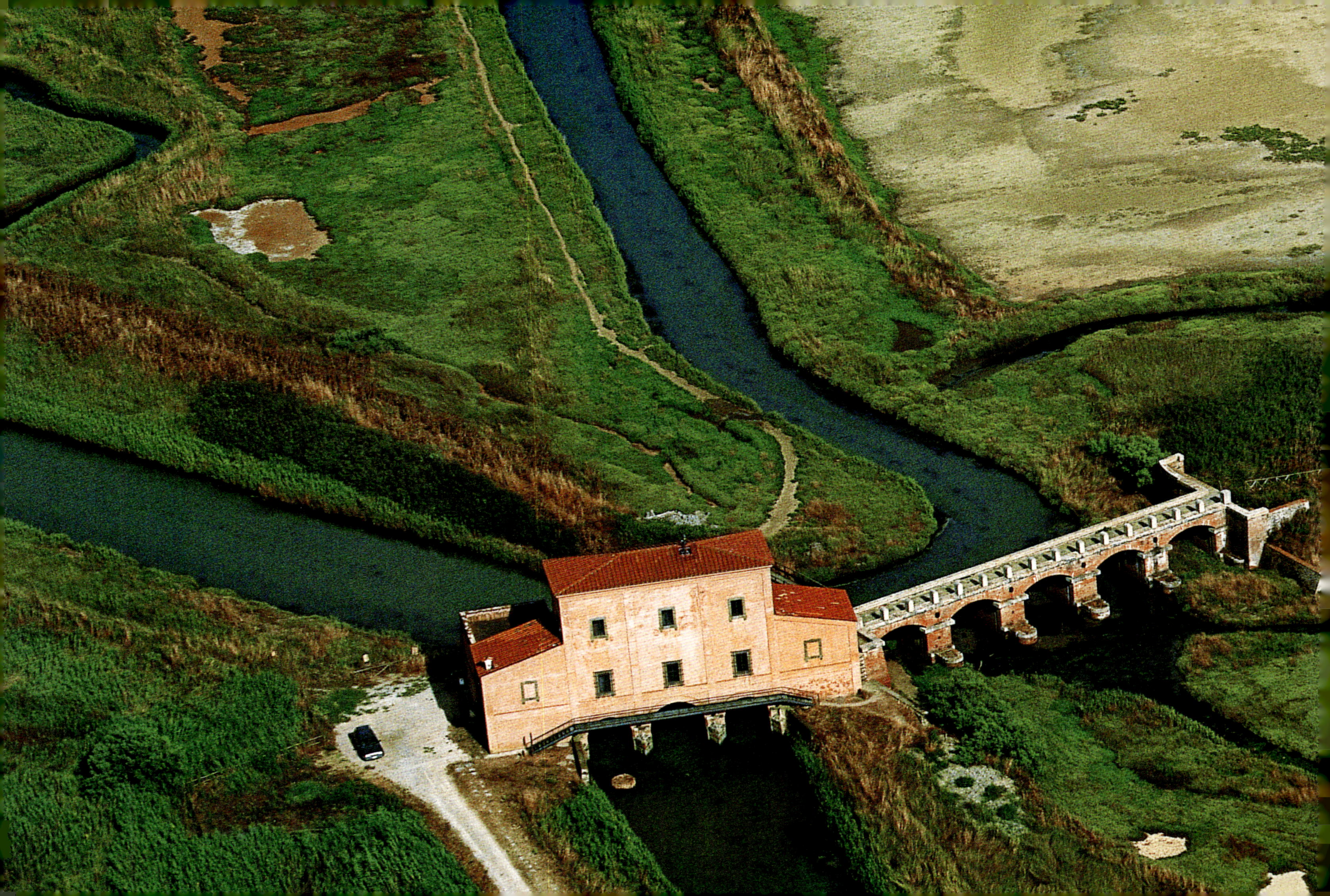

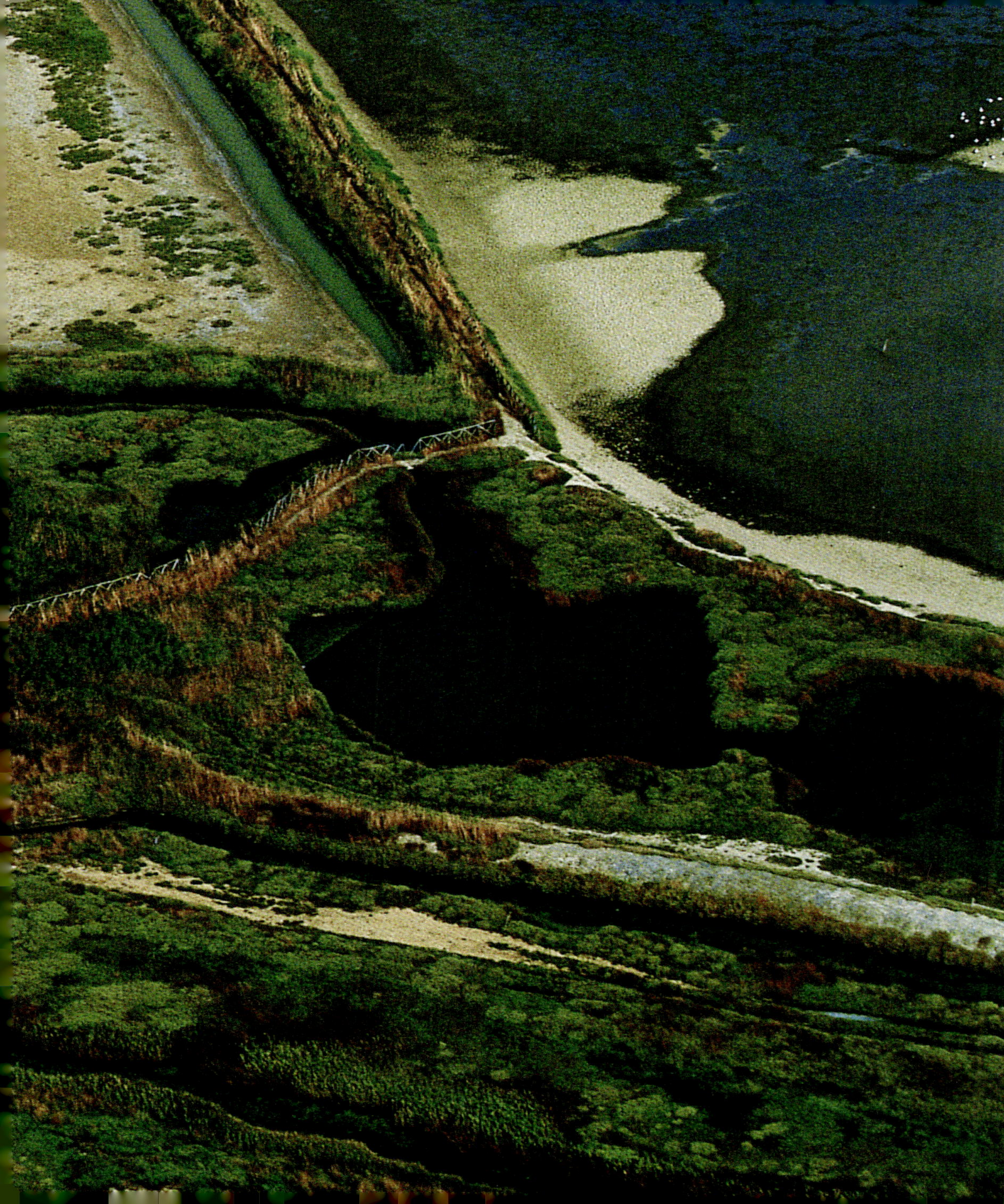

154-155 The Diaccia Botrona Wildlife Sanctuary occupies part of the plain between the city of Grosseto and the coastal resort of Castiglione della Pescaia. The protected area, a marshy valley, is what remains of the old Lake Prile (Lake Preglio), which was almost entirely drained in the 18th century by the Lorena dynasty, by means of water canalization systems. The Ximenes Red House (below) is one of the symbols of this reclamation and hosts a thematic museum on the Lorenas' drainage activities.

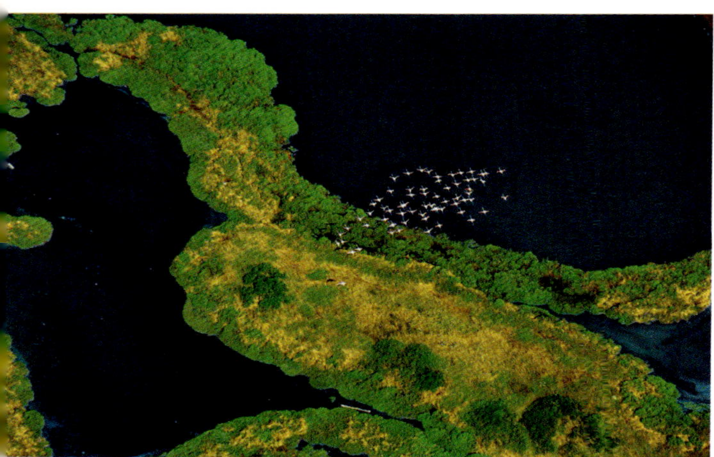

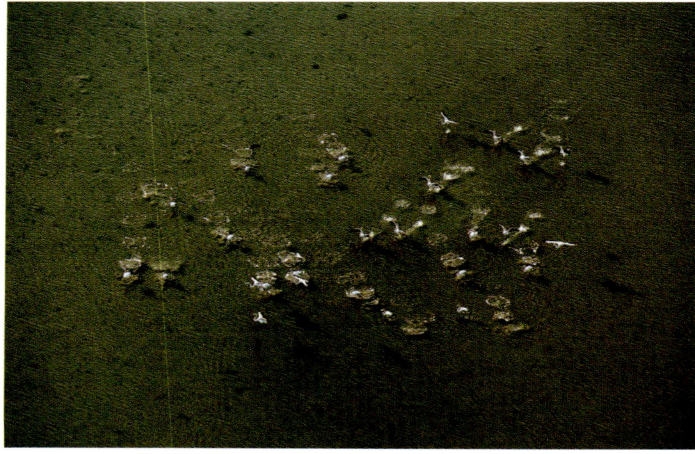

156 and 157 The Orbetello Lagoon, separated from the sea by the Giannella and Feniglia sand bars, extends along the the Maremma coast around Grosseto for approximately 10.5 sq. miles (27 sq. km). The lagoon's waters are rich in excellent fish and eels and host several species of birds, including the black-winged stilt, the great white egret and the osprey.

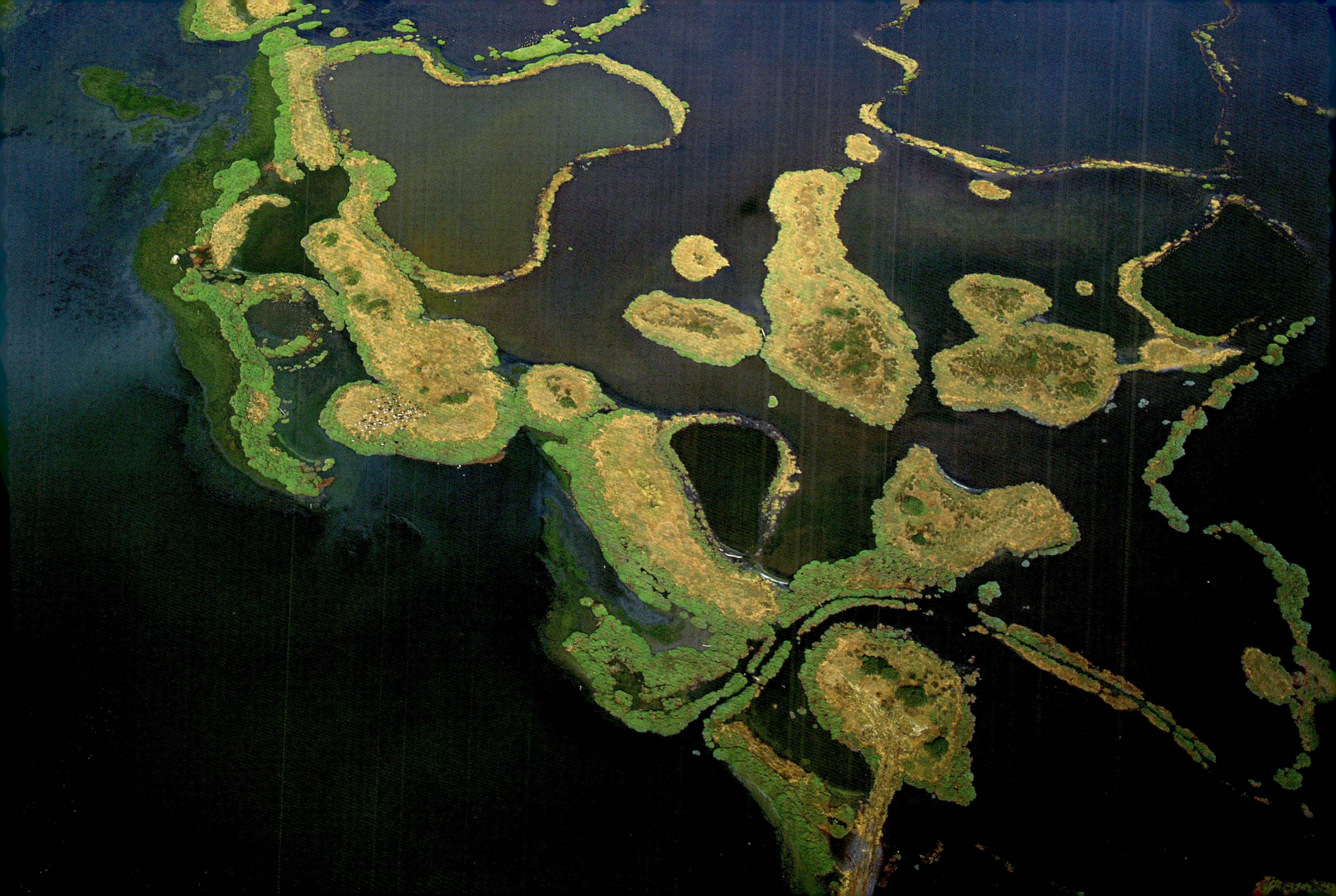

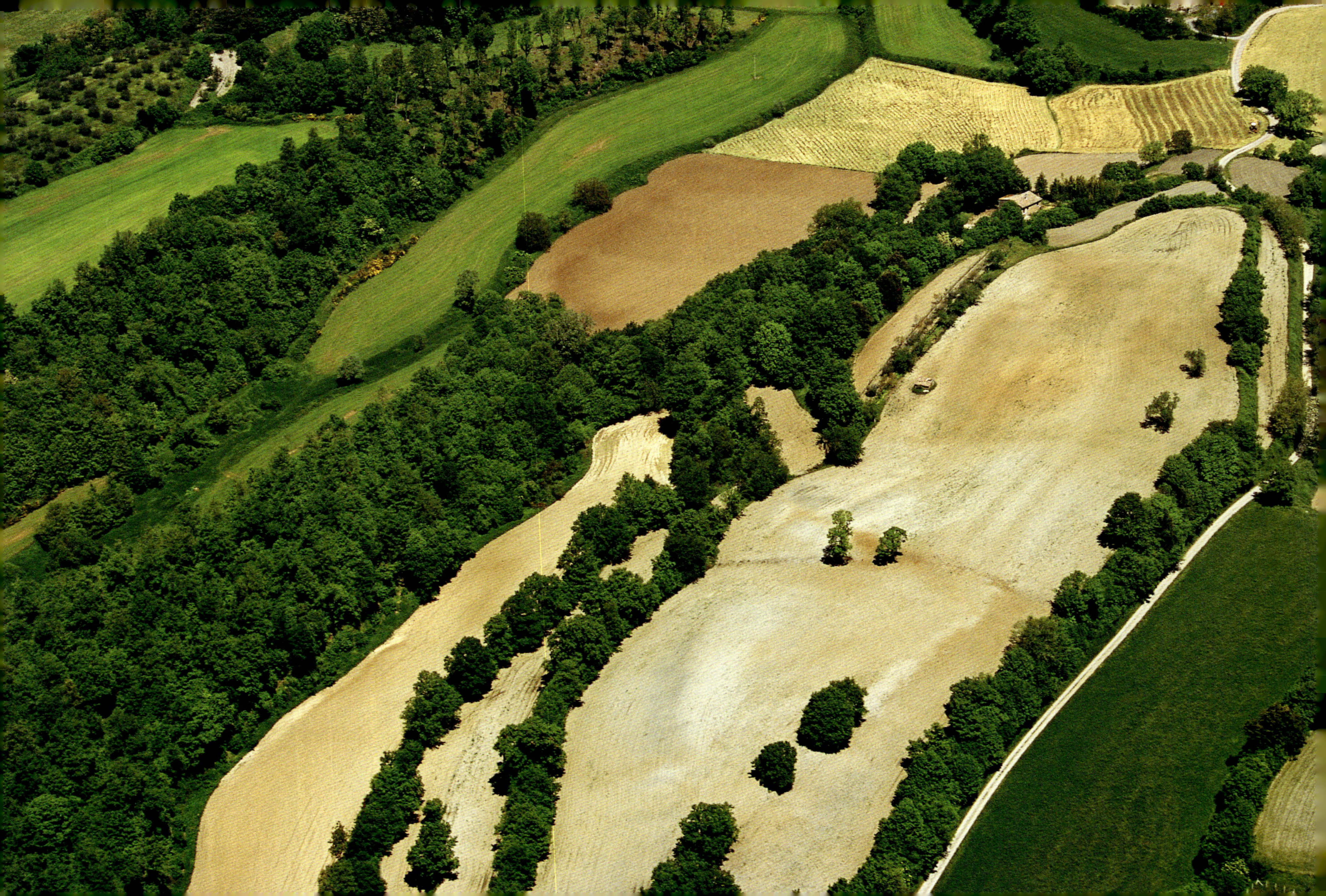

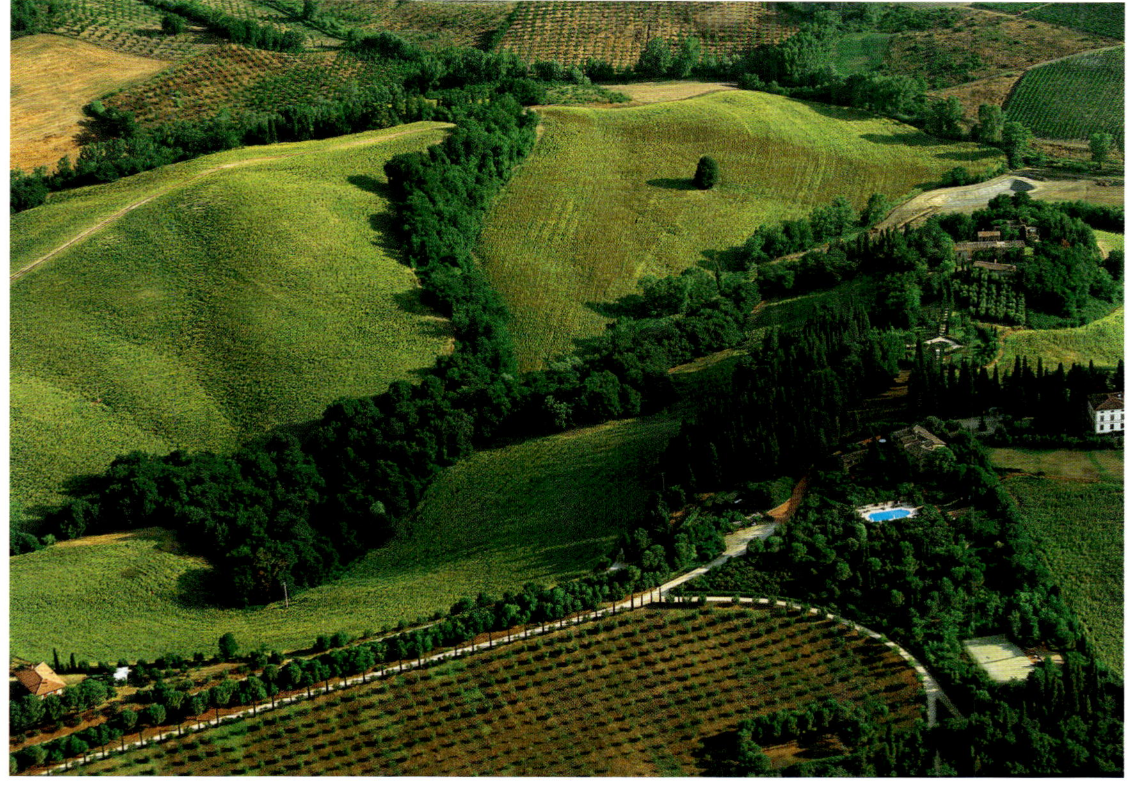

158 and 159 The more we descend toward Umbria and Lazio (left), the more the Tuscan countryside loses the neat and picturesque features of the Chianti region to become "strong and genuine," just as the Latin poets used to describe it. As we enter Umbria (right, near Orvieto), we will notice that more land is used for pasturing or is covered by copses; there is less and less intensively tilled land and the hills become increasingly steep.

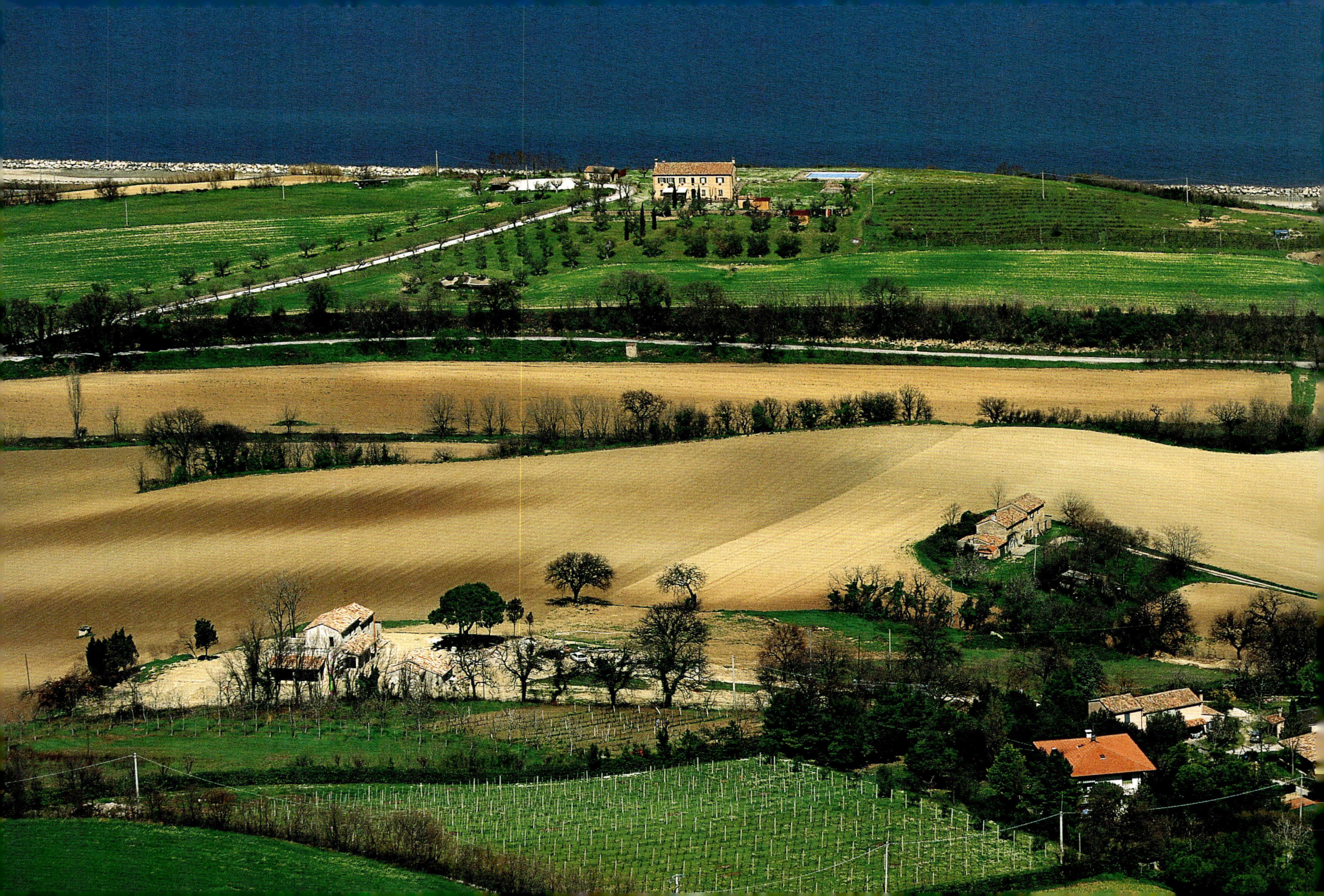

160 and 161 A number of Renaissance painters chose the scenery of the Marche as the background for various portraits; because of its mild shapes and colors they liked it better than the hills around Florence. These pictures, depicting the countryside south of Ancona, show that nothing has changed over the centuries: unsurfaced paths, farmhouses scattered on land, olive trees, cereal fields and, in the distance, the sea.

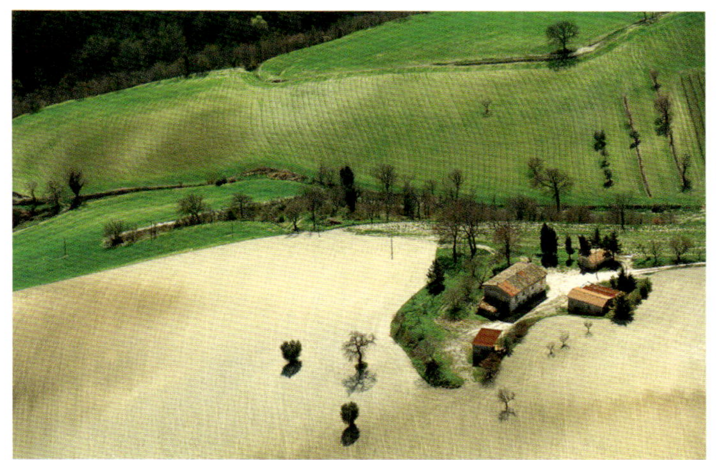

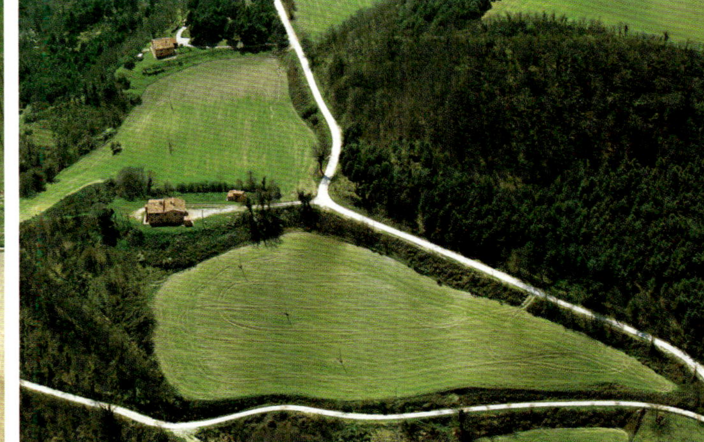

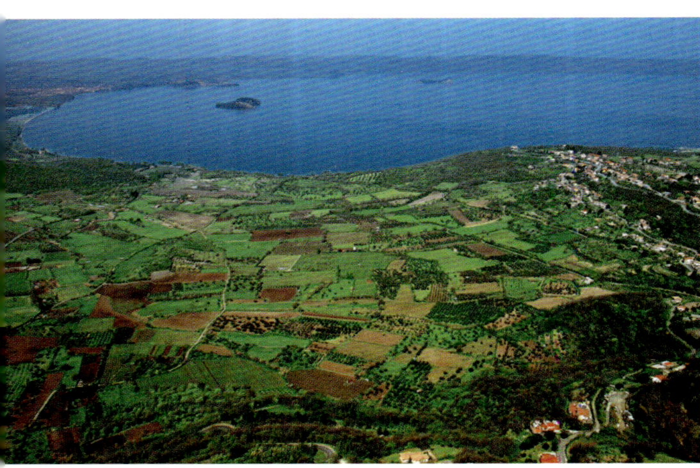

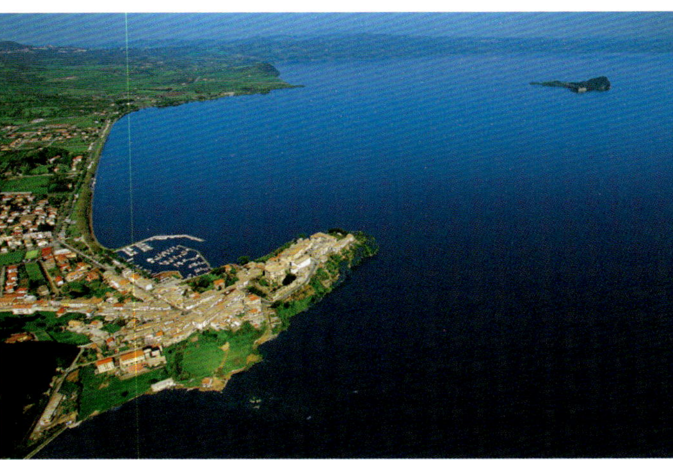

162 Lake Bolsena is one of the few large lakes in Italy where swimming is unrestrictedly permitted. The lake is near Mt Amiata (Viterbo).

163 Lake Trasimeno (Perugia), is Italy's largest non-Alpine lake and the fourth largest after Lake Como. In the middle is Isola Maggiore (in the picture), covered by a thick wooded bush of olive trees, holm oaks, pines, cypresses, and poplars.

164-165 Because of its oval shape and volcanic origin Lake Bolsena can boast only few proper promontories: Mt Bisenzio, which surrounds the Volsini Mountains to the west, Capo San Bernardino, Capodimonte peninsula (in the picture), and Punta Sant'Antonio.

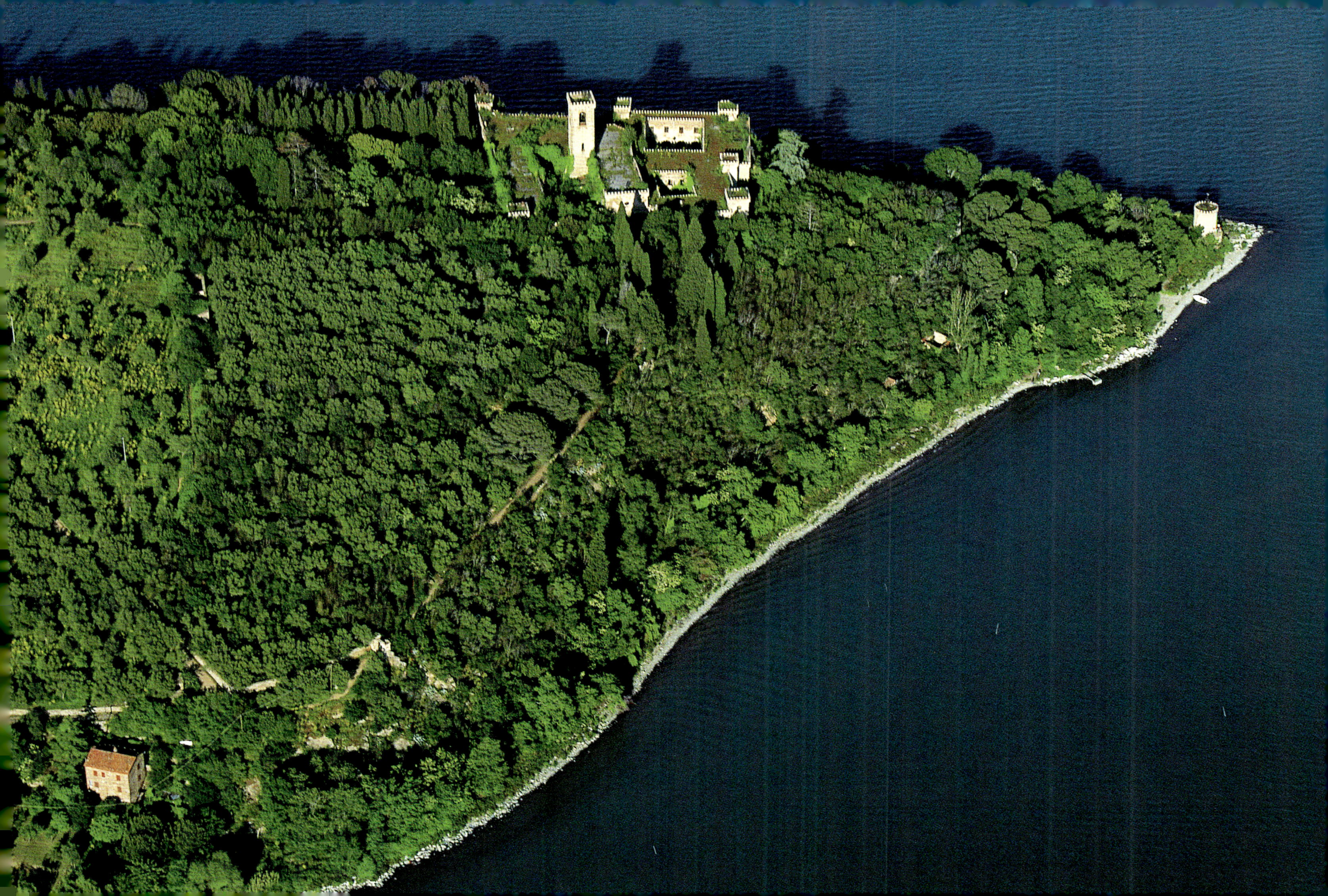

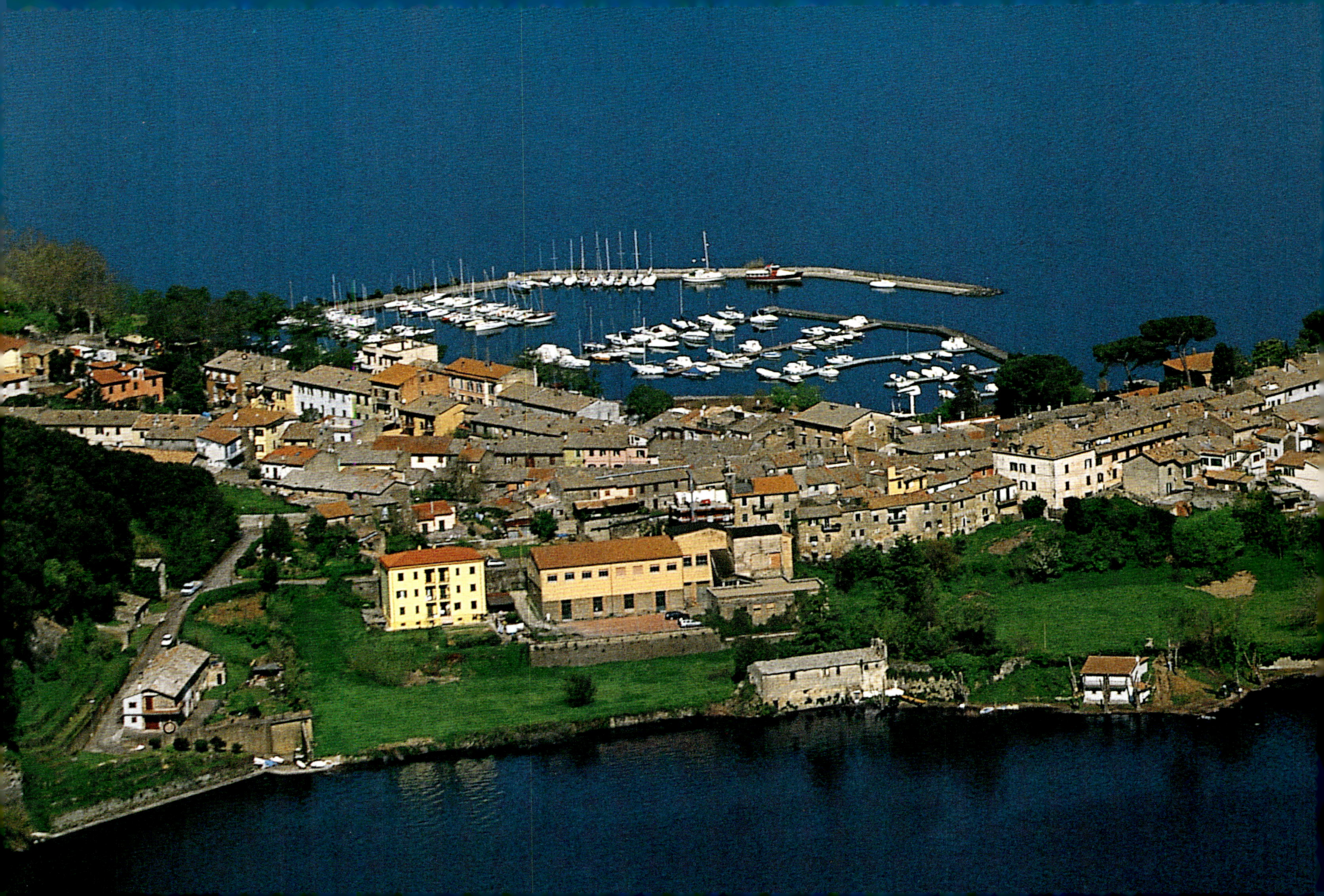

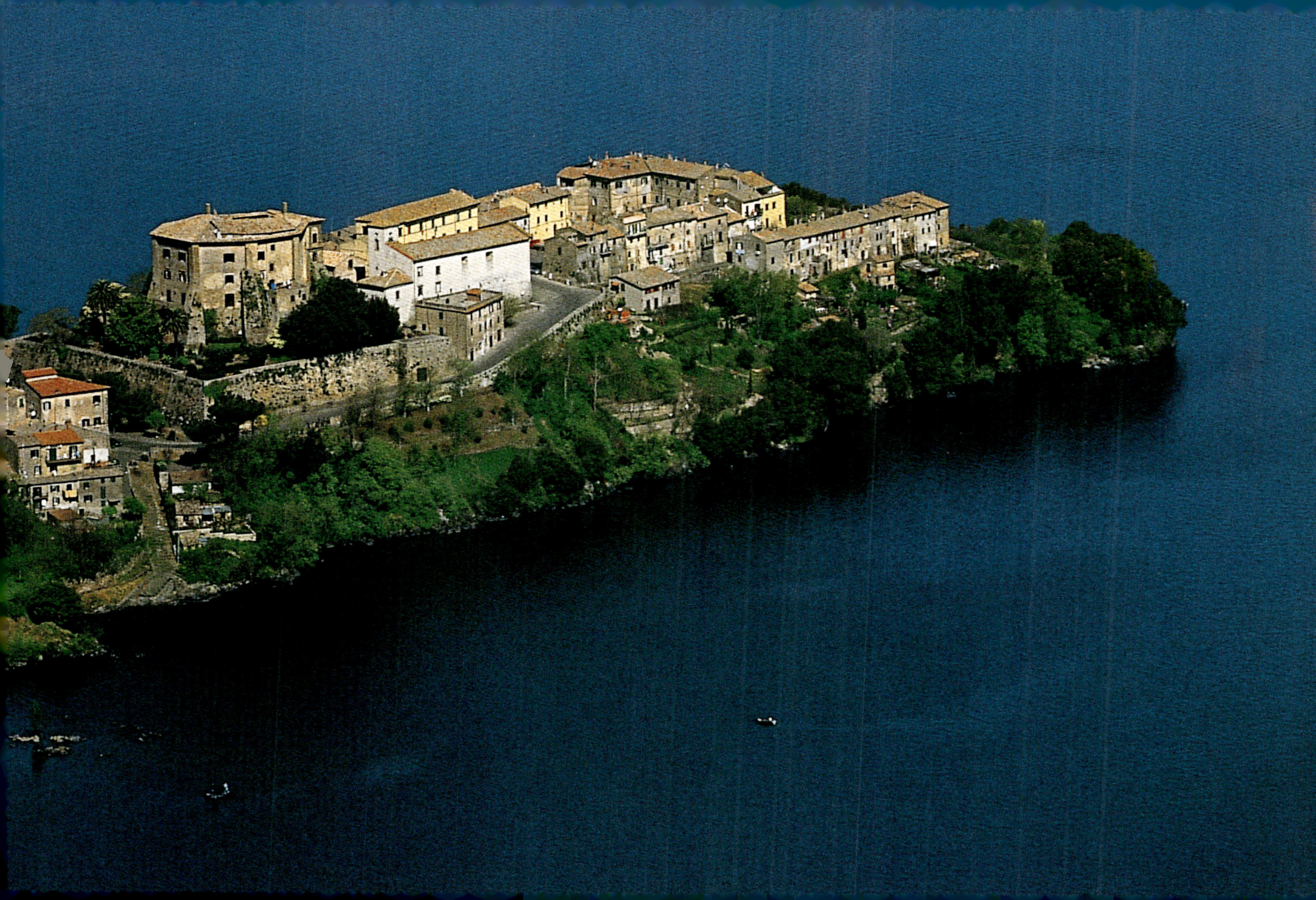

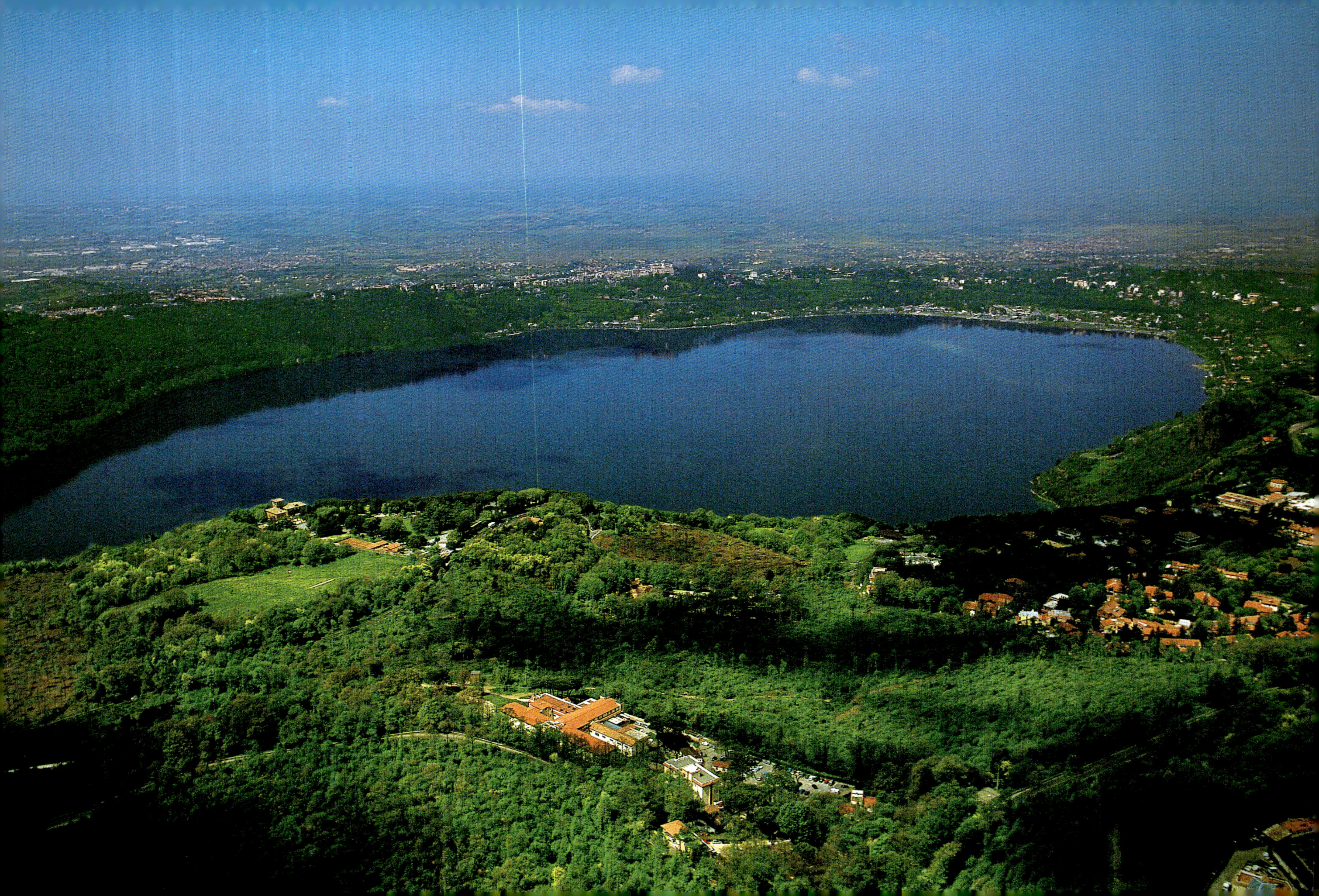

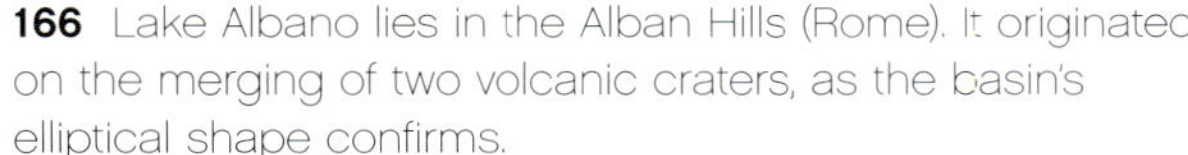

166 Lake Albano lies in the Alban Hills (Rome). It originated on the merging of two volcanic craters, as the basin's elliptical shape confirms.

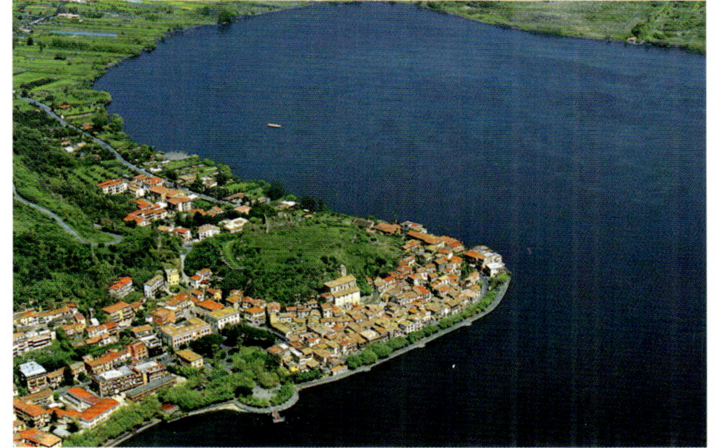

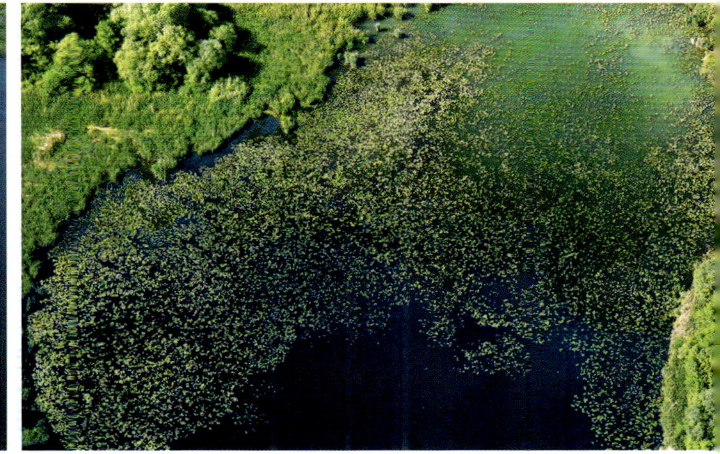

167 Lakes Bracciano (left) and Martignano (right), both of volcanic origin, lie within one of central Italy's most important wildlife sanctuaries. The park primarily protects the last stretches of the forest that originally extended from the Sabatini Mountains to the Tyrrhenian Sea.

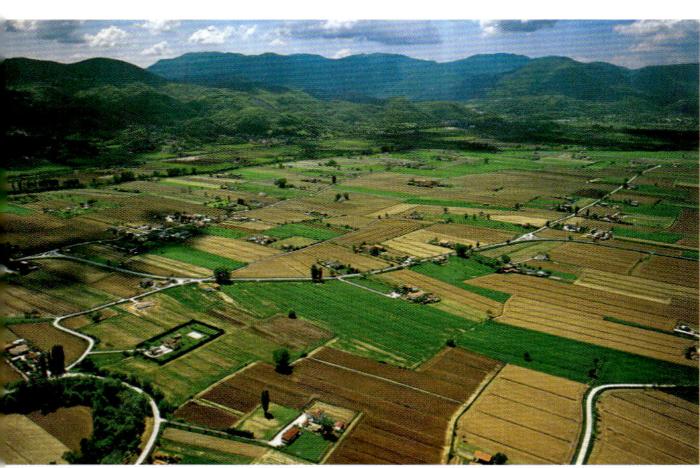

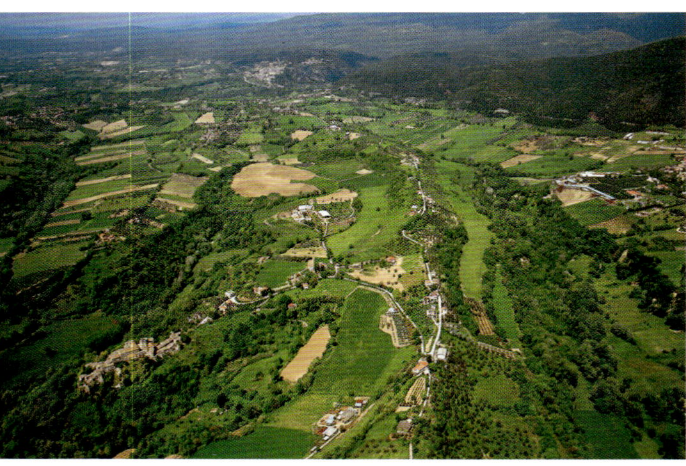

168 The Sabina, the countryside around Rieti, commonly considered the geographical center of Italy, is flat and rich in crops (left); as the country becomes more hilly, the fields are covered by thick woods, penetrating the Velino Valley (right) and proceeding north toward the Marmore Falls.

169 The southern Sabina area, from Rieti to the Salto and Turano lakes, is a verdant strip of mild mountains and hills which are almost uninhabited, except by wild boars and raptorial animals.

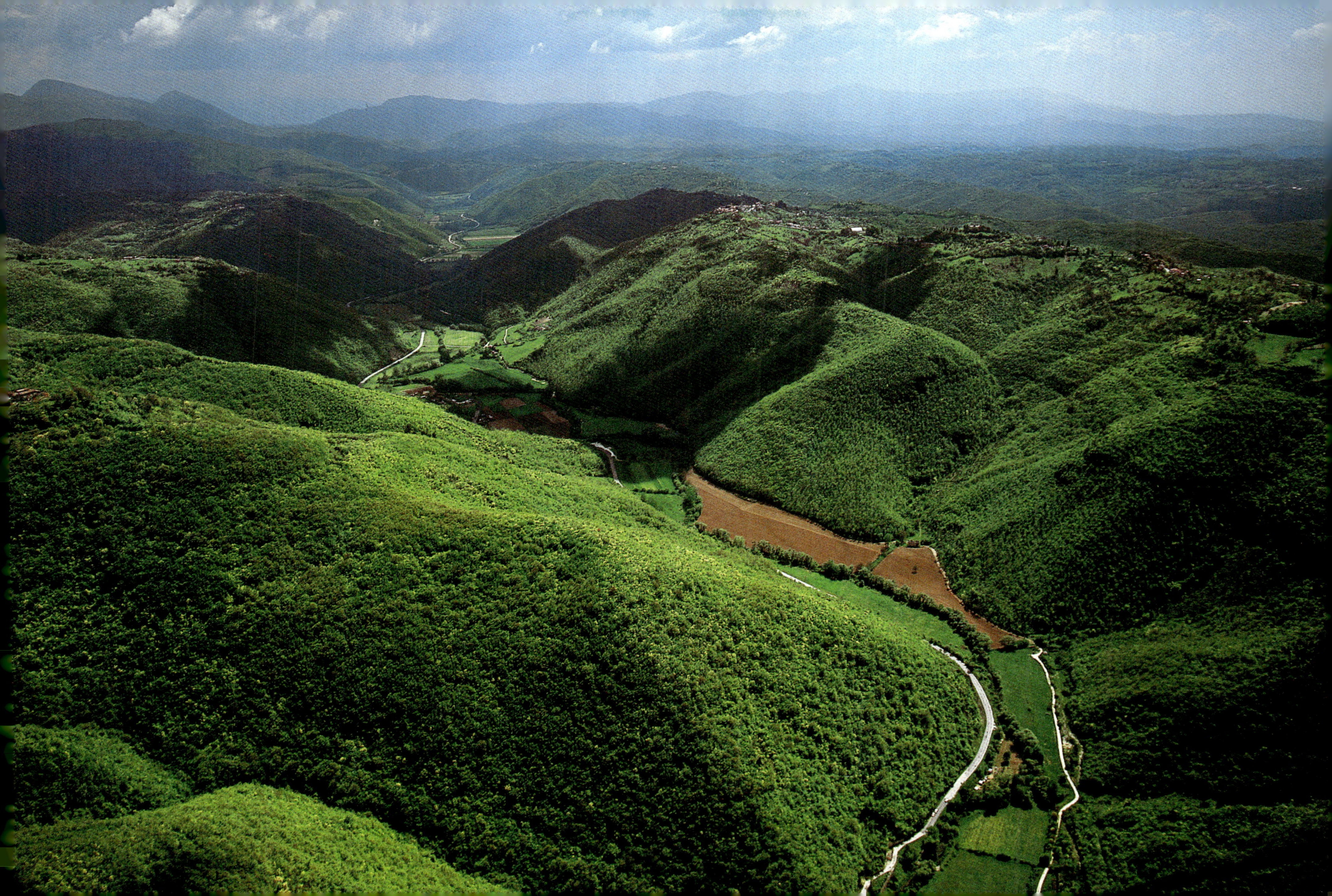

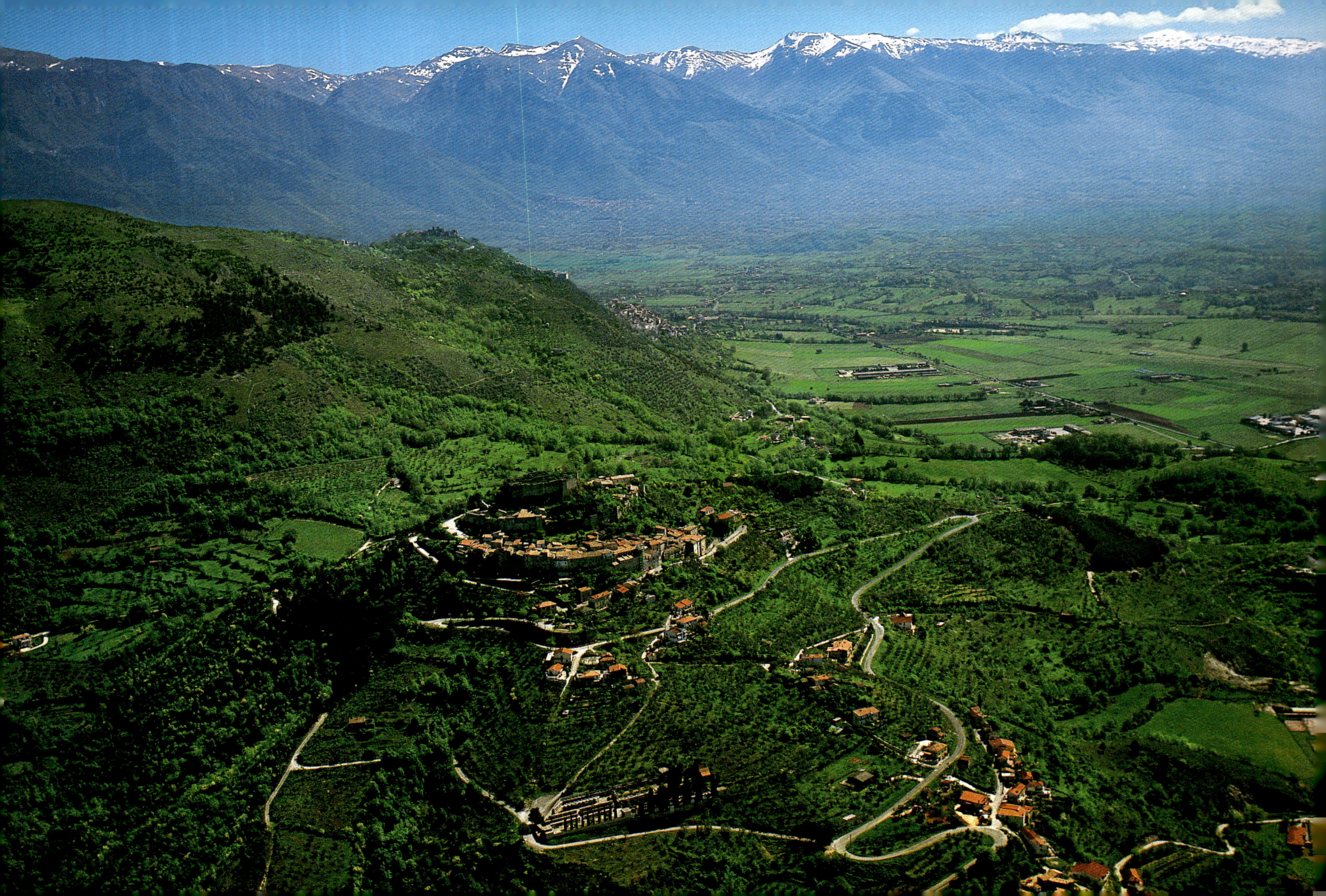

170-171 Comino Valley (Frosinone), is very close to the Abruzzi Apennines: it is a wide, regular basin, mostly surrounded by mountains, and extends over a historically seismic zone. In the post-WW II decades, many inhabitants left. Today the area is big attraction for visitors who love hiking and are looking for pristine sites.

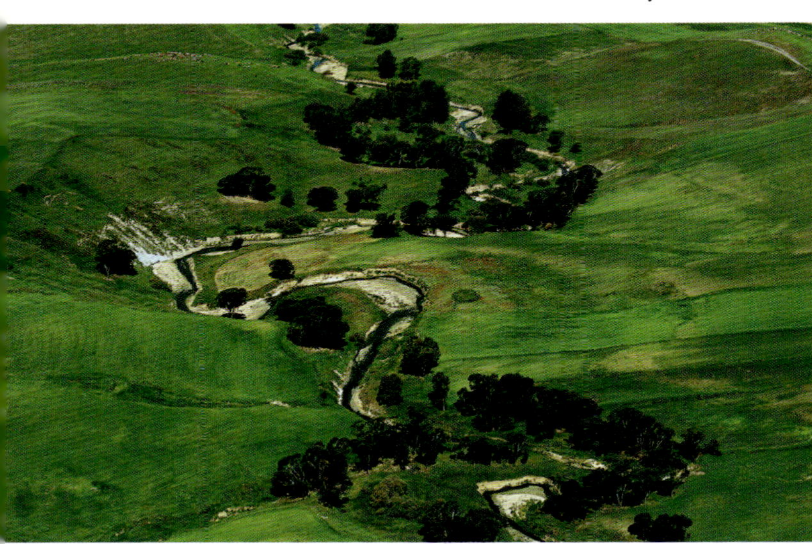

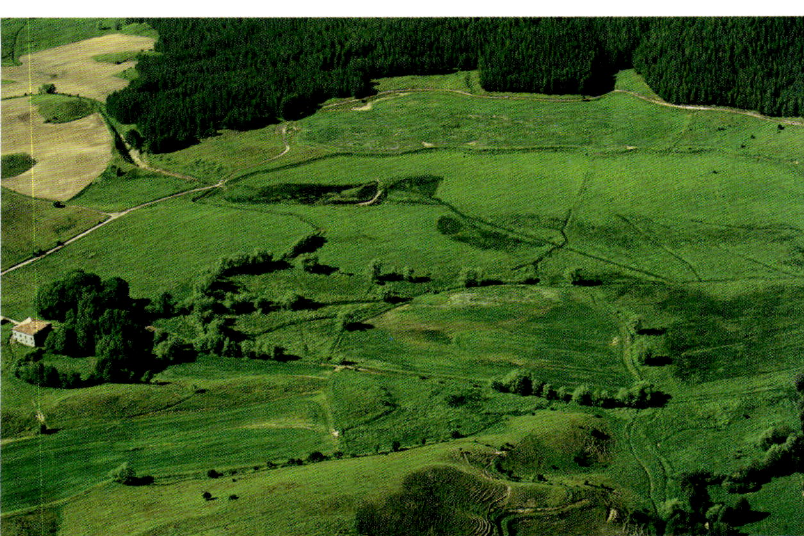

LANDSCAPES OF THE SOUTH

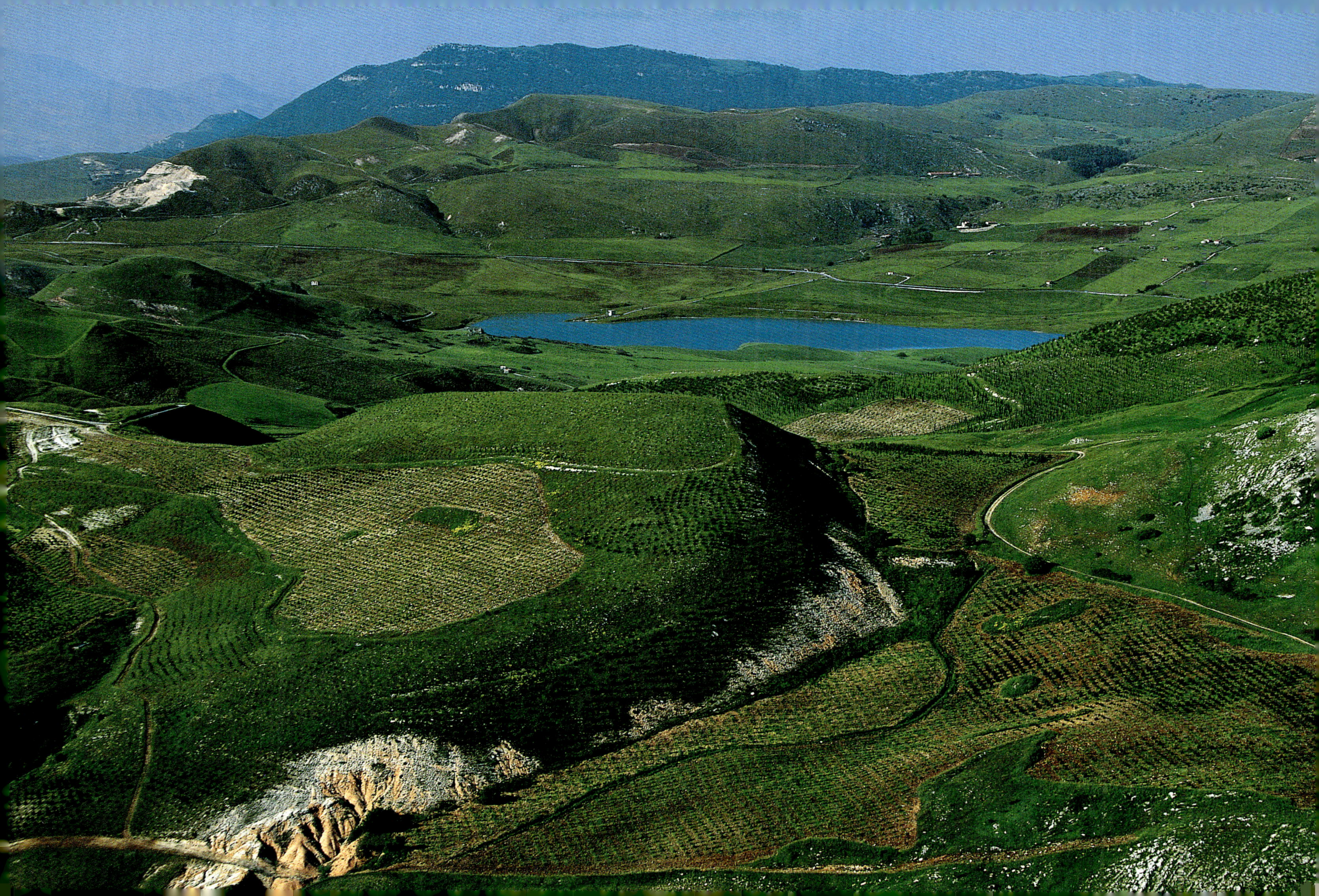

According to Dante, the south of Italy begins at the Maremma, the part of Tuscany that extends from Cecina to Corneto (Tarquinia). After World War II, many of the large agricultural estates disappeared, and in their place were created collective properties called Università Agrarie, which continued the traditional activities of raising animals and growing timber. As a consequence, although the villages have grown and a few roads now traverse areas once only accessible by horse, the region preserves its untamed appearance, featuring vast forests of oak alternating with rocky pastures scattered with enormous oak trees and wild prickly pear trees that have vibrant white blossoms in March and April. The coastal plains that still have luxuriant dune forests gradually change to a gently rolling land of modest elevation, much of which is covered by woods, olive groves, and vineyards. Wide valleys unfold among these areas, marked by the lazy meanderings of the Albegna, Fiora, and Ombrone rivers, which all flow toward the Tyrrhenian Sea. Farther inland and just reaching elevations of 3280 ft (1000 m) are the mountains, with forests of oak and beech. A few farmhouses, which are made of masonry in the zones of reclaimed land, and of stone in the hilly regions, are visible on the usually enormous farm properties. The villages, located in sunny, dominant positions, are built from the same stone on which they stand.

The region still has immense wooded areas where it is possible to walk for an entire day, and even become lost; torrents that turn into rivers without suffering the intrusion of dams, wharfs, and canals; cliffs that not even the most expert rock climbers would dare climb; vast agricultural areas cultivated in the old-fashioned way, where predatory birds make their nests and quails sing among the fields of grain; internationally important wetlands; and beaches of the finest sand that stretch for miles without umbrellas, bathing establishments, parking areas or roads. Today, the landscape is striking for its vastness. From the heights behind Capalbio, Orbetello and Grosseto one can see the cultivated plains in severe geometrical patterns that lie below. These are the same plains that until recently were basins where the muddy waters from ditches and torrents overflowing with rainwater would accumulate and stagnate. On the low sandy beach, for miles there is no promontory or shelter where a secure landing can be constructed. People avoided living in this "unhealthy" area where the "unwholesome" air of the swamps claimed lives.

172 left The Molise region offers numerous glimpses of the countryside in its traditional form, where short, practically dry streams cross the undulating landscape.

172 right Pollino National Park (the view is from Basilicata), located between Basilicata and Calabria, is Italy's largest natural park.

173 The Agrigento region contains the Sicanian Mountains, whose highest peaks are Rocca Busambra and Mt Cammarata.

175 The Posta Fibreno Nature Reserve extends across 1000 acres (400 hectares) in Frosinone province; it offers splendid panoramas like this one.

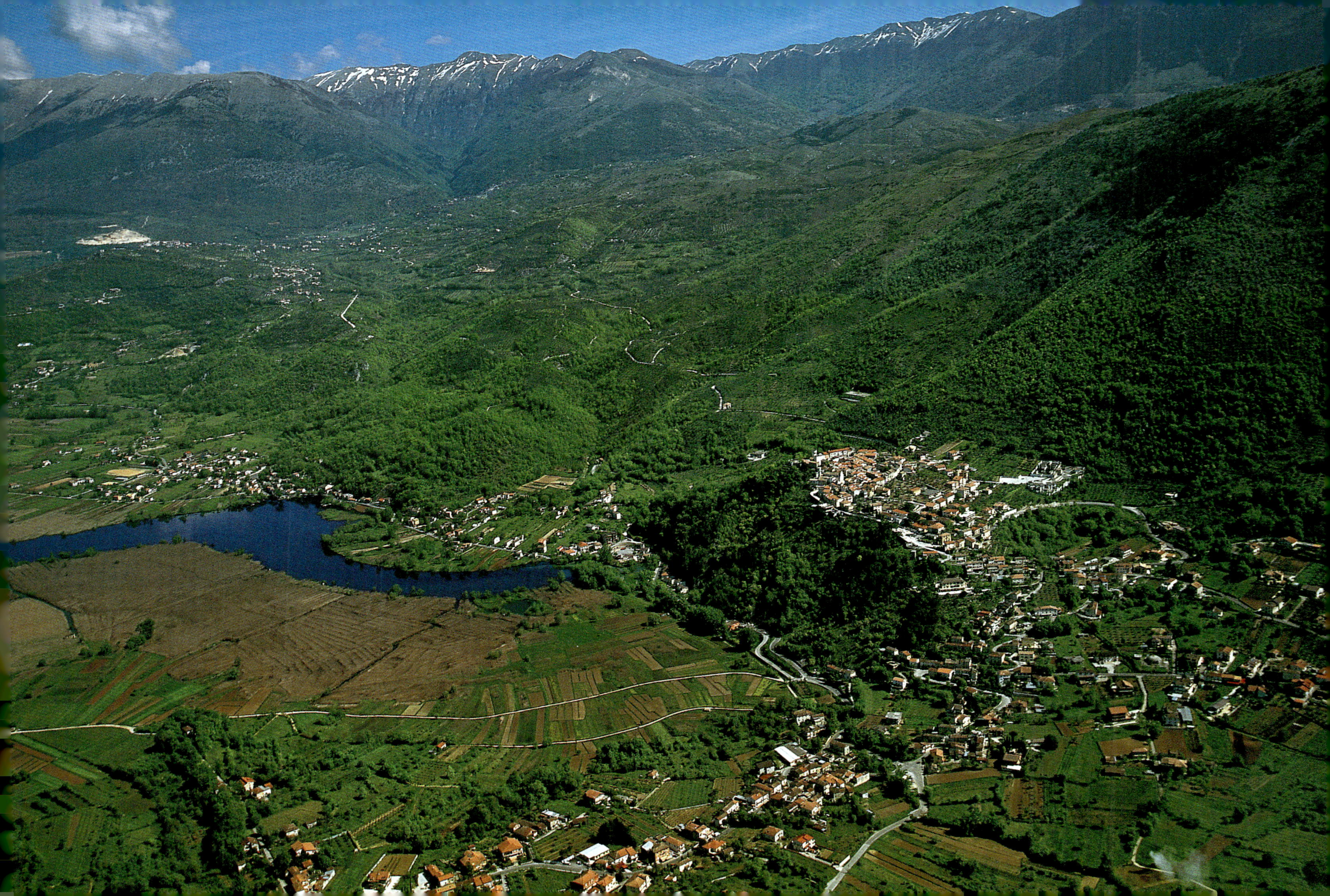

The heart of the Maremma is the Uccellina mountain range, a long chain of green hills, forests, and scrub, whose peaks are surmounted by the square silhouettes of ancient stone towers that are visible from the Via Aurelia, which runs alongside the mountains heading toward Grosseto. Next to the hills, the cliffs end in an almost sheer drop to the sea, and are covered by an impenetrable growth of thorny, forbidding brush. Then, as the heights give way to the Ombrone plains toward Grosseto, the elevation decreases, making the coast more accessible; it is here that the beaches of fine sand begin, enclosed from behind not by the usual houses and noisy seaside streets, but by thick pine forests, fragrant with resin, where saltwater ponds lie.

Heading south, the Via Casilina leaves one of the most heavily developed parts of the metropolitan area and reaches Ciociaria, the gentle agricultural heart of the province of Frosinone where nature, art and culture still find a way to co-exist in the small villages and the agricultural lands of the high mountains. For nature lovers, this area is also the access point for two important nature reserves that feature lakeside scenery. The ancient cities of Fregellae and Fabriateria Nova and San Giovanni Incarico Lake and the Lake Canterno Nature Reserve they all attract many visitors. Located at the base of the Ernici Mountains, not for from the noted Trisulti Abbey, this lake is surrounded by oak forests and has numerous aquatic birds. The heart of the Ciociaria region, which contains important urban

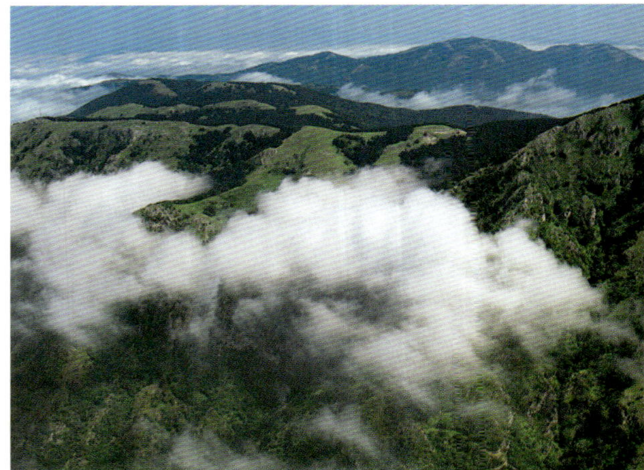

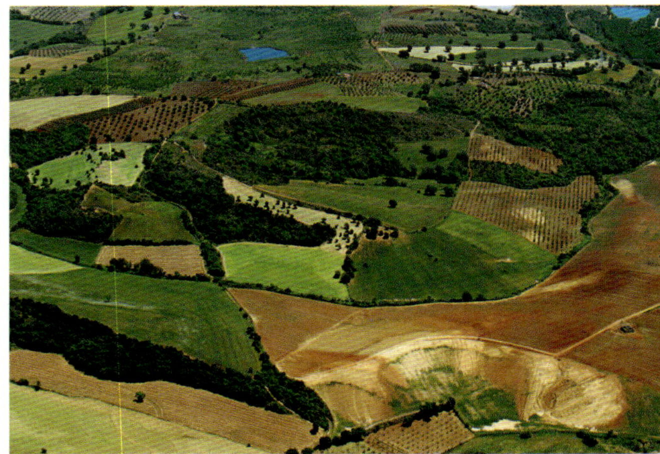

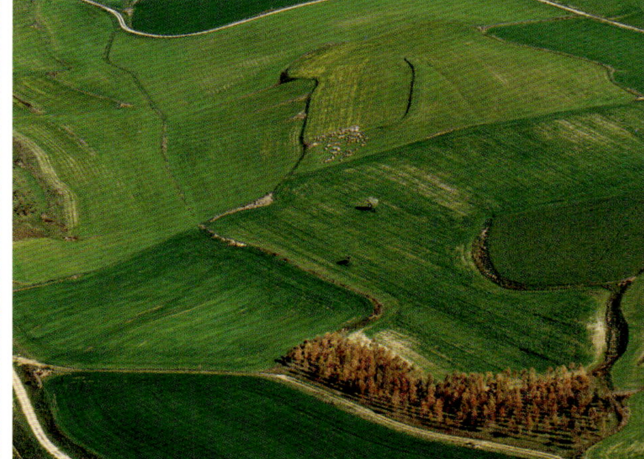

176 left Mt Taburno is a limestone mountain in the Campanian Apennines. From the mountain's base flow the Fizzo Spring; they at one time provided water for the cascade in the Royal Garden at Caserta Palace.

centers such as Fiuggi and Anagni, is Posta Fibreno Lake with its crystal clear waters inhabited by trout and another fish endemic to the region, a type of carp found in the Fibreno and the Comino Valley. This valley is a wedge-shaped area that extends from Ciociaria toward Abruzzo and constitutes the Lazio portion of the large, historical national park that was created in 1922 to preserve the territory of bears, wolves, chamois, and eagles that still populate the rocky areas and woods of maple and beech.

The road from Sora, passing Alvito and then San Donato Val Comino, ascends through woods and small cultivated fields, entering ever farther into the mountains, and finally reaches small stone villages that overlook the western slopes of the Meta and Mainarde Mountains. This realm of sheep farming is evidenced by the almost complete absence of forests, which were progressively eliminated to supply firewood and to make room for the pastures that were necessary to support growing flocks.

The mountains were radically transformed over the centuries and this portion of the Apennines became an integral part of the transhumance system that extends from Abruzzo to Apulia.

Until the 1960's, the traditional area for wintering the Apennine herds was the Foggia Plateau, the largest plain in southern Italy. Its 125,000 acres (50,000 hectares) of pastureland have subsequently been replaced by grain cultivation. The Foggia Plateau, at one time the bottom of an ancient sea, now connects the limestone promontory of Gargano to the rest of the peninsula, yet still separates it from the mountains of the Daunian Apennines. Until the second half of the 20th century, the plateau, characterized in the higher regions by the urban centers of Lucera and Ascoli Satriano and in the lower coastal regions by Manfredonia, Zapponeta, Trinitapoli and others, was a large expanse of meadows similar to the steppes of Eastern Europe; it was an expanse of grass that was green in spring, yellow in summer, and brown in winter, that rippled in the breeze like the liquid surface of the sea or a lake, punctuated by the thousands of colors of beautiful wildflowers such as cornflowers, daisies, sage, buttercups, lupin, and narcissus. However, on the plateau there are still arid meadows that, being unsuitable for any use other than pastureland for sheep, have preserved the same fascination as the American prairies, the African savannas or the Asian steppes. It rains very little in these areas, in fact so little that the Foggia Plateau is as dry as Lampedusa Island or the inland areas of Tunisia.

176 center The countryside of Saracena (Cosenza) is known for its strong, sweet muscat which is produced from the grapes cultivated here, and also for its renowned olive oil.

176 right The Orroli region (Cagliari), famous as home to some of Sardinia's most important traditional buildings (the *nuraghe*), is verdant and enjoys an abundance of water whose supply is ensured by one of the two Flumendosa dams and the Mulargia dam.

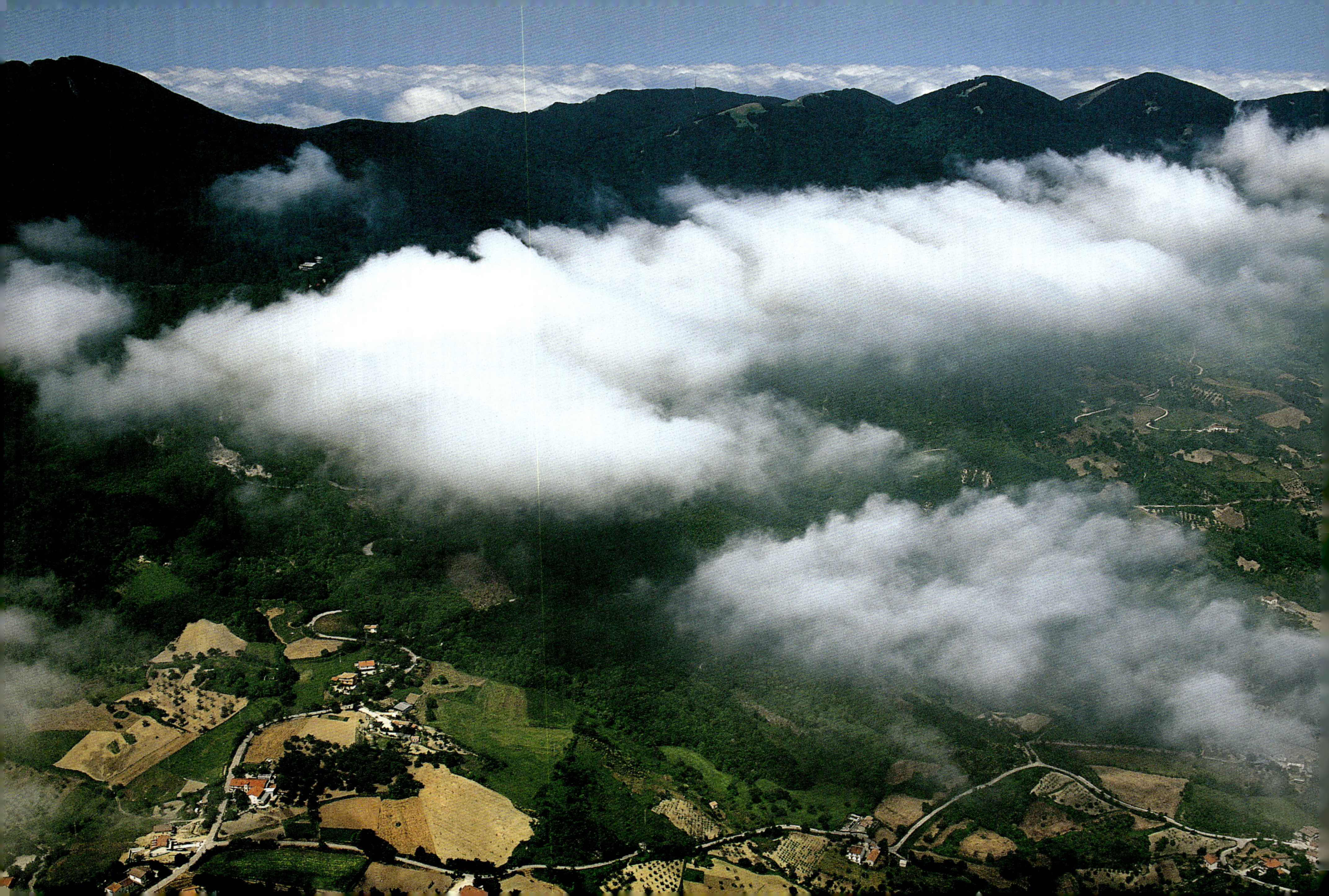

Sicily is one of the Italian regions that has been most changed by human activity. Once covered by a thick forest of oak and holm oak, the island was deforested as early as the Roman Period in order to create Italy's granary. It thereby became a stark territory used primarily for growing grain, except in the less accessible mountain and coastal regions where forests and scrub survived and where man has planted crops on the small areas of level ground, creating a unique landscape of gardens, small orchards, vineyards and fields that are bordered by a series of dry stone walls and rows of prickly pear trees. The predominant landscape features are the dark green of the citrus fruit trees, the blue of the sea, and the white of the rocky spurs that loom over the coast from the interior. Such is the beautiful landscape of the Conca d'Oro, which perfumes the air with orange blossoms and lies sleepily under the hot sun of the Sicilian summer. The rivers, insubstantial and unreliable, are actually dry riverbeds for much of the year.

Just as the heart of Sicily is characterized by the Conca d'Oro, Sardinia too is best characterized by a particular region, that of Barbagia, which is still based on a pastoral economy and an archaic sheep-grazing culture.

Sardinia is considered to be a haven for Mediterranean nature. Sparsely populated, mountainous and fairly inaccessible, it has preserved ancient wooded and pastoral landscapes. Sardinia comprises a series of granite and sometimes limestone elevations (particularly in the areas of Mt Albo and the Gennargentu Mountains) that alternate with large forests of holm oak and English oak, and with smaller undulations of granite covered in a blanket of low scrub that is made even more tangled by recurring fires. The hills and mountains are interrupted by the high plains and also wide plains, which are used for extensive agriculture and, more importantly, as pastureland for the herds. Included among these are the Giara Plateaus, the most renowned of which is the Gesturi Plateau because it is inhabited by a herd of wild horses that are unique in the world, a breed that is on its way to extinction.

Sardinia's ancient interior is composed of granite, strong yet also delicate, that emerges from a blanket of myrtle and broom. The sea, wind, and rain have, over time, shaped strange figures towering amidst the vegetation that gradually covers them. This represents the intimate character of the Sardinia far from the sea, ancient and austere.

Silent reminders of a past characterized by both hard work and celebration are the sheepfolds, the ancient pens where sheep were shorn to collect their valuable wool, which mothers gave as dowries to their daughters who were to marry.

178 The Taburno-Camposauro Regional Park protects wide expanses of Mediterranean scrub, which has been destroyed in other areas by the encroachment of crops. In this region orchards, vineyards and olive groves co-exist with pine, beech, oak and chestnut forests.

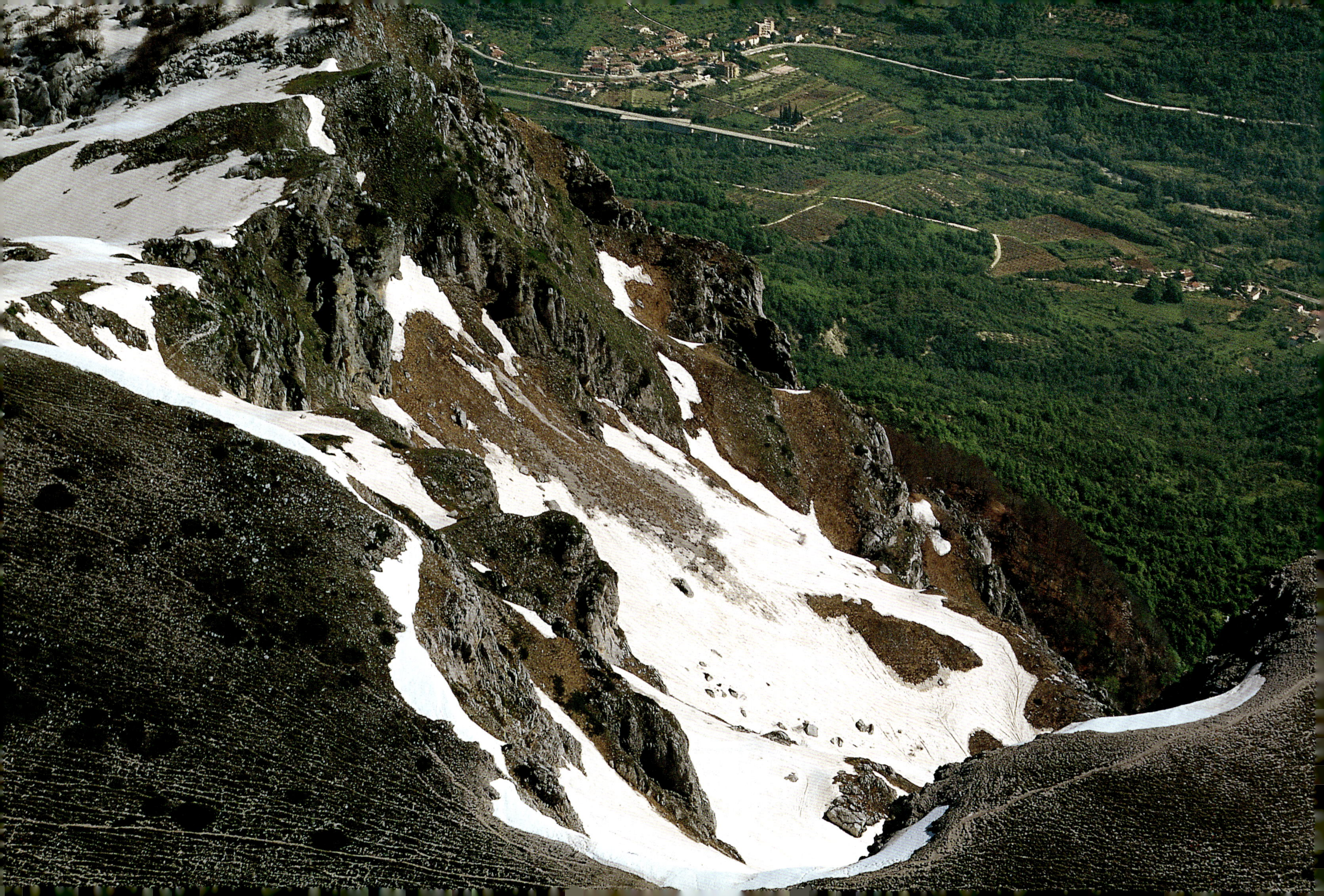

180 The Abruzzo National Park was established in 1922 and extends over 108,726 acres (44,000 hectares) of land, portions of which are located in the Molise and Lazio regions. The park's mountains have a wild appearance characterized by gorges, areas of karst and high plains. It is not unusual for the snow on the northernmost slopes to last until the end of spring.

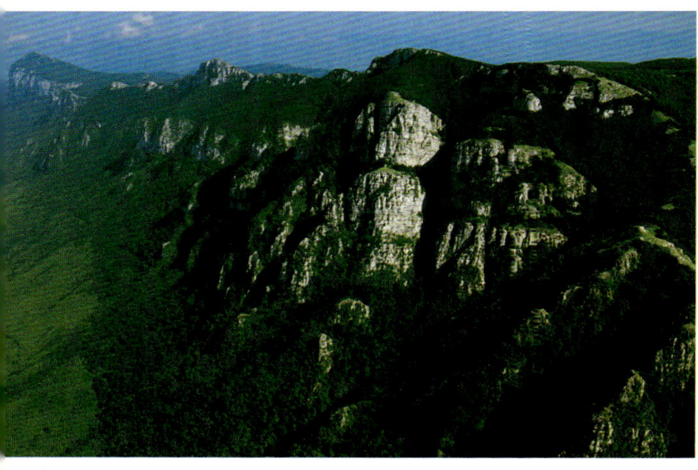

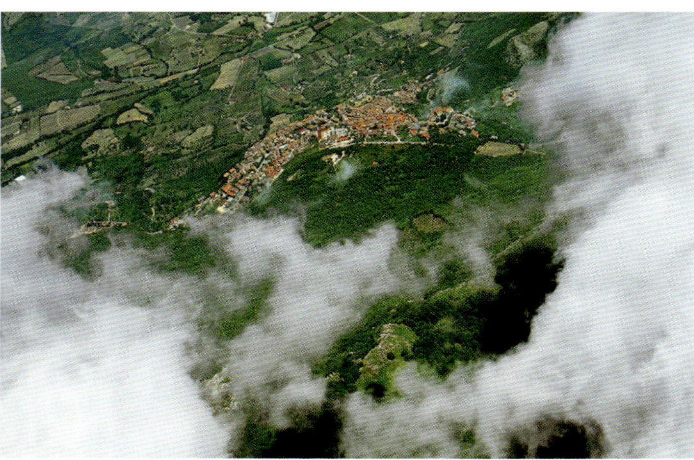

182 The Alburno Mountains have the typical appearance of a karst massif. The mountains, which contain many caves, grottoes and sinkholes, are located between the Sele Valley and the Tanagro, in the Campanian Apennines. They are known as the Campanian Dolomites, although the dense vegetation that covers their slopes makes their morphology unique and unmistakable.

183 The Molise area is divided into mountainous zones (55.3% of the territory, and hilly zones (44.7%). The eastern portion of the region slopes toward the sea in gentle, rounded hills, and enjoys the benefits of a temperate climate and medium-sized rivers, factors that have contributed to the survival of an agriculture that has been of historical importance to the Molise economy.

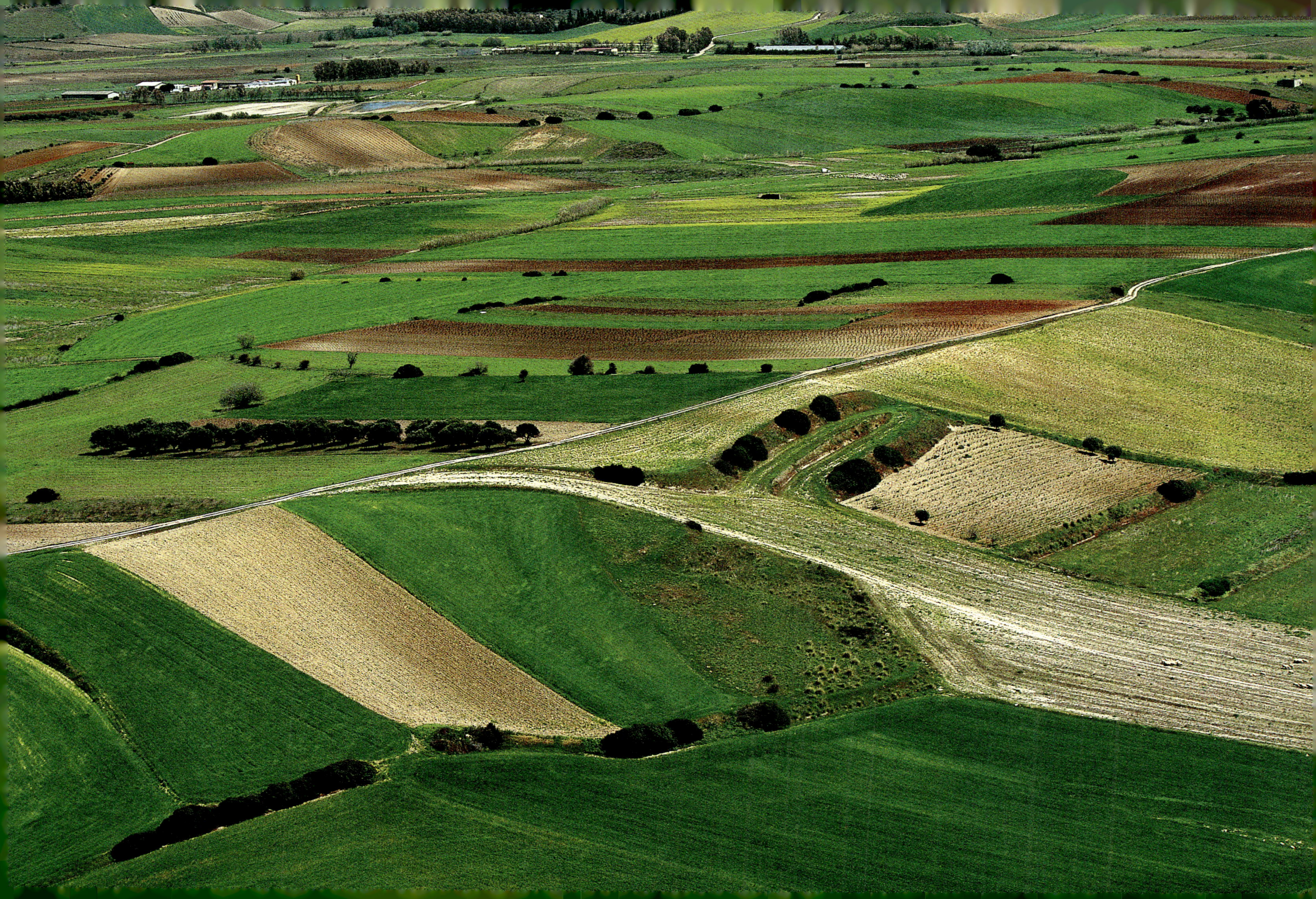

184-185 The system of migration paths that crosses Molise and other regions of Adriatic Central-Southern Italy, enabled the development of transhumant sheep farming. In Molise, transhumance always conflicted with other agricultural interests, and has now almost completely disappeared.

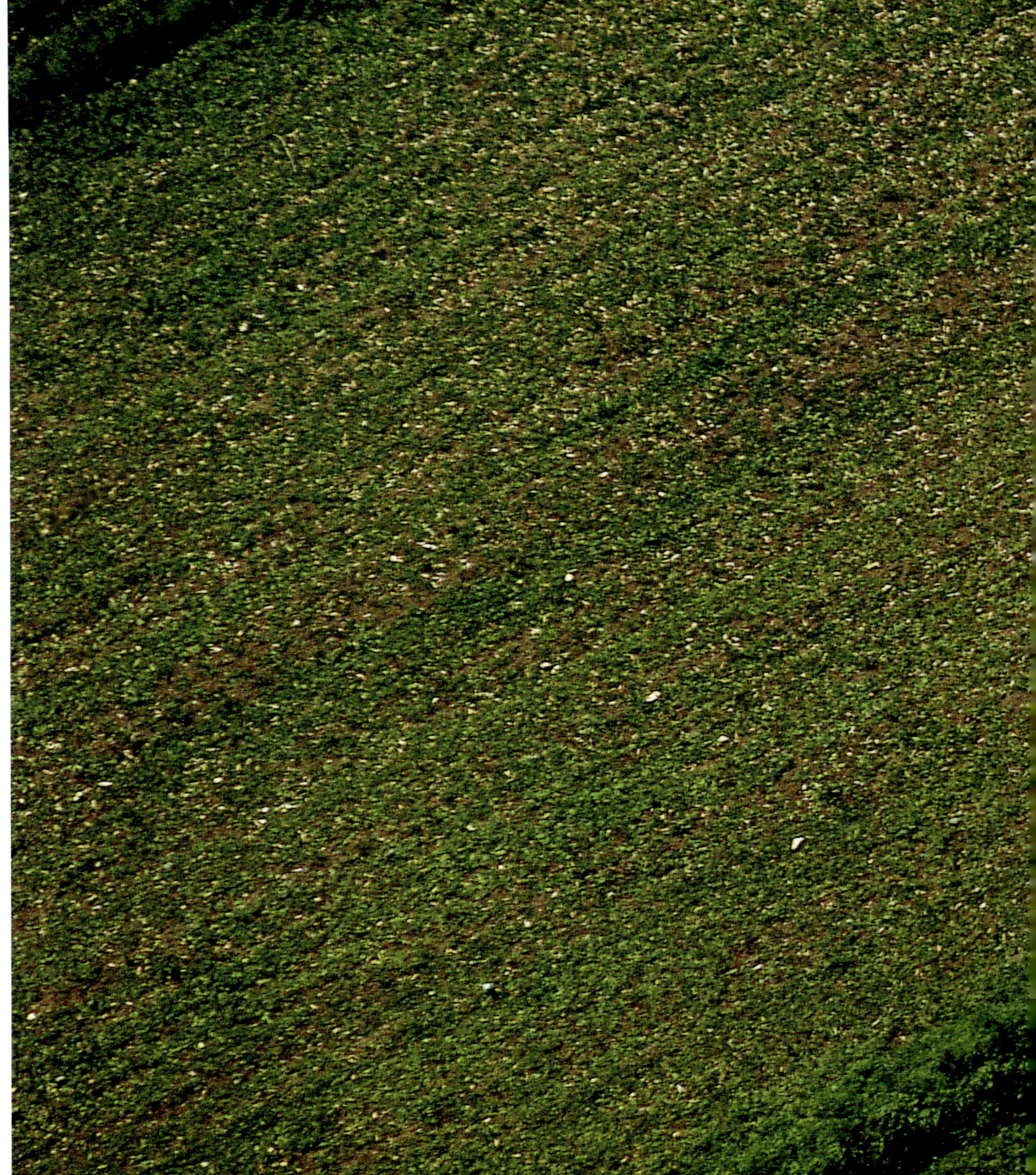

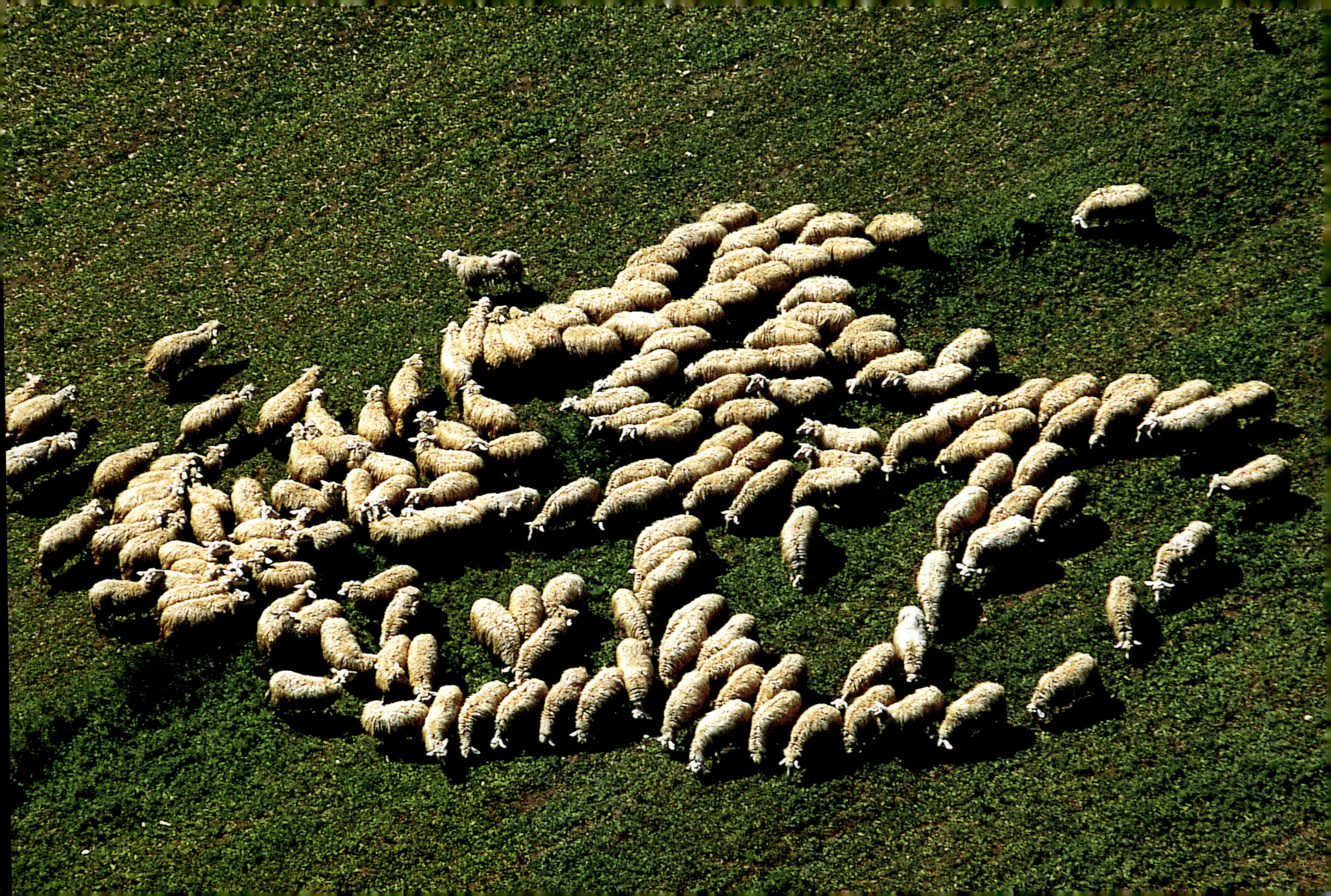

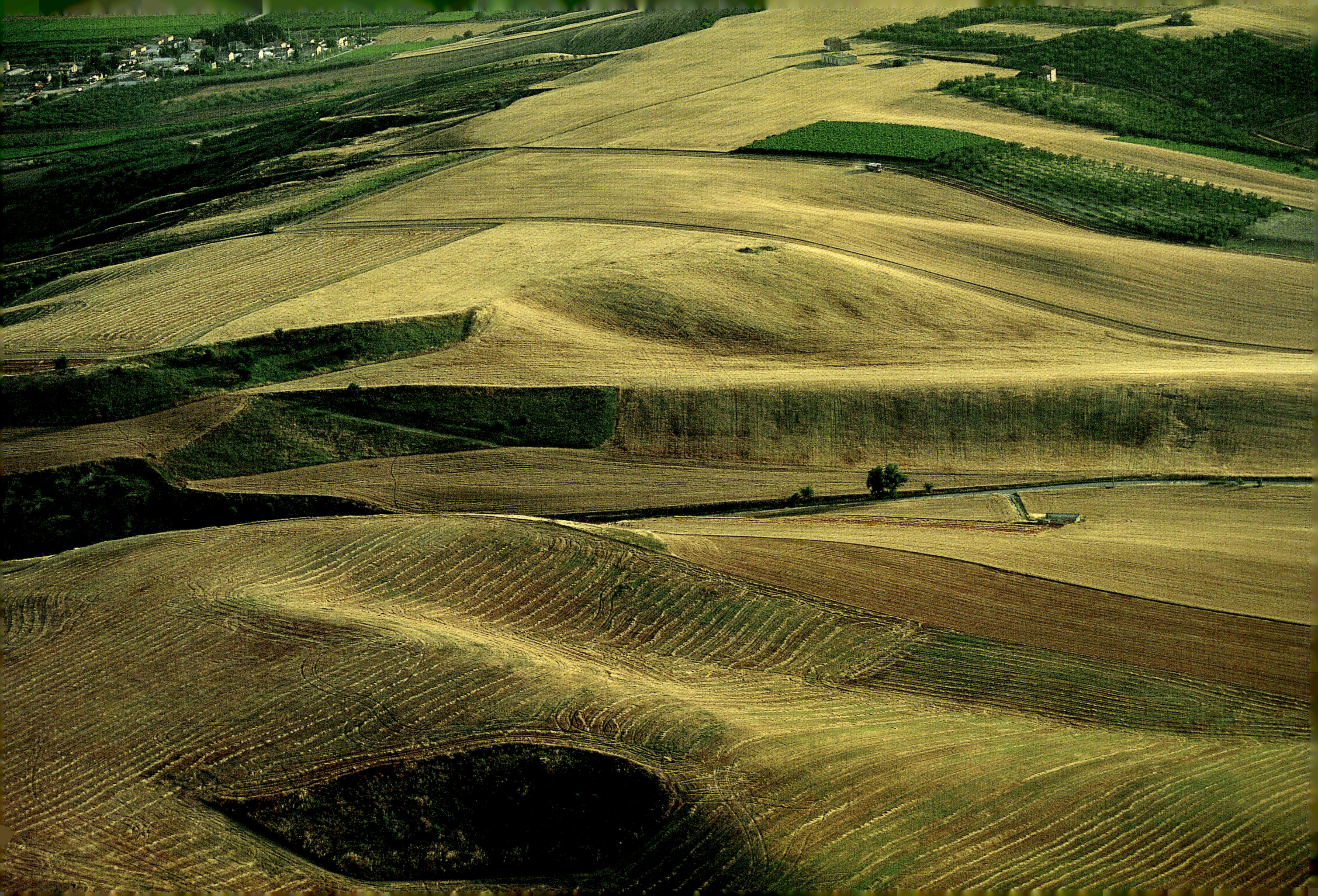

186 and 187 The Murge form a rectangular-shaped high plain of karst that occupies a large portion of central Apulia. The countryside shown here is located near Altamura (Bari), and is characterized by two long rows of gentle hills planted with grain. The name derives from the Latin word *murex*, which means pointed rock (like the shell of the murex).

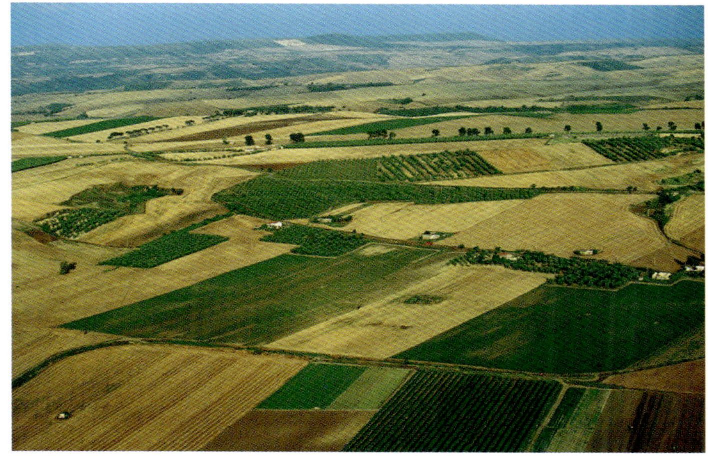

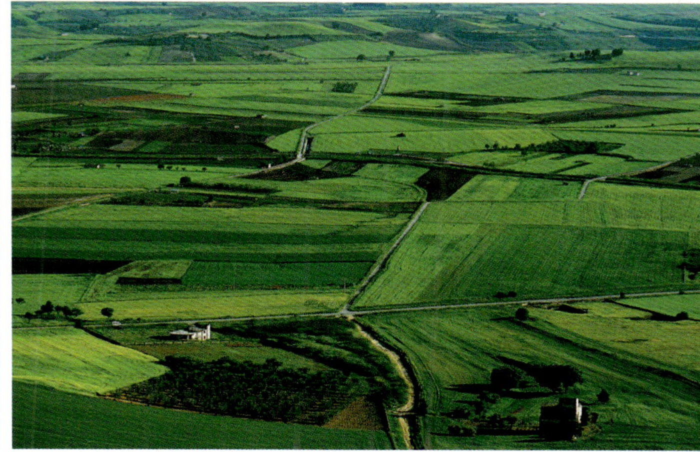

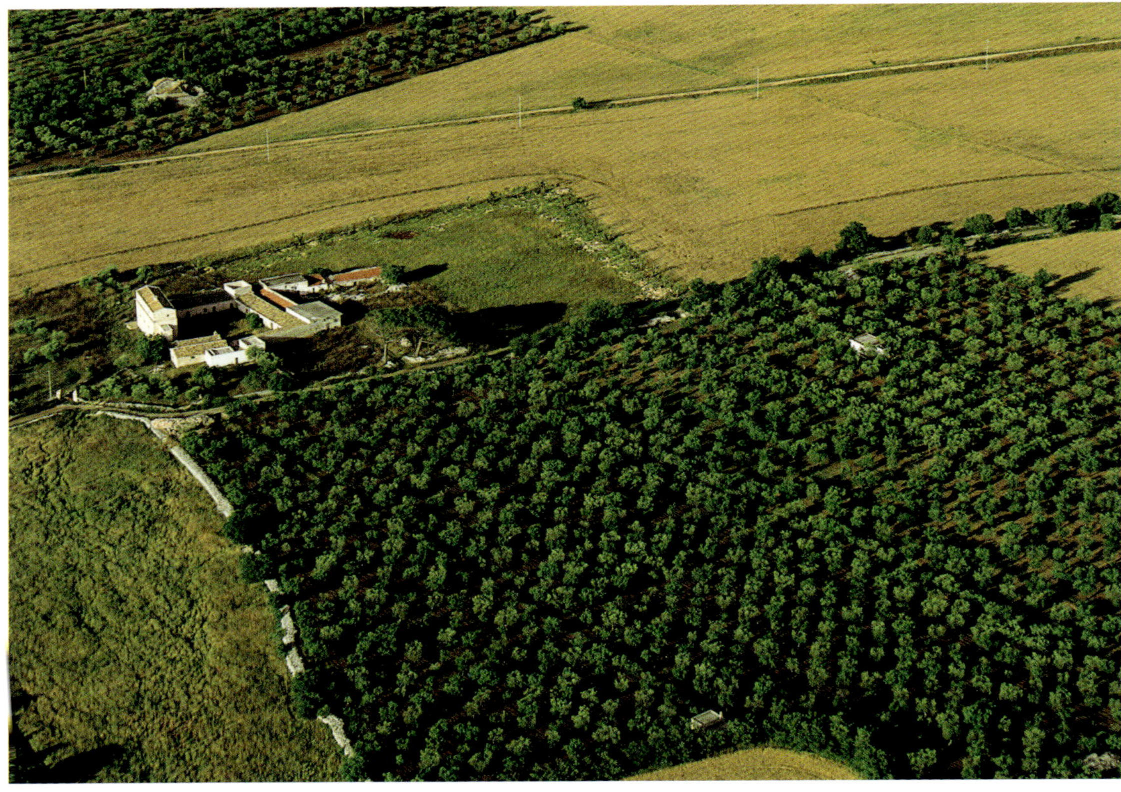

188 and 189 The Apulian Plateau, around Lucera (Foggia) is a completely flat elevated plain that extends for approximately 1545 sq. miles (4000 sq. km) to the west of the Gargano Promontory. It is the largest plain in the country after the Padana Plain, and is considered to be "Italy's granary."

190-191 The operation of the Margherita di Savoia salt pans, which are the largest in Europe and the second largest in the world, dates to the Roman Period. Today the salt pans form part of a nature reserve that is cherished by nature lovers and birdwatchers alike.

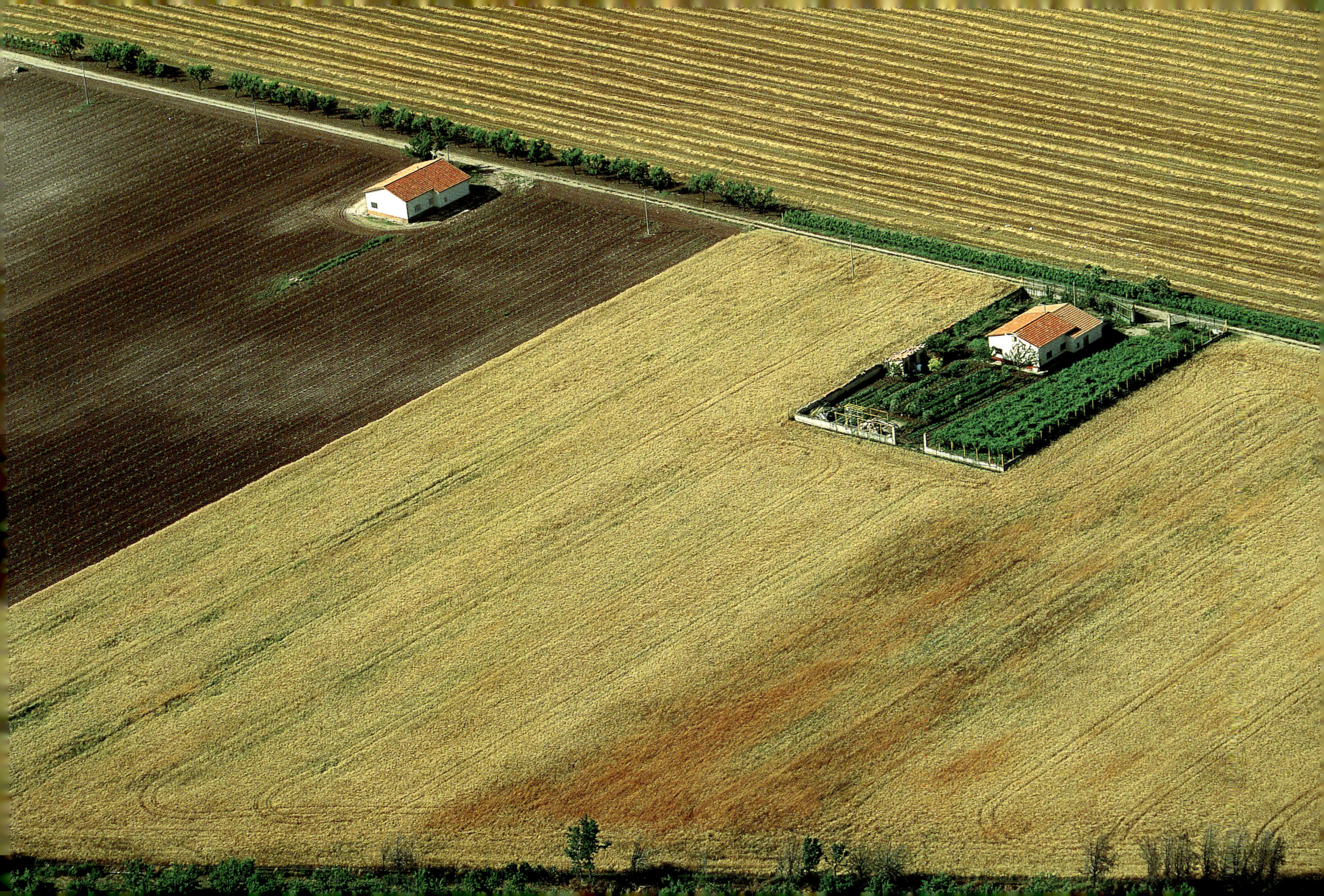

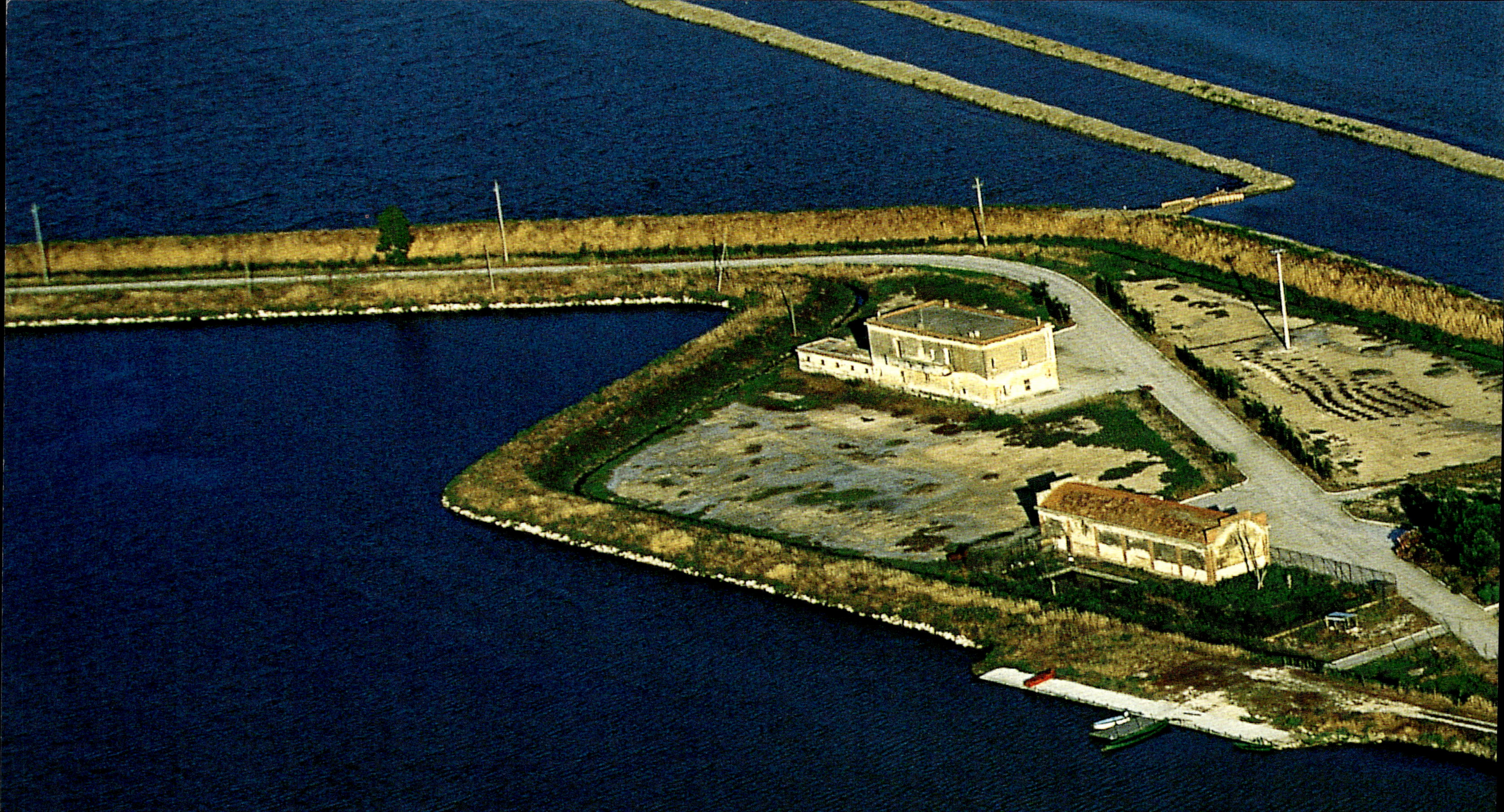

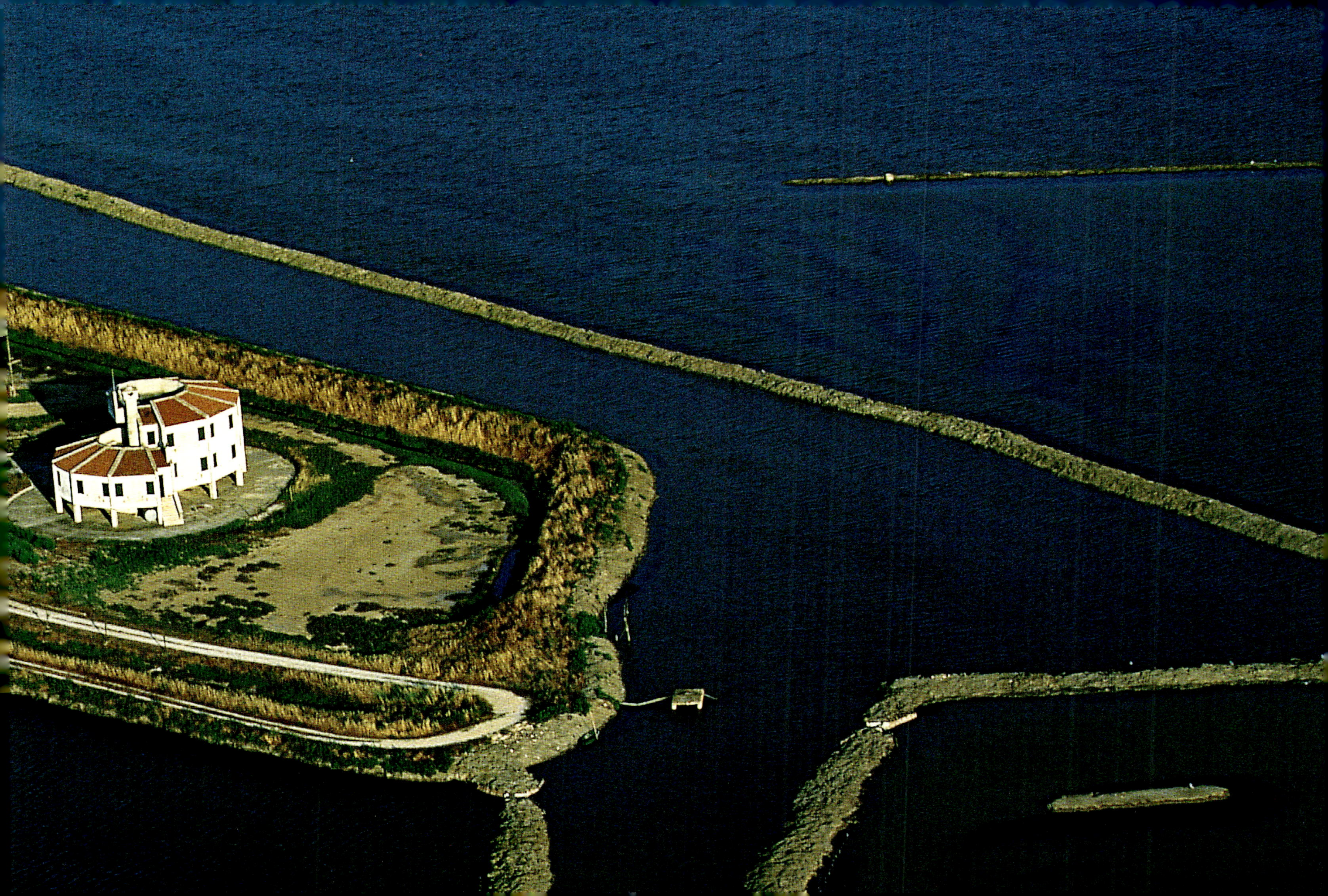

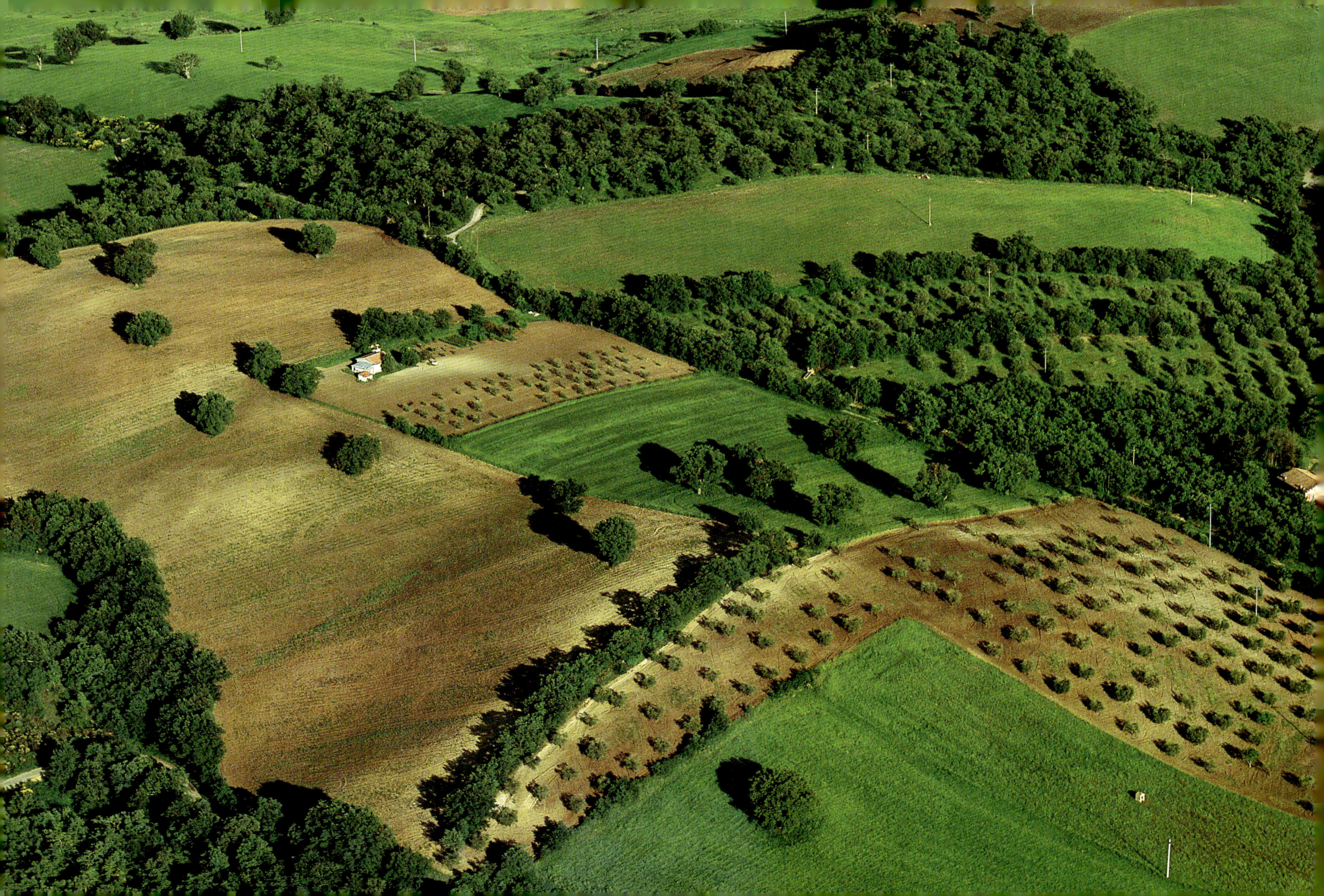

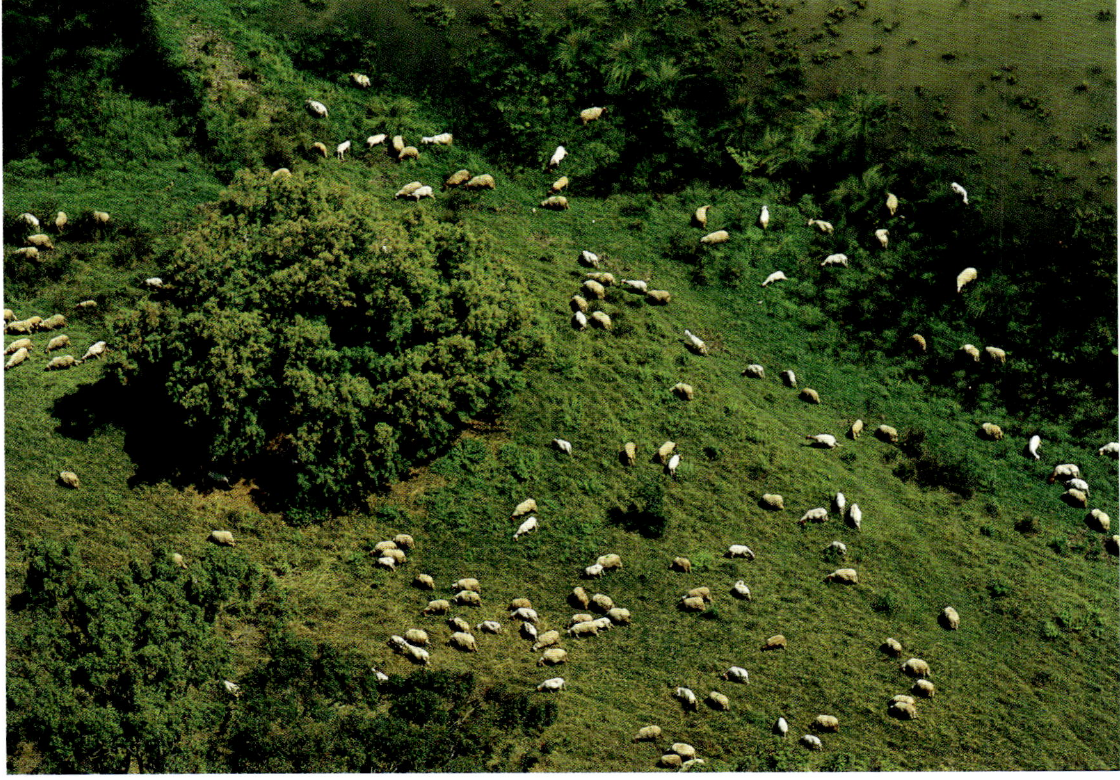

192 and 193 Two economies co-exist in Lucania; particularly in the interior region of Matera: the developed system of grain production also leaves large areas open for sheep raising. As can be seen in these photos, the effects of the incomplete mechanization of agriculture are apparent in the landscape, which contains ample areas of still uncultivated land.

194-195 Basilicata is predominantly mountainous (46.8%) and hilly (45.13%). Plains occupy only 8% of its territory, in the area near the mouths of the principal rivers that form the Metaponto Plain. The cultivation of wheat, corn, barley and oats is widespread in this area, and panoramas such as this are common.

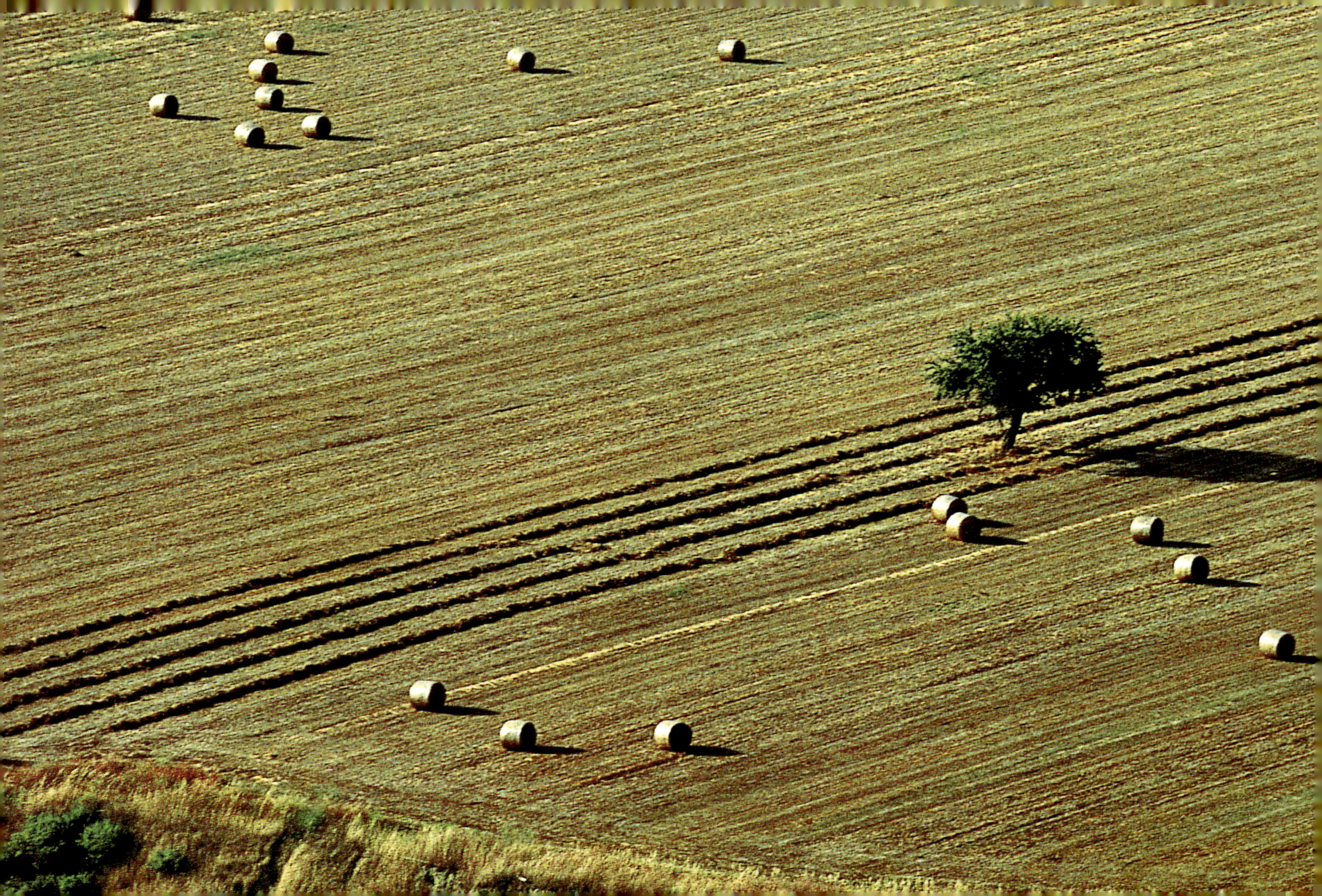

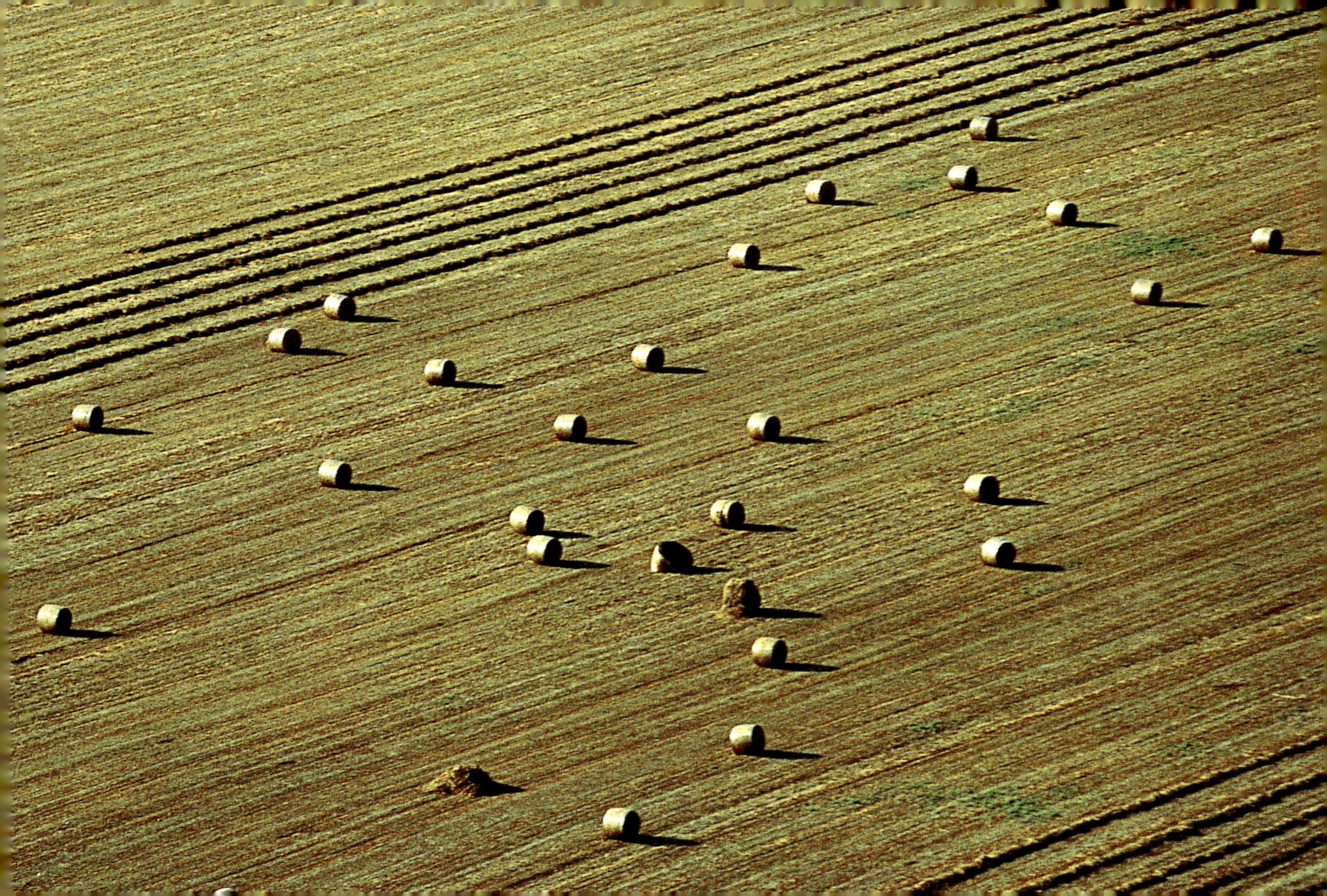

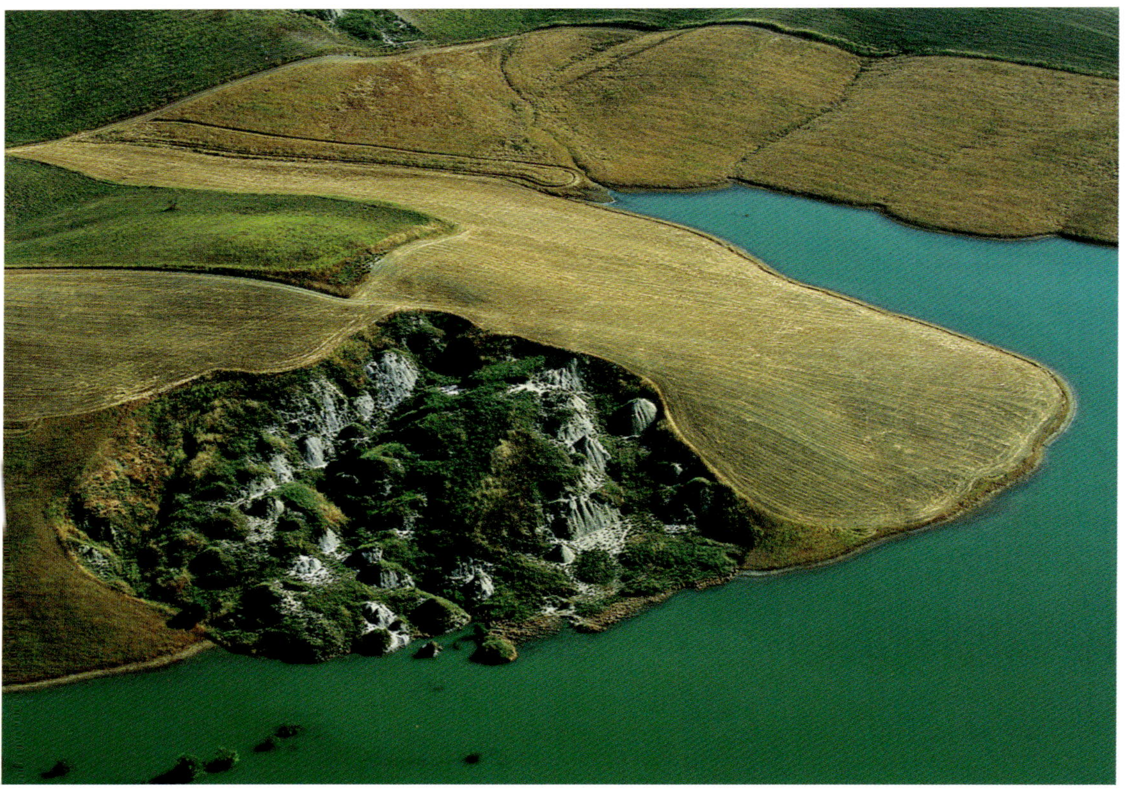

196 The Senise Dam (Potenza), which has blocked the Sinni River since 1983, forms Monte Cotugno Lake, a mirror of water created to meet agricultural and energy requirements, but which is now also considered particularly important from an environmental perspective.

197 The Lake San Giuliano WWF Oasis, located in Basilicata, is an important wetlands environment that is home to numerous aquatic birds, otters, and the Egyptian vulture, a small vulture now extremely rare in Italy. The history of the oasis is connected to that of the artificial lake of the same name, which was created by blocking the Bradano River between 1950 and 1957.

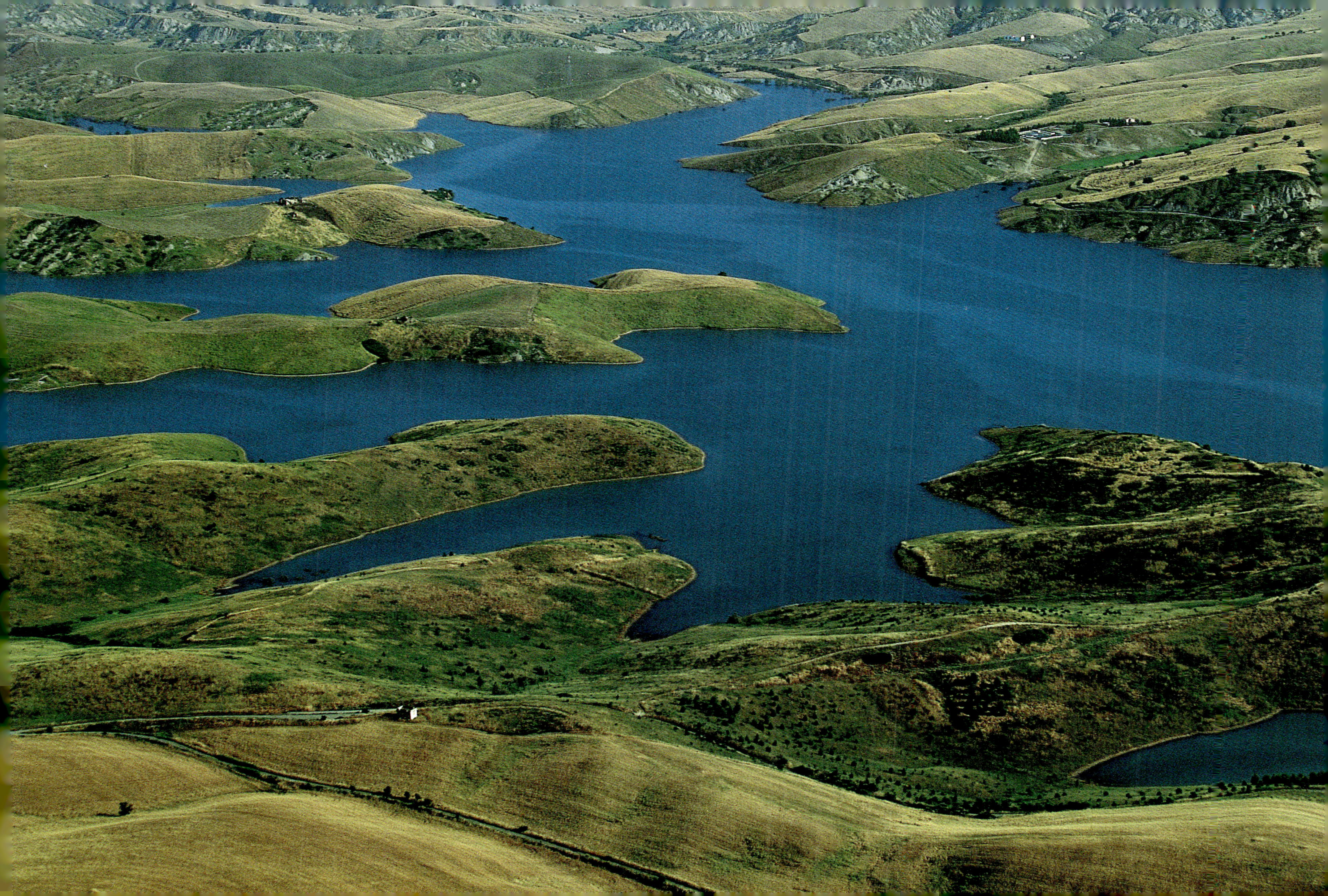

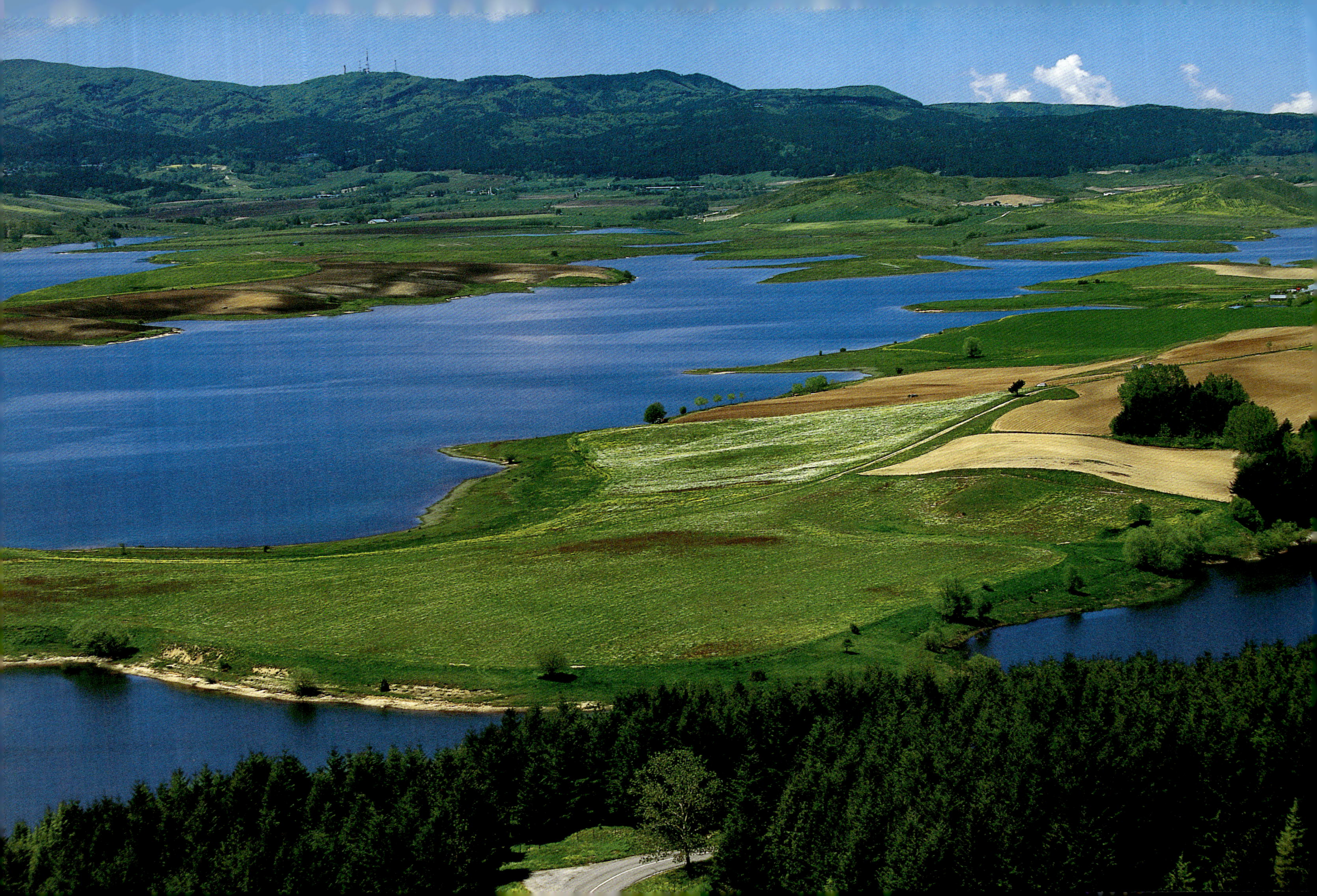

198 Lake Cecita (Cosenza) is an artificial lake created between 1950 and 1955 – the Mucone, Vaccarizzi and Cecita all flow into the lake and supply the Acri and Bisignano hydroelectric plants. Like the other artificial lakes of the Sila, it was created for purely economic reasons, but it has acquired a certain environmental value over the years.

199 The Sila is rich in water – this availability prompted the construction, in the 1950s, of artificial dams for the production of electricity or (as in the case of Lake Votturino) for irrigation.

200-201 The countryside near Crotone, called the Marchesato, has in recent years been experiencing a revival connected to agritourism and to the revaluation of the landscape's natural beauty.

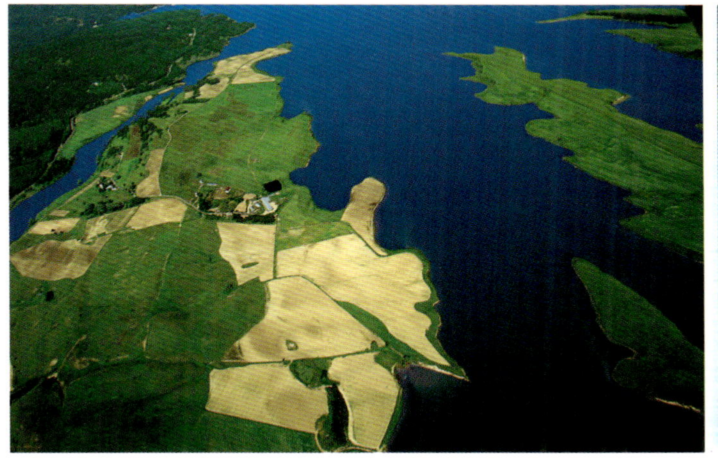

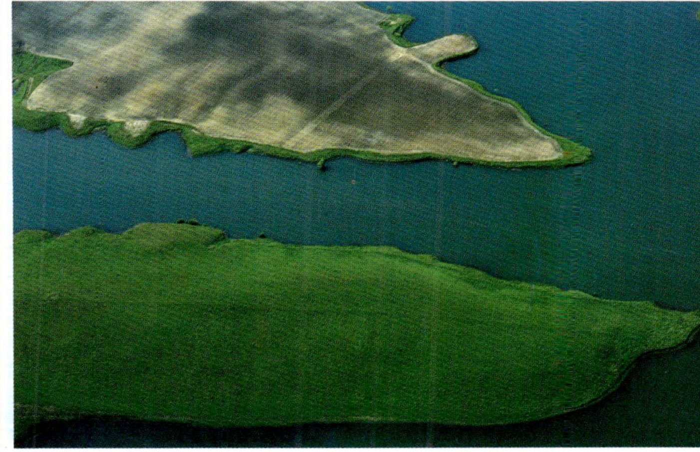

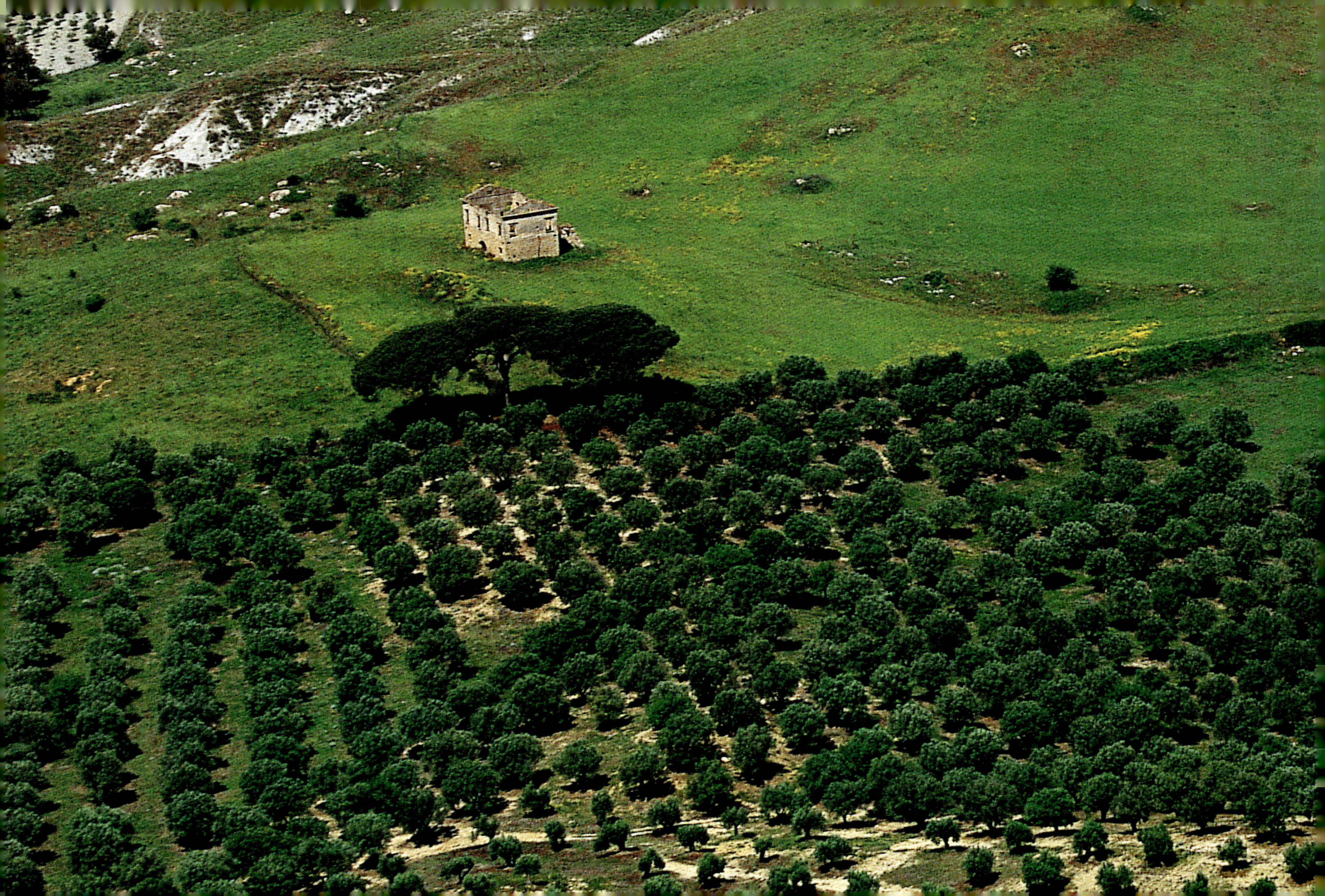

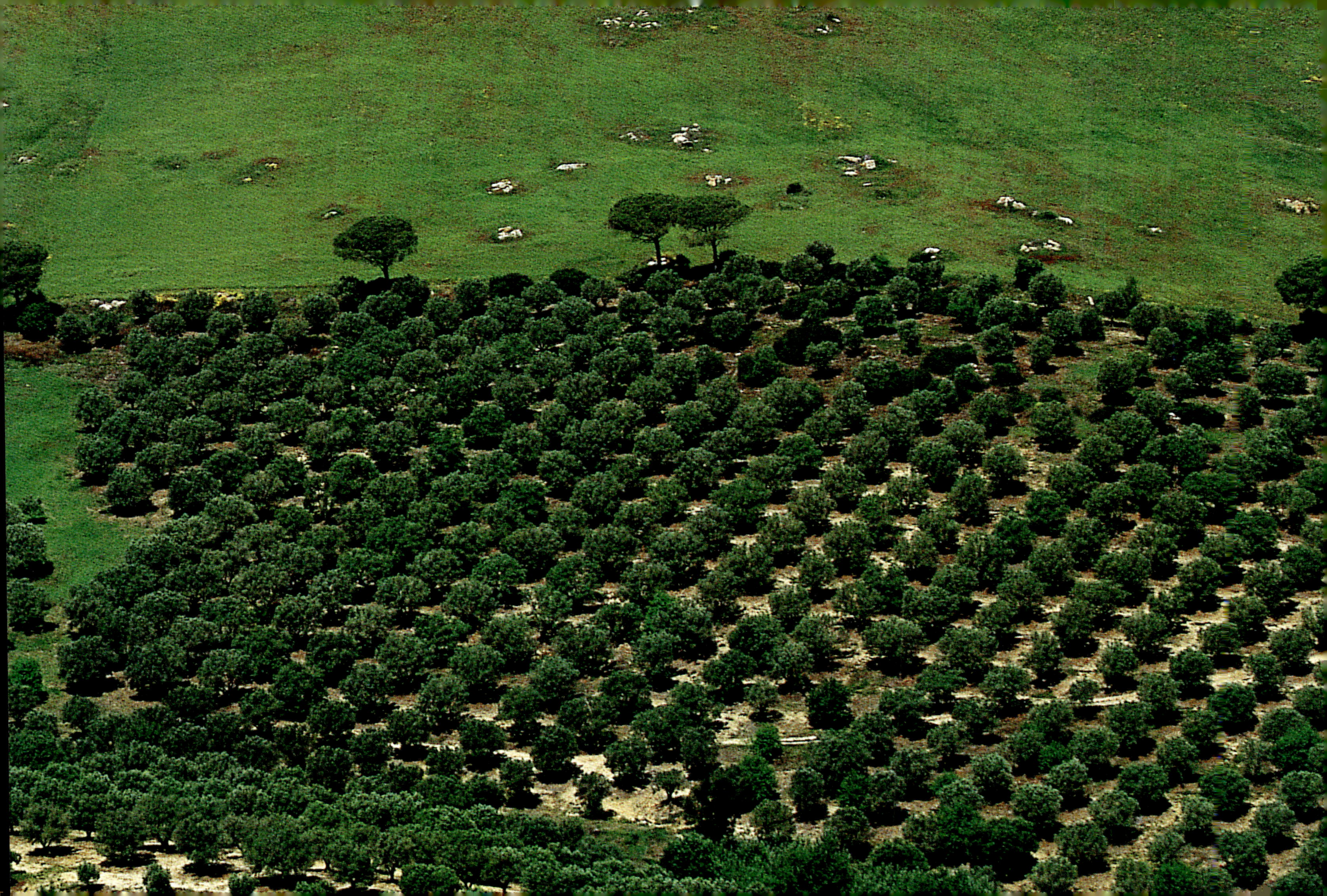

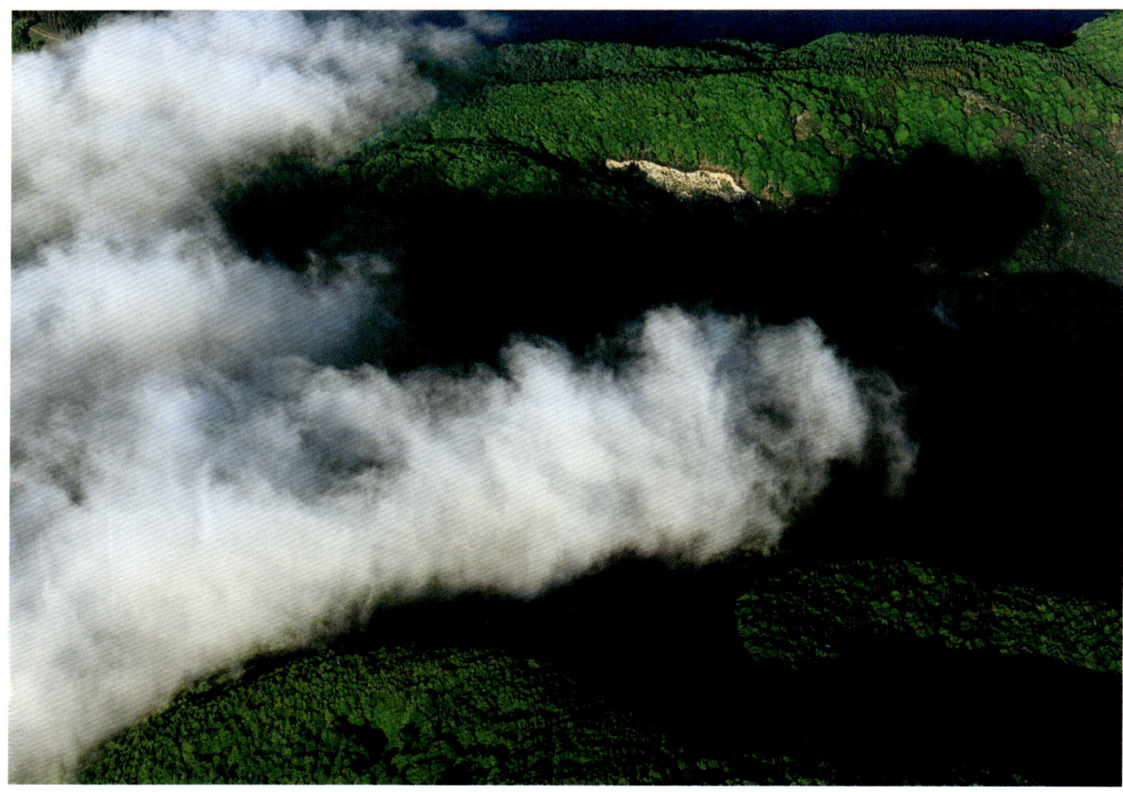

202 and 203 A mountainous massif, but also an important part of the identity of the entire region of Calabria, Aspromonte is a complicated tangle of peaks and valleys arranged in terraces. It is the final section of the small chain of Calabrian Mountains, which according to geologists are not part of the Apennines, that extends to the south of Pollino and Reggio Calabria. Not all of Aspromonte is arid and bare – the slopes that form part of Aspromonte National Park (in the photos) are covered by forests of oak and holm oak, and at elevations above 3280 ft (1000 m) by fir and beech forests. Established in 1989, the park is the largest situated entirely within Calabria.

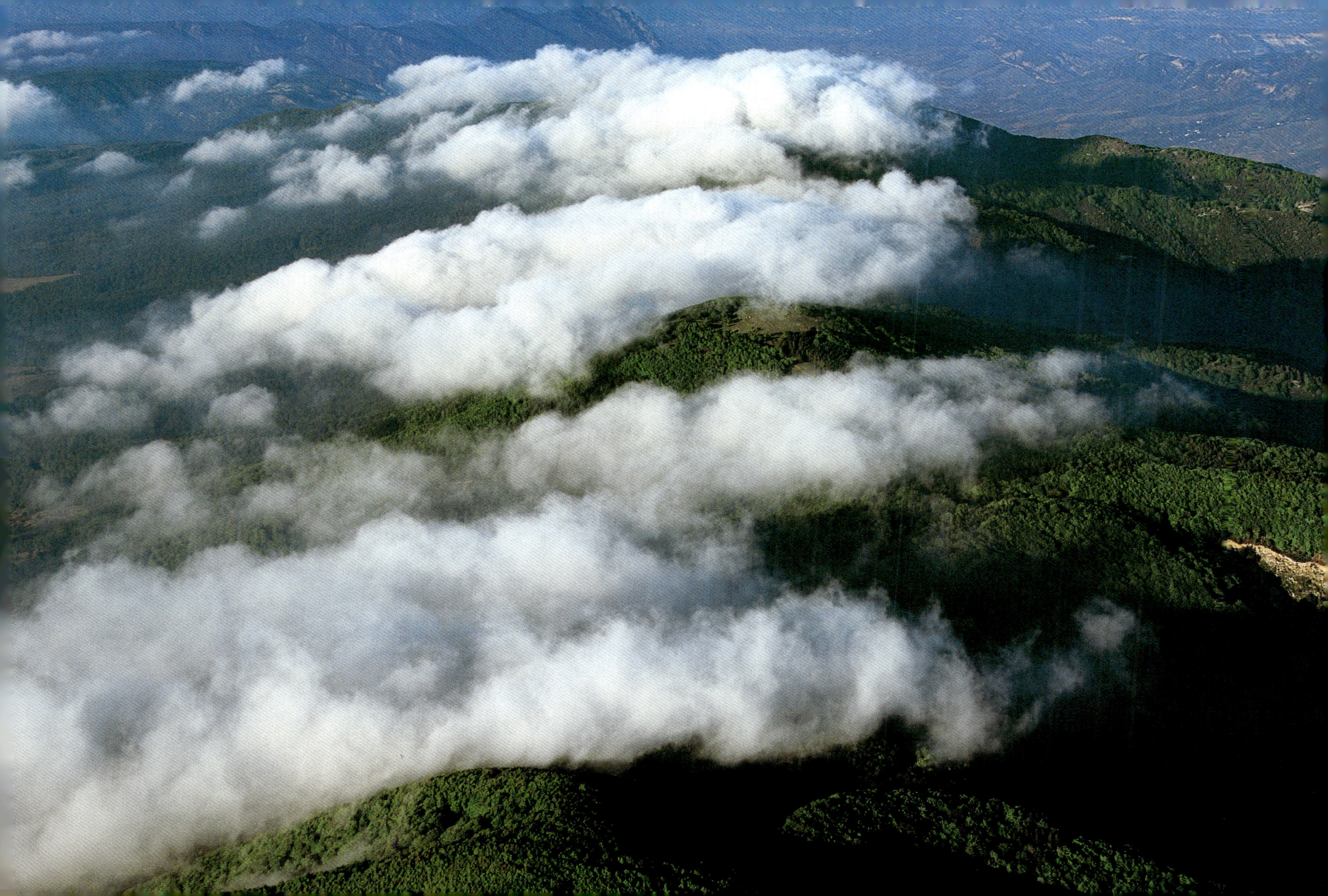

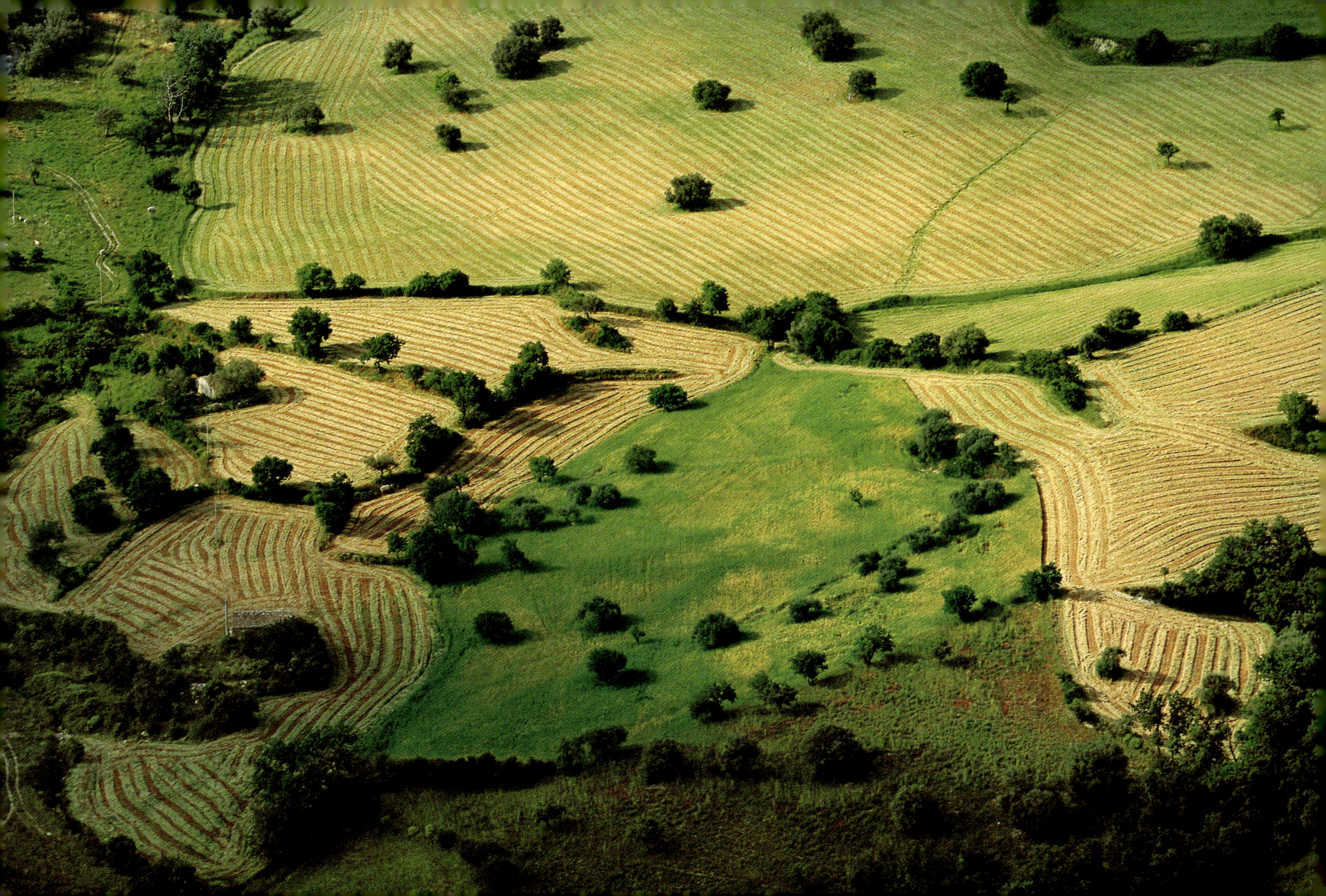

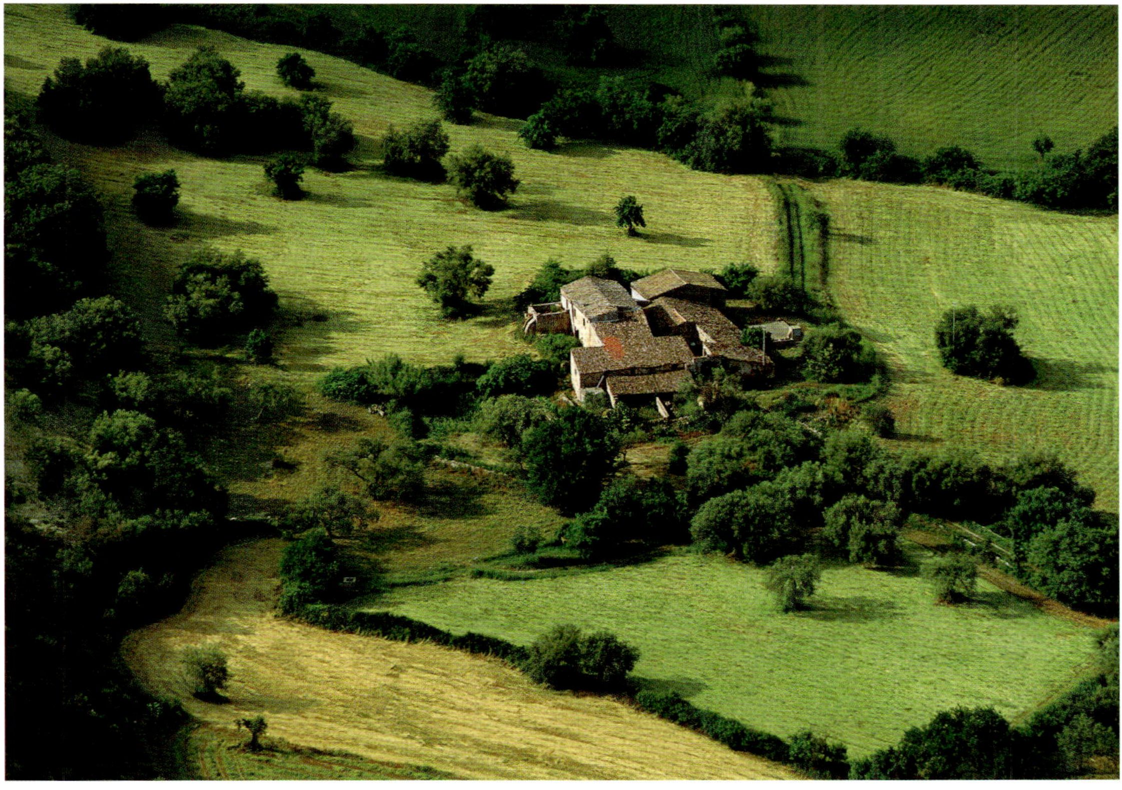

204 and 205 Located near Ragusa, in the heart of Sicily, is the Ragusa Plain, an ancient land of large agricultural estates that maintains a notable historical and natural charm. From the agricultural plots, which alternate between grain crops, olive trees, orchards and copses (left), to the large farms (right), this is the legacy of a still active rural civilization from a time that, at least in this part of the island, does not belong to the past.

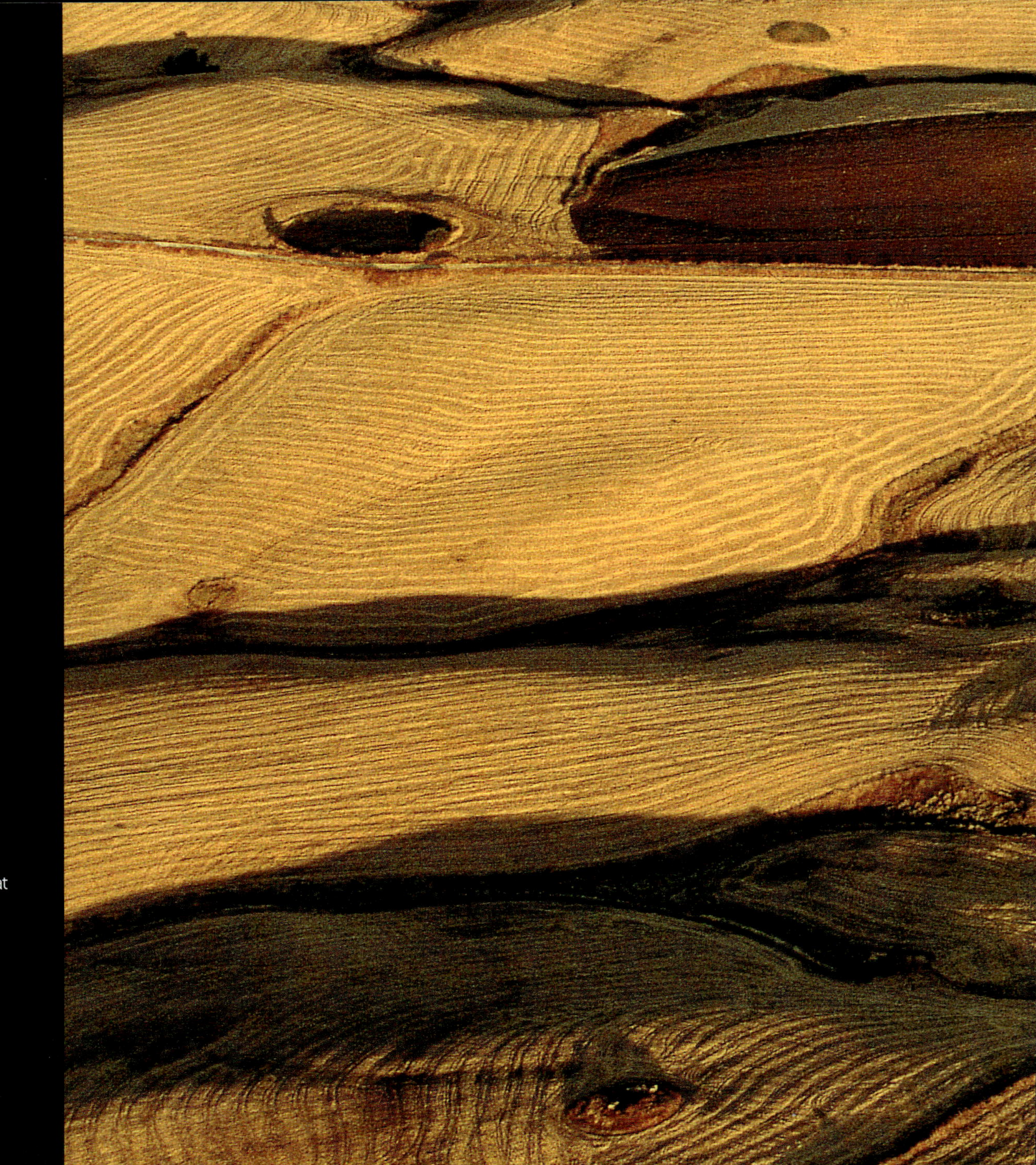

206-207 The grain fields of Ragusa, combed at the end of summer by the work of men and machines, relate the ancient connection between agriculture and the environment, and the continuous adaptation to the forms of nature, as is readily apparent in the walls that surround the perimeters of irregularly-shaped plots of land.

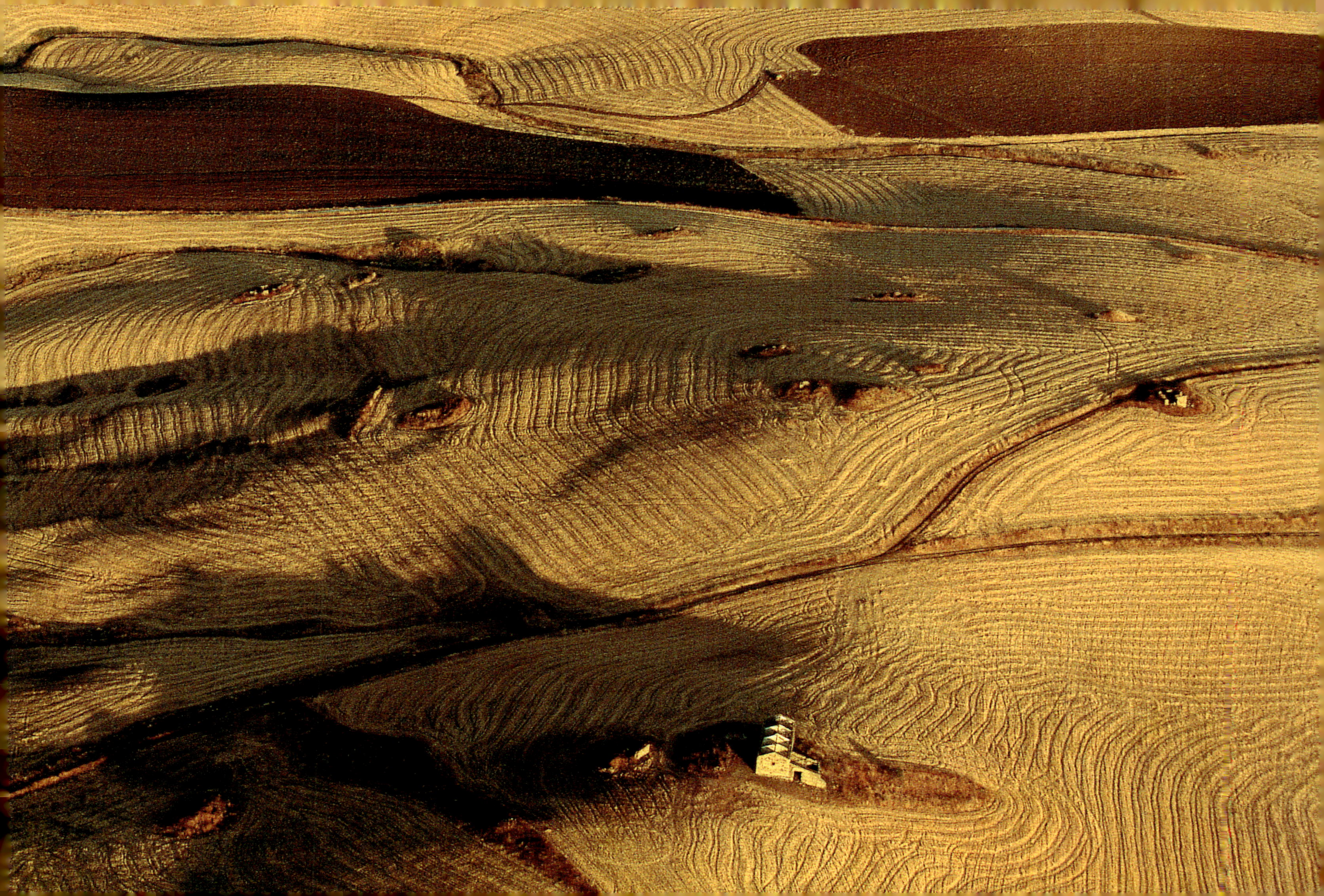

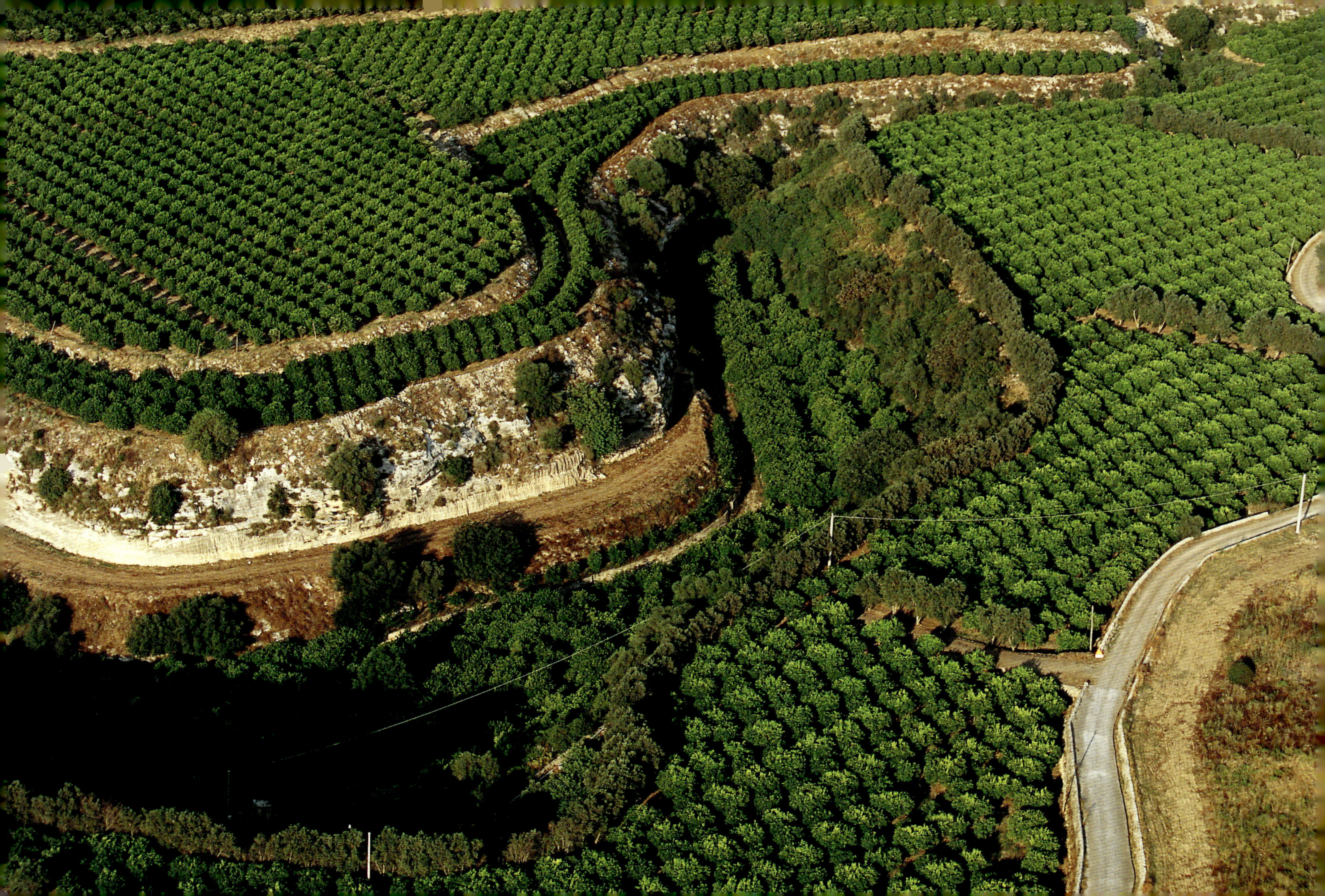

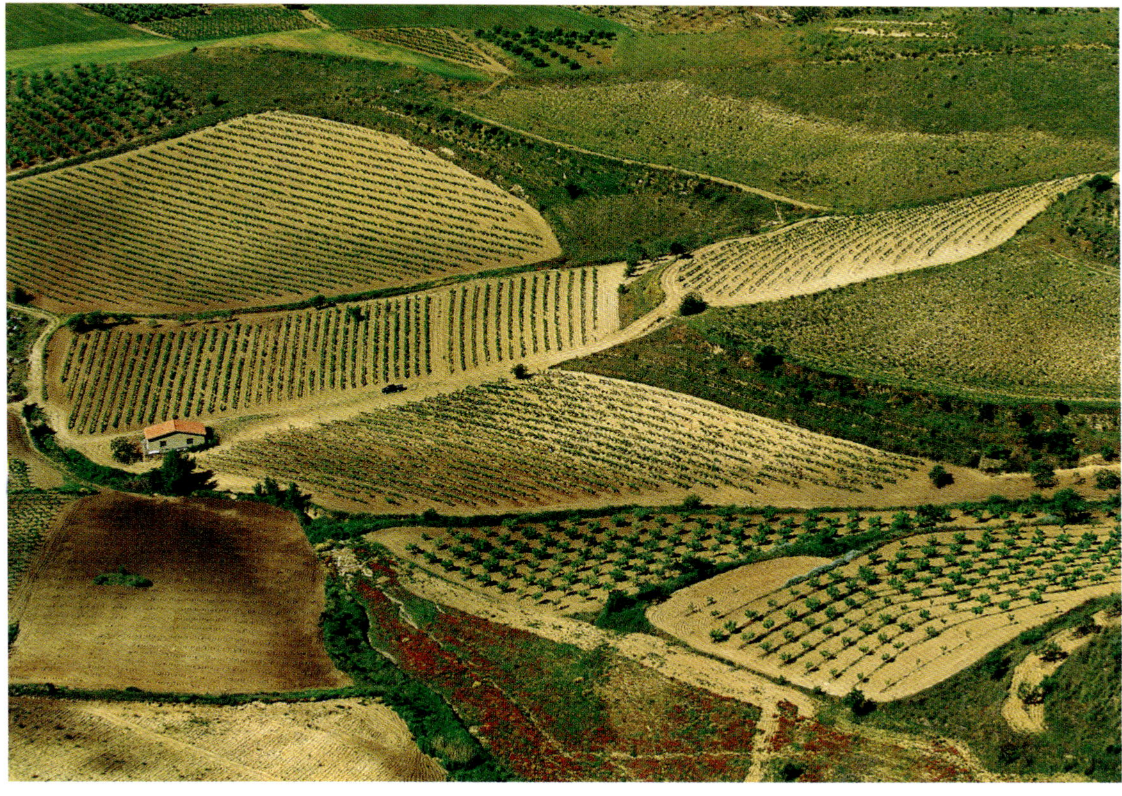

208 and 209 The Agrigento countryside reveals its agricultural nature from the first glimpse – almond trees, olive trees, vineyards and fruit trees, grown in small plots, stretch over the inland hills and offer the magnificent spectacle of a Sicily that is rural, but which is already in step with the needs of modern agriculture.

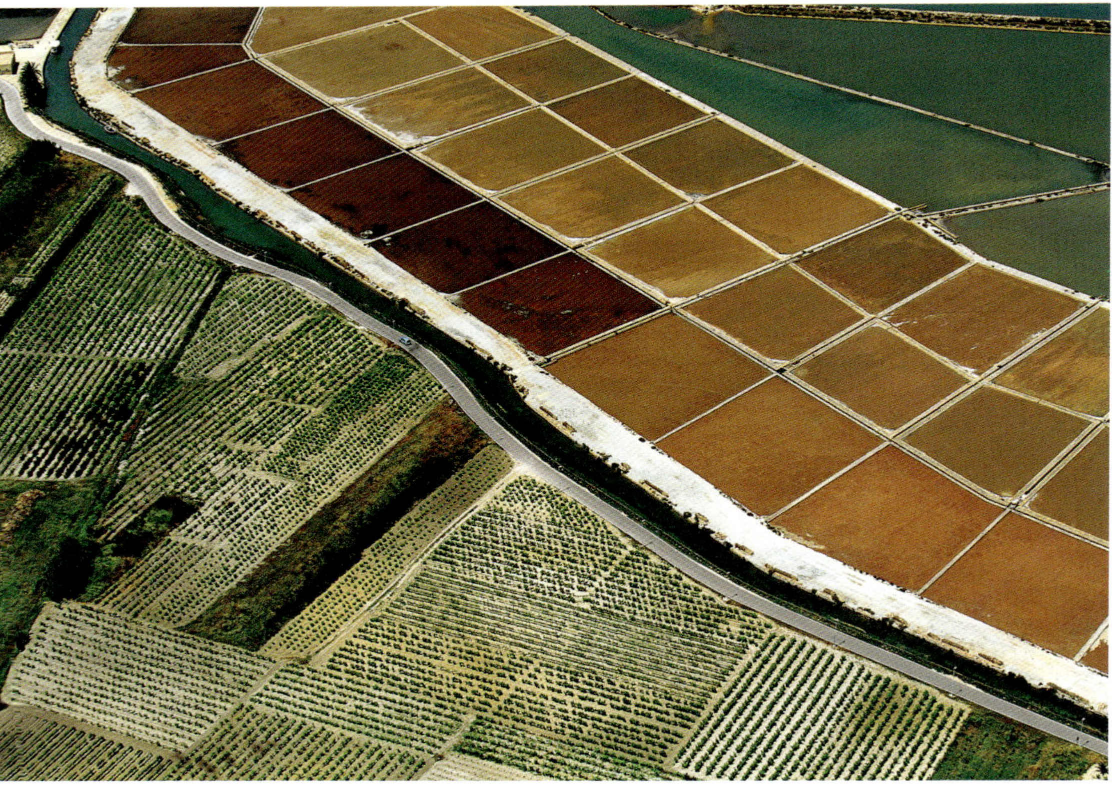

210 The Marsala salt pans are a magical sight even today. The colored basins, divided into regular sections, and the mounds of incredibly white salt that are aligned and ready for transport, are set into a traditional agricultural landscape composed of rows of trees and orchards.

211 The Stagnone Lagoon in Marsala is one of the most beautiful "wetlands" areas in Europe, and the largest lagoon in Sicily. Pink flamingos and numerous other birds stop to rest here. Salt pans extend around the lagoon, while located at the center of the mirror of water is the small island of Mozia, which guards the remains of the ancient Punic-Carthaginian settlement of Motya.

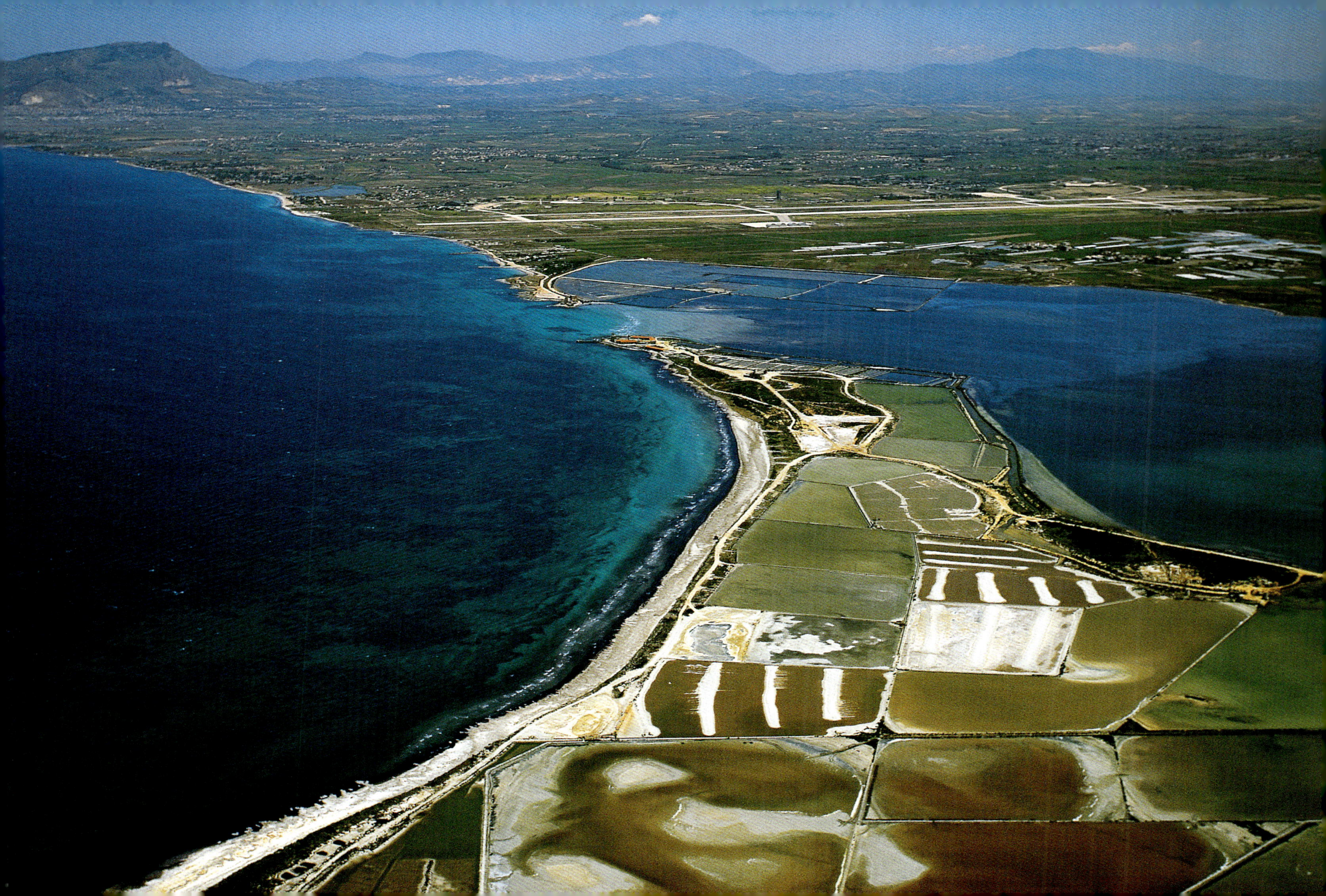

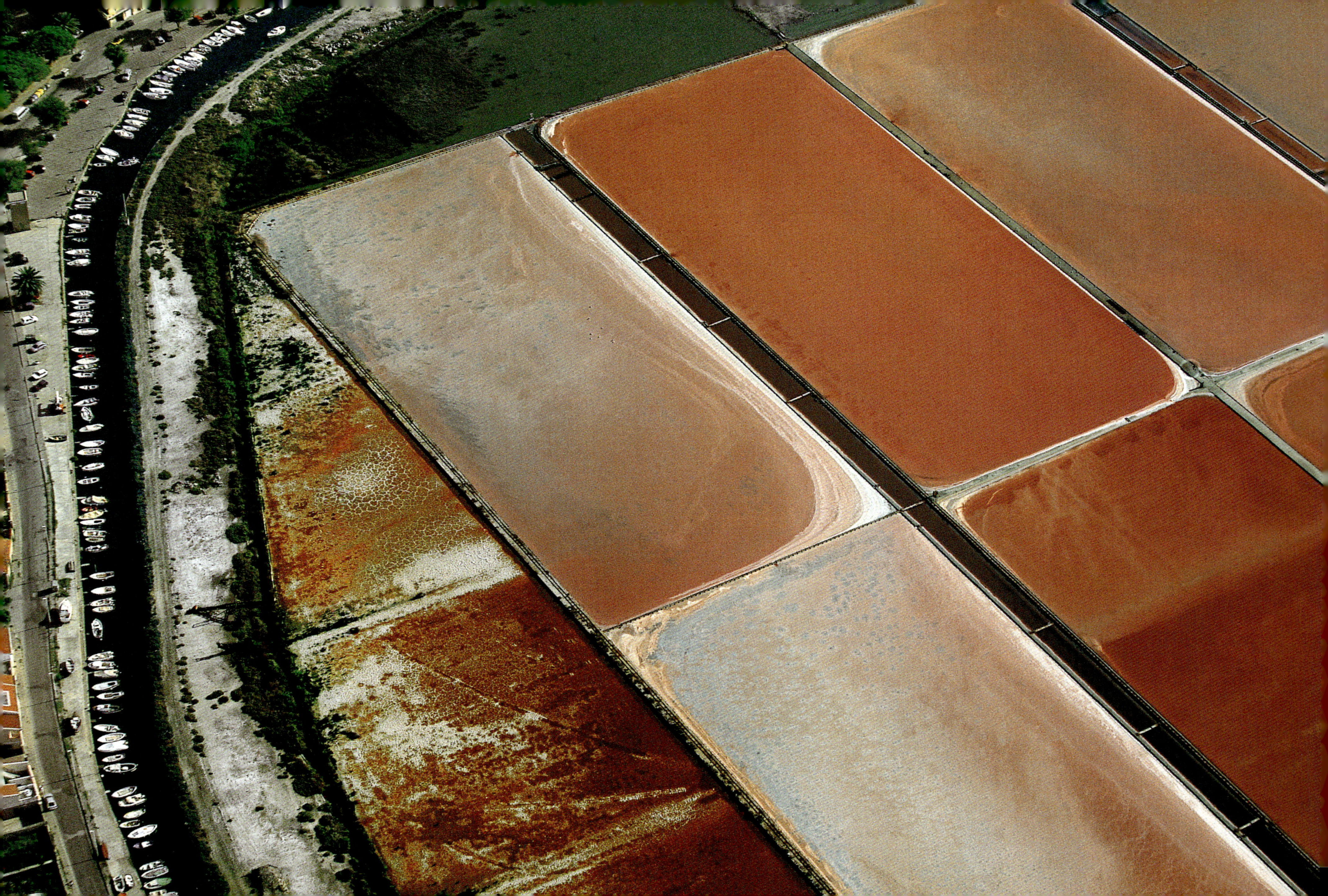

212 The Carloforte salt pans (on San Pietro Island, off Sardinia), located next to the inhabited center, have been in disuse for years and constitute a true paradise for flamingos as well as birdwatchers. Included in the species nesting among the saltwater ponds are the avocet, pied stilt, tern and egret; there is also a small colony of Corsican gulls nesting here.

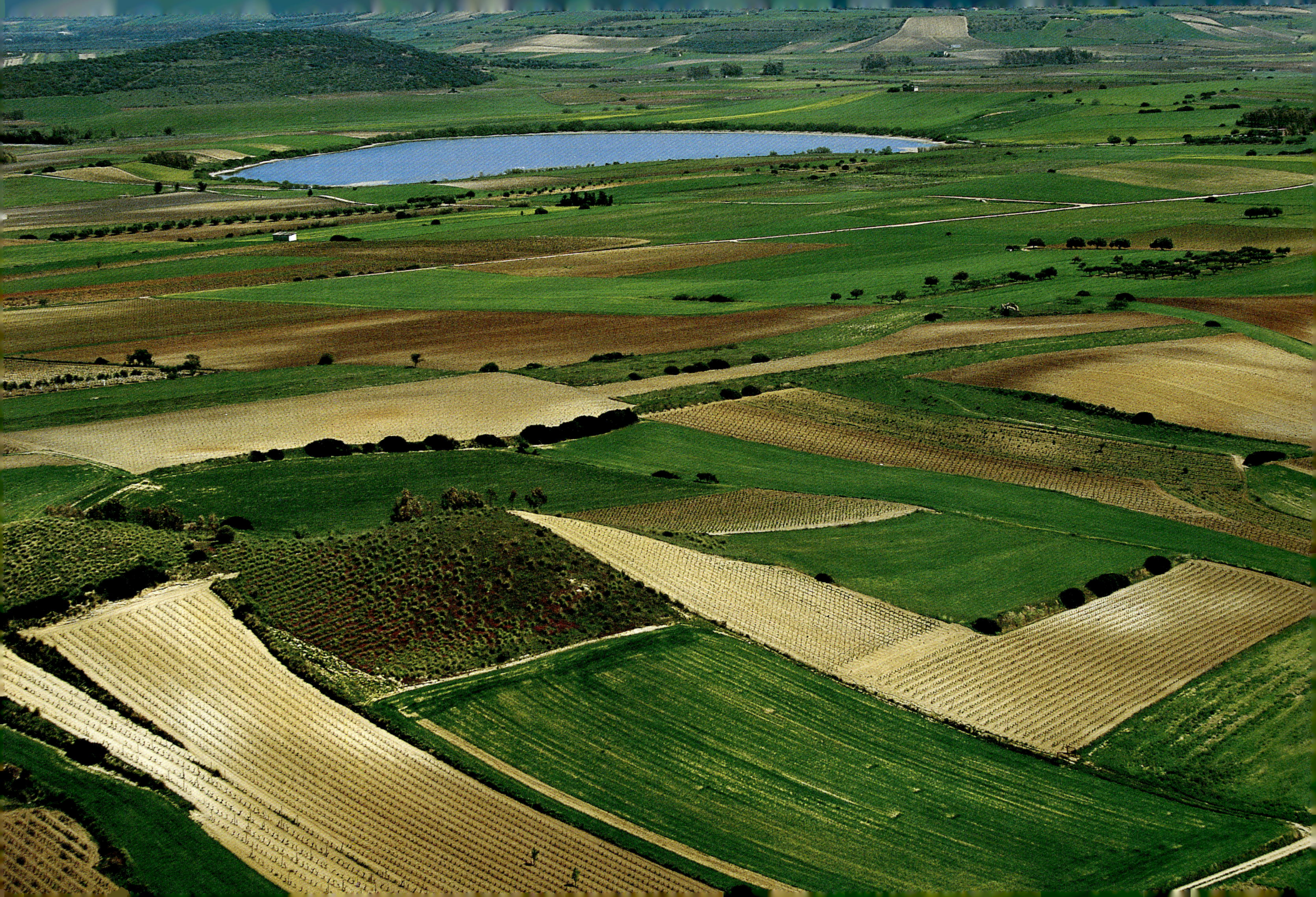

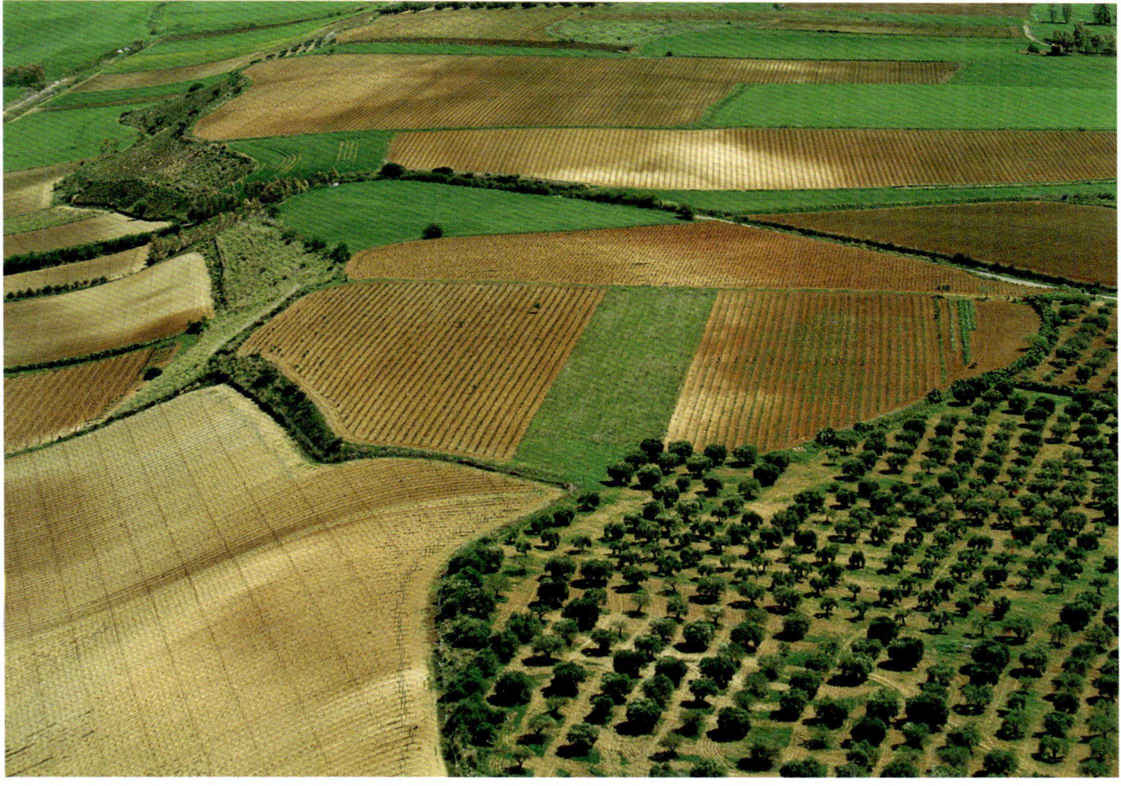

214 and 215 Campidano, the largest plain in Sardinia, was created by a tectonic sinkhole, or rather a sinking of part of the terrestrial crust that occurred approximately 4 million years ago. Subsequently filled with alluvial sediments, the sinkhole became a singular plain animated by gentle hills, shown in these photos, which connects Cagliari to Oristono. The plain is extremely fertile: grains and grapes have been grown here since antiquity.

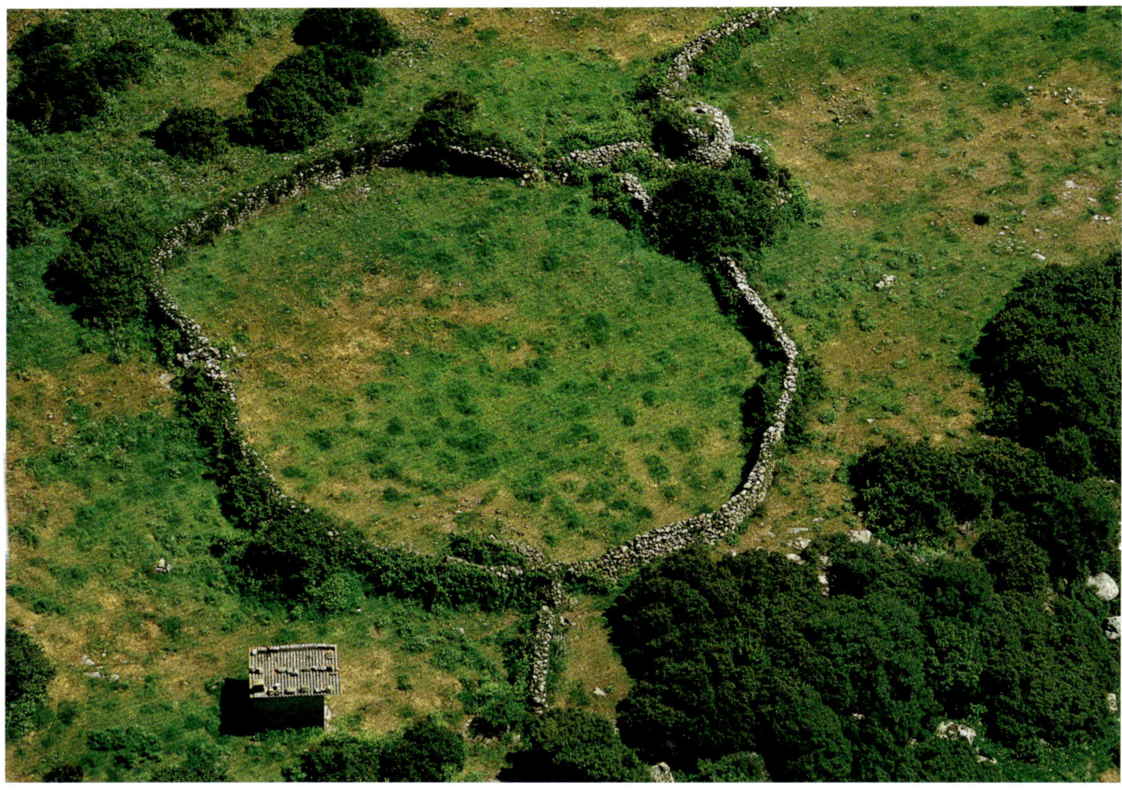

216 and 217 The Gesturi Plateau is a basaltic high plain of volcanic origins, situated in central-southern Sardinia at the border between Bassa Marmilla and Sarcidano. Over thousands of years, the wind and rain have eroded the rock surrounding the zone protected by the basaltic shield, thereby creating an "island." For this reason, it has been inhabited since time immemorial, as illustrated by these scattered remains of traditional structures. Its 17 sq. miles (45 sq. km) are characterized by rocks, oak forests, Mediterranean scrub and a blanket of rare botanical species. The soil's nature causes the formation of swamps of various sizes, which dry up in the summer (right).

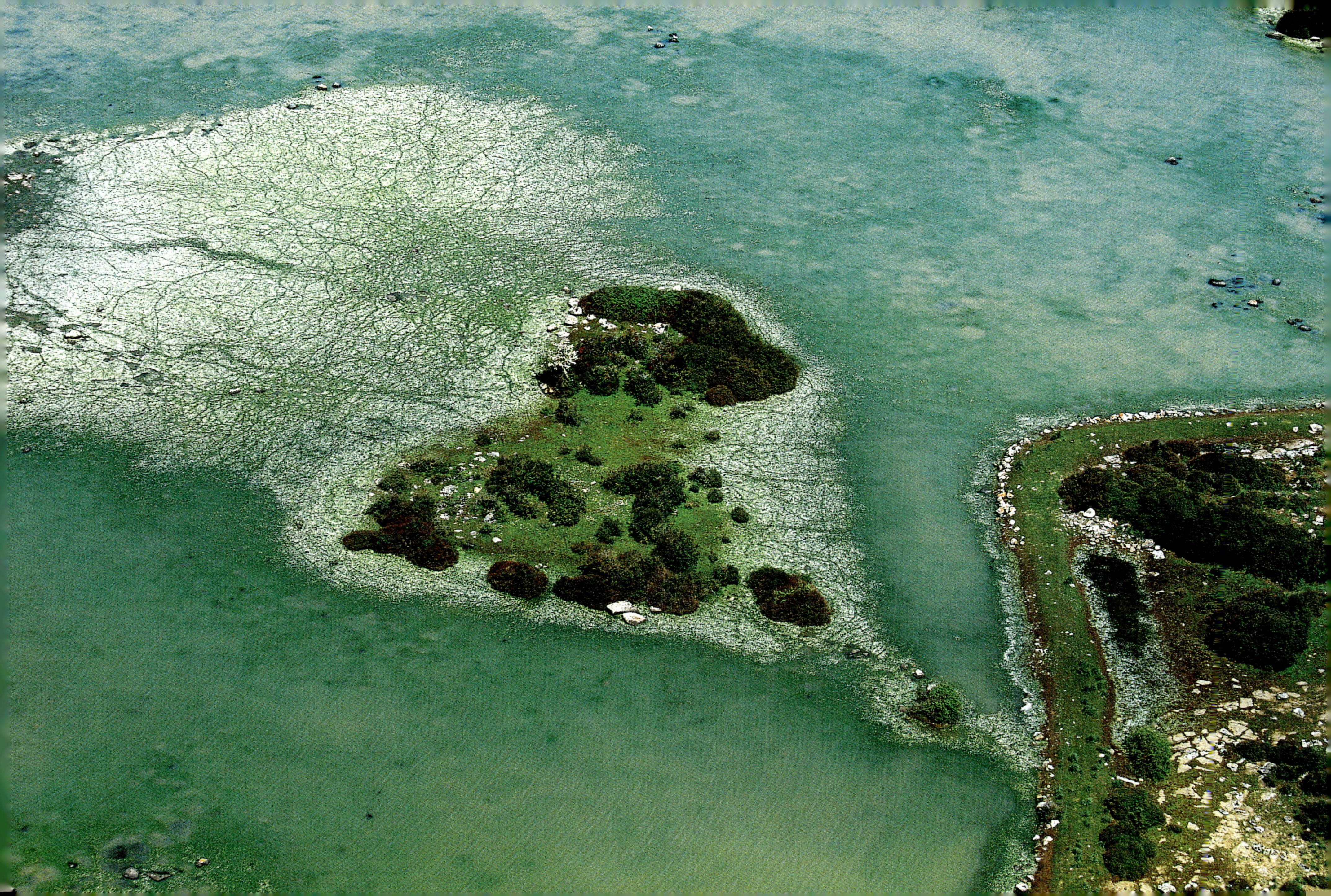

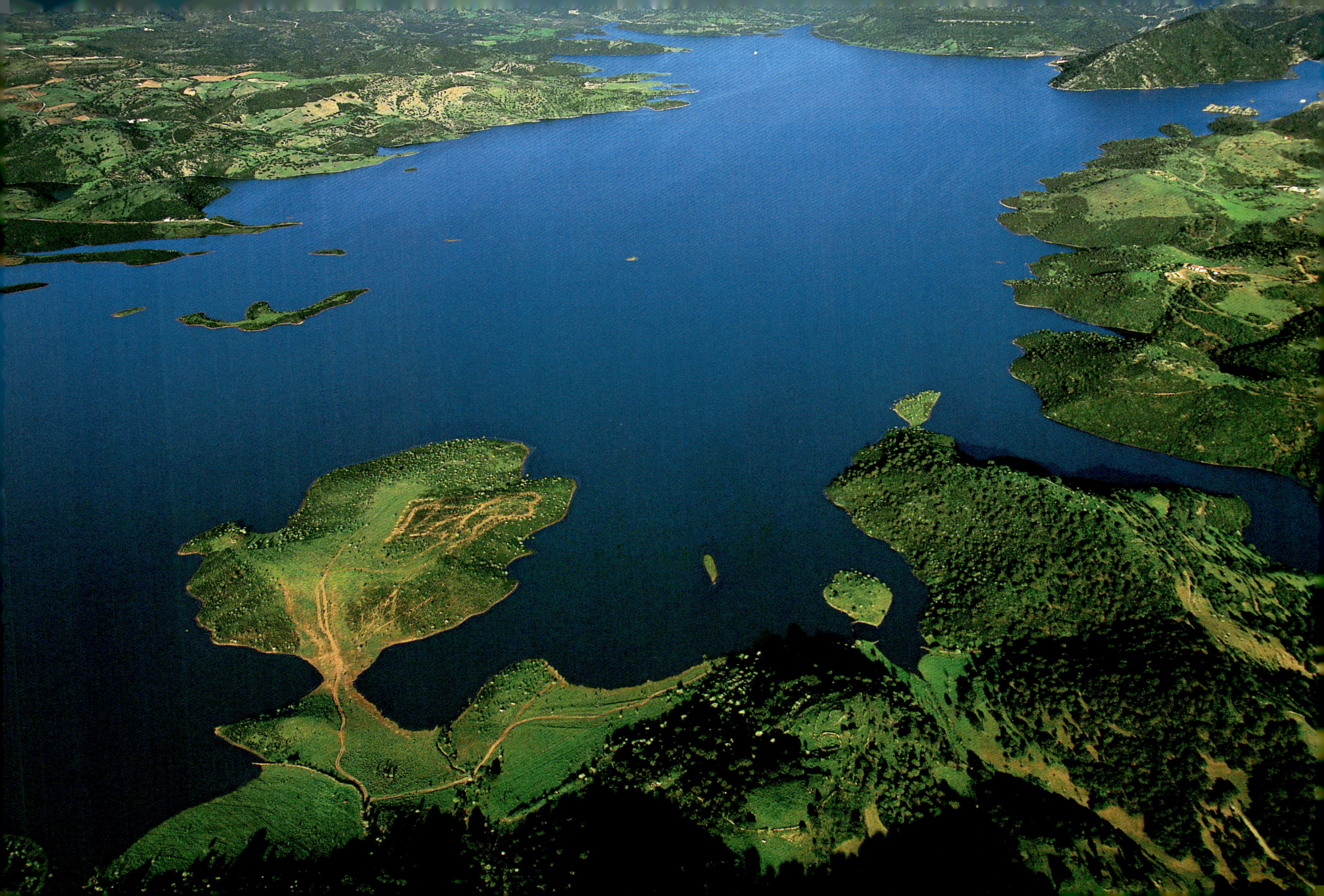

218 Flumendosa Lake, which is divided into an upper and a lower basin, extends along the Sarcicano at an elevation varying between 2624 and 656 ft (800 and 200 m). It was created between 1949 and 1952 after the construction of two dams on the Flumendosa River, built for the production of electricity and the collection of water for irrigation of Campidano.

219 Lake Gusana, like the other lakes of central Sardinia, was also created in response to economic needs. The dam was built in 1960 – from then on the Rio Taloro Valley has reaped new benefits from tourists, who are attracted by the oak and poplar forests reflected in the waters of the lake, which is located not far from Gennargentu.

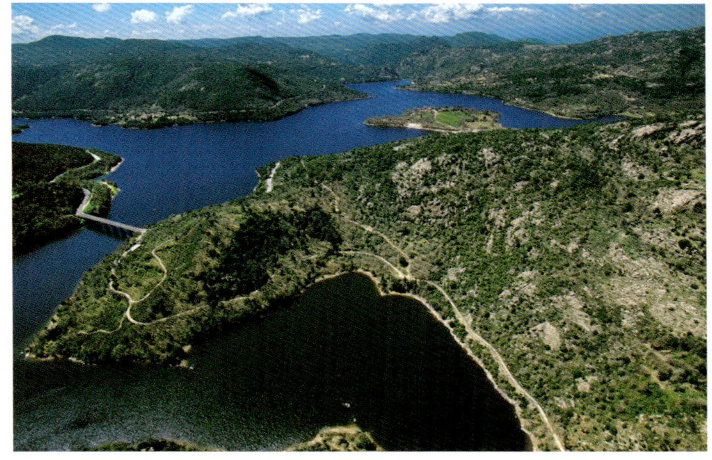

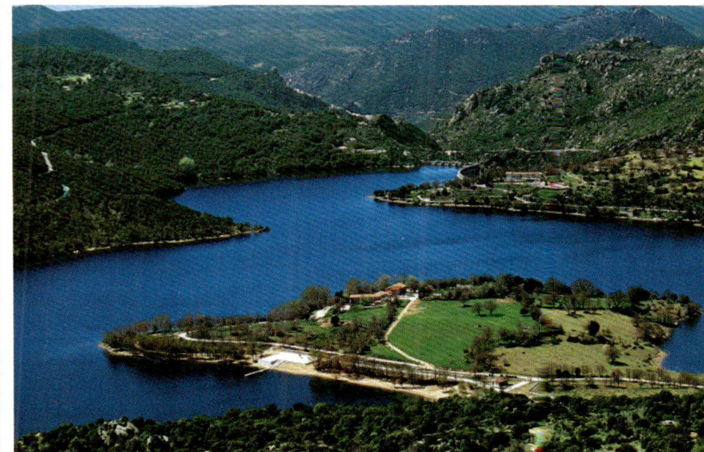

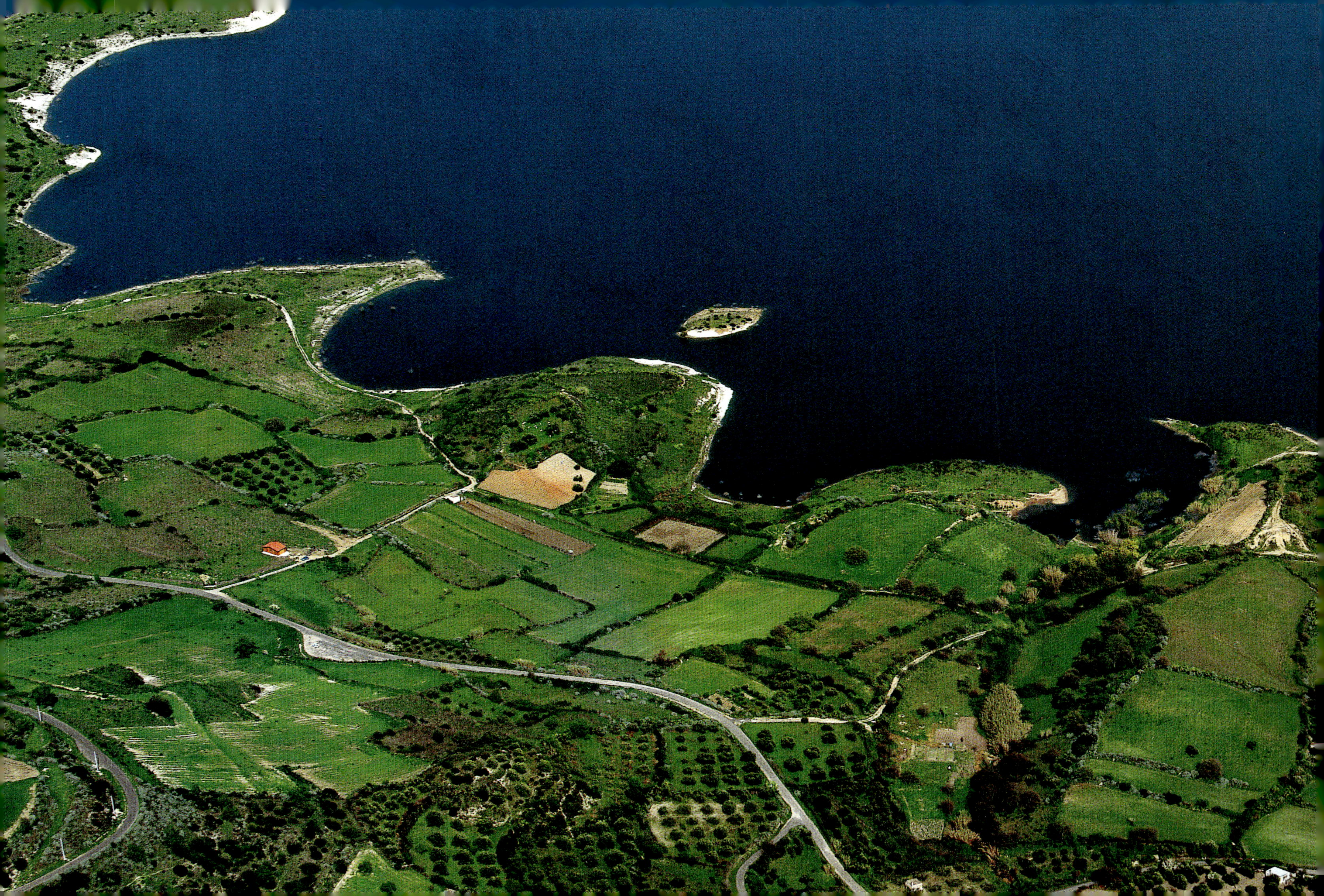

220 Omodeo Lake, in central Sardinia, is one of the largest artificial lakes in Italy. It is named after the engineer who, in 1924, designed and built what was at the time the largest dam in Europe.

221 left Created in 1927 by damming the Coghinas River, Lake Coghinas is the second artificial lake in Sardinia. Although it is manmade, the lake has enriched the environment of Mt Acuto, creating a habitat for numerous species of aquatic birds, as well as an important resource for tourism.

221 right The countryside surrounding Lake Omodeo, which is called Marghine, is still marked with the dry stone walls that once defined the boundaries of small rural properties.

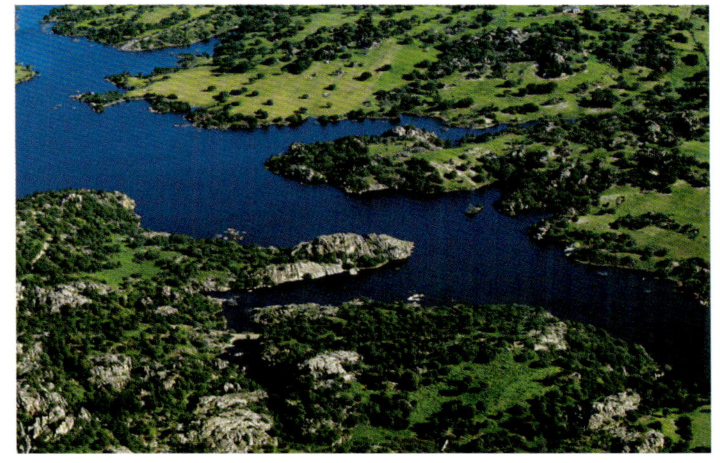

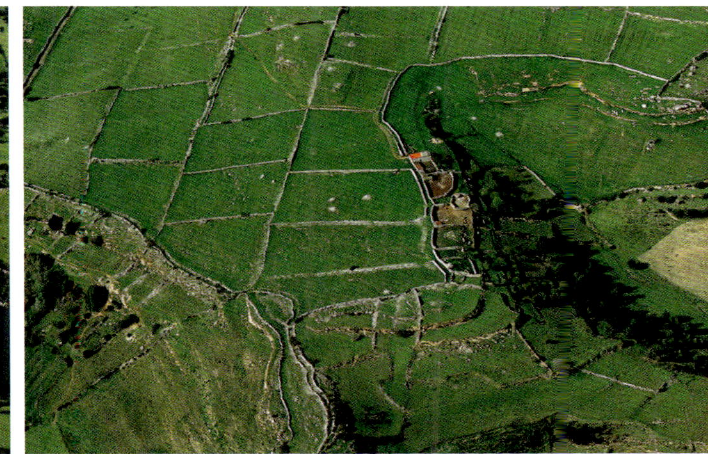

Index

Index

Credits:

Antonio Attini/Archivio White Star: pages 2-3, 4-5, 8, 10, 12 left, 12 center, 12 right, 15, 18-19, 20-21, 22-23, 24 right, 27, 43, 45, 52-53, 54, 55, 56-57, 58, 59 left and right, 60-61, 63, 66 left, 66 center, 66 right, 69, 73, 74, 76, 77, 78-79, 80, 81, 82, 83, 86-87, 88, 89 left and right, 90, 91, 92, 94 left and right, 95, 96 right, 100 right, 103, 104-105, 106, 107, 114-115, 116, 117, 118, 119 left and right, 120, 121, 122-123, 125 left, 126 left and right, 127, 128 left and right, 129, 130, 131, 132-133, 134 left and right,135, 137 right, 146, 147, 150 left and right, 151, 152, 153, 154-155, 156 left and right, 157, 158, 159, 160, 161 left and right,162, left and right, 163, 164-165, 166, 167 left and right,168 left and right, 169, 170, 172 left and right,173, 175, 176 center and right, 180, 183, 184-185, 186, 187 left and right,188, 189, 190-191, 192, 193, 194-195, 196, 197, 198, 199 left and right, 200-201, 202, 203, 204, 205, 206-207, 208, 209, 210, 211, 212, 214, 215, 216, 217, 218, 219 left and right,220, 221 left and right

Marcello Bertinetti/Archivio White Star: pages 40, 41, 42, 75

Marcello Libra/Archivio White Star: pages 6-7, 24 left, 25, 32-33, 35, 36 left and right, 38-39, 44, 62 left and right, 65, 70-71, 72, 97, 99, 109, 110 left and right, 111, 112, 113

Giulio Veggi/Archivio White Star: pages 9, 46-47, 48-49, 50-51, 84, 85, 96 left, 100 left, 100 center, 124, 125 right, 136, 137 left, 139, 140, 141, 142, 143 left and right, 144-145, 148-149, 176 left, 178, 182 left and right

Worldsat International Inc.: page 16.

Photographs
Antonio Attini

Text
Francesco Petretti

Editor
Valeria Manferto De Fabianis

Editorial coordination
Alberto Bertolazzi
Maria Valeria Urbani Grecchi

The publisher would like to thank:
Stefano Travaglia, Mimmo Potenzieri, Roberto Barsotti,
Paolo Barbieri, Roberto Botti; Francesco Orrico,
Emo, Francesco and Lanfabio Bientinesi by Volitalia.
Special thanks to Valentino Benvenuti and Elio Rullo.

Via Candido Sassone, 22/24
13100 Vercelli, Italy
www.whitestar.it

Translation: Maddalena Neale

ISBN 978-88-544-0404-5

Reprints:
1 2 3 4 5 6   12 11 10 09 08

Color separation: Mycrom, Turin
Printed in Thailand